To Debra
~a kindred spirit~
all blessings
Sheri Crockett

DOORS TO HIGHER CONSCIOUSNESS

MEETING ANGELS AND ASCENDED MASTERS THROUGH THE QABALAH

SHERI CROCKETT

BALBOA.PRESS
A DIVISION OF HAY HOUSE

Balboa Press books may be ordered through booksellers or by contacting:

Balboa Press
A Division of Hay House
1663 Liberty Drive
Bloomington, IN 47403
www.balboapress.com
844-682-1282

Because of the dynamic nature of the Internet, any web addresses or links contained in this book may have changed since publication and may no longer be valid. The views expressed in this work are solely those of the author and do not necessarily reflect the views of the publisher, and the publisher hereby disclaims any responsibility for them.

The author of this book does not dispense medical advice or prescribe the use of any technique as a form of treatment for physical, emotional, or medical problems without the advice of a physician, either directly or indirectly. The intent of the author is only to offer information of a general nature to help you in your quest for emotional and spiritual well-being. In the event you use any of the information in this book for yourself, which is your constitutional right, the author and the publisher assume no responsibility for your actions.

Any people depicted in stock imagery provided by Getty Images are models, and such images are being used for illustrative purposes only.
Certain stock imagery © Getty Images.

Print information available on the last page.

ISBN: 979-8-7652-4669-6 (sc)
ISBN: 979-8-7652-4671-9 (hc)
ISBN: 979-8-7652-4670-2 (e)

Library of Congress Control Number: 2023920798

Balboa Press rev. date: 11/28/2023

For my daughter, Jessica, and granddaughters, Violet and Scarlett,
my closest links in the love that unites all creation

CONTENTS

Preface xi
Acknowledgments xv
Chapter 1   Who Are the Ascended Masters and Angels? 1
Chapter 2   How This Book Came to Be....................................23
Chapter 3   Methods to Expand Consciousness............................42
Chapter 4   Recognizing When Angels and Ascended
                    Masters Make Contact....................................57
Chapter 5   Preparing for Ascended-Realm Contact: Forgiveness....72
Chapter 6   Preparing for Ascended-Realm Contact:
                    Choosing Love...86
Chapter 7   Introduction to the Qabalah 104
Chapter 8   Understanding Different Levels of Mastery................130
Chapter 9   Identifying Potentially Helpful Masters and
                    Angels Using Tarot and Western Astrology.................146
Chapter 10 A Method to Invite Specific Ascended Masters
                    and Angels Closer in Meditation........................157
Angel and Ascended Master Profiles..175
    Abraham: Judaic Founding Patriarch............................175
    Ailill mac Mata: Celtic Lineage 177
    Aine: Celtic Lineage 179
    Amoghasiddi Buddha: Buddhist Lineage............................181
    Angel Chamuel: Angelic Kingdom 182
    Angel Hasdiel: Angelic Kingdom 183
    Angel Nuriel: Angelic Kingdom 184
    Aphrodite: Greek Lineage..186
    Apollo: Greek Lineage 188
    Archangel Ariel: Angelic Kingdom 190
    Archangel Azrael: Angelic Kingdom 191
    Archangel Camael: Angelic Kingdom..............................192
    Archangel Gabriel: Angelic Kingdom 194
    Archangel Haniel: Angelic Kingdom 196

Archangel Jeremiel: Angelic Kingdom 197
Archangel Metatron: Angelic Kingdom 199
Archangel Michael: Angelic Kingdom 200
Archangel Raguel: Angelic Kingdom 202
Archangel Raphael: Angelic Kingdom 204
Archangel Raziel: Angelic Kingdom 205
Archangel Uriel: Angelic Kingdom 208
Ares: Greek Lineage 210
Ariadne: Greek Lineage 212
Arianrhod: Celtic Lineage 215
Arjuna: Hindu Lineage 217
Artemis: Greek Lineage 220
Asclepius: Greek Lineage 222
Athena: Greek Lineage 224
Avalokitesvara: Buddhist Lineage 226
Baldur (the Beautiful): Norse Lineage 229
Belenus: Celtic Lineage 231
Bernadette of Lourdes, Saint: Christian Lineage 232
Brigit: Celtic Lineage and Christian Saint 234
Buddha (Siddhartha Gautama): Buddhist Lineage 235
Cerridwen: Celtic Lineage 238
Charlemagne: Christian Lineage 240
Clare of Assisi: Christian Lineage 242
Dagda (Tuatha Dé Danann): Celtic Ireland 244
Danu: Celtic Lineage 245
Deborah: Judaic Lineage 247
Demeter: Greek Lineage 249
Durga: Hindu Lineage 251
Eir: Norse Lineage 253
Enoch: Judaic Lineage 254
Ezekiel: Judaic Lineage 256
Fionn mac Cumhail: Celtic Lineage 258
Forseti: Norse Lineage 261
Francis of Assisi, Saint: Christian Lineage 262
Freya: Norse Lineage 264

Frigg: Norse Lineage...266

Ganesha: Hindu Lineage 268

Gefjun: Norse Lineage...270

Guinevere: Celtic (Arthurian) Lineage.................272

Gullveig/Heid): Norse Lineage 274

Hera: Greek Lineage..276

Hermes (also known as Thoth or Hermes-Thoth): Greek
   Lineage...278

Hildegard von Bingen, Saint: Christian Lineage.....280

Huldah: Judaic Lineage 282

Isaac: Judaic Lineage...284

Jesus (also known as Yeshua or Jeshua): Christian Lineage......285

John the Baptist, Saint: Christian Lineage 288

Kali: Hindu Lineage...290

King Arthur: Celtic (Arthurian) Lineage 292

King David of Jerusalem: Judaic Lineage...............294

King Solomon: Judaic Lineage...............................296

Krishna: Hindu Lineage 298

Lakshmi: Hindu (and Buddhist) Lineage............... 300

Leah: Judaic Matriarch, Wife of Jacob/Israel.........302

Locana Buddha: Buddhist Lineage 304

Lugh/Llew/Lugus: Celtic Lineage.........................306

Machig Labdron: Buddhist Lineage.......................308

Mamaki Buddha: Buddhist Lineage 309

Manjushri: Buddhist Lineage................................. 311

Mary, the Mother of Jesus, Saint Mary: Christian Lineage 312

Mary Magdalene: Christian Lineage......................315

Mira Bai: Hindu Lineage.......................................317

Miriam: Judaic Lineage 319

Moses: Judaic Lineage..321

Niguma: Buddhist Lineage.....................................324

Njord: Norse Lineage...326

Nuada: Celtic Lineage 327

Odin: Norse Lineage 329

Oengus mac Og: Celtic Lineage 331

Orpheus: Greek Lineage 334
Pandara: Buddhist Lineage 336
Parvati: Hindu Lineage..338
Penthesilia: Greek Lineage 340
Persephone: Greek Lineage 341
Plato: Greek Lineage.. 344
Radha: Hindu Lineage 346
Rama: Hindu Lineage 348
Rebecca: Judaic Matriarch 350
Rhiannon: Celtic Lineage 352
Sarah: Judaic Lineage 354
Sarasvati: Hindu Lineage...355
Shiva: Hindu Lineage 357
Saint Germain: Christian Lineage 359
Tara, White 361
Tara, Green: Buddhist Lineage 364
Teresa of Avila: Christian Lineage....................................366
Themistoclea: Greek Lineage..368
Thor: Norse Lineage...369
Tyr: Norse Lineage 371
Vairocana Buddha: Buddhist Lineage................................373
Vishnu: Hindu Lineage 375
Yeshe Tsogyal: Buddhist Lineage 377
Yogananda (Paramahansa Yogananda): Hindu Lineage..........379
Zeus: Greek Lineage 381

PREFACE

Many of us have learned and grown spiritually from masters and teachings within our preferred spiritual tradition. It became clear to me in working with the ascended-realm beings who brought this book into existence that they are inviting us to actively seek their presence in new ways. By saying this, I am not advocating a new cult practice. You can work with ascended-realm beings along with whatever tradition you follow. We owe great thanks to every spiritual tradition that brought their names forward.

I am simply observing that when we step into higher consciousness and learn from the beings there, it quickly becomes apparent that there are no spiritual or religious rivalries in the higher dimensions. All masters reach ascension through their own culture, time, and tradition, yet once there, they extend their gifts of energy and experience side by side, serving the divine plan.

The cross-cultural approach I was guided to use for this book gives anyone an opportunity to learn what facets of higher wisdom the masters of other traditions might provide. They are available to support any of us when we move toward them without judgment and when we have developed our inner readiness to receive their communications.

By using the Qabalah to understand the gifts each being extends, we have a means to appreciate them side by side. The Qabalah (spelled with a Q) is the backbone of the whole Western esoteric tradition. From it, many other wisdom systems arose. There are also Judaic and Christian approaches, which are spelled *Kabbalah*. My approach to the angels and masters came through the Western esoteric tradition, so I use Qabalah spelled with a Q in this book. The spheres and paths of the Qabalah are like interdimensional doorways to reach the angels and masters in higher consciousness. This is the meaning behind the book's title.

This book is an invitation from the ascended realm, extended to those at all levels of spiritual experience. As a reference, it does not have to be read from start to finish. I recommend you begin by reading the first chapter, so you understand where the chapters lead. To apply the system in chapter ten with the greatest understanding, you will ultimately want to read what all the chapters outline. Following chapter ten of the book consists of the 108 ascended master and angel profiles, arranged alphabetically.

Chapter 1 introduces the group known as ascended masters, explains how they achieved spiritual ascension through a human lifetime, and introduces the angelic kingdom.

Chapter 2 addresses how the book came to be and the methods I used to identify and confirm the existence of ascended masters and angels in the higher dimensions.

Chapter 3 provides a brief overview of methods to expand consciousness into the higher dimensions, where the angels and masters are encountered.

Chapter 4 describes how one can recognize contact with an angel or master through the subtle intuitive senses known as clairvoyance, clairsentience, clairaudience, and claircognizance.

Chapters 5 addresses how to prepare one's consciousness for ascended master and angelic contact, through the practice of forgiveness.

Chapter 6 addresses how to prepare one's consciousness for the higher dimensions by learning to identify with love rather than fear.

Chapter 7 introduces the metaphysical concepts symbolized by the Qabalah, including its correspondence in Western astrology and the tarot. Keywords are given to understand the purpose of each sphere and path as a basis to recognize the type of help the masters and angels extend.

Chapter 8 introduces the four levels of mastery possible within the Qabalah structure: two emotional levels, the mental level, and the spiritual level. Spiritual ascension is possible at one of these four levels. The profiles of the beings recognize which level of mastery they extend. Having this information helps you to recognize which masters may be most accessible to your consciousness currently and those who will require greater spiritual sensitivity to contact.

Chapter 9 offers methods of correspondence drawn from tarot and Western astrology (which derive from the Qabalah) so readers can use their own tarot lifetime symbols, growth years, and Western astrological birth charts to identify potentially valuable allies among the masters and angels to invite forward in consciousness.

Chapter 10 provides an understanding of how to apply the simple color-and-symbol visualization system offered in this book, which can be incorporated into your meditation practice to invite the presence of specific angels or masters forward in your consciousness.

The Angel and Master Profiles

The heart of the book is found in the descriptions of the 108 angels and masters. The number 108 is sacred in several traditions, a microcosmic representative of the vast amount of spiritual help available to support human evolution. You may want to read about your favorite ascended masters or angels or discover others who are unfamiliar. Even opened at random, their stories can provide a moment of inspiration and guidance when we need it most.

Each brief description includes a bit of what I experienced when I contacted them, simply as one example of what is possible. I also share some of the methods I found most valuable to arrive at those experiences. The most important question to hold as you read this information is the following: What might occur *for you* as you build working relationships with your higher spiritual team? May actions that help you answer that question bring forth profound blessings.

ACKNOWLEDGMENTS

I did not suspect that spiritual practice would one day lead to the blessed opportunity to create this book. I wish to thank some who made this possible.

First, to those who served as teachers so I could answer the knock of the Spirit in my own form, I extend admiration and respect. The spiritual teaching-learning relationship is itself a high holy adventure with many dimensions. May the light you extended bless you.

I send thanks to my sacred sisters in groups and classes who have been willing to share their exploration of spiritual reality with me. You know who you are. The experiences we shared—and will share together ahead—bring me the greatest joy. One of those dear sisters is the gifted illustrator Jenifer Novak, who brought my vision for the book cover and the Qabalah drawings into form.

I also salute a dear group of spiritual companions, male and female, who shared valuable learning assignments together. Whether once or many times, each of you mirrored lessons about the spiritual journey that increased my learning exponentially. Wherever the four winds carry us, I remember you in my heart. I send you thanks for being the unique models of radiance that you are.

I am grateful for my editor and the Hay House publishing family for their dedication to help authors contribute to a wealth of different topics.

My deepest gratitude is to the ascended masters and angels from many traditions who appeared and reappeared in my consciousness, teaching me and patiently correcting my understanding over and over. Their unconditional love, support, and inspiration are part of the vast spiritual wealth available to all humankind.

In parts of the opening chapters, I speak about the value of prayer. If that word isn't your favorite, you can substitute another. In my experience, prayer is not restricted to a single form. I have prayed on my knees, while beating a drum or shaking a rattle, and during extended eyes-closed sessions in a Brazilian spiritual center. I have chanted prayers, painted some, and danced others. Prayer takes form when our heart and soul are gathered up in a deep communion with Creator. It is a gift that becomes more precious the more ways we express it.

In that regard, I intend this book as a form of prayer. It is a gift from my heart to the Light that surrounds us all. May it support your own deepest connection with the loving presence of Source consciousness in whichever forms are authentic for you.

Namaste.

CHAPTER 1

WHO ARE THE ASCENDED MASTERS AND ANGELS?

Who Are the Ascended Masters?

Humankind has had divine help ever since we appeared on earth. Some of that help came through souls who took on a physical form to bring certain ideas and types of consciousness to our planet. They are part of huge waves of spiritual light sent to assist human evolution.

I first encountered the term *ascended masters* in 1988 as I began to study shamanic practices. In the tradition I was learning, the masters include a well-known group of enlightened beings who can be experienced directly—when sufficient healing and fear resolution carry our energy into the higher realms, where only love exists. Whether one understands them as experienced elder brothers and sisters on the spiritual journey of awakening or as aspects of one's higher spiritual family (or higher self), the masters are recognized as advanced guides and teachers who are a great blessing to experience directly.

When I began my spiritual journey, I had no idea how many masters exist and how personally one could come to know them!

My First Experience with an Ascended Master

I was new to spiritual practice and to these ideas, when a dramatic experience occurred. At the time, I was still working as a jeweler and gemologist. I was sitting in my jewelry salon between clients, going through a parcel of turquois stones that had been cut by a dear friend and mentor who had passed on. I held the stones in my palm and closed my eyes for a moment, fondly remembering him.

Behind closed eyes, my awareness was immediately present inside a large tent. I was beside a tall, lovely First World woman dressed in a long buckskin dress. I could tell she saw me, and then she communicated in my thoughts that I should learn spiritual healing techniques. My eyes flew open in shock, and the vision ended. What had just occurred? All the years and the thousands of gems I had held previously had never produced this effect.

I looked for information about the subtle energy of minerals but could find nothing that connected to the gem science in which I had been trained. My instinct told me there had to be a link between the chemical, physical, and optical properties of the stones and their subtle energy. At the time, I had no idea that finding the answer to this question would occupy the next twenty years of my life.

My experience with the female master certainly got my attention, but it was not something I could re-create, although I tried repeatedly. It was a long time before regular contact with beings in the ascended realm occurred. As I continued spiritual development, they gradually came through more frequently to guide me. Spiritual support is available to all of us when we do our part to prepare our consciousness and turn toward the higher realms for help.

What Is Ascension, and How Did the Masters Achieve It?

The term *ascension* refers to a unique spiritual attainment that is the culmination of being in a physical body on a planet. Beings who have reached ascension no longer feel the need to be born into a physical lifetime, having learned all that can be learned in a bodily form.

To achieve ascension, each gained a certain type of mastery during his or her lifetime, sometimes by facing a certain human challenge repeatedly. A master may have been an artist, a mother, a philosopher, a scientist, or a temple priestesses, but all the masters' paths required them to overcome obstacles typical of human life. Now, in the higher realms, their hard-won success makes them exceptionally effective guides for us when we are attempting to fulfill a similar life mission. They are fully cognizant of the challenges everyone faces in human life and are dedicated to helping us succeed.

How Can They Guide Us?

Even though ascended masters no longer animate physical bodies, their consciousness remains accessible. They can communicate with us through dreams, as we lift our consciousness to the higher realms in meditation, or anytime our mind becomes still enough to hear them.

The masters are our higher spiritual family, and they love and care about us more than we believe we deserve. They believe in us because they see the divine spark in each of us and hold that view while we learn to claim it for ourselves. They understand that all of our lives matter and attempt to arrange opportunities for us to express what we came into physical incarnation to accomplish. They not only help with spiritual matters but also support us in every area of human life.

Learning Whom to Call Upon

The profiles in this book include ninety-three ascended masters drawn from seven of the world's great spiritual traditions. Finding the masters who can be most helpful to you begins with understanding their energy in the metaphysical system known as the Qabalah. This book introduces a Qabalah-based method that can be incorporated in your meditation practice to invite the presence of specific masters into your direct inner-world experience.

Masters Begin to Work with Us as Soon as We Ask for Their Help

Seers, mystics, and spiritual adepts have always been aware of the angelic realms and the masters. However, these enlightened beings are not just for a spiritual elite but can assist all of us—as soon as we want that. They won't intrude without our consent, as that would violate our divinely created free will. Wherever we are in our spiritual journey, they respond best when we invite them to come closer while we do our part to prepare our consciousness to receive their messages. How much we can experience from them is up to our own inner readiness.

For many years, I didn't realize that masters were indeed helping me! Later, I could look back and appreciate that many seemingly subtle events had unfolded under their influence. Chapters 5 and 6 outline two keys areas of inner preparation that have been essential for me to develop greater receptivity to their guidance. These two practices can be added to whichever spiritual path you follow.

The Angelic Kingdom

As our consciousness expands into the higher-dimensional realms in meditation or trance, we may also become aware of the presence of angels. There is something so universally appealing about angels that attention on them has gradually extended from religious traditions worldwide (in which they are still honored) into many different forms of spiritual practice. Many human beings are comforted by the thought that angels exist as evidence of a higher level of reality that cares about humankind.

How Do Angels Differ from Ascended Masters?

Both angels and ascended masters are extensions of divine Light consciousness. The most obvious difference between them is that angels do not require physical bodies to fulfill their spiritual functions, while the masters embodied physical forms during their earthly lifetimes. (Angels can assume a humanlike appearance when their mission with us makes that helpful, though that form may not have the same density as a human body.)

What Do Angels Look Like?

There are different orders of angels, and in spiritual vision, they differ in appearance. Often, they appear to me as radiant, abstract fields of colored or white light in motion. Like the ascended masters, when I see any of the angels in this book, they show colors or white light in their energy fields, which correspond to a particular part of the Qabalah. Having learned to understand each of the Qabalah dimensions (see chapters 7 and 8), I immediately know something about how each angel can be helpful.

Beyond the color and light, sometimes I have an abstract visual impression of warrior angels either with a flashing sword cutting away negative influences or wearing armor (Michael, Nuriel, Camael, and Raguel). Others appear massive in size (Raguel), and others are quite tall (Metatron). Many appear with an impression of simple flowing robes. Sometimes I see faces that possess tremendous radiance and ethereal, androgynous beauty.

Although angels were never in a human gendered form, visionary artists typically portray them as male or female so we can relate to them easily. The polarity-based nature of human language makes it difficult to describe individual angels without using *he* or *she* pronouns. The best way I can describe them without gender pronouns is to say that each angel extends energy that has a yin or yang quality. Since, in human life, we need to learn to express both polarities, it is helpful to know that there are angelic emissaries who extend both types of energy.

Ascension Is Possible Independent of Sexual or Gender Identity

Since ascended masters embodied a physical form during their ascension lifetime, their experiences were shaped by various human polarities, as ours are. These include some experiences shaped by sexual or gender identity, which can provide profound learning experiences.

However we identify on the spectrum of gender identity, it's important to recognize that at the level of higher self, there are no gender distinctions. During our lifetime, each of us will have opportunities to express both dynamic and receptive energies. While I use the terms *masculine* and *feminine* in parts of this book, the terms *yin* and *yang* are also appropriate to understand the nature of the energy we experience from individual masters and angels.

As one expands the lens of consciousness through spiritual practice, it is possible to become aware of aspects of one's multidimensional soul journey. At that level, those who were born in a female form may remember transpersonal or interdimensional lifetimes as males and vice versa. Experiences with both yin and yang masters not only are possible for everyone but are valuable, in my experience.

For these reasons, it was part of my intention to present a gender-balanced group of masters for this book. Together they can show us how to express both yin and yang qualities while we continue to evolve beyond all polarity.

The Spiritual Assignment Shared by Angels and Masters

Every human being born into a physical body at a certain time on a certain day temporarily forgets his or her eternal identity. This temporary spiritual amnesia is necessary so we can focus on the purposes that brought us into incarnation.

Developing individuality requires that we learn from the data provided by our five physical senses. We each build a strong identity based upon our body and personality to discover and develop the nuances of how we are unique from others. As a result, at first, we grant final authority to human perception. We learn the collective story of our family, nation, culture, and gender and come to accept different forms of human limitation.

At a certain point, the identity we have assumed becomes a barrier to further development. Once we learn them, we tend to remain identified with these definitions of what is possible for us—until some life event or breakthrough from the spiritual world sends us spinning out of our former orbit and encourages us to seek a higher-level answer.

If we use such times to step into spiritual practice, we invite the presence of masters who support us to awaken from the sense of human limitation into our own higher spiritual essence. This is the journey of awakening from the sometimes-disturbing perceptions of human life into the presence of love, which is eternally ours, no matter what seems to occur during our earthly sojourn.

Angels and Masters Can Assist with Every Dimension of Human Life

While all higher beings collectively serve spiritual awakening, they also have individual gifts of mastery that serve every dimension of human experience symbolized by the Qabalah. Some are protective, and others provide prophecy, help with healing, or deliver divine messages. Some serve as initiators into higher consciousness. Some help us refine and express creativity. Some oversee the development of harmonious relationships with lovers or friends. Others arrange "accidental" meetings with others who are important for us to meet or help us find a new home or job when we need one. There is higher help available for everything we undertake in human life and for all unanticipated challenges—when we remember to ask.

Moving Toward Our Own Ascension

Part of the spectrum of human potential available to all of us within our lifetimes is to claim our own potential for mastery and move toward ascension The masters who had life assignments like ours can gather near to inform us. In learning from them, we increase our chance of success.

Archangel Gabriel is the angelic link to Christ consciousness and the higher self. As such, he holds the knowledge about the special mission we have chosen to fulfill during our human lifetime and can remind us of what it is and the next step we can take toward it when we are ready to step onto that path.

In the Presence of Angels

While this book introduces just fifteen of the most familiar angels and archangels, I have experienced more than forty angels and archangels individually. Each of those experiences was precious. While there are more ascended masters than angels in this book, that does not imply that angels are less important. I am deeply grateful to experience the pure gifts of light and love they extend to all life.

All the angels and archangels included in this book work with large groups of individuals simultaneously, as do the masters, though we can experience them personally. One of my most dramatic angelic encounters began as I walked into the guest room of my home one day. I had the strongest reaction of goose bumps, over my whole body, that I've yet experienced. This physical reaction in the nervous system is understood by science to relate to the vagus nerve. I didn't see my angelic visitor, but every other subtle sense let me know he was there. It was like walking into an invisible mountain of spiritual energy that hadn't been present there the day before.

I sat down in a chair and immediately quieted my mind, reaching out to discover who he was and find out why he had come. He communicated his name (which I recognized from my study) and that he had arrived to provide another layer of divine protection for me and my home. I had recently asked for greater protection after there was an intruder in my backyard late one night. The angel I encountered has been with me ever since. It is possible to request and receive higher help when it is needed.

I have also experienced angels as spheres of diaphanous light that can be captured in a photograph or as cloud-angel forms that appear briefly in the sky overhead. The cover of this book depicts two angels hovering beside a Qabalah diagram. My wonderful illustrator created this image from a photo of a cloud angel that appeared for my camera during a spiritual retreat in Brazil.

Finding a Common Language to Describe Nonphysical Spiritual Helpers

There are different terms used to describe the nonphysical emissaries of divine help. Some traditions refer to *deities* or *demigods* and *goddesses*. Others use terms such as *avatar*, *Buddha*, and *bodhisattva*. Human language can provoke further divisions and controversies, or we can look for what unites us.

To present a single reference that can be used by practitioners of different traditions, I will use the term *ascended master* to refer to an enlightened being who ascended at the end of his or her physical lifetime on earth and remains accessible in the higher realms to assist humankind. I will use the term *angel* or *archangel* for divinely created beings who did not take on physical, earthly forms to fulfill their roles in assisting humankind. You can use whichever terms you prefer, but it is important that you understand what I mean when I discuss them.

Using the Qabalah to Understand the Energy of Ascended-Realm Beings

The Qabalah, mentioned briefly above, is one of the most well-known metaphysical systems representing the spectrum of spiritual light that connects humans with the spiritual realms. If you are new to the Qabalah, chapters 7 and 8 provide the basic information that will allow you to use the method outlined in chapter 10 to invite individual angels and masters toward you.

Understanding what the Qabalah demonstrates helps us to recognize that we are not separate from our Source and left to deal with life's challenges alone. The various parts of the Qabalah provide a means to understand the universal energy matrix available to human consciousness. Its quadrants provide potent psychic doorways through which we can experience contact with beings in the ascended realm.

Are Ascended Masters Saints?

Before you read the profiles of the masters in this book, it is important to realize that most ascended masters do not fit our definition of saints. A few of the masters in this book are found on lists of Catholic saints, and if so, I have included the word *saint* after their names to respect that tradition.

In a parallel way, I include the designation *Buddha* after enlightened beings known that way in Buddhist traditions. The masters themselves do not require us to address them with those terms, and they will work with our consciousness independent of the spiritual path we follow— when we can approach them without judgment. They have reminded me that it is important to respect each tradition that brought their names forward, whether we practice the tradition in which they are featured or some other.

The Masters Gained Ascension Despite Human Imperfections

Every human life offers a chance to grow and evolve amid the potent and sometimes challenging dynamics of earthly life experience. During their physical lifetimes, ascended masters displayed some superior quality of strength, courage, power, accomplishment, or wisdom— along with human foibles. Just like us, they did not live perfect lives, and they didn't always make the best choices.

Part of the human learning journey includes learning how to make corrections. They were required to do this during their physical lifetimes, just as we are. Facing a certain challenge or assignment, perhaps repeatedly, is what produced their mastery. Like us, they had to pick themselves back up and start again at different times in life. Yet somehow, from the unique raw material of their lives, they built a spiritually elevating path. They learned to use human life challenges as fuel for spiritual growth. Their ascension demonstrates that this is possible for us also.

Not Every Remarkable Human Lifetime Produces Ascension

While living a perfect human life is not a requirement, it is equally true that garnering worldly fame and glory does not automatically lead to ascension. What does it take to ascend? Part of the territory likely includes fulfilling the spiritual mission chosen for the lifetime and mastering some ability to forgive and extend love and compassion to others along the way. In addition, there are also individual elements that address the individual's multidimensional aspects, bringing completion and peace to matters that would otherwise remain unresolved.

Why Is a Cross-Cultural Approach to the Ascended Realm Helpful?

Since this book is intended to serve practitioners of many spiritual traditions, I was guided to identify masters from Buddhist, Celtic, Christian, Greek, Judaic, Hindu, and Norse traditions, plus the angelic kingdom, one group at a time. After I completed the research and classification steps, I moved to contact each master in that group. Through experience, I confirmed the colors of their Qabalah placements. Last came obtaining their preferred symbols to use to reach them in meditation. It is helpful to have multiple models of how each energy available in human life can be expressed.

A Vast Number of Ascended Masters Exist

Each of the lineages I surveyed produced more contacts with masters than could be included in this book. In addition, I also identified and contacted masters from additional traditions who are familiar to some spiritual practitioners. A few of these are mentioned below.

- Ancient Egyptian masters contacted include Isis and Osiris, Sekhmet, Hathor, Horus, Egyptian queens Nefertiti and Hatshepsut, Ptah, Bast, Amun-Re, Atum and Aten, and others.

11

- Indigenous North American masters contacted include White Buffalo Woman, Cochise, the Iroquois Great Peacemaker Deganawida and his collaborator Hiawatha, Chief Seattle, Sitting Bull, Mangas Coloradas, Metacomet, and others.
- Taoist masters contacted include Laozi, Quan Yin, Sun Bu'er, Yuanashi Tianzun (one of the Three Pure Ones), and Xiwangmu (Celestial Queen of the West).
- Mesoamerican (Inca, Maya, and Aztec) masters contacted include Viracocha, Kukulkan, Inti, Supay, Illapa, Cabraken, and Tohil.
- Sumerian masters contacted include Shamash, Ishtar, King Sargon of Akkad, Ninti, and King Ashurbanipal.
- Inuit masters contacted include Kinak, Tekkeiterstok, and Tapasuma.
- Katsina masters contacted include Blue Star Katsina, Eagle Katsina, Bear (Hon) Katsina, Blue Corn Grandmother, Spider Woman, and Snow Katsina.
- Masters known from a recent ascension lifetime include Annie Besant, Dolores Canon, and Jose Arguelles, among others. Masters known in other ascended master traditions include those mentioned by Blavatsky (DK the Tibetan, Kuthumi, and El Moyra) and other ascended master teachings (Melchizedek, Lady Nada, Serapis Bey, Hilarion, Paul the Venetian, Lord Lanto, Commander Ashtar, and Oshun).

> Each of the beings who made contact provided a precious experience that taught me more about each quadrant of the Qabalah and the higher dimensions than I would otherwise have understood. Divine help for humankind extends through every spiritual tradition.

Moving Past Comparisons

It is natural that many people have both preferences and aversions for different religious or spiritual traditions. This may arise from the fact that we have learned from a trusted spiritual teacher and have made progress through his or her form of practice, because of our own cultural ancestry, or for some other reason. Unexamined, this bias can lead to unproductive comparisons about whose masters are more enlightened and, thus, limit our potential to learn from all of them.

One of the central principles in this book is that to move toward experiences of unity (oneness, or spiritual connection to Creator Source), we must look toward the things that unite humankind. The existence of beings who have ascended—from among all cultures and spiritual traditions—and who extend love and evolutionary support equally to all of us can point us toward that unity.

Embracing Human Experience While Opening to Spiritual Reality

There is indeed much to enjoy and be grateful for in human life. The marvels we perceive through our five physical senses provide a unique way to experience the wonders around us. However, we are not only a personality in a body, though we experience life *through* a body.

Beyond the stream of impressions from our five physical senses— physical sight, touch, hearing, smell, and taste—some people become aware of subtle senses through which experiences of the spiritual world can be received. More about the extended range of those subtle intuitive senses is the subject of chapter 4.

The point is, no matter how grateful we are to experience life on this remarkably beautiful blue planet, no one's earthly experiences are entirely joyous. We extended into a physical body to learn and grow, and sometimes the process of evolution is less than smooth. Each experience has a purpose in life, yet we will want to gently lay some experiences down when their lessons have been learned. To achieve lasting peace and discover our own higher essence, we must seek and find what lies beyond the Third Dimension: the eternal Self in union with Creator.

The Limitations of Physical Sight

It can be helpful to understand something about the limitations of human perception as we prepare to meet the angels and masters who exist in the higher realms. The Hindu teachings of Advaita Vedanta use the Sanskrit word *maya*, meaning "illusion," to describe what we experience in the sensory world. Buddhist teachings as well as the text of *A Course in Miracles* also refer to the illusion or dream, or the sights and sounds perceived by physical senses, distinguishing that view from ultimate reality. Learning that what we perceive isn't ultimate reality gives us an opening, but only by going through that opening do we discover what lies beyond.

The spiritual mystics of every tradition report on a reality different from what physical senses perceive. The term *ineffable* is sometimes used for experiences of the divine. *Ineffable* is defined by Oxford Languages as "too great or extreme to be expressed or described in words." This is because those experiences have come through the temporary dominance of the right hemisphere of the brain, which is nonlinear, holistic, and nonverbal.

Explorers of higher spiritual realms often use poetry, symbol, or simile to describe what their subtle senses report. These forms provide the closest that language can come to describing transcendent experiences.

Scholars in many disciplines today still struggle to find adequate definitions for the word *consciousness*. Putting aside many of the unanswered questions about how it exists, there is compelling evidence that it does exist. One common experience is that consciousness is a complex series of energy fields that exist beyond time and space. Within our human potential lies the ability to directly experience expanded states of consciousness and to remember that we have done so.

What Lies beyond Human Perception?

As the spiritual mystics of every tradition demonstrate, it is possible to glimpse a broader spectrum of reality through spiritual practice.

Although x-rays and ultraviolet light lie beyond the band of human perception, we have come to understand they exist. Science has also discovered that certain animal species on our planet can see more than the human eye can register. A natural next step for human beings is to open to the possibility of developing our latent subtle spiritual senses.

The Model of Dimensions of Awareness

Having acknowledged the limitations of language to talk about phenomena that can be part of spiritual experience, we need an expanded vocabulary. Metaphysical discussions sometimes use the term *dimensions* to describe the spectrum of consciousness human beings can experience, which links the physical plane with higher states of awareness.

Briefly considering this concept gives us a means to prepare for spiritual experience and a system to later note the levels our consciousness has experienced. This gives us a framework to begin learning the Qabalah in an experiential way, as described in later chapters.

The Third Dimension

Every journey in consciousness has a beginning point. Within the dimensional model, human beings begin the spiritual journey from the Third Dimension. This is the earth plane reported by our five physical senses, where time (past and future) is experienced and where objects and people appear to be separate from us in space. Angels and ascended masters have, at times, appeared to those in the Third Dimension to fulfill some important mission, yet it takes a great deal of energy for them to enter this density.

As our spiritual development continues, our baseline consciousness gradually rises toward the dimensions where the angels and masters exist. This is why many sources advocate raising our vibration, so contact with the higher beings becomes easier for them and for us.

We are affected by experiences of higher dimensions in positive, expansive ways. As experience unfolds, we no longer believe that the five-sense-perception view of the world is all that exists, because we have glimpsed some of the wonders that lie beyond it. As our baseline consciousness rises, we open to an expanded perspective about ourselves and our relationship to all creation and develop both compassion and wisdom about the purpose of human life. The desire for more of these experiences increases.

Beyond the Third Dimension

All spiritual growth, through any tradition, is a process of expanding consciousness from what we already know to a next level of awareness. Like a hermit crab successively outgrowing its shell and moving into one larger, our consciousness grows by giving up formerly limiting beliefs.

Spiritual experiences can reveal a wholly different existence that is omnipresent at metalevels beyond time and space. All the higher dimensions exist as interpenetrating fields of energy accessible wherever we happen to be, within our own consciousness. Many of the world's great mystics (the poet Rumi, for example) evoke a tiny taste of what can be known. There is an eternal spark in each human heart and mind that remembers a tiny echo of eternity. Even while in the human experience, we cannot entirely forget our spiritual origins. As we fan the flames of our divine spark, we are attracted to discover yet more about our eternal connection with divine Source.

Finding Helpful Models to Develop Understanding

It is important to recognize that we approach an understanding of the higher dimensions from a human perspective. In direct experience, our mind's understanding is bypassed by the profound experience of the vast Self. We recognize that lifetimes of thinking could not possibly approach comprehensions of transcendent reality, but it's where we begin.

To understand the model of the dimensions, we can compare them to different types of energy that science has helped us understand.

The electromagnetic spectrum includes waves of energy, such as radio waves, infrared, ultraviolet light, and microwaves. We have come to understand that all these forms coexist as interpenetrating vibrational fields, wherever we may be in space. We can't see them with physical sight, but we have come to understand that they exist.

Higher states of consciousness—which, in this discussion, we are calling metaphysical dimensions—can become part of our experienced reality as we clear inner obstacles and develop meditative concentration. We all have the innate capacity to do this, but it takes practice over time to achieve. As we do this, we discover that all of those dimensions also exist as interpenetrating fields accessible with our consciousness, regardless of where our physical body appears in time and space.

Ascended Masters and Angels in the Fourth to Twelfth Dimensions

In the **Fourth Dimension**, the vibrations are higher, faster, and more subtle than in the Third Dimension. One is less limited by the seeming limitation of the Third Dimension's laws (time, space, and so on). This is the first level where the ascended masters and angels at emotional level one (none of whom are included in this book) can be experienced. At this level, we still perceive forms, but as inner vision opens on the astral plane, we begin to see color and light behind closed eyes, as well as phenomena with eyes open. Awareness is nonlocal and can shift across a broader spectrum of existence, visiting different scenes (and apparent time periods) and gathering a wealth of information.

In the **Fifth Dimension** (a higher vibration in the astral), awareness is yet more subtle and abstract. Many of the emotional-level-two masters and angels included in this book are encountered in this dimension. The key to admission into the Fifth Dimension (and, thus, to dimensions still higher) is an open heart that has forgiven the hurtful experiences of human life. Doing this inner work lifts our vibration and allows us to welcome some degree of oneness with all existence. As we cultivate this quality, we become willing to lay down the notion of separation, in favor of the truth of the higher realms where love and unity are the single experience.

Our willingness is crucial because what we believe isn't possible creates limits on what we can experience. As we open to the belief that we are not separate (usually facilitated by forgiving others and releasing perceptions about our own guilt), we can then experience the higher realms as our own senior reality.

As we move into those higher-dimensional experiences, it becomes clear that not only are we welcome there, but part of our consciousness is already there. The masters who extend energy in the Fifth Dimension offer great strength and support to those in the process of awakening to claim their senior spiritual identity.

Currently, many individuals who have been devoted to spiritual practice are shifting into a Fourth- to Fifth-Dimension baseline consciousness. This allows them to be less restricted by the notions of time and space, more able to hold a consistent vibration of love, and more aware of angels and masters and their own multidimensional existence. They are thus able to assist the spiritual world and their fellow humans toward collective spiritual awakening.

In the **Sixth Dimension** and **Seventh Dimension** (which pertain to the mental plane), many illustrious masters and angels extend energy. In spiritual vision, these masters may appear as moving abstract patterns of color and light with consciousness, rather than in human or other forms. These masters are a great blessing to experience and greatly accelerate our spiritual progress. Collectively, they help us to purify and release remaining limiting beliefs and accelerate our vibration to align with still-higher energies.

The **Ninth Dimension** includes masters and angels who are yet more subtle, representing the spiritual planes of consciousness. Their proximity to spiritual Source is a clear and wondrous experience. Here are some of the greatest teachers of teachers, who support the final stages of spiritual development for humankind.

The **Eleventh Dimension** and **Twelfth Dimension** include beings who can be met at the Gateway of Kether. At this high level, there are still slight nuances of gender as we meet extensions of Source energy.

Higher dimensions beyond this exist, but for practical purposes, at this time, beings from the Twelfth Dimension are among the highest vibration we can experience in consciousness while still experiencing life through the body.

Angels and Masters Support Our Spiritual Journey with Profound Love

Before we begin any journey (even within our own consciousness), it is helpful to understand the nature of the territory we will be visiting. Higher-dimensional experiences are universally characterized as enhanced awareness of love's presence. Divine love is the single animating force that flows through the ascended and angelic realm, just as it flows to and through each of us. We don't recognize this at first, but as we clear the inner obstacles, it becomes clear and builds into a certainty that sustains us.

While beings in the ascended realm have many individual assignments, all share in the universal mission of extending love. Love is the essence of Creator Source as well as our own true nature. From love, we were created, and it is all that exists in Truth. We can temporarily deny it, though we can never be apart from it, because it is what we are.

The angelic kingdom and ascended masters understand and love us exactly as we are right now. They do not share our limited human beliefs about ourselves, because they see who we really are. Their help does not come from the fact that they are more powerful than we are—they simply don't share the stories of limitation with which we have temporarily identified. They are in perfect communication with Creator Source and hold this as an ongoing state, modeling what is also possible for us. They want to help us to remember our higher levels also while we are still animating a physical body. Doing this makes our journey much sweeter and more meaningful.

We don't have to earn divine love; it is ours already. Our part is to claim it. Doing this requires a shift in perception, but part of our mind is there already. As we shed limiting beliefs, we learn to unify with our own higher levels. The angelic realms and the ascended masters guide us toward glimpses of that experience until we realize this state is all we truly want: to walk through the world while remembering human perception is not the final arbiter of reality, free of self-limiting thoughts, suffering, and fear and able to deliver inspired gifts to the world. Spiritual awakening reflects the attainment of this blessed state.

Opening Our Heart to Receive Unconditional Love

When we have asked for angelic and master support and are doing our part to move toward it, it becomes more accessible. Releasing the weight of old emotions, including blame, guilt, and fear, from our energy field gives the ascended realms a clear path to make their presence with us known (see chapters 5 and 6 for our part in this process).

As meditative concentration grows, we can interact and dialogue with the masters, receiving information and insight about our lives and matters of current concern. Our higher self is fully aware of what we need, and therefore, the masters and angels address far more than spiritual matters. We are helped to recognize our next steps, with activities that are part of human life. Along the way, the masters can show us some of the moves they made in life to successfully address various challenges. They become trusted guides who whisper in our consciousness, providing practical information, support, and love.

We all have a nonphysical team, or spiritual family, who support us as we develop higher awareness. Perhaps you already have experienced some of those who work with you. May you discover others as you work with the methods in this book! Chapter 9 provides some methods based on tarot and astrology to discover likely members of your higher nonphysical team.

What Do the Masters Want Us to Know?

The masters and angels sent the impulse for this book forward not to be known for their own sake (they have no human egos that require acknowledgment) but as a tool to help us elevate our consciousness. They are wondrous companions who invite us to discover and develop the spark of divine potential within our heart and mind.

Nothing valued by the collective world compares to learning about our own spiritual reality and how to fulfill the life purpose we came to achieve. Despite the temporary spiritual amnesia that arrives with physical birth, in our creation, we have been given free will to direct the light of our own consciousness. The press of energy present in the world today is an optimal condition for dynamic spiritual awakening. Many beings in the ascended realm are actively helping humankind currently, communicating during meditation, bringing messages through different authors, and working with us in our nighttime dreams and in many other ways, so we can claim the light and love that are our truest essence.

Support for the Spiritual Journey—but Not the Final Goal

Those who develop a working relationship with members of their higher spiritual team come to realize they are not the final goal of spiritual practice. There are yet-higher states of spiritual awareness. Experiencing one's own higher spiritual essence in union with divine Source is the ultimate goal for some. As consciousness unifies with that profound quadrant beyond the limits of language to describe, the spiritual quest is fully satisfied as the spark of Light rejoins the eternal Flame.

While we grow toward that ultimate reunion with divine Source, it is our choice to call the angels and masters toward us or not. They will not intrude in our consciousness without our say-so. If you wish to do so but have not yet invited your higher spiritual team forward, take a quiet moment to ask for their close participation with your life and consciousness. Saying whatever words come to you out loud or holding them silently in your heart is fine.

Important to Remember

Angels and ascended masters are divine help sent for human spiritual awakening, but they only come forward when we ask for this.

They love us unconditionally exactly as we are.

We can use the model of metaphysical dimensions to understand the range of consciousness that can be experienced by those who practice meditation.

Each human being has a higher team, or spiritual family, of nonphysical beings who work with us. We may work with others at higher levels as we continue to evolve.

Their specific mastery can be understood through the metaphysical system called Qabalah, which is introduced in chapters 7 and 8.

CHAPTER 2

HOW THIS BOOK CAME TO BE

By 2016, when the idea for this book came forward, I was beginning to experience regular contact with various angels and ascended masters. I had long ago given up working as a gemologist, but in the years following my experience of a master when holding some turquois stones, gradually, a deeper sensitivity to subtle mineral energy emerged. Learning to work with crystals to enhance meditation was a natural next step.

I had been around gems and crystals all my life, as my family business included fine jewelry. As an adult, I obtained the two most respected degrees in the jewelry industry: the graduate gemologist degree from the Gemological Institute of America and the FGA (fellow of Gem-A) from the British Gemmological Association. I spent the first fifteen years of my professional career as a gemstone buyer and appraiser.

As the years passed, my desire to understand how gems and minerals could be used in spiritual practice led me to undertake a deep study of the ancient hermetic tradition (part of the Western esoteric tradition) and develop a modern system to classify the subtle energy of the mineral kingdom, based upon chemical, physical, and optical properties. Doing this took twenty years. Along the way, I received guidance that finally allowed me to understand the bridge between gem science and metaphysical principles. During this period, I made many trips to major gem markets to experience the energy of more mineral specimens. Ultimately, I classified more than five hundred mineral varieties to identify those most available and effective to use for spiritual development. I expected to write a book on the subtle energy of minerals; however, all of this was simply preparation for learning to work with the ascended masters in a unique way.

As I sat in meditation one day, two of my spiritual guides brought forth the idea of writing a book about the ascended masters and angels, using the mineral kingdom species to invite them forward in my consciousness. Like most people, I found every experience with enlightened beings in the higher realms to be a deep blessing. The opportunity to continue these contacts and to use the knowledge about the mineral kingdom I'd gained for this purpose was immediately appealing.

As soon as I agreed to the project (within my inner-world consciousness), the spiritual realm turned up the volume on my spiritual experiences. Both the frequency of contact and the number of angels and masters coming forward in my meditations increased dramatically.

Guidance on the Book Methodology

I quickly realized I would need an organized approach to be able to remember and understand all the contacts with angels and masters I was experiencing. I asked for guidance and was given the first three steps of the four-step approach outlined below. I will share a bit about each step so you can understand the method used to identify the masters and angels in this book and identify their primary area of expertise.

Book Methodology Step One

Research the cultural myths and spiritual texts of many traditions to identify potential ascended masters.

To understand why myths would be a helpful resource for ascended masters, we must appreciate that there are different definitions of the word *myth*. Some use the word *myth* to describe something that is not true. The primary definition of the word, according to Oxford Languages, is "a traditional story, especially one concerning the early history of a people or explaining some natural or social phenomenon, and typically involving supernatural beings or events."

As I began to read books describing mythical interpretation, I soon encountered the term *euhemerism*. Euhemerism is the theory within the field of mythology that the belief in gods derives from the worship of human beings whose deeds were immortalized—recorded by the mythical traditions of later cultures—and who came to be regarded as divine.

The term *euhemerism* came from a Greek master known as Euhemerus of Messene (317–298 BCE), who coined the idea. Euhemerist approaches have been in and out of favor as a theory within the discipline of mythology ever since. As I discovered by contacting the masters, many—but not all—characters in myth can be met in the ascended realms.

Who Were the Mythmakers?

As author Mircea Eliade points out in his monumental classic study *Shamanism*, some of the original storytellers were tribal seers, oracles, and shamans who visited the higher realms in their own spiritual journeys and later described in their tales some of the beings they encountered there. Thus, myths that originated from such sources might include descriptions of ascended masters who once walked this planet, living lives as leaders, warriors, priestesses, seers, oracles, avatars, and sages.

Some mythmakers included bards who witnessed great historical battles and remembered them in verse. Others were initiates in various ancient spiritual traditions who passed ancient knowledge down to posterity or were storytellers who performed for entertainment in courts or at festivals.

Eliade's information on ancient seers as the origin of tales about ascended-realm beings dovetailed with the concepts of ancient Greek Euhemerus. This helped me to understand why guidance had directed me to begin my search for ascended masters within cultural myths as well as spiritual texts and histories, which were more obvious sources.

Fortunately, I did not know in advance the number of different spiritual lineages I would be asked to explore, which would have been too daunting! As I completed research into one cultural lineage, guidance would direct me to a next one. Along the way, I compiled the names of potential masters on an ever-growing Excel spreadsheet. (The beings themselves must have found this a bit humorous!)

Clearing Preexisting Biases for or against Certain Lineages

As mentioned briefly in chapter 1, recognizing that everyone is subject to preexisting biases, to do justice to each of the masters I hoped to encounter, I found it important to attempt to move past my own preferences. I didn't realize in advance what they might be, but as I began to study each tradition, I felt certain judgments surfacing. As they came up, I became willing to forgive and release my opinions about how (accurately or inaccurately) each being had been interpreted—both within and outside his or her tradition. I also discovered that the roots of some my aversions lay in some of my own interdimensional lifetimes still in need of healing.

I use the words *transpersonal healing* and *interdimensional healing* to mean the same thing. This area is commonly known by the term *past lives.* That term isn't entirely accurate because while human consciousness interprets experience in a time sequence, there is no past or future when consciousness views reality from a higher spiritual perspective. At that level, there is only the present, the eternal now.

Whichever term we use for our interdimensional experiences, if we hold a powerful emotional charge that remains unaddressed, it can exert powerful unconscious influences. As I applied the spiritual healing methods I'd learned and shared to clear these levels, each group of masters came into clearer focus. Sometimes the difference was amazing.

I cannot claim to have eliminated every personal bias perfectly, but in every case, the more I was able to release my judgments and clear the blocks in my own consciousness, the more graciously the masters came forward to connect with me (in step three). Frequently, my direct experiences provided a different way to understand each master. The information that some beings provided was clearly not from my own individual repertoire of thoughts and feelings, yet it resonated. Releasing my judgments was a healing process, and I share some of my inner shifts in the masters' profiles ahead.

Book Methodology Step Two

Determine which type of mastery a being gained during his or her physical lifetime. Use this information to identify his or her correspondence with a specific part of the Qabalah.

In addition to my gemological knowledge, by the time I began this project, I had a twenty-year background as a consulting Western astrologer and had also worked with tarot. Both Western astrology and the tarot are branches of the Qabalah. As an interest in the Qabalah emerged, I also read books on the system itself. All of this was just preparation for the deeper experiential learning about the Qabalah through the masters and angels, which I describe in chapters 7 and 8, and my experiences in the profiles.

To identify the likely Qabalah correspondences of masters, I read their myths (many in translation), some sacred texts that featured them, and, when available, books about specific masters written by other authors. I focused on one spiritual lineage at a time to get an overview of the roles each being played and how their interactions were described. Sometimes archaeological investigations provided helpful evidence to confirm the roles they played among those who honored them.

However, it is not always easy to understand masters' Qabalah correspondences from their existing myths or archaeological artifacts. Within the earthly time dimension, as oral traditions gave way to written accounts, errors in copying or translating arose, and changing cultural overlays appeared (frequently through the new influence of Christian religion). This altered the character of myths, and sometimes it is necessary to peel back some layers to discover a deeper truth about the ascended masters than their stories reveal at face value.

The result of my research allowed me to classify each master and angel by his or her primary life assignment and mastery (as it corresponds in the Qabalah). However, all of us have a secondary emphasis in our energy field (echoed in the work of Jack Scwartz, author of the book *Human Energy Systems*). Our secondary ray (*ray* describes an influx of subtle spiritual light that flows into our energy field and relates to our life purpose) is also expressed during life. The masters are classified in this book according to their primary ray (strongest quadrant of spiritual light), but their secondary ray is not given. Sometimes I noticed it in their energy field but not always. I received a lot of guidance that helped me to carry out their Qabalah correspondences, which I cross-confirmed by contacting them using minerals in step three below.

Sometimes it took me more than one attempt to locate and confirm a master's Qabalah correspondence. In some cases this revealed dimensions of their energy that are not commonly known. When that was the case, my description of that master in their profile shares the process I followed. You can continue to understand individual masters in any way you choose; I simply ask that you keep an open mind as you read what I discovered and how that information arrived.

Similar yet Unique: Masters Who Share the Same Qabalah Correspondence

It was fascinating to observe that masters who share the same Qabalah correspondence (but are known through different spiritual lineages) share some core similarities, yet each expressed the energy in his or her own unique way.

I came to understand these subtle variations like the unique light that emerges through each face of a single crystal. Having many expressions of each energy to learn from taught me deeply the range of ways that each Qabalah energy can be expressed. Understanding how others before us have expressed the energies highlighted within us provides a powerful array of models from which to craft our own lives. Learning from their level of mastery at emotional, mental or spiritual levelm (see chapter 8 for the full discussion of levels) shows us what the next step in the refinement of each energy can look like. This helps us to recognize the optimal direction to follow as we continue to refine our expression of that quality.

Book Methodology Step Three

Confirm each master's and angel's existence in the higher planes through direct contact in my inner-world experience, using mineral crystals.

This step in the process required a great deal of time for inner-world exploration. Most of my experiences with masters were intentional, meaning I would reach out to certain beings in a focused way to invite contact. However, some beings seemed to be seeking me.

It was not unusual, after a long day of research, to step into the shower and experience contact with a master who showed up spontaneously. When this occurred, I would add the master to my list and later attempt to confirm him or her by using a mineral.

Other masters came forward in dreams or during a walk. It was as if an invitation had been sent out throughout the ascended realm, and various masters came forth to let me know they exist.

Using Mineral Crystals to Determine Qabalah Correspondence

It would have been impossible for me to determine with certainty each master's and angel's Qabalah correspondence—and especially his or her level of mastery (emotional, mental, or spiritual)—without using mineral crystals.

While I came to this assignment with twenty years of work that allowed me to understand the vibrational spectrum of energy present in the mineral kingdom, now I was learning to link each mineral to the masters and angels whose vibrations harmonized with it. When I got the correspondence right, the gift was a profound contact. Then I felt certain about his or her Qabalah correspondence and level of development. Working back and forth, reading different descriptions of the masters from different sources and trying different crystals, was like solving a gigantic spiritual puzzle—a process I enjoyed!

If beings didn't respond to the crystal I thought was correct, sometimes they would arrive in my inner world anyway and tell me which crystal to use. Or I would receive an intuitive nudge to try a certain correspondence that hadn't occurred to me before. While my method may have been unusual, it was effective.

Looking back, I was amazed at the long path that had prepared me to carry out this assignment. This is exactly how Spirit works with each of us: the various chapters of our lives come together at last, and their overall purpose can be seen.

Ancient Esoteric Knowledge Has Reappeared in Our Time

A few translations of works by ancient authors exist that suggest the esoteric correspondence of angels and ascended masters with the Qabalah. I encountered such works written by seventeenth-century German Jesuit polymath Athenasius Kircher, sixteenth-century English alchemist John Dee, and fifteenth-century German occult writer Cornelius Agrippa. There are others who write about systems of esoteric correspondence. None of them, however, provide a complete system or explain how they arrived at the knowledge—because for the most part, the ancient sages who knew this information purposely did not publish it. In their time and for centuries following, this type of esoteric information was reserved for initiates of a particular spiritual tradition.

Today times have changed. Some bodies of formerly restricted sacred knowledge are appearing in new forms to facilitate human evolution at a crucial stage in our collective development. To my knowledge, this is the first book to distinguish a substantial list of masters by Qabalah correspondence and level (emotional, mental, or spiritual level) presented along with a system to invite each being forward individually in one's consciousness. May this information serve all those it is intended to assist.

Master Contacts Help Us Tune the Dial of Consciousness

When we turn toward the higher realms, asking for help and insight, the benefit of knowing each angel's and master's specific expertise helps us to focus attention on the ones who can best assist us.

For example, when we are working to create greater harmony and balance in a love relationship and overcome relationship challenges, it helps to be able to turn toward a master who earned his or her ascension by focusing on that type of evolution. Greek Hera, Judaic Rebecca, Hindu Radha and Parvati, and Celtic Queen Guinevere are masters who can be helpful.

Similarly, when we are working to align our thoughts and beliefs with spiritual reality, working in a spiritual capacity in the priesthood, writing a spiritual text, or engaging in advanced spiritual practices, we want to be able to turn to a master who achieved proficiency with those assignments. Francis of Assisi, Moses, King David, Krishna, Ganesha, and Plato could be important allies.

Whatever life assignment is our current priority, it helps the masters to help us when we turn to them with understanding of their specific mastery.

From Identifying Potential Masters and Angels to Contacts with Four Hundred Beings

The method I was given to determine potential ascended masters elicited a list of more than 1,600 names! While this is a larger number than I expected, the ascended and angelic realms are truly vast. In some of my earlier spiritual experiences, vision had revealed the ascended masters grouped together—row upon row of faces—in the form of a vast, arching amphitheater over my point of view.

Some of the same masters were known by different names in different cultures. I didn't attempt to sort out all the name overlaps, although sometimes a master would communicate that information directly when he or she made contact.

Guidance to Select the Beings to Be Included in This Book

Without knowing in advance the final number of masters and angels I would ultimately include in the book, I contacted more than four hundred angels and masters during a six-year period. From these contacts, the 108 beings in this book were chosen according to guidance received.

Not all the members of my personal spiritual team are included in this book, so if some of your beloved beings are not included here, that does not imply they are somehow of lesser importance. To profile the ones included in a meaningful way, I had to limit the total number, and guidance selected many whose names are well known in our time. (The names of many others remain in my files, and I will share them in other ways as opportunity permits.)

Ascended Masters from Every Spiritual Tradition Work Side by Side

As I mentioned in chapter 1, a striking fact arose from meeting more than four hundred masters and angels in direct inner-world experience: there are no spiritual or religious rivalries among them.

On many occasions, I experienced a master associated with one tradition working side by side with masters known in other traditions. This is different from the attitudes of some human beings, who argue, fight, and even die to uphold the supremacy of their own traditions.

When we approach this amazing group of beings without judgment about which are better, imagine the wealth of wisdom, experience, love, and learning we can tap. Why are so many masters needed? None of us hear, digest, and apply information in exactly the same way. Recognizing that humankind consists of many different types of learners, we can appreciate that collectively, the spiritual realms have provided diverse and abundant teachers who are dedicated to serving the highest good of all humankind.

Which Masters Serve as Members of Our Spiritual Family?

Everyone wants to know which ascended masters and angels are part of his or her higher team or spiritual family. Logically, the masters who are part of any spiritual tradition we follow in life are attracted toward our consciousness. We think about them, our heart reaches out for them, we read about them, we meditate and pray toward them, and they respond.

I have also discovered that if we have an interdimensional relationship with masters (in some other layer of incarnation, whether we consciously remember it or not), they will come forward to assist us now. The only requirements are that our consciousness can lift into their dimension and that we come with a worthy purpose and an open mind free of judgment.

Masters who ascended on the primary ray we came into life to express are also naturally attracted toward us. They can be amazing allies when we are able to recognize and receive their communications.

Asking for the members of your spiritual family to come closer to your consciousness is one way to discover them. Trust your instincts and move toward those who capture your attention in some way. The correspondences in chapter 9 will let you use your astrological birth chart, and your tarot lifetime symbols and growth year symbols to identify potential masters who may be attuned to assist you.

Working with the Ascended Realm
Accelerates Inner Development

As you might imagine, working on this project required continuing spiritual development to contact the masters who correspond to the subtlest levels of consciousness. While the work to clear my own inner obstacles was challenging at times, as our personal work can be, I am infinitely grateful for the result. I can say with certainty that working with the ascended and angelic realms as part of anyone's spiritual practice will accelerate spiritual development.

Masters versus Fictional Characters, Archetypes, and Humans Who Didn't Ascend

Clearly, not every character in a myth is an ascended master. It was necessary for me to be able to recognize that some names in myth were fictional characters created by the storyteller or bard for entertainment. Other names in myth (or those known to history) refer to humans who did not ascend from that lifetime. I ultimately took such names off my list when repeated attempts to contact them in the ascended realm (through many different potential correspondences) did not yield contact. I cannot say that no errors were made, but the sheer number of clear contacts was enough to satisfy me that I understood the difference.

Archetypal energies and personified cosmological principles are also found in myth. They are helpful to reveal archaic forces of nature or transmit important information to ensure humankind's survival, such as the correct seasons for planting and harvesting or how to deal with earthquakes, storms, eclipses, and other natural phenomena.

One example of archetypal energy is Indigenous American Corn Mother, a symbol of planting and earth's abundance, who is portrayed in many fetishes and artistic forms. She conveys a powerful tradition and is important to transmit knowledge about planting and abundant harvest but does not communicate with us in consciousness in the same manner as an ascended master.

In contrast, Sheela-na-gig, an ascended master whose worldly identity remains unknown but who is graphically portrayed as a stylized figure opening her large vulva, appeared in consciousness one evening. She is one of the emotional-level-one masters at the sphere of Hod, none of whom are included in this book. The energy of Hod at that level includes humor and sexual-erotic inspiration. She was chuckling in ribald humor with me about how amusing and amazing it is what human beings do with their sexual parts.

Ascended Masters or Deities?

Returning to our definition of ascended masters and the ideas of Greek Euhemorus mentioned earlier in this chapter, if beings whom some traditions refer to as deities, demigods, or goddesses lived in a physical form during some remote period of antiquity and ascended at the end of their lifetimes, does this take the divinity out of our traditions?

My personal answer is an emphatic no. Direct contact with them in the higher realms is what confirms their connection to divinity. They succeeded in their ultimate spiritual awakening and are part of the continuum of energy connecting us directly with spiritual Source. Those who lived in physical bodies on earth can be especially inspiring, as their ascension demonstrates that this is possible for us also. As is said in some traditions, we can metaphorically stand on their shoulders as we awaken to our own highest spiritual potential.

Book Methodology Step Four

Develop a method to invite contact with specific angels or masters that is simple to use and accessible to anyone.

I had spent five years working on this book by the time step four arrived as inner guidance. I had learned much more about the spiritual purpose of the mineral kingdom and still intended to share it in the book.

In the ancient hermetic worldview, every earthly kingdom (plant, animal, and mineral) plays a role in the evolution of humankind. Minerals are part of the vast network of spiritual light that connects us to our Source. However, using a crystal is not a substitute for the personal spiritual evolution that is required for us to experience our higher spiritual levels. No gem or mineral can override or compensate for what needs clearing from our energy field to raise our vibration. A mineral can energetically nudge us in the right direction as we do our part.

Gem and mineral specimens are not required to experience angels and ascended masters. While it was essential for me to use crystals to confirm subtle differences between masters at different parts and levels of the Qabalah, I experienced many times that we can connect to a master without the aid of a stone. In step four, I was given a method to share in this book that does not require the use of crystals. Below, I will outline why this occurred.

The Challenges of Using Mineral Crystals to Contact Angels and Masters

The system I developed to recognize which mineral crystals correspond with which masters is specific. However, it is far from simple. Communicating how to use it would require a lengthy book of its own. Specialized training in gem science (gemology or minerology), along with experience of the range of gems and minerals that exist, would make it most understandable and applicable.

In the absence of a great deal of additional information, the name of a mineral variety that corresponds to a master is totally useless. General correspondence to a specific part of the Qabalah is complicated enough, including far more than the visible color of a crystal, and then there is another whole set of criteria to learn to contact specific masters.

Some minerals for masters are relatively inexpensive, while other masters correspond to major gem species that are much rarer and, consequently, more costly. Not every specimen of ruby, emerald, and sapphire, for example, is equally effective for working with masters who can be contacted using those stones. Quality matters to ensure a strong connection.

The existence of lab-grown, synthetic gems, and the enhancement of natural gemstones (an accepted industry practice which sometimes dramatically alters a mineral's earth-born color) complicates matters further.. Trade names used by metaphysical dealers for branding purposes (also an accepted trade practice) sometimes make it hard for a potential crystal buyer to understand the species of mineral being offered for sale.

As a gemologist with years of experience in buying gems and minerals, from years of receiving guidance relating chemical correspondence and the Qabalah, and by using intuitive senses, I was able to wade through mineral crystals available for sale from a variety of sources and find those suitable for my purpose.

Some mineral varieties, such as the familiar purple amethyst and golden citrine quartz, occur at different energy levels (emotional levels one and two and the mental level) according to the specimen. Understanding how to recognize these differences is essential to find those that enhance contact with specific masters. Twenty-one of the masters included in this book require a specific specimen of amethyst or citrine quartz. Learning to recognize the subtle emotional level versus mental level differences between specimens of these stones requires a thorough background knowledge, plus developed intuitive senses. Without those abilities, finding the correct crystal to contact a specific master would likely be a frustrating experience.

The Special Case of Colorless Quartz Crystals

Forty of the masters and angels included in this book correspond to a specimen of colorless (rock crystal variety) quartz. Colorless quartz forms in a vast energetic range all over the earth. Spiritual practitioners of every ancient culture have recognized that specimens of colorless quartz can enhance the human-spiritual energy interface.

Many people today who become sensitive to crystal energy can select high-vibration stones. However, *high-vibration* is a subjective experience, and there are twenty-seven possible Qabalah correspondences among colorless quartz crystals (plus a few more if we count the Hidden Paths). To contact a specific master who can be met using colorless quartz, one needs to be aware of what those differences are, and be able to recognize the correct crystal, among thousands of specimens. These were some of the matters that the masters taught me, so that I could obtain crystals suitable to contact them.

Yes, there are many clues in crystal habit (the outer form in which it grew, number and arrangement of crystal faces, and more) that reveal the special uses of a specimen. To match with the most ancient masters, crystal surface features such as record keeper markings are important. Elestial crystal habits also are consistent with some of the more ancient groups of masters. Alpine quartz, Himalayan quartz and specimens that formed under metamorphic conditions also are suitable for the masters who were on earth in remote priomordial periods – however all these types occur in specimens that have a wide range of Qabalah correspondences.

Some crystal locations tend to produce high-vibration specimens in more volume than others—which also, unfortunately, leads to some crystals being sold with popular location attributions that are not accurate. The mined location of a crystal (where exactly it formed on the earth) must be compatible with certain groups of masters. With those specifics in mind, I bought some crystals from professional mineral dealers, who track and can guarantee the mined source of some individual specimens.

I also developed the intuitive ability to verify whether a crystal formed in a compatible location for the master I was seeking, so I was able to purchase some fine crystals from dealers that cannot guarantee the exact mined location of every specimen.

Qabalah Correspondence for Colorless Quartz Crystals

The most essential part of using a colorless quartz crystal to reach a specific angel or master is recognizing its exact Qabalah correspondence. As I mentioned above, there are twenty-seven possible different possible Qabalah classifications of colorless quartz for the conventional scheme of Spheres and Paths, plus a few more if we consider the Hidden Paths.

It took some time for my spiritual team to teach me how to recognize the Qabalah correspondence of the colorless quartz specimens. I was taught that one energetic basis for the different Qabalah correspondences (and level – emotional, mental, or spiritual) arises from the presence of submicroscopic chemical elements – known as trace minerals, - within the quartz crystal lattice.

Every quartz crystal is basically SiO2, silicon dioxide, yet within each crystal is a unique, sub-mircroscopic world of trace elements! We cannot see trace elements – even with a gemologists gem microscope but I developed the intuitive sensitivity to recognize their presence enough to match a crystal to the masters who can transmit energy through it.

How was this possible? Those who become sensitive to mineral energies feel the unique vibration of a stone through their subtle senses. That vibration is impacted by several factors, including the chemistry of that mineral. The chemistry of minerals has been known to science for a long time now. The opaque pink mineral Rhodochrosite, for example, contains a high percentage of manganese. When one becomes familiar with the energetic feel of many manganese minerals (including Rhodonite and the pink variety of Inisite), a next step in sensitivity is to be able to recognize manganese within a colorless quartz crystal, by it's vibrational feel. Sensitivity to many things has been problematic in my life (I cannot tolerate many medicines for example) but to identify the crystals I would need to confirm each masters Qabalah correspondence and level, that sensitivity was essential!

Guidance, along with a great deal of practice, gradually helped me develop a key to link chemical trace elements with each part of the Qabalah (and thus with specific angels and masters). Using that key, I was able to acquire quartz crystal specimens to contact all the masters in this book. Diamond color grading, performed by gemologists, uses a master set of diamonds whose slight nuances of color have been carefully pre-determined. As I worked on this book, I developed a master-set of quartz crystals, to use for the angels and masters. Finally, I was eventually able to develop the ability to purchase colorless quartz crystals online (by photos alone) checking with my guides about their trace element chemistry and then have them work to reach a specific master.

Differences in Quartz Crystals
Observed by Mineral Sciences

While this ability developed, with my background in gem science, I naturally explored whether there was any current, non-destructive, scientific test that could determine the trace-element profile of a colorless quartz crystal.

In the case of rare and valuable colored gem and mineral species, sophisticated laboratory tests, performed in major gem laboratories such as the Gemological Instituted of America, have been developed to chemically analyze specimens with incredible specificity. However, quartz is not valuable enough to justify the cost of such research. While slices of a crystal can be profiled (at a significant cost) there is no current nondestructive test that can provide the overall chemical trace-element composition *for a whole quartz crystal.*

A final issue in using crystals to enhance ascended master and angelic contact, and one of the most significant, is that in addition to the individual master you are attempting to contact, others who share the same Qabalah correspondence and level may also respond through the same crystal. I experienced this many times and it was helpful for this book since I needed to confirm many different masters. However, to have a system to invite a specific master or angel forward in your consciousness, a different approach was necessary.

Arriving at the Method Shared in Chapter 10

As I contemplated the issues that arose with recognizing and communicating how to locate the correct crystal, the masters told me to leave the mineral correspondence out of this book.

At first I was surprised, since this was the very method that I had been guided to use. However, the masters and angels want to be accessible to all who are seeking them and want that process to be as simple as possible. In the time it has taken you to read some of the information above, the whole purpose of contacting ascended-realm beings who can support and guide your life has faded into the background, and crystals have become the focus!

When I agreed to be open to another method, the approach that emerged took one more year to develop and confirm and is presented fully in chapter 10. It will allow you to reach out to a specific ascended master or angel in meditation, without crystals or any other external tool, using your mind's own ability to visualize a color combined with a symbol.

Important to Remember

There are a vast number of ascended masters and angels who exist in the higher dimensions.

Some of their names can be found among the cultural myths of different traditions.

For optimal contact experiences, it is important to release any preexisting biases and judgments about the spiritual traditions that have brought their names forward.

There are no spiritual or religious rivalries in the ascended realm, where all masters and angels serve divine Source and the course of human evolution together.

Considering angels and masters from a cross-cultural perspective provides multiple examples from which we can craft our own life journey.

Working with beings in the ascended realm (masters or angels) accelerates spiritual development.

While certain mineral crystals can be used to contact specific masters, the masters can make contact in our consciousness without the use of crystals.

A simple method to contact specific masters and angels in meditation is fully described in chapter 10.

CHAPTER 3

METHODS TO EXPAND CONSCIOUSNESS

There can be many different reasons to begin a spiritual journey. When we read the inspired poetry of Rumi, Buddhist or Taoist songs that arose spontaneously at masters' enlightenment, or the divine love poetry of Hafiz and Mira Bai, something within the human spirit yearns to reach those higher perspectives also.

This desire can be understood as a mystical quest. According to Evelyn Underhill's classic book *Mysticism*, mystics are those who serve as the spiritual pioneers in every age. Mystics follow many different paths yet arrive at the same goal: a direct experience of spiritual Source.

Underhill identifies mysticism as the art and science of establishing a conscious relationship with the loving presence of Creator. She observes that mystics can unite with the Absolute, proving to themselves through such experience that their spirit is divine. Whether they share their experiences in poems, songs, or autobiographies, their works are always written in the firsthand language of personal experience.

All Religions Have Mystical Traditions, but Not All Mystics Follow a Religion

Many individuals who are acknowledged as founders of the world's great religions had direct experiences of the divine. Abraham, Jesus, and Buddha, all of whom are included in this book, had such experiences. In some manner, each of them established his consciousness in a direct relationship with the higher realms. After their lifetimes, others collected their teachings so they would be available for others to follow.

Whether or not codified teachings always faithfully honor what the spiritual founder taught is a valid question, but that is not my point here. When we prepare our consciousness through spiritual practice, including meditation, and release limiting judgments, it is possible to have our own direct experience with these masters. Their minds, and those of many other masters, are still available, extending to help us awaken to our own divine nature.

Modern-Day Mystics

The essence of the mystical journey remains the same today as it always has been. The desire for direct experience of the sacred has not disappeared from the human spirit. Collective evolution has opened new vistas within human consciousness, and more individuals are ready to experience what can be discovered there.

The array of different practices available to expand consciousness can be bewildering. There are many types of teachers offering many different practices. Recognizing which spiritual path serves us best requires discernment and genuine self-honesty. We need to persist through inner obstacles, develop the discipline to practice, and recognize when our ability to learn a path is complete. At some point, the inner teachers—from the angelic and ascended master realms—can come forward to carry our consciousness further, through a very personal curriculum.

Does Mystical Experience Differ from an Altered State of Consciousness?

The term *altered states of consciousness* has become familiar to many today. It points toward a variety of means to temporarily move past one's personal-ego identification to gain an expanded view. Some altered-state experiences are challenging and require assistance to integrate. An experience that opens the heart as well as the mind while allowing you to feel safe and nurtured, helps you to achieve greater self-love, and builds compassion for everyone else engaged in the human drama may be worthwhile. However, not every altered state moves toward a spiritual experience of Creator Source—the goal I continue to choose.

To be sure, mystics also experience temporarily challenging shifts of energy as consciousness learns to soar beyond former bounds, as well as states of temporary physical discomfort. It is helpful to have the support of someone who understands the special territory of energy changes that may be experienced along the way. Those who arrive at any experience of union with Source find that no questions remain about whether the journey was worthwhile, despite any challenges faced along the way.

The Power of Intention and the Role of Belief

The single most important factor in every type of experience of expanded awareness is intention. Intention is far more than a goal you are seeking. It is an inner attitude that is held as an unwavering core, around which actions consistent with it are arranged. Intention involves the heart, the mind, what we say, and what we do, held in a state of alignment. Many wisdom traditions suggest that we wait until an alignment of heart, mind, and gut arrives before acting on a potential opportunity. Intention is powerful. When we are consistent in holding and acting according to intent, real results will follow.

Belief is part of the foundation for intention. Since we are powerful cocreators along with spiritual Source, what we believe is possible for us to experience determines what can manifest. Things we do not believe are possible will not become part of our experienced reality, even though we might see them occur for others.

Spiritual development includes opening to possibilities we are willing to entertain beyond our current experience. While we are developing our spiritual capacities, we are not asked to grant blind faith to experiences of heightened awareness. However, we must be open enough to discover if they are possible. Finding skilled practitioners can help us learn how to cultivate energy. Develping intention requires discernment. As spiritual experiences unfold, an inner attitude that extends the invitation "Show me more" to the higher realms will eventually result in experiences that carry us forward.

Means and Methods

The sections below briefly highlight some of the methods that spiritual practitioners have used to train their consciousness to reach the higher realms. Some of these may already be part of your current form of spiritual practice. Reading about additional methods will allow your guides and inner wisdom to direct your attention toward other practices that may be helpful for you to consider.

Clearing the Channels

To create an inner opening for Spirit, the mystics of every age have learned to become active participants in clearing their inner storehouses of self-limiting emotions and mental patterns. Doing this makes it far easier for spiritual agencies to contact our consciousness. This clearing occurs in stages, which radically changes our receptivity to spiritual energy.

Doing my part in this inner purification has been one of the most powerful tools to deepen contact with the higher realms of consciousness. Chapters 5 and 6 describe two important means to do this, and they can be added to any form of spiritual practice.

Preparing the Energy Body for Ascended Master and Angelic Contacts

Another focus that develops our capacity for higher consciousness is to consciously work on improving the functioning of the subtle energy centers in our energy body, known as the chakras. The seven chakras that align with the human body (root chakra to crown) allow us to express all the basic functions of human life and turn toward the infinite. It is possible to discover which of our chakras are naturally strongest and to work to clear and balance the others. I had the privilege to facilitate chakra-development groups with women about twenty years ago. It was a powerful process for all of us!

45

When we have cleared any blocks and honed the functioning of the seven chakras, then the transpersonal chakras—those over the crown of the head—and the Merkabah levels connecting us all the way to spiritual Source are ready to be activated. Learning to work experientially with the Qabalah, as outlined in chapter 7, can be a next step to develop those higher chakras and deepen one's capacity to experience the angels and masters.

Shamanic Traditions

Spiritual lineages that began with First World peoples—the indigenous elders and shamanic practitioners present in every part of the globe—include drumming, rattling, fasting, dancing, vision quests, sweat lodges, and the use of sacred plant medicines to enter states of expanded awareness.

A vision quest can break the bonds of normal perception when fasting is rigorous and the body is kept awake for a twenty-four-hour period in a wilderness setting. I experienced this enhanced vision profoundly on one occasion and received precious ascended master visits during another.

Rhythmic drumming, rattling, or dancing allows practitioners to enter trance states. Such practices have been used over tens of thousands of years because they successfully bypass the thinking function of the left-brain hemisphere and create a state of brain-wave entrainment that allows consciousness to soar into nonlinear, intuitive awareness.

We can understand this form of entrainment as the brain's natural tendency to self-synchronize or be drawn into a current or flow of frequency or rhythm, presented via music or another environmental stimulus. It taps into an ability known today as frequency-following response, which recognizes that human brain waves tend to align with the frequency of instruments or other sound technology perceived by the individual. Entrainment has been utilized in many forms of sound healing, both in ancient shamanic cultures and in the present day.

Neoshamanism

While traditional shamanism arose in First World cultures worldwide, today there are also practitioners of neoshamanism who were not born within an indigenous culture but have skillfully adopted some of the elements of shamanism for the purpose of expanding consciousness.

Modern neoshamanic practices may include drumming, breathwork, and other means to enter trance states. Finding qualified guides to learn such practices is important, and discernment must be used. Many different spiritual traditions offer ritual or ceremonial forms in which beings of the higher realms can be experienced. However, the single most important factor in producing experiences remains one's intent, along with the inner state of readiness of the practitioner.

Seasonal Rituals and Ceremonial Forms

Many people enjoy rituals and spiritual ceremonies. Traditions that honor the moon cycle and the changing seasons of the year and include times of ritual celebration have primal roots. In many ancient cultures, building an altar or tending a home shrine was the responsibility of female wisdom keepers entrusted with ensuring the quality of life for family or tribe. Many traditions in the present day continue to honor such celebrations as part of their spiritual practice.

Rites of passage, such as coming-of-age traditions for both men and women, were once part of every society. So too the arrival of menopause was celebrated as a woman's entry into an expanded state of wisdom and power. Since we live in a time when many of these ways have been abandoned, we enter various life stages without traditions that validate our changing status and level of responsibility within our culture. This denies us the value of our lived experience. It has long been part of my practice to re-create female rites of passage and to encourage other women to create them for themselves. Doing this is empowering, raises energy, and allows one to enter the next life phase with renewed dedication and meaning.

47

Brain-Wave Levels and the Availability of Consciousness

As noted above, mystical explorers over the ages developed some consistent views that allowed them to navigate consciousness with skill. One of their most enduring truths is that eternal consciousness exists independent of the physical body. Books about near-death experiences written over the last twenty years by physicians and scientists seem to have clearly confirmed the idea that consciousness, whatever it is, exists independent of the brain's electrical activity. This confirms what mystical explorers have always known: consciousness *is*, both before and after the experience of human life.

While present-day experts in many scientific fields cannot agree on the definition of consciousness modern science has helped us understand the spectrum of human brain-wave levels, which can be scientifically measured. Each brain-wave state represents a different vibrational level and is useful for specific functions. Our consciousness typically moves in and out of them naturally many times a day.

Brain Wave Frequencies

Beta is the common frequency that best serves the busy tasks of daily life. It also is present when we are afraid or worried.

Alpha is present when we are working in a creative flow, during some meditations, and during nighttime dreaming

Theta is a level that can be reached in meditation, and it's also present during deep sleep.

Gamma may correlate with heightened brain activity that can bring forth various experiences of inspired intelligence.

Delta correlates with deep and dreamless sleep.

Where do these different levels of consciousness exist? Spiritual traditions point to the senior existence of Mind, omnipresent and unrelated to the physical location in space and time of the physical body. This is a meta-level of existence, which can be directly accessed through the development of higher consciousness.

Reenvisioning the power of Prayer

Like some people, when I first began a path of spiritual development, I came toward it having had some less-than-ideal experiences with my birth family's religion (which was Christianity.) It took some healing to be willing to discover a different approach to prayer that I could embrace.

There is a thin volume adjunct to *A Course in Miracles* called *The Ladder of Prayer*, which was helpful. It introduces prayer as a whole spectrum that begins with praying for something needed and desired but can move toward subtler levels. Prayer can ultimately cross the boundary into what some of us might call meditation, where, in inner silence, we offer up a time of concentrated listening that allows our eternal relationship to the divine to blossom.

Some of the most well-known female Christian mystics were noted for advanced abilities with prayer, which they described using the term *contemplation*. Teresa of Avila was known to levitate when her consciousness was gathered up in divine grace. This is reminiscent of abilities that would be known as *siddhis* among advanced yogis in the Hindu world. You can read what Teresa offers about the stages of contemplation in her book *Interior Castle*. An excellent translation is currently published by Waking Lion Press and the Editorium.

Trance States

The general term *trance states* includes many forms, some of which were mentioned under shamanism above. Trance facilitates a shift in awareness, as attention on the physical body and environment is diminished. Trance is one of the time-honored forms of connecting with higher spiritual forces, as it allows the practitioner to temporarily bypass the rational mind (left hemisphere of the brain) to tap into a holistic, nonlinear, nonverbal channel of intuitive consciousness via the right-brain hemisphere.

The female seers who served the ancient oracle centers throughout Greece typically entered a trance state either by their own innate ability or with the aid of some agent, such as fumes arising from a natural fissure in the earth at the Oracle of Delphi. Some of the most famous oracle priestesses delivered prophecies in verse, which was considered a sign of being in inspired communication with a nonphysical, enlightened being.

In one deep contact with Phemone (a female master not included in this book), who is acknowledged as the first priestess who served at the Oracle at Delphi, the term *mantic consciousness* was delivered to my awareness. The term was not familiar, and I had to look it up. As described on *Wikipedia* under "Greek Divination," the Greek word for a diviner is *mantis*, which is generally translated as *prophet* or *seer*. Mantises were internationally recognized professional oracles, such as the women who served at sites such as Delphi. Contact with Phemone's mind was an unforgettable experience for me.

An esteemed Judaic female named Huldah (included in the profiles ahead) is mentioned in the Old Testament of the Christian Bible (2 Kings 22:13–20; 2 Chronicles 34:22–28). She was skilled in entering trance, and her word carried unquestioned spiritual authority, which was quite remarkable in her time and culture.

Many ancient Norse female masters, practitioners of the art known as *seidr*, were also noted for their capacity to enter trance states and bring through prophecy. Some individuals today practice this form of spiritual contact. The book entitled *Trans-Portation: Learning to Navigate the Inner World*, by Diana L Paxon, is a comprehensive book on trance states, written from the northern pagan perspective.

Scrying, a technique most well known in pagan circles (and used by some indigenous practitioners), involves entering trance by staring at a crystal globe; at the reflective surface of water or oil; or into a mirror, fire, or candle flame to receive a vision.

Group trance can be induced by a facilitator who reads a guided-meditation script that features symbols, colors, and guided imagery. When the script relates to one of the twenty-two paths of the Qabalah, the technique is known as pathworking.

Use of Trance States by Mediums, Psychics, Channels, and Intuitives

Individual practitioners usually prefer one of the terms listed above rather than the others, although the terms can describe overlapping abilities. Each practice involves entering some form of trance to receive and deliver communications from beings in the higher realms as a form of spiritual service.

This ability was profoundly demonstrated by famous American psychic medium Edgar Cayce (1877–1945). He performed some seven thousand readings for individuals during his lifetime. The text of his readings has been published in various forms by the Association for Research and Enlightenment (ARE), and both his books and access to ARE's online database of individual readings (searchable by topic) are available today.

Information about mediumship can also be found in the writings of Allan Kardec (see *The Book on Mediums: Guide for Mediums and Invocators*). Kardec's work is applied in some Brazilian spiritual traditions today.

Some individuals learn to channel messages from a specific spirit entity, whether angelic, an ascended master, or a being from an extraterrestrial race. In each of these forms, the ability of individuals receiving such communications varies, and greater clarity is achieved as they continue their spiritual development.

Binaural Sound Technology

The development of binaural sound technology, which involves musical recordings and guided meditations that work with both hemispheres of the brain in a specific way to induce higher consciousness, has been available during recent decades. One of the pioneers in this technology is the Monroe Institute in Virginia, USA. I have enjoyed using their products many times in the last twenty-five years. Currently, they offer residential training programs, an outreach of seminars worldwide, and an app called Expand to help people explore states of consciousness beyond the physical.

Chanting, Toning, Sacred Songs, and Music

Many spiritual traditions use chanting to raise and focus energy toward a specific higher-vibrational being. Whether using deity names, seed syllables, or phrases from a sacred text, chanting may be done in Sanskrit, Hindi, one of the Tibetan languages, or another language. Tibetan monks are renowned for their polyphonic throat-singing chants. Chanting features in Buddhist, Taoist, Hindu, and Jain traditions, among others.

Whether chanting is part of a devotional practice or not, virtually every form of spiritual practice uses hymns or sacred songs. All of these are based on the vibrational power of sound, fueled by breath, to induce a frequency-following response in the human brain to raise one's vibration.

Modern musical performers Jai Uttal, Krishna Das, Carlos Nakai, and many others use the power of sound to consciously raise spiritual energy. At her concerts, Deva Premal often invites her audience to join in some of the Sanskrit chants her songs include. It's easy to feel the collective vibration in the room lift as attendees chant together. The Monroe Institute uses toning, along with a specific frequency, to achieve the same purpose.

Spiritual Pilgrimages and Wilderness Retreats

Since ancient times, people have made spiritual pilgrimages either solo or in focused groups to ancient sacred sites worldwide. Stonehenge;

the Great Pyramid of Giza; Machu Picchu, Peru; Assisi, Italy; Santiago de Compostela, Spain; Lourdes, France; Chichén Itzá, Mexico; Angkor Wat, Cambodia; many sites throughout India; and Jerusalem in the Holy Land are just a few locations still popular today. Some ancient sites were built over a yet more ancient ceremonial site or an underground confluence of powerful ley lines and earth energy.

Sometimes group visits to these sites are led by living energy masters from various spiritual traditions, who assist participants to focus on healing or lifting consciousness. Depending on an individual's readiness, the skill of the group facilitator, and the means and methods used, one can have profound experiences of the higher realms and beings.

Individual spiritual practitioners may also find suitable wilderness sites that offer spiritually useful configurations of energy. My husband and I made many visits to a site in a remote wilderness area of central Nevada that supported our spiritual evolution and growth.

Meditation

All forms of meditation are beneficial, however they do not all lead to the same experiences. Saying this does not imply judgment that some are better; they are simply different—by design.

Mindfulness meditation is a popular form that arises from Buddhism yet has been modified to remove the spiritual elements and offer in corporate or health care settings. It is intended to reduce stress, promote health, and help one to develop greater self-mastery of emotions, grow in self-acceptance and compassion for oneself and others. All of these are certainly worthwhile goals.

Working with mindfulness as a practice can help you to develop concentration and inner stillness. By design, mindfulness is not theistic, meaning it does not include the existence of divine beings. Those who do wish to reach experiences of the angels and masters may need to include, rather than disregard, some of the subtle signals through which the spiritual world attempts to contact us. We can take all skills learned in any meditation practice—clarity, calm, focus, and the power of breath—into the domain of spirit when that becomes our purpose.

Breathwork

Some attention on the breath is an entry point for most types of meditation. This is because our breath is the most available tool for us to center, clear our minds, and become receptive. It helps us shift from the beta brain-wave level of everyday life concerns toward the levels at which we are receptive to subtle energy (e.g., a trance state).

Stanislav Grof, MD, a psychiatrist and researcher into nonordinary states of consciousness, identified one method to do this; Holotropic breathing, which is available through accredited teachers.

Techniques of pranayama (alternate-nostril breathing) arise from yogic practices. There are various practitioners who teach these techniques, including an online course available through Sounds True Publishing, Colorado, USA.

There are many more variations using breath to enter trance, involving the speed of inhaling and exhaling, the holding of the breath for various counts, and the circulation of the breath within the body. Some breathwork combines visualizations. Any of these can be effective to tap into layers of consciousness that temporarily bypass the discursive mind. It is helpful to experience different methods to find the ones that are most effective for you.

Cultivating Nighttime Dream Recall

Consciousness moves into the astral planes every night during sleep and dreaming. People who develop the ability to remember their dreams may wake up with awareness about information communicated to them by one of their higher spiritual team.

The hypnagogic state—the transitional, liminal state that one experiences between waking and sleep—can also be a powerful opening through which angels and masters can communicate with your consciousness, delivering information that has not reached you in another way.

Symbol and Color Visualization

Visualization is one of the classic tools employed in different forms of healing, meditation, and spiritual practice. Symbols are the vertical bridges that establish a relationship between different levels of consciousness. They bypass the intellect, tapping deeper levels of knowing.

When symbols and colors arise from a system that recognizes specific dimensions of metaphysical energy, such as those presented in the Qabalah, and are used with consciousness and intent, the system becomes an effective bridge to the dimensions where angels and masters exist. This is the principle that gives rise to the approach presented in this book, which is discussed in chapter 10.

Powerful Life Experiences That Open Doors in Consciousness

For some individuals, a sudden, temporary shift to a metaperspective of consciousness can occur through a near-death experience or a life-threatening illness. Such experiences can literally propel consciousness into new terrain. There are many books that describe the personal experiences of people from all walks of life who've experienced complete life transformation through such events.

The transition of a dearly loved family member at the end of his or her physical life can also open the doors of consciousness. A great many people worldwide, including those with no previous interest in spiritual matters, experience the presence of departed loved ones who visit them after their physical lives have completed. Those experiences can alter one's perception about the reality of the spiritual world and lead to shifts in belief and attitude that direct his or her life in new directions.

When Your Heart Desires a Personal Connection with Creator Source

In briefly surveying some of the many avenues that can expand the lens of consciousness, we can appreciate that there is a strong drive within the human spirit to experience more than the five-sensory world. Cultivating our capacity for awe (see *Awe*, the recent book by Dacher Keltner) enhances health and happiness and feeds the human spirit.

In exactly this way, everyone contains a spark of the mystic. Finding the path that helps you develop your natural abilities and asking meaningful questions before embarking on any practice will help you make informed choices. Becoming clear about the type of experience you seek and listening within for the quiet voice of inner guidance will help you find your optimal path.

Important to Remember

Every human being has the capacity for mystical consciousness that, when developed, leads to direct spiritual experience of ascended-realm beings.

There are many ways to expand the lens of human consciousness, some of which include shamanic practices, rituals, visualization of symbols, breathwork, chanting, certain forms of meditation, and intense life passages.

Ascended-realm beings can contact us anytime our mind becomes silent enough to become aware of them (when we desire that contact and prepare for it).

When one's goal is a direct experience of the sacred, it is important to learn which practices lead toward that experience.

The most important factors are always one's intention, inner preparation, and ongoing commitment to a spiritual practice.

CHAPTER 4

RECOGNIZING WHEN ANGELS AND ASCENDED MASTERS MAKE CONTACT

This chapter discusses the means to recognize our experiences with the higher dimensions when they occur. It concludes with a discussion of the four basic types of subtle intuitive senses so you can recognize and develop the forms that are naturally strongest for you.

Recognizing Spiritual Guidance

There is a difference between inner guidance and the voice of the personality self. Guidance often arrives in a gentle tone, like a quiet thought that doesn't go away, in contrast to the more strident tone of the ego.

As we are learning to recognize the difference, it is helpful to incorporate a spiritual wisdom text (such texts exist within many traditions) into our daily practice. This helps us to release ideas based on fear, blame, and guilt and build an elevated thought system that allows the voice of Spirit to be recognized.

Learning to try out the inner messages we believe to be guidance is part of the learning process. We will discover that genuine guidance will not always produce the results our personality expects, because sometimes important lessons are meant to be learned. However, over time, it is easy to recognize that following inner guidance results in the best outcomes.

Signs and Synchronicities That Confirm a Spiritual Contact

The spiritual worlds are in constant communication with us, but our attention is often too distracted to be aware of it. The first step on any spiritual path is to free up enough energy and attention to notice when our guides are attempting to reach us.

There are many ways the spiritual realm gently confirms its presence with us. Signs (the inner ones) come in many forms: numbers that consistently appear, animals we encounter as we walk in nature, found feathers, books that tumble off a shelf at our feet, or lyrics of seemingly random songs that address exactly what we've been asking for guidance about. We might recognize guidance orchestrating meetings with others who appear in our lives at the perfect time. The basic purpose behind a spiritually oriented daily meditation—and, for some, a daily practice of journaling—is to provide a regular time when we make our attention available to listen for the quiet voice of Spirit.

Spiritual contact registers in the human nervous system and can be experienced through the physical body in sensations such as shivers, the hair raising on our arms, or tears that fall when we are not sad but have been touched by something profound.

As many sources report, these reactions come about through the vagus nerve, the longest nerve in the body. It emerges from the medulla, the lower part of the brain stem, and it branches off the right and left sides of the body, interfacing with the automatic responses of the parasympathetic nervous system. It helps to regulate our internal organs; digestive system; respiratory rate; heart rate; and certain reflex actions, such as sneezing, coughing, and swallowing.

The vagus nerve can flush our body with light. Developing it, through stretching, yoga, meditation, and other means, produces a healthy connection between the head, heart, and gut; enhances our natural empathic and telepathic skills; and helps us trust the flow of our intuition. Clearing out the inner obstacles (turbulent emotions and thoughts) to increase inner calm and receptivity helps those signals enter our awareness with greater clarity.

Experiences with Angels and Masters
Are Individual and Anecdotal

As we develop the inner calm, clarity, and focus to begin to access the higher realms directly, it is important to highlight the fact that anything we experience in meditation or trance is always a subjective inner-world experience. It is anecdotal, meaning it is our personal account of what we experienced, which always lies beyond the realm of objective proof.

I cannot guarantee you will experience angels and masters in any of the ways I have, which I share in their profiles. Whichever way you receive their communications is the best method for you, and your ability will deepen as you continue your spiritual practice. There are some basics that help us prepare for those direct experiences, which are discussed in chapters 5 and 6, to develop greater readiness.

The best evidence for any profound spiritual encounter lies in one's approach to all the matters of life after such experiences. The experiences should—and do—have lasting transfer value across all areas of one's life. Mystical experiences have a way of reshaping us from within as we realign our outer lives with the heart of the wonders we were shown.

Learning to Extend and Deepen the Moment of Contact

When we do our part to prepare (see chapters 5 and 6), finally, in some precious moment, the consciousness of an ascended master interacts with us directly, and we are aware of it. At first, the mind says, *Wow, that really happened!* This type of reaction usually terminates the moment of contact. With practice, we learn to keep our thoughts still, prolonging and deepening the experience, and reflect upon it afterward.

At first, the masters seem so lofty that part of the human personality feels less than the energy they extend. However, they won't long allow us to be less than they are. They will often convey in some form that we are just like them in terms of potential, long before we can fully accept that fact.

Humor is one of the classic hallmarks of communicating with ascended masters. Masters might joke with us in a gently teasing way, and we might dissolve in belly laughter as we see exactly what they have so adroitly pointed out about us. This is a form of teaching that is truly helpful, because we can feel the love behind the message rather than take it as criticism.

Other experiences with masters or angels are like energetic showers (or torrents!) of love and light, and we can feel the energy move through our whole energy field. Our awareness might soar with them in the higher dimensions, taking in views filled with exquisite colors and information. Whatever forms our experiences take, learning to improve our receptivity is worth every effort.

I can say with certainty that if you continue to seek a form of spiritual practice that is suited to you, and incorporate it in your daily routine, some type of spiritual experiences will result. The timing in which they arrive will be whatever serves your highest good. Spiritual reality wants to be known and has met all sincere seekers through some form of experience in every age. The masters at the heart of this book are the evidence that the journey can be fruitful.

Developing Discernment to Guide You in the Astral Plane

As one prepares to experience the higher dimensions, knowing a bit about what is called the astral plane is essential. Diverse types of nonphysical beings may be encountered there by our consciousness. Each of them is part of the continuum of spiritual light that links us to our Source.

When we encounter nonphysical entities that once animated physical bodies, they represent a wide spectrum of evolutionary development. While we can bless every soul's evolutionary learning journey, being able to distinguish spiritual masters from other less-helpful, disembodied spirits is essential so we know which ones are worth listening to.

Experiences in the astral plane can be deceiving, and things may not be as they first appear. The astral light reflects the higher planes and pure archetypes, but it isn't only that. Since it is a fluid medium between the higher planes and man's thought faculties, it became, over time, a storehouse of both light and dark. It simply mirrors all the impressions it has received from collective humanity.

For this reason, it is wise to put intention into inviting contact with only those beings who will provide a positive learning experience for you. To do this effectively, you will want to learn techniques to create a sacred space and shield yourself from less-evolved energies. You will want to come toward any experience seeking the higher realms, with a calm and purified inner state and worthy intent (healing, forgiveness, and personal spiritual evolution are always worthy intents). Each spiritual tradition has developed approaches to do this, which are usually best learned from an embodied teacher.

When one is working with a group, there are additional means that may be necessary to keep the group energy focused on a high trajectory, ensure that everyone feels safe, and guarantee that the confidentiality of anything participants share is maintained.

Forms of Spiritual-Intuitive Sensing: The Four Clairs

As our spiritual abilities deepen, they are quite individual, according to the life assignments we came to fulfill. For general understanding and so we can recognize our natural strengths, they are grouped into four general categories known as the "four clairs": clairvoyance, clairsentience, claircognizance, and clairaudience. There are some additional variations, but these four are the basic group. Reviewing the descriptions of each type below can help us become more aware of the ways in which intuitive information comes to us, so we can recognize when the ascended-realm beings are communicating with us.

Some individuals manifest strong intuitive senses from an early age, and children born in the last few decades are arriving with profound early abilities. It took me many years of spiritual development to arrive at the level of contact shared in this book, but there were enough blessed experiences along the way to keep me dedicated to my practices. Everyone who is truly committed to spiritual awakening will be guided by his or her higher team, developing in whatever way is best.

Clairvoyance: Clear Seeing through Spiritual Vision

People who have the potential to develop clairvoyant vision tend to be highly visual and frequently remember their nighttime dreaming experiences. They can easily learn to perceive subtle nuances of color and mists, and they notice gradations of sparkling light. The higher spiritual worlds are exquisitely beautiful! Clairvoyants who are artistically inclined may create visionary art to share a bit of the wonders they have seen.

Like any of the subtle intuitive senses, clairvoyance may develop slowly over time, or it may arrive suddenly with a major life event, such as following the death of a loved one or a traumatic health incident. Some people see so many nonphysical entities that their challenge is to bring this experience into balance with physical world activities. For others, a gradually deepening ability arrives through spiritual practice.

Not every clairvoyant sees the same type of information. Some (who tend to work in fields related to healing) become adept at observing the energy fields of individual human beings, or can notice changes in their physical organs. An energy field surrounds the human physical body and can take various shapes and sizes. Subtle layers and colors can appear within the overall energy field that present specific information about the individual's state of health, career path, spiritual development, emotional state, and many other topics. A few individuals, such as author Jack Schwartz (1924–2000), could see the great rays extending from higher dimensions, entering directly into the crown of an individual's head, and revealing the specific energies they came into life to express.

Some clairvoyants see symbols or receive a whole spiritual vision behind closed eyes, while others can see entities in the spiritual world while their physical eyes are open. Those who work with clients by phone can see as clearly as if the client were physically present. As spiritual vision develops, angels and ascended masters stand out, because their colors are pure and light, and their luminous radiance is splendid.

What do angels and masters look like? Sometimes we see them in a form that has become ubiquitous in collective thought. The concentration of many minds over eons builds up human-appearing forms in the astral. When one sees the pure energy of these beings, the appearance is much more abstract. There may be suggestions of form, gender, and, frequently, there are patterns of color and light, but they are essentially without form. (Form is perceived in the Third Dimension and less so in the Fourth Dimension and Fifth Dimension, giving way to formlessness beyond that.)

When masters' faces are visible, sometimes their eyes look at us with consciousness—we know they are aware of us. On occasion, their eyes can become a portal that opens into yet higher dimensions. Similarly, angels may appear as spheres, in abstract forms we identify as human-appearing, or simply as fields of colored light in a constant state of motion.

On occasion, spiritual vision with a specific master can carry you to observe a sacred site, such as Stonehenge, the pyramids of Giza, or Machu Picchu. This type of vision can be accompanied by kinesthetic senses of walking on the ground, awareness of whether it is day or night, and the context for the information being presented to you. This type of visionary experience can be described by the terms *astral travel*, or *bilocation*. Clearly, the shift is entirely in consciousness as the physical body has not gone anywhere. Such experiences tend to underscore lineages and sites that were significant in the lifetime of masters who are part of your higher spiritual family. If one has transpersonal lifetimes in that culture, the experience can be profound, and the master may convey specific information that provides deep insight.

Fear is the great block to clairvoyant vision, since the spiritual world will not show us things that increase our fear. Many years ago, I had just experienced my mother's death transition. I was feeling exhausted from the intensity of her sudden health crisis: three weeks from cancer diagnosis to end-of-life transition. The second or third day after she left her body, I was watching TV with my husband, just appreciating the comfort of his arm around me more than paying attention to the screen. Into the brightly lit afternoon daylight came a tiny bubble of light, which got larger as it drew closer. In its center was a tiny figure of my mother, appearing just as I had known her in life but much younger and more vital. The moment took me completely by surprise. Something in me wasn't ready to hold that level of spiritual experience, and I felt a stab of fear. The vision closed instantly, and I could not recreate it, much to my sadness. It took years of further development until I was able to experience the visions I describe in each master's profile.

Clairsentience: Clear Perception through Emotional Feeling Senses

Those with developing clairsentient abilities are extremely sensitive to physical body sensations and sudden changes of mood and are likely to feel the emotions of others. In the beginning stages of developing this ability, you may unconsciously pick up the subtle emotional energies of others everywhere and not be able to distinguish which are yours and which belong to others.

To give a personal example, many years ago, my husband took me to stay at a five-star hotel in Arizona designed by the famous architect Frank Lloyd Wright. He intended it to be a special treat. We checked in, and I stayed in the room while he was away for four hours at a business meeting. When he returned, I was insistent that something terrible had happened in that room—because I could feel it—and said I couldn't possibly sleep there. At that time, I didn't understand much about clairsentience, but he got us another room. That sensitivity also occurred occasionally when we traveled to our favorite small hotel in the village of Mulegé, Baja California Sur, Mexico. I learned to clear the energy in places I visited and to surround myself with light, but some places were so emotionally toxic that it was easier to switch rooms.

Another way clairsentience can be experienced is by feeling discomfort in your physical body that mirrors a health problem or coming traumatic event for someone close to you. This occurs because the physical body of a clairsentient is a powerful receiver of subtle energy. This information comes up into the energy field through the soles of the feet and through the root chakra. Those who use clairsentience to work as intuitive counselors learn to decipher and use this information on behalf of their clients and then release it from their own energy field. A different type of clairsentient experience is feeling the presence of a deceased loved one who may be near you at times. We all become familiar with the unique feeling of energy associated with those we love, and we can still recognize them near us even when they return to spirit form. It is also possible to simply know when masters, or departed loved ones, are near you. You may not see, feel, or hear them, yet you absolutely know they are close.

When clairsentient abilities develop into a full link between your consciousness and someone in the nonphysical realm, through which information can be transmitted, this is known as mediumship. Mediums (some individuals with this ability prefer the term *intuitive* or *psychic medium*) may experience any of the subtle senses at work to allow them to receive information from nonphysical entities.

As mentioned earlier in this chapter, for your own highest good, it is important to be able to discern the evolutionary development of spiritual entities *before* opening your energy field to connect with them. Each angel and master in the ascended realm has his or her own distinctive energy signature, just as our individual loved ones have theirs. Clairsentients feel naturally drawn toward beings who are highly evolved, since contact with their energy is so elevating. Holiness, wisdom, love, strength, and the feeling of minds connected directly with divine Source itself are just a few of the highly attractive characteristics that a clairsentient can feel in the energy fields of specific masters. As we align with that same high vibration in ourselves, this naturally accelerates our own evolution, and we learn that we too carry that vibration of divine light.

Those with clairsentient abilities might be able to feel the emotions that masters experienced during their key life-learning assignments. When clairsentience combines with clairvoyant vision, we can also look through a master's eyes in a visual way. They can show how experiences looked and felt from their perspective. For example, when Sir Perceval, one of King Arthur's knights—not in this book but an ascended master—connected with my consciousness, I could feel the rush and raw courage that allowed a knight to charge toward his opponent in a jousting tournament. He was demonstrating "Try it like this," a lesson I recall whenever I face a situation requiring courage in my life today.

Also, through clairsentient senses, one can directly feel the love that still exists between sacred relationship partners who are now part of the ascended realm (see my experiences with Guinevere and Arthur; Radha and Krishna; and Jesus/Yeshua, and Magdalene in the profiles ahead). I have also felt the love shared between ascended master mothers and their ascended master children. (John the Baptist and his mother, Elizabeth, and King Solomon and his mother, Bathsheba, have occasionally arrived together in my inner-world contacts.) Each time I feel the love still present between some of the ascended masters, I'm reminded that when we lay down physical form, the love we have shared with others continues with us into eternity. Love is the one experience that is forever!

Claircognizance: Simply Knowing, Direct Downloads of Information

Claircognizance allows us to simply receive a body of data and know that it is accurate, with no evidence to corroborate it. Sometimes our spiritual team needs to convey specific knowledge to help us carry out a specific life assignment beyond the present scope of our learning. The information can come through in an instant, in a whoosh, through consciousness. This can occur for authors as they receive specific information to include and even the exact words to use. The information wasn't there a moment before, and you may not have even been thinking of the subject, yet suddenly, it's there in your mind, whole and complete. Those who develop this ability can bring innovative ideas, concepts, or even scientific inventions into form in this manner.

Even in early stages of spiritual development, claircognizant information can arrive to avert a potential life crisis. Years ago, during a workday at my jewelry store, I suddenly knew I was urgently needed at home. I leaped into my car, drove the short distance home, and walked in to discover my young daughter choking. Her babysitter was out of earshot at the other end of the house. Suddenly, the information came, and I knew I had to go, though I did not know why. I was grateful I acted!

Over the past twenty years, claircognizant information has come through many times as I was learning and writing about esoteric systems, such as the Qabalah, and being taught how to use gems and minerals to accelerate spiritual development. My research would take me to a certain point, and I wouldn't know how to go further; then, suddenly, I would receive a whole new download of information.

As this ability first develops, you may be startled to notice information coming to you this way and initially doubt its validity. There are various methods of applying discernment to see if information you have received comes from a higher spiritual source. You can always ask for confirmation through other means and pay attention to your own best ways of receiving such information. It can be helpful to notice if the message you received was a completely new idea that your mind did not already have in its inventory or if the message answers a question you had been asking about, although not necessarily at that moment. When you feel confident that it came from a higher source than personal ego, it is highly advisable to take action to put it into effect in your life.

In experiences with the masters, claircognizance allows you to know exactly who they are, even if you have never experienced or heard of them before. This occurred more than a few times as new masters came forward to connect with me. Sometimes I also suddenly received knowledge of exactly where I would be able to find further information on them to deepen my understanding.

Clairaudience: Clear Inner Hearing

As clairaudient abilities develop, some might find they receive answers to their spiritual questions by audible synchronicities. This can happen by hearing the lyrics of a song or accidentally tuning in to a radio or TV program or podcast that is discussing something you have been asking for guidance about. You might also wake up from the experience of hearing something spoken to you in a dream. (A few new ascended masters brought me their names in dreams so strongly and repeatedly that I woke up remembering them and immediately looked up more information on them.)

Or, in the middle of a conversation with someone, you might hear words come out of your mouth that, the moment before, were not present in your mind. This occurs with some intuitive counselors who deliver spiritual insight during client readings.

In some northern pagan traditions, it is called *prophesy* when the communication relates to likely timelines and probable outcomes that have not yet manifested. It is important to note here that the prophetic information an intuitive may relay to a client is based on his or her ability to perceive which of multiple possible timelines is most likely to manifest in that individual's life. The ongoing choices and development of the client can quickly shift him or her toward another of the potential timelines, so predictions do not always hold up. This fact reaffirms the power of our own choices in the moment to shape the course of our lives.

The ability to receive and deliver inner information again touches on what is known as mediumship. Those who are full-trance mediums may not be aware of the words they are speaking, because their individual consciousness has completely withdrawn, allowing a higher being to communicate through them. This was the case for famous American psychic Edgar Cayce, who was completely unaware of the words he spoke to clients, until he later heard what had been recorded by others who were present. Other mediums and channels step aside partway in consciousness and are thus able to be at least partially aware of the information coming through them.

When I encounter ascended masters in a direct experience, clairaudient senses allow them to communicate their names directly in my mind. This occurred more frequently for me in contact with the masters in this book than the number of claircognizant experiences wherein I simply knew who they were. No way is intrinsically better than any other, and in both cases, I needed to confirm by repeated contact and by my experience of their energy through other senses that these contacts were who they claimed to be.

Clairaudience might also allow you to hear a distinctive inner musical tone, though there is no physically audible sound. I have experienced this with only two masters to date, but the experiences were memorable. I have received some immensely helpful clairaudient communications from masters who communicated with my consciousness as clearly as if I were listening to an inner voice speaking. These messages included instructions in a specific spiritual practice or guidance about the best way to deal with a current life situation.

When the masters communicate with me this way, the words are simple, clear, and easy to remember, though I also recognize the high evolutionary development of the masters by how succinctly they can convey spiritual principles or practices. They know exactly the best words to use so that I understand them, because they are aware of my mind's already existing knowledge and use it as a framework. There is no grandiosity or superficiality in what is being communicated, and I always appreciate how timely the message is for me when it arrives this way.

Some people receive ongoing messages delivered at a pace that allows them, or a colleague, to transcribe them. Whole channeled books can arrive in this fashion. (See *Absence from Felicity*, which details how *A Course in Miracles* was received and transcribed by Helen Schucman.)

The members of our higher teams might choose to communicate clairaudiently at critical times in our lives. I once received a striking inner message this way, telling me what to do about an emergency that came up when I was free diving along the Northern California coast with my husband. I was a novice diver, and he was experienced, but the new snorkel he had bought the day before was faulty, although he had not known that before entering the water. The calm ocean we had entered turned suddenly rough, and he was in trouble, swallowing seawater. I only learned this after the inner message I received. It was the first time I had heard an inner voice, and it was amazingly clear. It told me to swim toward him and tell him I could get myself to shore safely. This would allow him to focus on taking care of himself, rather than being concerned about me, and we both made it safely back. It is wise to act on such messages immediately!

Hallmarks of Communication with Higher-Dimensional Intelligence

Subtle intuitive senses take time to fully develop within anyone. Along the way, each person is given a means to distinguish communications that arise from a deeper level than his or her personality's intelligence. As such communications arrive in consciousness, they can bring an influx of greater light, information and knowledge that were not present previously, and guidance at crucial transitions in the personal life.

These communications do not always conform to what the personality believes it wants or needs. Yet even when this is the case, they carry some note of authority for the individual that allows him or her to accept and embrace what is given and discover its life-enhancing value as he or she applies it.

Important to Remember
Using Subtle Senses to Connect with the Ascended Realm

Many nonphysical entities occupy various levels of the astral plane, and you will want to develop discernment to recognize those who are highly evolved. This gives you insight about whose advice is worthy of following.

It is important to seek higher contact in a calm state, with a worthy intention, and ask for protection from lower energies.

Individuals who have clairvoyant abilities may experience the exquisite beauty of the higher realms in spiritual vision and be able to visually recognize masters by their radiance.

Those with clairsentient abilities will feel, kinesthetically and emotionally, the loving and beneficial energy of ascended-realm beings in a powerful way and be able to recognize individual masters through their feeling senses.

Those who are claircognizant may receive a download of information from the ascended realm that they can recognize did not come from their own minds, or they may simply know something with certainty without having any outer-world evidence that it is true.

Those with clairaudient abilities use inner subtle hearing to receive the name of a master their consciousness is contacting, along with complete messages and guidance.

It is important to develop personal inner criteria to distinguish genuine experiences with members of the ascended realm and to ask for confirmation along the way. Everyone does that based upon his or her strongest subtle senses.

CHAPTER 5

PREPARING FOR ASCENDED-REALM CONTACT: FORGIVENESS

The first chapters of this book have offered a lofty vision of the potential for human consciousness to experience angels and ascended masters while we still animate physical bodies. While the spiritual realms strongly support our ability to do this, our individual preparation is essential.

As discussed earlier, to experience these beings directly, we must lift consciousness from five-sense perception toward the higher realms. It's easy to notice that the collective world currently still operates within paradigms that are fearful, create experiences of scarcity, and project blame onto others. This very unpleasant energy becomes the fuel that pushes some of us to discover a better way.

Patterns That Hold Us in the Third Dimension

When we first begin to meditate, some of the unconscious and unresolved mental and emotional charges we carry in our energy fields hold our awareness in the Third Dimension. It's like trying to take off in a hot air balloon while holding on to lead weights. Memory and angst about those charged past experiences keep our consciousness earthbound, tethered to the personality self, and we cannot see that there is so much more. It's like wearing blinders, because they block us from experiencing the brilliant light, joy, and peace consistently experienced in the higher realms.

This dilemma isn't personal, though to resolve it requires personal effort. Every human being grows up within a paradigm that defines existence from the viewpoint of a personality identity in physical body on a planet.

When you came into your body, you inherited its operating system, the human ego. As an operating system, it allows you to move the body around and attempts to keep you safe. However, the type of safety it offers comes with the cost of perceiving a limited and fearful world.

The parts of the operating system that ensure the ego's survival are based on the false idea that we are separate from our Source and separate from brother and sister humankind. Unexamined, this belief eclipses awareness of our connection to our own spiritual levels. It can also attempt to make us fear what we might find if we turned to clear obstacles within. As a result, the pattern directs our attention to past hurts and future fears, believing that changes outside ourselves are the only answer to relieve inner distress. While we listen to the ego's logic, we are denied powerful choices that open wholly new trajectories in life.

Regardless of the ego's patterns, we surrender only pain and suffering to claim our divine birthright. We don't have to fear or fight the ego, because it is not our ultimate reality. As we grow in spiritual experience, eventually, we reach a point when our own consciousness becomes a trustworthy vessel for the higher self. As certainty about our eternal nature solidifies, we can simply thank the ego and turn toward the more certain guidance of our higher levels and spiritual team.

Life Changes Are Necessary to Experience the Changeless

Whatever motivation sends us to explore a spiritual path, at first, we encounter a seeming paradox. To experience the changeless, eternal essence that we are necessitates some inner and outer changes at the level of the individual. Why is this so?

Some human patterns are simply part of the territory of entering into a body, with its physical senses. Physical senses are helpful, and sometimes we delight in the beauty they reveal in nature and how we can perceive the loving gaze of another. However, they do not reveal the full extent we can experience during human life. We can only discover this by learning to move beyond the five senses.

Some of our personality's seeming limitations arise through life

73

experiences that leave a charge (e.g., shock, fear, guilt, blame, or self-judgment) that remains in our energy field. When these charges are triggered, they produce automatic responses to situations, which can trip us up. Some of those patterns have been present long enough that we believe they are us. (They are *not* us!)

Everyone experiences some lingering effects from past experiences in one way or another, but we can learn how to clear them. When we approach them with spiritual tools, we come to appreciate that they are simply overlays that don't accurately reflect our true essence.

Finding Means and Methods to Clear Inner Obstacles

We experience life through a physical body, but it is not our senior spiritual identity. As many spiritual explorers of higher-dimensional reality (from different spiritual traditions) have discovered, our eternal essence remains unchanged no matter what we experience in physical life.

When the means to reach higher states of consciousness arrive, the blessed truth of our eternally unchanging spiritual reality is confirmed in direct personal experience. The relief this produces is amazing. It returns us, and everyone else, to eternal innocence. We are relieved of all the burdens we have been carrying overlong about things done and undone during our life. All of them were part of the learning, growing environment that our human life includes, but their effects are not final in harming anyone.

Until we reach this blessed experience for ourselves, we can open to the possibility that it is so and move toward a practice that brings the experience of it closer. That is where forgiveness plays an essential role.

Forgiveness as Part of Spiritual Practice

In collective human understanding, the word *forgiveness* is still commonly interpreted as a practice to release *others* from blame for harm they have done to us. Instead, forgiveness is a process that helps us to release *ourselves* from the effects of troubling situations we have experienced. A great many spiritual disciplines offer various types of forgiveness practices, which, like the many forms of meditation, differ in means and methods.

The circumstances in your life that can benefit from forgiveness might include a recent situation, something you experienced a long time ago, or a whole pattern you seem to experience in different ways. As soon as you notice yourself upset, applying methods drawn from mindfulness can be immediately helpful. For example, if we stop to take a few deep breaths, observe, and name the feelings that have arisen (e.g., irritability, anger, a sense of being out of sorts, tension in the solar plexus), we interrupt our typical emotional response. We can use the same approach to name mental patterns (e.g., judgment, distrust, blame). In that momentary pause as we do this, we might become aware of the circumstances that triggered the feelings and thoughts, but we don't need to figure all that out, since clearing them lies in what we do in the present.

The method of forgiveness shared in *A Course in Miracles*, and in many other books based on the course's understanding written over the past half century, begins with recognizing that we have lost our inner peace and, thus, become willing to see the situation another way.

How Do We Arrive at Willingness to See Things Another Way?

With genuine humility, we must acknowledge that no matter how intelligent or savvy we are, no matter how powerfully we can run a corporation, no matter the intuitive skills or spiritual insight we possess, there are events that will evade our earthly understanding. The good news is that we don't need to understand the higher spiritual purpose of everything to return to inner peace. We just need to be willing to see things a different way.

The human ego wants to make the forgiveness process complicated, but that is only to mask the reason why we don't try forgiveness—at first. Attachment to being right can predominate over our desire to be peaceful! I will admit that getting to willingness to see things differently wasn't always an easy process for me in the beginning. Being right and remaining upset seemed natural!

Applying forgiveness bypasses the human ego, opens the channel to our senior spiritual identity and guides, and brings forward our ability to trust the higher realms to use every situation for the highest good. The ego may resist this attempted bypass, creating resistance. Depending on your ego patterns, the resistance can be subtle ("I just don't understand how to do this") or overt ("That person doesn't deserve to be forgiven").

Usually, the difficulties we carry unforgiven in our energy fields become such a burden over time that we eventually arrive at willingness to explore change. It is tiresome when these feelings get triggered; we know exactly where our typical emotional reactions lead; and ultimately, we become willing to find a better way. Forgiveness renews youthful vitality, makes us smile more often, and deepens our compassion for everyone who shares the human journey.

Forgiveness Becomes Easier to Apply as Soon as We Experience the Benefits

Once I experienced the tremendous relief, not to mention the return of energy, and heightened spiritual ability that forgiveness produced, it became my number-one spiritual tool.

As we become willing to open the door to wisdom beyond our intellect and experience, insight can arrive in whichever form we are most open to receive. With our deepest forgiveness assignments, it may arrive in layers over time. Ultimately, each shift helps us undo the roots of our suffering until the pain is entirely gone. We gradually make peace with whatever appeared in those scenes, claiming the gifts of learning they produced while shedding any lasting negative effects. Doing this is a gift that only we can give ourselves. Any life circumstance or issue can be completely cleared from our energy fields through forgiveness. As we clear our inventory of experiences from the past, we become quicker to reach for forgiveness to apply it to any perception of the world around us that does not reflect love and light.

Are There Angels and Masters Who Help Us Forgive?

Absolutely! All the higher beings recognize that human perception is where forgiveness is needed, and they will do their best to help us realize it also. Archangel Raphael is one of my favorite allies in forgiveness, but there are many others one can call upon.

I happened to be working with angel Teriaple, who corresponds to the emotional level of Yesod in the Qabalah. (She isn't in this book but was helpful to me that day). I had just discovered that difficult life circumstances were unfolding for a dear one who means a lot to me. While I have learned over many years that human life offers learning assignments for all of us and that they are important for our growth, there are times when my heart wishes someone's learning assignment wasn't quite so challenging.

This reaction can occur when we judge that something that's happening shouldn't be happening. It signals that we are reacting from a limited human perspective while temporarily forgetting that there is a higher view. Compassion is always appropriate when anyone is challenged, and I needed to first acknowledge what I was feeling before I could forgive it and return to peace.

As I turned inward to connect with Teriaple, my whole emotional field lit up as if a switch had been flipped. I could see that my emotions were activated, rather than peaceful. Pretending we are not upset does not help us to return to peace, so her spotlight was a bright one.

She gently supported me while I felt what was there in my emotions. I found myself playing out an imaginary conversation with someone involved, saying exactly what I saw and felt would be helpful (though it was not my place to do this in an actual two-way conversation). At other times, when faced with something like this, I have journaled my feelings or written a letter that I burn after, rather than send. Sometimes tears are a quick release that helps clear a limited perception and so I can return to a higher perspective.

As I moved toward being willing to see the situation differently, in that moment, I remembered that my personality's perception did not have access to what might have been a life-defining moment for my friend. Since it was occurring, it could be used for a higher purpose in my friend's life. I realized the situation might present an important opportunity for soul growth (and life change) that was being offered. These thoughts came forward to help me reframe the situation as a powerful opportunity, rather than something wrong. Yes, I have studied and practiced holding this perspective, but perhaps one of my spiritual team brought it to mind at that moment.

With that shift I was able to lift the whole situation up to Spirit, surrendering it for everyone's highest good—without knowing what that would look like in physical life circumstances. I forgave everyone involved and myself for the way I had seen it initially. Since I was willing to change my mind, I was shifted out of judgment. The angst melted away, and I moved into extending compassion, love and light to surround those involved.

In this situation, angel Teriaple didn't offer guidance about how to resolve my emotions; she simply let me see them—as clearly as if in a spotlight—so I knew where to apply forgiveness. Other masters I call upon to help with forgiveness assist in other ways. Jesus/Yeshua, Mother Mary, and many other masters and angels have been great help at different times. When we are truly willing to see a situation from a different perspective, guidance will gently flow in to help us do that.

Forgiveness Opens the Lens of Perception

As we transform our consciousness through extending forgiveness, our vibration lifts, and we might receive expanded glimpses into higher reality. Experiences of the higher self begin to arrive, revealing our essence eternally whole and complete, shining in innocence, and eternally connected to our Source. In the greater light of such experiences, any self-judgments, guilt, and blame simply dissolve. We don't fight them; we simply turn away from them, seeing they are not justified. This choice allows our senior reality to direct the path of our life moving forward.

Any profound spiritual experience you have that reveals a glimpse of higher reality is a golden link in the chain of certainty that leads you to claim your higher self as an ongoing reality. This leads to the end of suffering over *anything* that appears to occur in human life.

Forgiveness as a Spiritual Practice

Each human being likely has one major and a great many minor potential forgiveness assignments. Each one accomplished contributes to your spiritual awakening.

In the beginning, start with something relatively small that you remember from past experiences. Notice how even seemingly small grudges—holding on to blame—interferes with your peace of mind. This is part of the process of cultivating willingness to see things differently.

When I got to my deeper lifetime forgiveness assignments, the issues were clearly beyond my personality's ability to solve, and there was clearly resistance blocking my willingness to change my mind. I could only offer the whole situation up in meditation and ask for higher help to arrive at willingness. Sometimes there was plenty of emotion to send along with that request. When strong emotions are present, we can learn to use that energy to literally send our prayers soaring. Help arrived at different times in different ways, and my perception gradually shifted. Watershed moments arrived with higher glimpses of reality that greatly assisted the process. Eventually, the last remaining charges from the past were gone, replaced by spiritual light.

Considering the amount of suffering our issues with the past produce in us, it is humbling to recognize that our willingness is the only thing asked of us to release them. Yet this seemingly small part is the key, for the reasons outlined elsewhere in this book. We are far more powerful in cocreating our experience along with the higher self or spirit than we typically recognize. Our say-so matters, whether it is opening to the possibility of experiencing ascended-realm beings or being willing to learn to shift from hurt to beyond the possibility of being hurt in any way.

Willingness to Forgive Doesn't Deny the Circumstances We Experienced

Choosing to extend forgiveness does not mean we are asked to deny our experiences in human life. Some of them are intense when experienced through physical senses. Employing the opposite of denial, we are asked to first feel the feelings those experiences included and then lift them up to Source so they can be resolved in the light of our eternal, unchanging, divine self.

To acknowledge our experience means we don't ignore or overlook whatever pain the experience produced in us. It's essential to allow time and a safe space (with professional support of various kinds when helpful) to discharge difficult feelings without judging ourselves for having them.

Practicing Forgiveness Does Not Ask You to Remain in Harmful Situations

We may also need to make a few dramatic life changes or set clear boundaries with others to end an ongoing negative situation. No one should remain in situations that are harmful physically, emotionally, spiritually, or in any other way. Taking appropriate action to change your circumstances, if that is the case, is essential.

After any necessary life changes have been made, when you are in a safe, nurturing environment and have acknowledged and discharged strong feelings, a willingness to see things a different way gradually arrives. (This stage should not be forced or attempted before you are ready.) Whatever you felt was a natural first reaction, but if you allow anger, hatred, rage, or grief to remain present in your energy field, these unpleasant states can become problematic. Unaddressed, our grievances remain as interference we must work around every day as we go about normal life activities. As we become aware of the cost of any unforgiven matters, we become willing to see what we experienced in a different way.

Forgiveness as a Final Step in Healing Trauma

There are many reasons for the experiences of our individual human lives. Some events we can understand at the time, and some we understand later. The most traumatic experiences often defy understanding from purely a human perspective—yet all of them can be completed, healed, and released through forgiveness. Some will take more work than others, but the bigger assignments are rocket fuel for spiritual evolution, carrying us to levels that could not be gained by a lesser effort.

When trauma occurs in childhood, we don't have the tools to resolve it at the time. It is a normal part of the psyche's protective response that memories of those events become buried at unconscious levels. At some point in life, they may come up for resolution. If those matters do come up, it is an opportunity for deep transformation. Those who facilitate different forms of trauma healing recognize that spiritual approaches are necessary so the last stage of healing can arrive. However, the means to invoke that spiritual help is often less clear. Forgiveness practice, inspired by *Course in Miracles* teachings, can provide that missing link.

Lifting the situation up to our own spiritual team and higher self, we invoke the highest spiritual help to clear any remaining energy from our energy field. When we embrace trauma healing with tools that carry us successfully through, we emerge empowered and filled with immense gratitude—for our own courage and personal effort and for the grace received that carried us through. The same forgiveness practice is also effective to complete and clear any distressing transpersonal or interdimensional life experiences.

81

How Forgiveness Works

Whatever one may have experienced in life (or in his or her multidimensional soul journey), no one is a victim without his or her mind's say-so. The concept of victimhood may be useful at an early stage of healing and is used in good faith by various well-intentioned organizations to help people. However, in the later stages of personal healing, the idea of victimhood is like a glue that holds us to the very issue we are attempting to heal.

Twenty-five years ago, the groundbreaking book *Why People Don't Heal and How They Can* by medical intuitive Carolyn Myss pointed out the cost of taking on ideas of victimhood. As she noted, when we accept a healing modality that permanently identifies us as victims of any sort of unpleasant experience, for as long as we remain identified there, we cannot arrive at the far shore of healing. That is the power of our own mind's say-so at work. When we become willing to see things a different way, forgiveness can carry us past victimhood, delivering us to our senior identity, which is eternal, innocent, and unchanged by anything human life can present. Spiritual practice is essential to arrive at the far shore. The difference is profound and affects the quality of our life experience moving forward.

The Importance of Compassion

My guides also remind me that extending compassion is always an appropriate response to situations of apparent distress. None of us gain the far shore of healing and higher spiritual wisdom overnight. It's a process, and we need to love and be patient with ourselves while it unfolds. Learning how much we are loved by all the angels and masters just as we are helps greatly while we gradually extend this to ourselves.

When we encounter others who appear to be suffering, it does not help them to join them in that emotional experience. What does help is remembering their own higher levels eternally present with Source. From our own healing journey, we can easily appreciate that human life presents many opportunities to practice and hold spiritual truth in the face of how things appear to us on the physical level. That means we can stand beside those who are doing their own spiritual heavy lifting, appreciating the inner strength it requires and seeing their ability to successfully face whatever situation is before them.

As you will see in the Profiles, under my experience with ascended master Tara, she is compassionate because she understands that humankind lives as if our perceptions about ourselves are the ultimate truth. She understands the suffering this entails—but she does not share our view. Therein lies compassion.

Extending Forgiveness to Our Perceptions of the Outer World

As forgiveness became a first-line spiritual practice that I use to this day, I found many occasions to apply forgiveness to my perception of outer world events. Politics, COVID, global warming, and a host of other topics produced judgment, cost me inner peace, and provided fuel for continuing willingness to forgive. While I held on to judgment, my access to the higher dimensions was temporarily restricted. Forgiving my perception of all outer-world situations doesn't lend my agreement to any troubling situations; it simply allows me to retain my center and, from there, take any actions that are authentic.

Claiming the Gifts of Forgiveness

Without minimizing the challenges of a deep healing process, when we fully incorporate the truth of our highest spiritual reality, we discover that far beyond the body, our eternal spiritual essence remains eternally radiant, changeless, and wholly connected to a divinely loving Source. Experiencing that truth requires dedication to spiritual practice, but it shines healing light through every challenging experience we have ever had.

So too, at the level of ultimate reality, our actions have not harmed any other being. When we enter states of higher awareness, we can see that we and everyone else are actors in one another's life dramas, providing fuel for mutual spiritual evolution. There are inevitable points of friction and conflict, through which we grow and evolve. Yet despite human perception, we all remain exactly as we were created by divine Source. The blessed news is that our actions have not produced any lasting effects for others, and theirs have not changed our eternal spiritual essence in any way.

Achieving Self-Forgiveness

Everyone has the most difficulty in forgiving him- or herself. The spiritual principle is that we can experience as much or as little of any quality (e.g., forgiveness, love, abundance, or peace) as we are willing to grant to another, since on the highest levels, we are not separate.

This means the ability to finally achieve self-forgiveness arrives through the many times we have been willing to forgive others. In extending what is true to them (their own eternal innocence, wherein we decline the role of victim), we realize we are forgiven also. This powerful act allows us to reclaim the eternal innocence we believe we have lost. Relieved of guilt, our energy fields can soar to new heights in meditation, joining the divine chorus of love.

As my nonphysical spiritual team has communicated through the years, we are already forgiven—forever. Eternity remains unchanged, despite our personalities' limited views. As we give the gift of forgiveness, we are released from all forms of suffering over what didn't occur in ultimate reality.

Forgiveness as an Ascension Practice

Once you have successfully forgiven one person, you will begin to realize the value of forgiveness. Clearing the past through forgiveness helps us become more diligent in clearing personal conflicts as they arise, because we know their weight will tie us to third-dimensional experience and, thus, hinder our ability for spiritual awareness.

On one occasion, a member of my inner team gave me a succinct perspective on forgiveness: "We learn forgiveness by encountering much that requires it!" It made me laugh because I could understand the higher purpose of the many forgiveness assignments that had been presented in my life. I really did learn the value of this practice!

As our inner storehouse of blame is cleared, our heart opens. We are more able to extend love universally, which is the key to entering the higher dimensions, where love is all that exists. When the inner slate where we noted our grievances with others has been wiped clean, there are no remaining obstacles. Energy flows to and through us at unprecedented levels. Of course, this raises our baseline vibration. It is a direct contribution to the possibility of our own ascension at the end of physical life and contributes to the highest good of all beings, our planet, and beyond.

Important to Remember

To prepare for ascended-realm contact, we must
do our part to clear our energy field.

True forgiveness
releases us from the shadows of the past;
helps us lift our vibration;
can improve health and vitality;
is a bridge between human perception and our own higher levels;
helps us reach the masters by clearing whatever isn't love;
provides inner peace to help us develop
greater concentration in meditation;
gets quicker and faster as it's practiced; and
can be applied to personal, interdimensional
healing or healing the earth.

CHAPTER 6

PREPARING FOR ASCENDED-REALM CONTACT: CHOOSING LOVE

In the previous chapters, I referred to divine love as the single state consistently present in the higher dimensions of spiritual reality. To apply the method given in this book to experience angels and ascended masters in meditation, one's ability to hold the truth of love present in consciousness is essential.

Clearly, not every appearance in the third-dimensional world arises from love. To develop our capacity to choose love as our ground of being, it can be helpful to examine what *A Course in Miracles* calls "love's impossible opposite": fear.

What Is Fear?

Fear is a lower-vibrational thought form present in the Third Dimension, where bodies appear to be separate from one another and from Creator Source. Fear colors the world we experience through the five senses with less-than-ideal appearances. Unaddressed, fear is a weighty obstacle that robs us of inner peace and holds us back from direct experiences of the angels and masters.

In contrast to experiences of fear, all mystical explorers of the higher dimensions report transcendent experiences of love, radiant beauty, and divine light. Love and fear cannot coexist simultaneously in awareness. How can we anchor ourselves more surely to love's presence?

Fear Arises from Our Stories about Past Experiences

Since fear is an obstacle that impedes spiritual awakening, some of the great spiritual adepts over the ages have examined the nature of the human mind in depth to discover the source of fear. They found that fear appears only in the mind's interpretation of the past, which then gets projected forward into a future dread. We fear a future like what happened in the past, and in holding tight to that view, we unconsciously misuse our divine cocreational abilities to invite the very outcome we fear.

If we stop and center in the present moment, fear is nowhere to be found. Take a few breaths, and notice you have everything you need at this moment. Fear is not present right here and right now. It can become a self-fulfilling prophecy only if we hold on to it. Returning awareness to the present moment, to the scene directly before us, helps us refuse fear.

Fear Arises from Our Condemnation of Others

Another important characteristic of fear is that it arises from our condemnation of others. Here is the connecting link to the spiritual practice of forgiveness discussed in the last chapter. While we have remaining issues with people and past experiences, we still hold judgments and blame. This is a form of unconscious attack that has a boomerang effect, harming us.

Holding onto a life story that is based on our grievances, our senses gather all the evidence to support that view. We do not realize that the interpretation we've given those circumstances, the story we tell ourselves about them, imprisons us. There is a direct relationship between what remains unforgiven from our past and the presence of fear. While we hold on to the right to condemn others, we give fear full permission to land in our consciousness.

Our Part in Refusing Fear

While no one enjoys remaining in a state of fear, we do not initially realize how it arises and that we can choose a different experience. We were given free will in our creation, so the power to choose love resides with us. No angel or ascended master can erase fear for us, as that would contravene our divinely given free will.

Breaking out of this loop is possible through forgiveness. When we forgive others and, thus, are returned to our own eternal innocence, this automatically returns our awareness to love's presence. Discovering that the lever to move past fear lies within us, we learn to become skilled in reaching for it.

Moving Past the Ego's False Logic about Fear

While we remain tied to the idea of a fearful world, we gather more and more justification for the various defenses we attempt to place between the perception of our small, seemingly vulnerable self and that which we believe can harm us.

The more defenses we gather, the more vulnerable we become. The ego mind believes it needs to figure out how we are to save ourselves from all apparent dangers. At the same time, it recognizes that it cannot assess all the variables to accomplish this. That seeming conundrum simply adds more fear to the loop. This condition is common in the collective mindset, though most do not recognize its basis.

Learning How to Face Fear

Though I had felt fear at certain times throughout life, as every human being does until he or she learns a different approach, I really knew nothing about it until I began spiritual practice. Once the subject came up, I tried to be courageous, yet I hadn't really owned that I was afraid. At times, I even sought out challenges that produced fear, mistakenly believing that facing them would eliminate fear.

One such adventure included free diving in ocean water so murky I couldn't tell up from down. I love the ocean, but I'm not at ease in it. I wasn't being foolhardy. The situation wasn't unsafe, and I was with my husband, who was an experienced diver, and two native abalone divers. Though I made myself do the free diving, it did nothing to alleviate fear. There were other adventures I undertook for the same reason, each of which demanded some courage, but none of them produced the result I had hoped for.

Those efforts failed for two reasons. First, I tried to overlook the roots of the fear I was experiencing. It arose because I was identifying only from the perspective of a personality in a physical body, rather than my senior spiritual identity. I wasn't sure of that senior identify in the beginning of my spiritual practice; thus, it was easier for fear to gain a temporary foothold.

The second reason these activities didn't allay fear was that I first made the fear real and then tried to overcome it. This is the same problem we encounter when we first recall challenging life events, decide that we have been irrevocably harmed, and then try to forgive them. This doesn't work! We need a means to recognize that the perceptions of human life are not as final as we once believed and move toward our eternal levels, which are beyond all harm.

By the time we grow to adulthood, most of us have experienced only our personality identities. To move into a completely fearless state, we need to get to know that our higher self exists and engage with a spiritual practice that can carry our consciousness toward it. When consciousness gains those metalevels of experience, even for a moment, we see and feel the love that exists beyond all perceptions of fear. Any brief experience of supramundane, transpersonal, or timeless awareness (use whichever term you prefer) allows us to experience that fear is tied to the illusion of human perception. Our eternal existence cannot be harmed or changed, no matter what appears to happen in human life. The physical body is finite, but our eternal identity is infinite.

As we shift into certainty about that higher truth, fear loses the ability to deceive us. Settling fear—and doing so on a continuing, as-needed basis—is what prepares us to enter higher states of consciousness.

How Do We Recognize Fear's Presence?

We can recognize fear is present anytime we experience anxiety or agitation and have lost our state of inner peace. Without judging ourselves for faithfully executing the fear pattern that our collective culture models, we can recognize that fear's presence simply means we have not yet experienced—or have temporarily forgotten—the sense of safety that arises from our connection to higher spiritual reality. With practice, we can shift right back to love simply by noticing we momentarily forgot it.

What Do We Fear?

Some fears are common throughout human experience: not having enough money, losing a job, losing a loved one, becoming ill, dying, going through a profound life change, speaking in public, or looking foolish. (Yes, those last two are feared as much as the others!)

All of us face times in life when the path ahead is not clear. Many ultimately beneficial transitions begin with our stepping into the unknown. However, the part of our mind that holds the ego wiring likes to believe it is in control and may be threatened by change. It might recall the last time something major changed and remind us how difficult that period was.

Rather than allow fear to dominate, in some stages of life transition, we must simply be patient, putting one foot in front of the other and allowing things to unfold. This makes it easier for our spiritual team to arrange matters in the optimal way for us and all concerned.

Learning to Be Patient with Our Growth Process

Everyone who begins spiritual practice becomes more aware of fear states. This is just like when we begin to meditate and notice the seemingly incessant arising of thoughts. We need not judge ourselves when we notice fear. These thoughts are simply part of the program operating within the human mind. Learning to be aware of the nature of our thoughts (fear-based or love-based) is an important first step. Becoming able to just observe that we are momentarily fearful, without going into judgment, we have made half the shift already.

Fear is a bit like a misty cloud bank that appears to block the sun. It doesn't have substance, and the light of love can always shine through it. To use a familiar metaphor, when we take off in an airplane during a cloudy day, we know from experience we will be back in the light as soon as we pass through the clouds. It's the same experience when we face fear. We can't go around it. It simply surrounds our consciousness until we turn to face it, recognize it is an illusion and thus move through it.

Dealing with Unconscious Fears

Sometimes we know and can quickly name what we fear. In some cases, the source of fear is not yet clear. To bring it to consciousness, where we can change our mind about it, we can track it down and question it: "Show yourself, fear! Where are you? What are you about?"

Those with kinesthetic abilities might track a fear to a particular part of their body. From there, they may receive deeper insight into the situation in which the fear was first present. That allows you to consciously extend forgiveness toward that past event, clearing the trigger for good.

Another way to unmask fear is to give it a voice and let it communicate with you through an imaginary dialogue. Seat it in a chair across from you, and open a conversation, asking a question and giving it time and permission to speak. Or you can dialogue with it in journal form, asking it what it has to say and recording those answers. When the fear comes up, forgive yourself for feeling it, as well as anyone else involved, as a first step to releasing it.

Praying for insight to arrive is also helpful. You can do this aloud, or in any way that is authentic for you. Call upon the members of your spiritual team to help you arrive at the core, so you can change your mind and let it go.

If we are really gripped by fear, we might need to rest for a night and check in again in the morning to see if it's still there. If you are overtired, haven't eaten, or are in some way in need of self-care, provide that for yourself immediately, and see if that lifts you past the fear state.

How to Recognize Progress

In the beginning, every step of progress from fear toward awareness of love's presence arrives with an enhanced sense of inner peace. That signals we are moving in a helpful direction.

At different times, every spiritual practitioner will experience turbulent periods of life when his or her ability to refuse fear is tested. We might find ourselves facing a life-threatening health crisis or the potential loss of something or someone we hold dear. When we find ourselves at such a point, we must recognize and name what we fear as the first step in turning it over to our higher levels.

A Spiritual Perspective on the Death Transition

All spiritual lineages address, in their own way, questions about what exists before and after a human lifetime. Teachings left by the world's spiritual mystics and masters stand beside current collections of near-death and other out-of-body experiences. There is much agreement that it is possible to experience a profound homecoming to the Source of love itself at life's conclusion. Those who pursue spiritual practices with dedication discover they don't have to wait until life's end, to become certain of the love that awaits them in the higher realms.

As spiritual practitioners contact angels and ascended masters, they grow more certain that union with an entirely loving Source is our senior spiritual identity. That is my experience also, underscored by hundreds of experiences with angels and ascended masters. From the earthly perspective, death appears to be an ending. Viewed from a metalevel reality. where our highest spiritual essence already exists, it is full awakening to love.

One experience with the Norse master known as Odin provided a simple but powerful illustration about the death transition that I found helpful. In one deep contact, he showed me a hand inside a glove. The hand represents our spiritual essence, what I refer to as our senior identity. When our earthly purpose is complete, the hand simply withdraws from the glove. The glove was a temporary sheath the hand found useful for earthly life. The glove, emptied of its animating spirit, collapses, while the hand arises, returning full awareness to its already existing spiritual levels.

As the lives of many masters demonstrate, one does not have to die to awaken to the reality that transcends human experience. Waking up while still animating a physical body brings greater light to the rest of your life journey and a peaceful homecoming at its conclusion. Awakening may not mean that data we perceives through the five physical senses will entirely disappear. However, it might shimmer a bit less solidly.

As one of my guides informed me, the most important question any spiritual practitioner can ask him- or herself today is "Who am I?" The way we answer this question—that we are either a personality in a body or a ray of divine light with infinite resources extending from Creator consciousness—makes a profound difference in everything we can experience.

Building Trust in the Spiritual Realm

Spiritual trust is based on awareness that we are not alone in facing the circumstances of our lives. Each of us has spiritual help to call upon when we remember to ask. We can look back at different times in life and remember serendipitous events that had *divine help* emblazoned all over them. A part of us recognizes that we couldn't have gotten through those scenes alone!

In passing through dynamic life events, the seeds of spiritual trust are sown. While miraculous help often arrives through the participation of some human agency, sometimes that help is so unexpected that the only reasonable explanation we can come up with is that it was divinely arranged. That conclusion is entirely accurate.

Spiritual Guidance

Trust builds as we listen for and follow spiritual guidance. When I began spiritual practice, the idea of receiving guidance was something of a mystery. How was I to recognize it?

The early years of spiritual practice involve a lot of inner sorting so that we learn to recognize the difference between guidance and our mind's thinking. Guidance is sometimes described as a quiet voice that gently comes again and again in our consciousness, rather than the more insistent voice of our ego.

In the beginning, we learn the difference by moving toward what we understand as guidance and noticing the results. We don't get it right all the time, and we grow more skillful from our mistakes.

Following guidance may sometimes produce results our personality didn't expect, but that doesn't mean we weren't on track. Developing trust in the guidance we receive builds an upward arc that helps us to stay on our path, and we are grateful when we discover the value of the information we can receive. Gradually we are delivered to blessed experiences beyond the parameters of the physical senses and ego mind. In those transcendent glimpses of love and light, the tight hold of fear gives way, at first a little and eventually a lot.

Choosing Again

Everyone possesses the ability to choose love over the perception of fear. Becoming aware of our thoughts, and recognizing our power to choose them, we can turn situations that potentially trigger fear over to our higher levels and Source. As we do this, we bypass our ego's default setting that suggests that its all up to our mind to figure out, even when we know we don't know which outcome is best. This allows our own higher levels and spiritual team to arrange things optimally, without interference, and helps us remain clear enough to receive whatever guidance is offered.

How Angels and Ascended Masters Support Us to Overcome Fear

We have no idea at first how beloved we are by all beings in the higher realms. To fully receive that love, we must shed some of the self-limiting beliefs that arrived when we took on the experience of being in a body on a planet.

Like most human beings, I didn't feel entirely self-loving in early adulthood, nor did I understand how precious everyone is to all beings in the higher realms. As I continued spiritual practice, the human notion of being unworthy of divine love began to fall away, and I experienced more and more of the love that is constantly extended to everyone.

The angels and masters gently remind us that bypassing the illusion of fear is simply part of the work of human life. They never judge us and are patient, gently whispering in our consciousness so we can make a different choice. While we are learning, they shower us over and over, with massive currents of love. Extending love is the core assignment of all beings in the higher realms.

The Happy Outcome

As we graduate from fear to love, our own experience confirms that the source of fear was simply a program running in our own thoughts. We no longer allow states of fear to dominate our experience. This is an enormous relief!

When we have resolved sufficient fear, the doors of our consciousness open to higher dimensions. Our experience with angels and masters deepens and they welcome our awareness with great love. We experience them more frequently in meditation and receive guidance with heightened clarity. We finally accept the truth that we are loved unconditionally exactly as we are. In love we were created, and part of love's extension we remain.

Eventually, we stabilize in a state where we remember love as a consistent state. This allows us to gently walk through every appearance human life can include, entirely beyond the reach of fear. As that state is reached, we have made a permanent dimensional shift. This is a hallmark of entering fifth-dimensional consciousness.

Advanced Practice: Shifting to the Neutral Observer or Witness

One technique useful to experienced practitioners of different traditions is called shifting to the neutral observer. This is a quick, metalevel shift, past the judging component of human ego. Everyone who develops this ability might describe the process in different words, but it is essentially the same. Shifting to the neutral observer, the individual can view the scene in front of them, looking through their body's eyes, from the perspective of higher self.

Doing this doesn't deny what you are witnessing; it simply anchors awareness in a higher spiritual perspective so you can respond compassionately and informed by guidance, rather than being emotionally reactive. The neutral observer isn't available to fear because they are certain that human perception is not the final arbiter of truth.

How Is the Shift Accomplished?

With an ongoing commitment to spiritual practice over time, one eventually becomes completely certain about the senior identity of the higher self existing in timeless awareness.

Then when an intense life situation appears, awareness pulls back behind the body's eyes to simply view the scene without judgment. It's a bit like looking through a mask in your human bodysuit, while senior identity, where you locate yourself, is firmly anchored in the love of Creator Source.

Those who master this technique learn to use whatever intense life events appear before them as opportunities to practice. They use the intensity of the scene as a powerful launching pad for consciousness to shift from the personality's perspective to that of its own metalevels. You may not always succeed in the beginning, but practice will develop it into an automatically available, helpful response.

If you are not yet certain of your own higher levels, you cannot expect to hold this perspective—yet. If this practice is a new concept, simply consider it as a possibility while you gather further spiritual experience.

Summary of the Journey from Fear to Love

1. Become vigilant to recognize when fear is present.

Name it. Say it aloud if you are alone or with a trusted other, saying exactly what you are afraid of. Denying we are fearful simply allows the fear to remain. As soon as you name it, forgive yourself for fearing this. Forgive the whole situation, including all those involved. Go global if your fear exists on that level.

2. Recognize that the source of fear lies within your thoughts.

The source of fear isn't whatever appears to be happening outside you; it's origin point is within your mind. Forgive yourself for reacting with fear. This puts you in the perfect place to change your mind about the whole situation and decide to trust that the situation is already being worked out by your higher levels and spiritual team. In many cases, fear is simply an old program running, but you are choosing not to listen to it.

3. When triggering outer circumstances appear suddenly, surprise can generate an automatic fear reaction. Calm your nervous system.

Take some deep breaths, releasing each one more slowly than the one before. A few minutes of slow, deep breathing can calm any state of anxiety. You might need a night's sleep to fully restore your energy field to peace.

4. If needed, reframe the experience with empowering thoughts

From thinking, *Oh no, I wish this wasn't happening,* take a breath, and release judgment that it should be other than what appears in the scene. Forgive what you perceived and your reaction.

97

Below are some of the core thoughts that have helped me, which you will recognize from the discussions in previous chapters. There are many similar ones, and you may already have your own tried-and-true versions.

- Life crises occur for every human being.
- Any demanding situation can be used for a higher purpose in my overall life, helping me grow.
- I have chosen to participate in this scene; it's not happening *to me*.
- Forgiving my perception can shift how I see this.
- I trust there is a way through. I will be guided to find it, and my spiritual team is helping.

5. Turn the situation over.

Recognize that you have the power to choose your thoughts and spiritual support to accomplish it. Lift any fear thoughts up to the divine and then pay attention for further instructions. Guidance may come to you during the next hour or day, that shifts your perspective in a helpful direction. If there is an action that is important for you to take, you will be told. Quiet your mind so you can listen for that guidance.

All fear thoughts have the same anatomy and can be resolved the same way. We may initially feel something is harder simply because we are more vulnerable in that specific area. If something feels harder, forgiving ourselves for that impression helps us to turn back to the one choice that can resolve it.

6. Choose love.

Turn away from fear to concentrate on something that fills you with light and love. A moment spent in gratitude for all the spiritual help and blessings you have already received can achieve this. Changing the channel of awareness by taking a walk, gardening, cleaning a closet, helping someone with something, talking to a friend, or thinking of those you love can also be helpful. Adding a method to open your heart more widely, especially in morning meditation, is beneficial. In doing so, you claim the day for love, which gives fear no space to land.

7. Repeat as needed.

If the fear thoughts return in the next hour or day, you can recognize this as an ego pattern, which likes to grind over the same territory, robbing us of peace. If guidance doesn't reveal any needed actions on your part, turn firmly back to love.

Two Exercises to Overcome Fear

Exercise 1: Life Crises and Turning Points

1. **Make a one-page list of the major crises and turning points in your life to date.**

Use a few words to describe each event, such as "father's death" or "moved to _____." You are not telling your whole interpretation of these events; you are just making a chronological list. It doesn't matter if anyone else would think these events were challenging; it only matters if you experienced them that way. Give yourself a time limit for this. An hour should be more than enough.

2. **When your list is complete, reflect on it to get an overall perspective.**

Are there any observations or insights that come to you? Write them on a separate sheet. Are you amazed at all you have been through? Can you extend yourself a moment of self-compassion, especially for those times that were difficult? We are all humbly learning how to negotiate life with grace and dignity. Some of those lessons are hard-won.

3. **Looking at your list, do you suspect you had spiritual help to find a way through obstacles?**

If so, how likely is it that the same help is still with you? In what ways do your spiritual team let you know they are with you? Even if you are just beginning your spiritual journey, you will have noticed something. Trust the first answer that comes to mind. Write it down. This is a demonstration to you and the spiritual realm that you are paying attention to guidance.

4. What things did you do to support yourself during each of these life events?

Write these down, even if you think they are obvious, such as taking a hot bath, talking to a trusted friend, gardening, or meditating. That list is your go-to reminder when something happens, and you can benefit from extra support. In a crisis, we don't always remember the obvious.

5. Do some of the events on your list still carry an edge?

If any events you listed still produce an edge when you remember them, then you have a list that will help you to apply forgiveness where it's needed. As you do this, you will defuse any remaining triggers and eliminate a lot of future fear.

6. Did you gain a new perspective about all the events you have come through?

All of them led to your current amazing, wondrous, one-of-a-kind self. Is there more trust present that you will be gently guided through any steep patches ahead?

Exercise 2: Remembering Love's Presence

This begins as a writing exercise and shifts to a guided meditation. Before you begin, read the instructions beginning with step three into a voice recorder (on your phone or other device) to play them back as a guided meditation you can listen to with your eyes closed after you complete the writing in steps one and two.

1. **Make a one-page chronological list of the times when you felt most loved.**
Even if your life has included traumatic events, it is likely you can identify some situation, person, or animal companion that helped you to feel love. Give yourself a one-hour time limit to write your list. If you can think of many times, people, or animals to list, great. If you can think of only one, that will be perfect also.

2. **Now focus on one situation in which you felt loved.**
How did you recognize this? Write a list of key words that would help you to describe this scene to someone who wasn't there. You can just choose key words, rather than writing full sentences. Choose words that set the scene in as much detail as possible.

**Now set your pen down and play your
prerecorded guided meditation.**

3. **Close your eyes, and take some slow, gentle breaths.**
Relax more deeply each time you inhale and exhale. Let your attention move into the center of your chest, into your heart. Allow yourself to shift into a gentle, open receptivity. Imagine or sense the energy field that surrounds your physical body. In that field, you can notice warmth, where some of the words that described your feeling of being loved are still resonating within you.

4. Let the energy surrounding one of those words grow, expand in size, and lift into a field that rises way above your head.

As this takes a misty form, in your inner world, it becomes a channel of white light that connects you directly to whatever you hold to be divine. It can be God, the Absolute, or a particular angelic or ascended master's loving presence. Experience the wonder that this channel of love connects to you in a personal way.

5. Now gently become aware of a little wall of tension you didn't realize you are holding that keeps that current of divine love at arm's length.

It's OK to let that go now in this moment and just see what occurs. Take a breath, and as you exhale, let it go. Receive what is eternally extended to you exactly as you are in this moment. It is truly unconditional. You don't have to earn it, and you can never lose it. In this moment you can choose again to remember love's presence exactly as it is. It is yours eternally because of who and what you are. Take whatever time you need to fully experience this.

**When you are complete, bring yourself gently
back into the room, and open your eyes.**

6. As soon as possible, journal what you experienced.

Important to Remember

Fear arises from our thoughts (conscious and unconscious) rooted in our interpretation of the past or as an effect of condemning others.

It can be present within third-dimensional awareness (the perspective of a personality in a body) but is not present in the higher dimensions, where only love exists.

Love and fear cannot be experienced simultaneously. Remembering to choose love undoes fear.

Noticing and undenying fear are the first steps to releasing it. Developing greater trust, love, and gratitude automatically diminishes the potential for fear to be present.

Since we were created with the capacity for free will, releasing fear is something we must do for ourselves. We have great support from the angelic and ascended master realms to accomplish it.

Moving past fear is essential to experience deeper contacts with angels and ascended masters, because their energy is present in dimensions where only love exists.

Shifting to the metalevel neutral observer is an advanced practice that helps us to fearlessly shine divine light into every life scene that comes before us.

CHAPTER 7

INTRODUCTION TO THE QABALAH

This chapter introduces the basic structure of the metaphysical system known as the Qabalah. While the Qabalah has a rich and varied meaning within various spiritual systems, in this book, it serves a practical function. It gives us a means to understand the masters and angels known from many traditions within a single framework and allows us to appreciate the individual gifts of spiritual light that each extends. This helps us to seek the guidance of those beings who can best help us with the matters that are uppermost in our lives.

As you grow in ability to work directly with masters and angels through the Qabalah, you stand on the shoulders of the initiates of various spiritual traditions who, over the centuries, have used its portals to experientially accelerate their spiritual progress. Learning to recognize each of the Qabalah's subtle energy quadrants as your consciousness connects with beings who extend those vibrations makes it easier for you to remember your own higher-dimensional experiences. As each of those energies awakens within your own consciousness, you build neural pathways that allow you to call forth that quality from within your own experience when life brings a suitable opportunity before you. Climbing the Qabalah tree in consciousness is ultimately an opportunity to move toward the possibility of full spiritual awakening and ascension at the end of your lifetime.

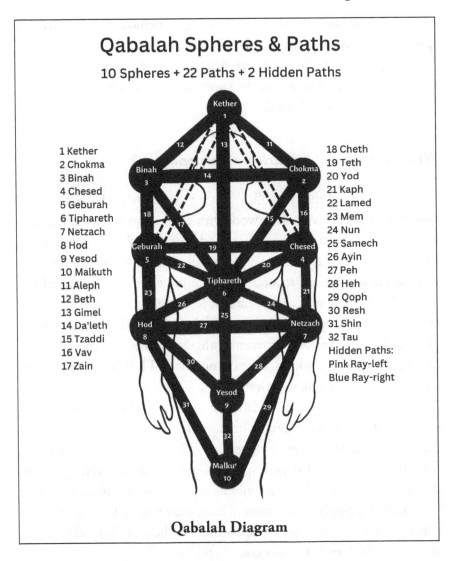

Qabalah Spheres & Paths

10 Spheres + 22 Paths + 2 Hidden Paths

1 Kether
2 Chokma
3 Binah
4 Chesed
5 Geburah
6 Tiphareth
7 Netzach
8 Hod
9 Yesod
10 Malkuth
11 Aleph
12 Beth
13 Gimel
14 Da'leth
15 Tzaddi
16 Vav
17 Zain

18 Cheth
19 Teth
20 Yod
21 Kaph
22 Lamed
23 Mem
24 Nun
25 Samech
26 Ayin
27 Peh
28 Heh
29 Qoph
30 Resh
31 Shin
32 Tau
Hidden Paths:
Pink Ray-left
Blue Ray-right

Qabalah Diagram

The Qabalah: A Diagram and an Interdimensional Matrix of Spiritual Light

The Qabalah diagram reduces a multidimensional matrix to a form that can be printed in two dimensions on a flat sheet of paper. The structure symbolizes a continuous loop of subtle spiritual light that extends from Creator toward human experience and from human experience back to Creator.

It is a metaphysical system, meaning it includes the nonphysical spiritual dimensions as well as the physical world in the same diagram. The diagram symbolically shows that earth and humankind are not separate from Creator, despite the views reported by physical sight, but are part of a connected whole.

What Is Meant by *Esoteric Correspondence?*

To understand the symbolic meaning of the Qabalah diagram and how it is used in this book to work with angels and ascended masters, it is necessary to consider it as a model of esoteric correspondence. Over the centuries, systems of correspondence have always been taught to students in mystery schools and to initiates of various traditions. Tarot offers a system of correspondence, as does astrology. The idea of correspondence simply means that different orders of things (e.g., certain planets, letters, numbers, minerals, angels, masters in the ascended realm, and human chakras) are harmonious and linked, all the way to Creator-Source, despite manifesting in different forms.

Understanding that these different forms arise from a metalevel of existence and share a common vibration, we are more able to work with them skillfully. Ancient practitioners typically used the term *sympathetic* for orders of things that correspond. Correspondence literally means that different orders of being vibrate together in connected lines of spiritual light. Applying a system of correspondence allows us to direct energy and attention toward individual members of these vast chains to invite them forward in our consciousness.

Qabalah and Its Branches: Western Astrology and Tarot

Working with any of the elements of the Western esoteric tradition helps us apply what we learn in one discipline to other branches—by correspondence. For example, if you have learned a bit about Western astrology or worked with the tarot, you will find that working with the Qabalah, the mother of your specialty branch, is a natural next step.

If you are just beginning your exploration of higher wisdom with the Qabalah, you will grow a deep knowledge that is a complete system within itself and allows you to understand Western astrology and tarot within a unified context.

Approached from either direction, your intellectual understanding, and ability to navigate the higher realms, can grow exponentially as you step through the Qabalah's portals in an experiential way.

The Qabalah as World Tree

Qabalah is also known as the Tree of Life, or World Tree. It is compared to a symbolic tree that grows upside down from spiritual Source toward earthly experience.

From the Qabalah's uppermost sphere, called Kether, the tree extends downward toward the realm of human earthly experience. This symbolizes how the descending energy of Source consciousness extends to meet the physical world, passing through various dimensions that are increasingly denser to ultimately appear in physical form. The descending energy passes through the four elements of fire, air, water, and earth as it enters the earth plane at the sphere of Malkuth at the bottom of the Qabalah diagram.

Since the roots of this upside-down tree are anchored in Creator Source, considering the diagram from the top down reminds us that our senior identity is eternal. We are each a divine spark that extends from the white light downward through the dimensions to embody an earthly experience. Our journey into incarnation includes a focus on several energies that will be important to fulfill our life purpose. The diagram symbolizes that we remain eternally connected to divine Source—through the Qabalah's multidimensional ladder of light— even while we embody physical form and engage in the experience of human life.

Approaching the Qabalah diagram from the viewpoint of human life means we are locating our perspective in the bottom sphere of Malkuth, looking upward on the tree. As we do so, we see a symbolic ladder by which consciousness can gradually realize, or awaken to, successively higher perspectives, culminating in our own already existing higher levels in union with divine Source.

Taking this symbolic meaning into meditation, as we calm the body and quiet the mind, we can learn to lift awareness beyond the physical plane. It is a process of gradual expansion of consciousness, learning about each of the higher dimensions as we experientially climb the Qabalah tree.

The Qabalah's Ten Spheres

Returning to the Qabalah diagram, we notice ten discs called *sephiroth* (which I will refer to simply as *spheres*) connected by twenty-two straight line paths. The spheres are numbered one through ten, counting from the uppermost one, called Kether, down to the one known as Malkuth at the bottom center.

At the most basic level, spheres one through nine correspond to the physical planets in our solar system. You will find their correspondences included below in the descriptions of the spheres. I have included a few keywords to provide an overview of the archetypal energy of each sphere and its correspondence in Western astrology and tarot.

Deepening your understanding of each part of the Qabalah is achieved by reading about masters who expressed the energy of a sphere or path (see the 108 profiles at the end of this book). Their lives provide concrete examples of how each energy represented in the Qabalah can be expressed. When you connect with any of them in inner-world experience, your understanding of each energy becomes experientially based. You no longer need to believe the interpretations offered by others when you can experience them yourself.

Qabalah Sphere Keywords
With Corresponding Angels and Masters in This Book

Malkuth (pronounced Mal-kooth): Kingdom
- Tenth (bottom) sphere
- Planet Earth
- The beginning and ending of the spiritual quest, grounding, earth ecology, personal integration of all higher spiritual experiences into one's life

> While Malkuth represents the domain of the five physical senses, occasionally, an angel or master can assume a form that can be perceived at this level.

Yesod (pronounced Eee-sod): Foundation
- Ninth sphere, central column, sphere above Malkuth
- The moon
- Emotions, female fertility cycle, intuition, psychic mediumship, manifestation, dreaming, ability to direct awakened kundalini energy toward healing and spiritual enlightenment

> Archangel Haniel, Huldah, Leah, Arianrhod, Themistoclea, Rhiannon, Aine, Artemis

Hod (pronounced like *bod* in *body*): Glory
- Eighth sphere, bottom sphere in the left-hand column
- Planet Mercury
- The human mind—language, grammar, history, study, learning, creative expression, rhythm, connection to divine mind and spiritual guidance

> Archangel Uriel, Archangel Jeremiel, King Solomon, Niguma, Sarasvati, Mira Bai, Orpheus

Netzach (pronounced Net-zatch, soft a like *hatch*): Victory
- Seventh sphere, bottom sphere in the right-hand column
- Planet Venus
- Love, beauty, abundance, the desire nature, images, artistic expression, healing through experiences of divine love

Archangel Raphael, Amoghasiddi Buddha, Tara (Green), Lakshmi, Aphrodite, Freya, Asclepius, Brigit, Radha

Tiphareth (pronounced Tiff-a-ret): Beauty
- Sixth sphere, central column above Yesod
- Our sun and the Great Central Sun
- Leadership ability, confidence, will, capacity for intellectual brilliance, philosophy, logic, science, mathematics, founding institutions and organizations, connection to higher self, Christ consciousness, Buddha mind, fulfillment of a unique life mission

Archangel Gabriel, Hildegard of Bingen, Teresa of Avila, Siddhartha Gautama (the Buddha), Vishnu, Mamaki Buddha, Paramahansa Yogananda, Apollo, Athena, Lugh, Belenus, Fionn mac Cumhail

Geburah (pronounced Geh-burr-a): Severity
- Fifth sphere, center sphere left-hand column
- Planet Mars
- Physical strength and courage, capacity for assertive action, concentration and self-control, sexuality, boundaries, the warrior, overcoming fear, protecting, destroying negative influences

Archangel Camael, Archangel Raguel, Penthesilia, Pandara Buddha, Kali, Tyr, Ares

Chesed (pronounced Chess-ed): Mercy
- Fourth sphere, center sphere in the right-hand column
- Planet Jupiter
- King warriors, politics and rulership, spiritual study, and teaching, founding temples or institutions of higher knowledge, writing sacred texts, sacred masculine, compassion, mercy, high ethical and moral principles, bringing heavenly values into earthly form

Archangel Michael, Angel Nuriel, John the Baptist, Francis of Assisi, King David of Jerusalem, Moses, Avalokitesvara, Rama, Krishna, Ganesha, Plato, King Arthur, Baldur the Beautiful, Zeus

Binah (pronounced Bee-na): Understanding and Spiritual Knowledge
- Third sphere, top sphere in the left-hand column
- Planet Saturn
- Gateway between eternity and human life, imparting form-building structure to new life and surrendering form to return to the formless at life's end; overcoming grief; divine Mother and divine Father; spiritual mystic founders of many spiritual traditions who bring teachings that help humankind realize the divine

Archangel Azrael, Jesus/Yeshua, Mary Magdalene, Saint Germain, Ezekiel, Isaac, Sarah, Machig Labdron, Demeter, Danu, Yeshe Tsogyal

Chokma (pronounced Hoke-ma): Transcendent Wisdom and Power
- Second sphere, top sphere in the right-hand column
- Planet Uranus (originally fixed stars)
- Omniscient wisdom about transcendent reality, will and spiritual power to uplift human consciousness, leadership that initiates needed radical changes in human affairs, male potency extending the energies of creation toward manifestation in form

Archangel Raziel, Abraham, Manjushri, Vairocana Buddha, Shiva, the Dagda, King Nuada, Odin, Njord, Ailill mac Mata

Kether (pronounced Ket-ter): The Crown
- First sphere, top central column
- Planet Neptune
- Gateway to Creator Source through the crown chakra, the source of spiritual blessings and energy that rain down upon humanity, the culmination of the spiritual journey of individual consciousness. In reaching it, we learn that it is also the beginning point of our incarnation into physical form. The truth of eternal oneness with our Source has reawakened in direct experience.

Archangel Metatron

The Twenty-Two Qabalah Paths (plus some Hidden Paths)

In this brief orientation to the Qabalah diagram, the paths are the straight bars that link the spheres. As we have seen, each Qabalah sphere has its own characteristic energy. Bringing any two adjacent spheres into balanced functioning occurs via the path that connects them. Masters and angels support us to achieve that balance, corresponding to the paths as well as spheres.

Typically, in an individual's consciousness, one of the spheres is innately stronger than the other one that each path connects. Bringing both connected spheres into a state of balanced functioning usually requires effort to develop the side that is weaker.

Each path is named for its corresponding Hebrew letter and corresponds to one of the major arcana cards in the tarot. Twelve paths correspond to astrological signs (Aries through Pisces), while the others are under the rulership of certain planets and stars. There are also correspondences to notes on the musical scale, colors, and more, which are not included here.

There are two paths included in the Qabalah diagram above that are not illustrated in conventional Qabalah diagrams. These have occasionally been described by others using the designation *hidden paths,* the term I also use. Each of the two has a specific function and some masters who express that energy. There are other hidden paths I have experienced, and some masters (such as White Tara included in this book) who correspond to those. It is difficult to show White Tara's path in a two-dimensional diagram, but it' is described under her profile.

In this book, and in my more extensive files, there are more names of beings who correspond to spheres than paths. I do not know why this is so; it's simply the result of the process of identifying them that I was guided to use. According to my guidance about the final selection of which names to include in this book, there are many masters who correspond to paths that could not be included. I will share information about more of them as opportunities arrive.

Qabalah Path Keywords
(Beginning from the bottom of the Qabalah diagram, moving up)
Only the masters and angels in this book
are mentioned, but others exist

Path 32: Tau (pronounced Taw)
- Tarot: The Universe
- Ruled by planet Saturn
- Inner purification to begin clearing the personal unconscious to become more able to lift awareness into the astral plane, glimpses of the wonders of the higher realms that lie ahead, ultimately growing an understanding of cosmic order and bringing it into earthly forms

Path 31: Shin (pronounced like the front of the lower leg)
- Tarot: Aeon, or Judgment
- Elemental fire

Primal fire to transform that which no longer serves one's life and reorient toward a more elevating journey

Path 30: Resh (rhymes with *mesh*)
- Tarot: The Sun
- Ruler sun
- A welcome influx of solar light to rest, regenerate, uplift, and support greater joy and collaboration with others

Path 29: Qoph (pronounced Koph)
- Tarot: The Moon
- Astrological sign Pisces
- Increasing astral light to reclaim lost instinctual wisdom, discern authenticity, develop compassion and the desire to serve others

Path 28: Heh (pronounced with a soft *e*)
- Tarot: The Star
- Astrological sign Aquarius
- Undertaking heroic quests or journeys to the underworld to reclaim something lost at the behest of higher spiritual forces, astral travel, assignments to develop confidence and allow the individual's gifts to shine and contribute to humankind

Path 27: Peh (pronounced Pe with a soft *e* and silent *h*)
- Tarot: The Tower
- Ruler Mars
- Spiritual fire to clear strong passions within the personality that inhibit further growth

Path 26: Ayin (pronounced Eye-een)
- Tarot: The Devil
- Astrological sign Capricorn
- For females, crone wisdom, the ability to laugh at one's bedevilments through the wisdom of maturity, channeling of sexual energy toward spiritual power

Cerridwen

Path 25: Samech (pronounced Sam-ek)
- Tarot: Art and Temperance
- Astrological sign Sagittarius
- Discovering systems of higher wisdom (tarot, astrology, Qabalah) to support the inner integration of opposites, which produce a first-level inner marriage within consciousness where lunar and solar forces are balanced and integrated

Path 24: Nun (pronounced Noon)
- Tarot: Death and Rebirth
- Astrological sign Scorpio
- Immersion in the unconscious (intuition, instinct, and feeling) brings forth a rebirth of truth, beauty, and new purpose

Persephone

Path 23: Mem (like in the word *memo*)
- Tarot: The Hanged Man
- Element water
- Reversal of former perspectives brings new awareness to former blind spots and limiting patterns to complete and release them

Path 22: Lamed (pronounced Lam-ed)
- Tarot: Adjustment and Balance
- Astrological sign Libra
- Strength to bring greater balance to all areas of life by making needed adjustments, the ability to resolve interpersonal conflicts (for oneself or between others) with fairness to create greater harmony

Deborah, Forseti

Path 21: Kaph (pronounced Kaff)

- Tarot: Wheel of Fortune
- Ruler Jupiter
- Providing opportunities to extend and receive spiritual grace, extending material resources to uplift those in need, commitment to uphold values that are guided by the eternal

Clare of Assisi

Path 20: Yod (sounds like *bod*)

- Tarot: The Hermit
- Astrological sign Virgo
- Healing abilities, herbal knowledge, folk remedies, personal healing and integration that arrives through divine resources, projects that require periods of isolation to complete, development of leadership to show others the way

Eir

Path 19: Teth (Tet, with a silent *h*)

- Tarot: Lust and Strength
- Astrological sign Leo
- Taming inner passions to become a trusted instrument to use unique gifts of personal leadership and inspired creative expression to serve higher spiritual forces and provide divine protection

Archangel Ariel, Durga, Thor

Path 18: Cheth (Chet, with a silent *h*)

- Tarot: The Chariot
- Astrological sign Cancer
- Developing expertise to navigate life changes by awakening higher spiritual awareness, assisting others to do the same,

compassionately supporting those who are transitioning at the end of physical life, and developing mediumship abilities

Bernadette of Lourdes, Enoch

Path 17: Zain (pronounced Zy-een)

- Tarot: The Lovers
- Astrological Sign Gemini
- A second inner marriage of opposites (the first was at Samech, Path 25) achieved by transcending intimate relationship conflicts, channeling of passion toward spiritual illumination, outstanding capacity to apply reason, production of inspired communications, team leadership, and mentoring skills

Oengus mac Og

Path 16: Vav (pronounced Va, with a soft *a* and *vv*)

- Tarot: The Hierophant
- Astrological sign Taurus
- Male priest initiates willing to endure personal sacrifice to gain and extend specialized knowledge of ancient traditions used to guide spiritual initiates into experiences of ultimate reality

Path 15: Tzaddi (pronounced Ts-zadi)

- Tarot: The Emperor
- Astrological sign Aries
- Warrior leaders who pioneer a new land, initiate a new body of knowledge, or otherwise establish a new frontier that allows humankind to evolve

Charlemagne, Arjuna

Path 14: Da'leth (pronounced Day-let)

- Tarot: The Empress

- Ruler Venus
- Integrating the polarities of masculine and feminine, contributing to healing relationship wounds still present in the collective (by seeking spiritual help), awakening relationship with the Source of love itself

Archangel Hasdiel, Rebecca, Hera, Parvati, Guinevere, Frigg

Path 13: Gimel (pronounced Gi-mel, with a soft *i* and soft *e*)
- Tarot: The High Priestess
- Ruler moon
- Potential to develop the ultimate state of connection with the spiritual world possible through a female lifetime, requiring inner strength, independent leadership, endurance, and detachment to carry out assignments received from guidance

Ariadne, Miriam, Gefjun, Lady of the Lake

Path 12: Beth (pronounced Bet, with a silent *h*)
- Tarot: The Magician
- Ruler Mercury
- High initiate esoteric knowledge and transmission of the cosmic codes and patterns that underly existence, which produce forms in the Third Dimension (physical world),

Hermes-Thoth

Path 11: Aleph (pronounced Al-eff)
- Tarot: The Fool
- Ruler air
- The transcendent, ecstatic, divine impulse to life, extending in wonder and fearless anticipation that initiates all new beginnings

Hidden Path of the Pink Ray

- No tarot equivalent
- The pink ray is not illustrated on the Qabalah diagram (thus, it was named a "hidden path" in certain Qabalah systems). It connects the sphere of Geburah (action) directly with the sphere of Kether (gateway to Creator consciousness). The spiritual purpose of this path is to learn the divine nature of love and to actively, compassionately extend it unconditionally to all humankind.

Angel Chamuel

Hidden Path of the Blue Ray

- No tarot equivalent
- This path was not illustrated on the Qabalah diagram (and, thus, was named a hidden path in certain Qabalah systems). It connects the sphere of Chesed with the sphere of Kether and is home to certain all-female masters who carry out protective spiritual functions on behalf of humankind.

Saint Mary/Mother Mary, Gullveig/Heid

First Hidden Path of the White Ray – Yesod to Kether

- No tarot equivalent
- This path is not illustrated on traditional Qabalah diagrams (and, thus, was named a hidden path in certain Qabalah systems). It connects the sphere of Kether with the sphere of Yesod and is home to a master who achieved full enlightenment through a female lifetime, and supports human females to achieve the same result

---

Arya (meaning White) Tara

Second Hidden Path of the White Ray – Yesod to Chesed

- No tarot equivalent
- This path is not illustrated on traditional Qabalah diagrams (and, thus, was named a hidden path in certain Qabalah systems). It connects the sphere of Chesed with Yesod and is home to a female master whose mastery of intuition can direct downloads of spiritual wisdom

---

Buddha Locana

The Human Outline in the Qabalah Diagram

As you look closely at some Qabalah diagrams (including the one above in this chapter), you will notice the faint outline of a human form behind the geometric pattern of spheres and paths. This reminds us of an important distinction.

We encounter the dimensions symbolically illustrated in the Qabalah diagram within our own consciousness. As mystics throughout the ages have suggested, the pathway to the divine lies within. Once those pathways are awakened within our own subtle energy system, when we quiet the mind and turn within, we can access multidimensional reality from wherever we are. To do that with skill, it is necessary to learn and practice the techniques that help us open the doors in our consciousness and develop focused concentration.

Qabalah Spheres and Masters Considered as Three Vertical Columns

On the Qabalah diagram, you will notice the spheres are arranged in three parallel vertical columns. The central column is sometimes understood to correspond to the central spinal column of the human energy system (called sushumna in yogic systems). The right-side column, called the Pillar of Mercy, and the left-side column, called the Pillar of Severity, represent the ida and pingala channels within the human energy system. The two outer columns illustrate the basic principle of polarity (opposites, such as night and day), which are part of human experience until consciousness arrives at Kether at the top, the gateway to oneness with Source.

Some systems of Qabalah associate the two outer columns with female and male energies, and the two sides of the human body are generally understood as more receptive (yin, or female, left side) or active (yang, or male, right side). *Expansion* (right column) and *contraction* (left column) might be better terms to describe the overall energies on the outer columns.

Nuances of Energy within Each of the Columns

Most spheres and paths, include both female and male masters, while some include only female masters and others include only male masters. The number of beings I contacted individually allowed these distinctions to emerge. The text below summarizes what I found.

Right-Hand Column

Two spheres on the right-hand column (Chokma and Chesed) offer masters who ascended from male lifetimes only. They are important higher-dimensional allies for both female and male spiritual practitioners.

The sphere of Netzach at the bottom right includes some masters who ascended from male lifetimes but many more who ascended from female lifetimes. Netzach is ruled by Venus, and we can meet Greek Aphrodite, Green Tara, Lakshmi, and Norse Freya there, as well as many other masters who were female. Yin energy doesn't entirely dominate Netzach, but even many of the male masters who ascended at Netzach extend a gentle, artistic, or healing type of energy.

Of the two paths that connect spheres of the right-hand column, the path of Kaph is decidedly home to masters who ascended from female lifetimes (Clair of Assisi), while Vav is home to male masters only (some of whom belonged to a male priesthood during their lifetimes).

Left-Hand Column

In the left-hand column, each of the spheres corresponds to masters who were either female or male in their lifetimes before ascension.

Binah, at the top of the column, is home to an extraordinary number of female masters who are acknowledged as spiritual mothers who usher consciousness into the formless eternal realms, as well as others who were founder leaders of earthly spiritual traditions or served as queens or empresses in physical life. The male masters at Binah also include powerful founders of spiritual knowledge traditions. The male masters at Binah extend energy in a vibrational style distinct from the male masters at Chokma, at the top of the right-hand column.

The sphere of Geburah, in the center of the column, includes spiritual warriors, male and female in physical life, who protected peoples, whole spiritual lineages, or earthly kings. Those beings at the spiritual level (Kali) extend lines of force to eliminate that which has become redundant, so evolution can proceed.

The sphere of Hod, at the bottom of the column, includes both female and male masters who allow many forms of information and creative inspiration to flow from the spiritual world into the earthly realm through the human intellect in variouus rhythmic forms.

The path of Mem, in the left-hand column, includes only male masters, while the path of Cheth includes both males and females.

Central Column

The first sphere above Malkuth in the central column of the Qabalah is Yesod. I have experienced more masters here who ascended from female lifetimes, but some were males.

The next sphere moving up the column is Tiphareth, which seems to offer more males, but female masters are also met there (Athena,

122

Hildegard of Bingen, Mamaki Buddha, and Teresa of Avila are included in this book).

The uppermost sphere of Kether represents the gateway to spiritual Source. Masters here still retain a tiny bit of yin or yang influence in their energy but are approaching the state beyond all gender polarities.

The connecting path of Samech between Yesod and Tiphareth includes masters of both genders, while Gimel, connecting Tiphareth to Kether, is the longest path in the entire diagram, including masters who ascended from female lifetimes only.

Qabalah Spheres Considered in Three Triangles

Returning to the Qabalah illustration at the beginning of this chapter, now consider the arrangement of spheres horizontally across the diagram. They are further described in Qabalah texts in terms of three triangles that denote the way those energies function together within human experience. You will understand more about these groupings as you begin to experience masters at each sphere, but below is the essential meaning.

As you contemplate these principles, it is important to understand that the Qabalah ladder is not a simple progression upward, since each energy has the potential to develop inward through emotional, mental, and spiritual levels of mastery, and there are masters and angels who developed one of those levels of mastery. This inward progression is one in which each succeeding level is closer to the pure energy of Creator Source.

This will be explained more fully in the next chapter, but it is important to include here so you don't jump to the conclusion that all the masters who correspond to the spheres in the lower two triangles are less evolved than those who correspond to spheres in the supernal uppermost triangle.

Summary: the Three Triangles

1. The **astral triangle** includes the three spheres at the base of the tree—Yesod, Hod, and Netzach—which correspond to the human personality (emotional orientation, thinking, and values-desires).

2. The **ethical triangle** includes the spheres of Geburah, Tiphareth, and Chesed. This triangle of spheres describes the energy we use to interact with the outer world around us (our capacity for action, the moral-ethical values that inspire us, and our orientation to our individual self and, eventually, to the higher self).

3. The **supernal triangle** includes the spheres of Binah, Chokma, and Kether. These are the energy domains of spirit—before and after physical life. (Kether is the highest sphere included in the Qabalah diagram, but there are domains still higher, faintly symbolized by the white shadows above the sphere of Kether, which lead all the way to Creator Source.) Chokma is the first transcendent gateway through which pulses of omniscient wisdom and power extend the forces of creation toward human experience. These transcendent energies first meet form-building energy at Binah, which serves as the gateway between the eternally unmanifest realms and the soul's journey into human incarnation. Binah is also the final gateway where form is laid down at the end of physical life to reenter transcendent reality.

Experiential Qabalah

Experiential practices using the Qabalah are attractive to all explorers of higher spiritual reality. The illustrious masters of every spiritual lineage, along with philosophers such as Plato and Aristotle, have always acknowledged that other levels of reality exist beyond what the five physical senses report. Becoming familiar with what others have experienced helps us recognize the territory when our own consciousness arrives there.

The abstract understandings that arise from Qabalah traditions are a helpful basis to begin. Many books written on the Qabalah can add to one's knowledge when consulted at a helpful stage. Adding the experiential dimension of Qabalah to your spiritual practice is a bit like putting a door into the two-dimensional diagram and using it to step into multidimensional reality. You can learn to use the Qabalah as a tool to navigate the matrix of spiritual light energy accessible to human consciousness and remember afterward what you have experienced. This is the reason the Qabalah has been an initiatory practice favored in multiple traditions.

Each of the Qabalah spheres and paths carries a particular frequency of divine energy. As we experience each higher dimension within our own consciousness, we learn to recognize its unique qualities and higher spiritual purpose. True understanding of the Qabalah is then grounded in direct personal experience, rather than intellectual understanding. We have more recall of what we experienced and can apply what we learned to enhance our ongoing lives in practical ways. Practices to utilize the Qabalah can be added to any spiritual path. The method I describe is the subject of chapter 10.

Opening the Qabalah's Doors to Higher Consciousness

The Qabalah is a living matrix of spiritual energy,
offering portals that can be accessed within our consciousness,
connecting us to ascended masters and angels
who help us develop a unique expression of our spiritual light.

As said earlier, the ability to experience the masters at different parts of the Qabalah happens internally as a movement of our consciousness into dimensions beyond the physical senses.

When we have prepared our energy body through spiritual practice, using intention, breath, trance, or meditation, we turn the dial of our consciousness to attune to a specific vibration and dimension.

As we contact a master or archangel who corresponds to a sphere or path, we briefly anchor our awareness in that unique vibration. We don't need to believe anyone else's interpretation but can confirm it for ourselves. Experience teaches more deeply than intellectual understanding, as it bypasses the mind's need to process.

What Do I Mean by *Direct Contact* with an Angel or Master?

When we have honed our own strongest spiritual abilities, we become aware of nonphysical beings through our subtle senses. When our consciousness recognizes highly evolved beings, it is natural to want to draw closer to them. As noted in earlier chapters, we must develop discernment to be able to distinguish the masters from less-evolved spirits. (You can review chapter 2's description of the four clairs to remind yourself how this might be determined.)

I experience masters and angels as moving fields of divine light and consciousness. Seen in spiritual vision, they appear in fields of colored or white light, sometimes with an abstract appearance of form. There is some quality present that my consciousness recognizes as highly attractive, whether it is the exquisite beauty of their light, the divine love they extend, or a sometimes elegant and at other times humorous, spiritually elevated communication. In some way or ways, their enlightened nature is apparent.

I typically use the word *merging*, or sometimes the word *attuning*, to describe my experience of contact. Others describe contact through their own strongest subtle senses with different words. No form of experience is intrinsically better than another; what is important is developing the clarity, as well as the depth of your best form of experience.

A commonality shared by most practitioners who contact beings in the higher realms is that they are a great blessing to experience. The angels and masters can teach us, show us, and allow us to feel or understand a specific form of subtle energy or way of being that is part of their Qabalah dimension, yet each expresses it in his or her own unique way. As it arrives in our consciousness, through whichever subtle senses are stongest, the communication is direct, clear, and unmistakable.

Contact can be gentle, profound, or powerful beyond words to express. The masters show us "Like this," demonstrating or communicating in a way that is designed exactly for us. They understand us better than we know ourselves and can recognize exactly what we are ready to learn. Knowing a masters' Qabalah correspondence before we attempt to contact them lets us refresh our memory about the specific type of energy they extend. This prepares us in a general way to receive whatever they can share with us.

In this way, the masters are like wise elder brothers or sisters or beloved coaches or mentors, willing and able to show us something that is helpful. They accelerate our spiritual learning and growth in miraculous ways.

Working with Multiple Angels and Masters

It may not be your path to contact multiple masters. Most people may reach out to only a few, which is perfect when that is what feels most helpful to you. Since it was necessary for me to experience and confirm all the masters included in this book, meeting so many was a massive opportunity to learn the Qabalah matrix at a depth I would not have otherwise been able to obtain.

One result was that I could recognize the likely Qabalah correspondences of new masters I had not previously read about when they appeared spontaneously in my inner-world experience. I could do this because I had come to recognize the unique vibrations they extend, from previous contacts with other beings who extend those frequencies of spiritual light. I am grateful I was able to add some significant masters to the book in this way.

The cross-cultural group of masters in this book provide many different models of how each basic energy can be expressed and how each energy evolves through emotional, mental, and spiritual levels. Together the angels and masters provide an amazingly rich database of wisdom we can access when our own lives call us to express one of those qualities.

Awakening the Entire Qabalah Matrix

Over time, if we contact multiple masters, we can gradually awaken the whole Qabalah matrix within our own consciousness. After many contacts with masters at different parts of the Qabalah, I experienced this occurrence.

In one meditation, I became aware of a stream of energy descending from an infinite height above my point of observation, coming toward me. A Qabalah diagram glowed in luminous white light against the blackness of the cosmic void. The light ray entered the sphere of Kether at the top and moved toward the bottom of the diagram, passing through each sphere consecutively, culminating at Malkuth. As divine light passed through, each sphere lit up. I realized I was witnessing the Lightning Flash. Having read descriptions of this in the abstract texts on the Qabalah, I understood that the practitioners who wrote about it likely had witnessed this phenomenon for themselves.

Another meditation experience unfolded as I became aware of the Qabalah tree diagram glowing against cosmic blackness. I could direct my consciousness to travel into each of the spheres and paths individually and follow a specific energy as it continued through successive levels of development—from spiritual to mental to emotional levels and toward the physical plane. I experienced the color of the light energy changing from the white light always present at the spiritual level (which is closest to Source) to a characteristic color of light at the mental level. It sometimes changed color again when my consciousness reached the emotional level. All such initiations are available in the higher dimensions when you can lift energy and sustain concentration—and if it serves your spiritual purpose.

You will not need to understand the sequences of colors to work with specific masters and angels, as their color is provided for you at the end of their profiles. The colors are part of their higher-dimensional addresses and knowing them in advance is part of the system outlined in chapter 10 to invite them forward in your consciousness.

Important to Remember

The Qabalah is a metaphysical symbol system that provides understanding of our eternal connection to Creator Source.

The Qabalah is also a potent matrix of spiritual light energy, which can be experientially navigated within our own consciousness.

Adding Qabalah to your spiritual practice can help you enter successively higher states of awareness, contact masters and angels, and accelerate your spiritual growth.

Experiential Qabalah allows us to awaken higher potential within our energy fields and remember what we have experienced afterward, so we can call more easily upon those energies in our lives.

It is possible to develop a comprehensive experiential knowledge of the Qabalah by focusing on each sphere or each path sequentially within the full series, through individual or group work.

It is not necessary to learn the Qabalah in this depth to use the method presented in chapter 10 to reach out to specific angels and masters in meditation.

CHAPTER 8

UNDERSTANDING DIFFERENT
LEVELS OF MASTERY

The last chapter provided a basic overview of the Qabalah spheres and paths as a framework to understand the specific gifts of energy the angelic kingdom and the ascended masters extend to humankind.

In that chapter, I briefly introduced the idea that each of the Qabalah's spheres and paths offers different levels of development. This means that while nearly all Qabalah diagrams show a single series of spheres and paths, we need to think of the whole pattern unfolding in four levels.

It would be a bit too complex to attempt to show this in a single diagram. Occasionally, one might see the Qabalah pattern repeated in a linked series of four repeating patterns. If so, the image might remind you, as it did me, of the biblical description known as Jacob's ladder.

Each of the four levels has a specific name and is described within Qabalah traditions. I will highlight the attributes of each level below. It is important to understand that each master ascended at a particular sphere or path *and* at a specific level of attainment. From that level, he or she extends energies to support us now.

The Unique Opportunity of Human Life

It is a human tendency to think and speak of the challenges life produces, as well as the things we are grateful to experience. Beyond the rich beauty and sensory experience available on planet Earth, human life offers a unique opportunity to rediscover our own higher essence, even while we remain in physical form. We were created with the potential to experience states of higher consciousness, along with the free will to develop that capacity—or not. If we answer the inner call, awakening that potential requires evolutionary development, which can unfold as we undertake some form of spiritual practice.

This was the same opportunity each of the masters accepted during his or her human life, which was accomplished through personal effort. In contrast, the angels in this book were given a certain type and level of spiritual energy to extend in their creation, rather than needing to evolve toward it.

What the Ascended Masters Achieved

Over the course of their lives, by transforming human personality patterns and developing their potential gifts, the masters created an elevating path that produced ascension at life's end. Now, in the higher realms, they remember the special challenges of human life and can offer us compassion and wisdom born of human experience. They appreciate how our human dramas can be compelling. They are sometimes compassionate and at other times humorous in offering us something that might help us. They meet us in a loving way wherever we are, seeing us more clearly than we see ourselves. To seek those who can be most beneficial to us now, I will now discuss the different levels of mastery and what each type entails.

Ascension Can Be Achieved at One of Four Possible Levels of Mastery

No human being masters all the energies—or levels—of the Qabalah in a lifetime. Spiritual ascension occurred at one of the four possible levels for each of the masters in this book.

Spiritual ascension is possible at
emotional level one or two,
the mental level,
or the spiritual level.

The Subtle Sheaths within the Human Energy Field

To understand the levels of mastery, let us first consider the diagram below of the human energy field. As was said earlier, behind the limitations of physical eyesight, each human being is an outpouring of subtle spiritual light. The physical body we animate in life is light that has been slowed by the density of the Third Dimension to the point that it appears solid. (Modern physics has come to agree that at the heart of matter is light.)

The physical body can be seen by the human eye, but it is not the entirety of what we are. The physical body gives us a means to show up on the earth plane and to intact through the five senses, communing with others who share the same journey of an eternal spirit animating a body on planet Earth. Surrounding the physical body are layers of increasingly subtle energy. These layers are part of the light we carry into life, through which we express our unique gifts.

Collectively, our subtle layers of light are known as our energy field, and they appear as interpenetaring sheaths, each surrounding the others. They are sometimes named, progressing from the physical body and moving outward, as follows:

-The etheric body
-The emotional body
-The mental body
-The spiritual or casual body

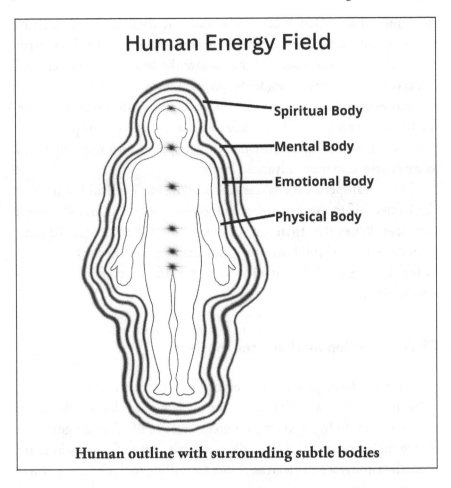

Human Energy Field

- Spiritual Body
- Mental Body
- Emotional Body
- Physical Body

Human outline with surrounding subtle bodies

The Human Chakras

I briefly mentioned the human chakras in an earlier chapter. The chakras, powerful, spinning vortices of energy in the human energy system, extend through the spiritual, mental, and emotional levels of our energy field. The most familiar are the seven main chakras, which are oriented parallel to the human spine. They are not visible to the human eye, but it is possible to learn to see one's own chakras with spiritual vision when one begins spiritual development. There are many smaller chakras also, in the palms of the hands, in the feet, and elsewhere.

Each individual has an additional group of chakras that are above the human head. One is called the soul star chakra, which contains the blueprint for the life we came to express. Another, called the earth star chakra, is about twelve inches below the feet. The transpersonal chakras over the head (outside the physical body envelope) are part of an even vaster subtle network of light (sometimes called our Merkabah levels) that connects us all the way to Creator Source. It is possible to glimpse the web of light above our crown chakra with spiritual vision as we continue to more advanced levels.

Those transpersonal chakras (those above the physical head) allow the higher self to eventually become embodied within one's physical container. When that final state of inner marriage occurs (an old term from alchemy but still descriptive), our higher levels then take the lead in life, helping us draw manifest inspired gifts that are of service to humankind.

Chakra Development and the Masters

Spiritual development, for everyone, is a process that is somewhat individual. When we place attention on how our chakras function, which we can do by observing different areas of life that are governed by the main seven chakras, we discover that some of our chakras are naturally strongest and clearest. As we are willing to work on the others we create a more balanced functioning. Everyone polishes the emotional levels first. As we progress, we might be working on emotional-level development at some chakras and have moved into mental-level development with others.

To assist this energetic development we become aware of what might be holding us back, let go of old patterns, and adopt new ones. Depending upon the chakra we are developing, our next step might include changes in the career path we follow, where and with whom we live, and the type of friendships we seek. It's a process of authentically discovering what works and does not work for us at each stage. We learn to recognize we are on the right path, because our adjustments are empowering and regenerating. We feel brighter, lighter, and grateful that new ease has flowed into areas that we have worked to improve.

To support a higher vibrational level, we learn to make more conscious choices about what we eat, what entertainment uplifts us, and how to modulate media and technology so that they do not eclipse the spiritual experiences we are coming to value. There are times when we grow best in a group environment and other periods in which our optimal growth is nurtured by solitude and introspection.

Gradually, changes occur in all our physical systems, cells, organs, brain, and bloodstream. The chakras develop their inherent potential to receive and transmit a faster, higher vibration. Psychic changes occur as well, and we are more able to access spiritual guidance to recognize the optimal path ahead. Our faces become more serene, and we are more resilient, better able to weather life's ups and downs as they occur. Over time, we reach welcome plateaus of inner peace that allow us to become aware of the masters and angels by our side, who have been quietly helping us all the way.

How Far Can Our Spiritual Development Go?

There is always a choice about how far we go with spiritual development. There are stages of evolutionary rest as we integrate what we have already accomplished. After a time, a sense that more is possible draws some onward. It becomes clear that further evolution is needed to fully embody the higher self's full potential in our physical form.

Just as it takes time for the initial stages of spiritual development to unfold, so too the advanced stages of development cannot be completed overnight. Neither our psyches nor our physical containers can assimilate our full spiritual light that quickly. Individual development proceeds at a pace that our nonphysical spiritual team and Source (and our own higher spiritual levels) carefully oversee. Their guidance along the way informs us about changes that will serve our individual processes. We can help ourselves best by cooperating with whatever information we receive.

For those who remain dedicated to the path of spiritual transformation, full integration with the higher self arrives. The result is worth everything it has taken to get there. Not every stage is easy or comfortable, yet along the way, the wonders of the multiverse awaken in direct personal experience. The angels and masters are yet more available in direct contact, and the experiences themselves become profound.

Which Masters Can We Experience?

Understanding that the vibrations of masters and angels are faster (and subtler) at each higher level of development lets us know why some are easier to experience than others. The mental level is subtler than the emotional level, and the spiritual level is yet subtler than the mental level. It will be easiest to connect with those who match our current level of development in the corresponding chakra or chakras.

There are exceptions to this, as from time to time, a master more advanced than our current range will extend to meet us as a special experience of spiritual grace. Experiences of spiritual grace are highly encouraging to our continuing efforts. We feel seen, and there is no doubt we are loved! Knowing they are by our side, it is no wonder such experiences help us remain committed to our practices.

As we continue to raise our vibration to meet them at their own vibrational level, it becomes easier for them to work with us. To make ourselves most available for guidance from the highest masters, our part of the bargain is to continue to uplift our vibration. Understanding more about the personal work that is part of each level can help us approach this in the most helpful way.

Everyone can reach out in meditation to any masters or angel, whether he or she is just beginning a spiritual journey or has been on a path for many years.

Understanding that it takes spiritual development to consciously receive what the masters and archangels extend helps us approach them with practical expectations. They are aware of our reaching toward them and will help us in many ways.

We may not be aware of their help directly in the beginning, but as we continue our spiritual practices deeper experiences will follow.

Emotional-Level Mastery

By the time we experience contact with ascended masters, we have generally been committed to some form of inner development through our spiritual practice. As we do our part to clear inner obstacles, at some point, the inner door of consciousness opens.

As we begin to access the ascended realms more frequently, we are most likely to meet the emotional-level masters first. The role of all emotional-level masters is to support us while we clear and complete anything that is not yet consistently harmonious in our emotional body. Working toward emotional mastery invites more ease and grace into our life.

No masters at emotional level one are included in this book, but I have experienced some of them. Therese of Liseaux, whose simple words of spiritual devotion are still popular today, and Brother Lawrence, who brought us *The Practice of the Presence of God*, are two masters who correspond to the sphere of Binah at emotional level one. Egeria of Spain or Gaul (her country of origin is still debated by scholars), who wrote about her ancient pilgrimage to the Holy Land, is met at the sphere of Hod at emotional level one. There are many other masters and angels at the first emotional level who can be encountered in consciousness, who correspond to every part of the Qabalah.

Emotional level two masters completed the entire process of clearing and uplifting their emotional body to its fullest potential before their ascension. What an accomplishment that is! We can reach out for their help even as we begin this inner work. Any of them can stand beside us, when we invite their help, as we complete all our forgiveness work so that only love remains. They also serve as ambassadors, welcoming our consciousness with great love to the Qabalah dimension of energy they extend. They can show us or otherwise communicate through our strongest subtle senses a thought, practice, forgiveness assignment, or way to approach something in life that is enormously helpful.

As we clear former disharmonies, we are more able to maintain a calm inner state, which helps in all areas of life. Our vibration lifts more easily when we meditate, and we are better able to concentrate for longer periods of time. We learn to bypass the ego's habits in favor of choices that more accurately reflect our inner light.

Over time, we learn with these masters how to navigate in the higher realms, and they inspire us to continue our spiritual practices. A relationship with one angel or master at emotional level two may provide enough support for an entire lifetime. Even when we move into work at the mental level, we may sometimes return to work more deeply at the emotional level. These masters and angels are profoundly strengthening each time we turn to them.

Mental Level

As anyone begins some form of spiritual practice, he or she encounters ideas that reshape thought and belief. Drawing from a sacred text or spiritual thought system allows us to make changes that undo the ego's program of judgment, blame, and fear. Gradually, this lifts our vibration, and we begin to experience the masters and angels directly.

If we continue spiritual practice past the welcome and restorative integration of emotional levels, we become receptive to mental-level masters. These include some of the most beloved teachers of teachers, who hold every form of higher knowledge. They support us to discover and release any remaining unconscious thoughts and beliefs that are inconsistent with our highest essence.

Becoming receptive to their subtler energy is possible when our energy centers develop a faster and higher vibration. In consistently seeking the divine, we awaken the subtle pathways that link our personal chakras to the transpersonal chakras over the human head. This allows us to draw increasingly on our higher-self levels for inspiration and guidance.

Mental-level masters and angels oversee the final purification of any remaining unconscious thoughts and beliefs that are inconsistent with our highest essence. This allows us to be fully aligned with the abilities we came to deliver to the world.

To move toward this, we bypass motivations such as ambition and the need for acknowledgment from others. We are stengthened from within, and deep gratitude to the spiritual world fuels a desire to contribute through the specifc gifts and talents that are strongest in our energy field.

Whether our gift lies in consulting, health care, art, science, motherhood, politics, or gardening doesn't matter. What matters is the intention to become an instrument for profound currents of higher energy that can come through us in service of the spiritual world and the highest good of all. In delivering them, we find meaning and resources that meet our personal needs.

When we connect with mental-level masters in meditation, we experience minds that have a highly developed awareness of the spiritual dimensions and hold this as a constant state. Developing certainty about their connection to Source allowed them to walk through every experience in human life while remembering their senior eternal identity. They are beside us as we seek to achieve this also. Contact with their minds can be electrifying, illuminating dimensions of wonder that are truly magnificent.

Each of the mental-level masters and angels corresponds to a specific Qabalah sphere or path. We can reach out for those whose skill lies in an area we are developing. Through contact with one or more of them, we begin to discover more fully the life mission we came to contribute.

They mirror different ways to express energies that are strong within our own field, and they are willing to show us how to polish our own unique expression.

Spiritual Levels

Few beings express spiritual-level mastery during an earthly sojourn. As we review available information on their lives, which is not always easy to accurately obtain, we observe those who came to fulfill a special purpose on behalf of the spiritual realms and humankind. Their vibrations are faster and subtler than those at the mental level.

Connecting to spiritual-level angels and masters evokes experiences of being blessedly close to Creator Source. Even an instant of joining with their consciousness erases all sense of separation, because their essence is one with those higher levels.

The spiritual-level beings included in this book extend energy that corresponds to many parts of the Qabalah. They are met in realms of radiant white light. Some, after their physical lifetimes, were acknowledged as the illustrious founders of earth's religions and spiritual lineages. Some are specially able to instruct us in advanced practices that assist ascension. It is an understatement to say that it is a deep blessing to experience them directly in one's consciousness.

How the Evolutionary Levels Are Described in the Qabalah

As mentioned in the beginning of this chapter, Qabalah diagrams typically show only one complete series of the ten spheres and twenty-two paths. However, there are four levels of Qabalah, which are named Assiah, Yetzirah, Briah, and Atziluth.

Assiah, the first level, relates to earthly experience. As said earlier, angels and masters can and do occasionally appear to physical sight when that serves some higher spiritual purpose. Most commonly, masters and angels are met at the next three levels. I find it is easiest to remember the terms *emotional, mental,* and *spiritual* regarding the levels, but the traditional names are also given below.

> **Assiah** corresponds to the physical body, earth, and the planets in our cosmos.

> **Yetzirah** corresponds to the emotional body and astral plane.

> **Briah** corresponds to the mental body and plane.

> **Atziluth** corresponds to the spiritual, or causal body, and plane.

I will describe the nature and evolutionary work at each of these levels below, which expands the previous descriptions of the different levels of masters and angels in a bit more detail.

Qabalah at Assiah: Physical Level

Everyone who comes into a physical body gains experience with the physical plane as he or she learns to express energy. This is the material world, where we animate physical bodies and experience life through the five senses: physical sight, hearing, taste, touch, and smell. At this level, the material world is perceived through appearances of difference (polarity and gender), time, and space. forms manifest through the four classical elements: fire, air, water, and earth. At Assiah, each of the Qabalah spheres corresponds to one of the planets observed in our solar system. We begin the process of developing expanded states of consciousness here and to integrate all we have learned into our ongoing life.

Qabalah at Yetzirah: Emotional Level

Every human being who is open to self-reflection explores feelings and desires, which are contained in his or her emotional body. It is part of human nature that we may experience conflicting desires when we begin to pay attention. Noticing what works and where greater harmony is needed, we can bring our energies into more harmonious functioning.

The emotional body is also the storehouse that contains any unresolved matters from the past. The experience of living in a human body on a planet, interacting with others, is not always smooth. It is important to learn self-compassion, rather than be self-critical as we engage in self-discovery. Meditation practices such as Mindfulness, can help us in the initial stages to simply be with what we are feeling, without blame or judgment. Cultivating self-love and acceptance, just as we are, gives us a strong foundation on which to stand as we approach any process of developing inner peace. The masters and angels love us exactly as we are right now, and so too, should we.

Every human being has emotional clearing to do, to create greater harmony. Finding the courage to do that inner work, creates renewal. Physical health can improve, artistic and creative faculties blossom; and a strong sense of self emerges that allows us to enjoy abundant and fulfilling lives.

Fine Tuning the Emotional Body

Personal healing allows us to arise from former limitations and claim the full potential of the human journey. Many disciplines can be helpful. Dance, movement, yoga, art or poetry therapy, journaling, and work with intuitives, hypnotherapy or healing energy practitioners can help us clear matters that no longer serve our highest good.

When a healing journey is paired with forgiveness, as described in chapter five, we bring welcome calm to the emotional body so that we can remain clear and centered and available to receive guidance from our higher spiritual team. We are more able to move into blessed experiences that expand our perception from the personality-in-a-physical-body view to receive glimpses of our own higher spiritual reality.

Qabalah at Briah: Mental Level

We may still be polishing the emotional body when we notice some of the accompanying thoughts and beliefs that have structured our experiences. Many of our thought patterns formed early in life or were assumed from family or cultural teachings.

As we begin to examine them, we recognize right away some that served us earlier might be holding us back now. Other beliefs are initially unconscious. Sorting out which beliefs still feel helpful and authentic is a necessary step that delivers us to greater coherence. We discover what works for us and act in accordance with our beliefs. Greater coherence means the ways we think, feel, and act are in harmony (coherence), rather than battling to fulfill different agendas.

Observing our mental operating system is best served by self-compassion rather than allowing the inner critic to make it difficult. Inviting spiritual help into the process, we by-pass the ego's settings in favor of our own higher levels. Every human being goes through a mental sorting process if they wish to grow and evolve. Everyone has patterns that no longer serve, and when they are unmasked, we have the opportunity to change our minds.

There are many good ways to examine our throughts and beliefs. Professional counseling, coaching, meditation, and journaling can provide insight, as can higher-wisdom systems, such as astrology, tarot, and Qabalah. It is only when we allow our minds operating system to run by default, without observing the settings, that diffficulties continue.

As we continue, our unconscious levels gradually become conscious, and purified. This deep work builds spiritual power. We are more able to maintain sustained concentration in meditation which allows experiences to become profound. Our vibration lifts into faster, higher, subtler dimensions.

143

Fine-Tuning the Mental Body

It is immensely helpful to work with spiritual texts as we uplift, purify, and reprogram our thoughts to a higher vibrational level. There are equistie ancient texts from many traditions as well as thoughtful modern approaches to choose from.

When our consciousness achieves the inner stillness and concentration to connect with mental-level masters, they can guide us to deep understanding and insight on many different topics. Some can answer the deep spiritual questions we hold and, in that way, guide us to accelerate our own evolution. Others can inspire us with ideas that can be expressed through our careers, relationships, and creative gifts and address the collective needs of our time. Direct contact with mental-level masters carries us toward our own higher-dimensional existence. We develop our ability to hold our spiritual reality as an ongoing state of being, no matter what physical sights and sounds come before us.

Qabalah at Atziluth: Experiencing the Pure Energy of the Spiritual Body

Within the Qabalah system, Atziluth represents the pure spiritual realm, the headwaters where each type of energy extended by Source descends toward human life.

Human awareness cannot experience this state continuously while we remain in physical bodies, but we can experience it in blessed moments outside time. Contact with a master at this level, at any Qabalah sphere or path, is a great blessing. The energy they extend is so light-filled that any brief experience with them in our own consciousness can move our evolution forward in a dramatic way. Discovering that it is possible to align our consciousness with these levels—even momentarily—teaches us with certainty that divine energy is part of our own higher spiritual essence.

The spiritual level masters included in the book are available to all, yet it may take considerable spiritual development to be conscious of connecting with them and able to recall what they communicated. Each one is unique, and their specific gifts are reflected in the meanings of their spheres or paths. Focusing a spiritual practice toward one or more of them can provide a meaningful path that shapes a lifetime.

Important to Remember

Every sphere and path in the Qabalah includes masters who ascended at either emotional, mental, or spiritual level development.

When our consciousness first rises into the higher Dimensions in meditation, we are met by Emotional Level masters who support us as we bring peace to any experience that isn't yet fully resolved in our emotional body.

We can reach out to any master or angel at any time but are most likely to connect with those who match ot level of development. They are the ones that can be most helpful for the life matters that are our current priority.

As an extension of spiritual grace, we might experience contact with a master at a higher level than we have yet attained. To connect with them more frequently and fully receive their help we will need to continue our spiritual practices.

CHAPTER 9

IDENTIFYING POTENTIALLY HELPFUL MASTERS AND ANGELS USING TAROT AND WESTERN ASTROLOGY

As said earlier, whatever your life assignments include, there will be members of your higher team who mastered the energies you are developing and can actively support you when you ask for this. When they contact your consciousness, you will learn exactly who they are. You might be instinctively drawn toward certain ones as you read the profiles of the 108 beings included in this book.

It is also possible to use the principles of correspondence to attempt to identify members of your higher spiritual family through tarot paths that are significant for you, or your Western astrology birth chart. You can use these methods as a guide, while following your instincts to reach out to any angels or masters you are drawn toward.

The information below will help you to identify potential masters and angels, using four different approaches. You can explore any of these methods as you feel drawn to do so.

1. Angels and masters to support your tarot lifetime path
2. Angels and masters to support your current tarot growth year
3. Angels and masters who correspond to your Western astrological birth chart
4. Angel and masters who support any current astrological outerplanet transits

---

Identifying Potentially Helpful Masters
and Angels by Using Tarot

In the system of tarot, an individual's lifetime symbol indicates one or two of the Qabalah pathways that will be a primary focus of development over their whole lifetime. Your lifetime symbol is determined by adding up the day, month, and year of birth and then adding the resulting number across.

Example 1: Birth date of January 6, 1982

Calculate the following:

> **month 1**
> **day + 6**
>   **= 7**
> **+ year 1982**
> **= 1989**

Then add the last digits together.

> **1 + 9 + 8 + 9 = 27**

If total is a double-digit number greater than 21 (the last of the tarot Major Arcana cards), Then add the two digits together.

> **2 + 7 = 9**

The number 9 is your inner and outer lifetime symbol.

Any single digit represents that your outer expression and inner expression are the same.

In the chart below, you find the corresponding Qabalah path (the Hermit), its connecting spheres (Tiphareth and Chesed), and corresponding masters and angels. If one of those mentioned calls to you, reaching out to him or her might help you to refine and balance your expression of that energy. Also, the Norse female master Eir corresponds to the Yod/Hermit path itself, indicating that her area of expertise may help you to develop the path.

Example 2: Birth date of September 9, 2014

9
+ 9
= 18
+ 2014
= 2032
2 + 0 + 3 + 2 = 7

The number 7 is the tarot lifetime symbol and inner and outer expression.

Path 7 in tarot is the Chariot, which corresponds to the path of Cheth in Qabalah.

Cheth connects the spheres of Geburah and Binah and also has masters and an angel for the path included in this book. See if any of those masters or angels call out to you.

Example 3: Birth date of January 20, 1959

1
+ 20
= 21
+ 1959
= 1980
1 + 9 + 8 + 0 = 18
1 + 8 = 9

Path 18 is your outer expression. Path 9 is your inner expression.

Path 18 in tarot is the Moon, this individual's outer expression. In Qabalah, this is Qoph, which connects the spheres of Malkuth and Netzach (Netzach only has masters and angels, some of whom may be helpful to reach out to).

Path 9 in tarot is the Hermit, this individual's inner expression. In Qabalah, this is Yod, which connects the spheres of Tiphareth and Chesed, both of which have corresponding angels and masters. Yod itself has one master in the book (and others in my files).

Correspondence Chart: Tarot/Qabalah/Astrology with Masters and Angels in Profiles

---

As discussed in the last chapter, levels of mastery differ, so pay attention to which level of being is most helpful for you at this time.

- Path 21 Tau, the Universe (connects Malkuth and Yesod)
- Path 20 Shin, the Aeon (connects Malkuth and Hod)
- Path 19 Resh, the Sun (connects Yesod and Hod)
- Path 18 Qoph, the Moon (connects Malkuth and Netzach)
- Path 17 Heh, the Star, Aquarius (connects Yesod and Netzach)
- Path 16 Peh, the Tower, lower octave of Mars (connects Hod and Netzach)
- Path 15 Ayin, the Devil, Capricorn (connects Hod and Tiphareth), Cerridwen
- Path 14 Samech, Art/Temperance, Sagittarius (connects Yesod and Tiphareth)
- Path 13 Nun, Death/Rebirth, Scorpio (connects Netzach and Tiphareth),
  Persephone
- Path 12 Mem, the Hanged Man, Hebrew mother letter, root of water
  (connects Geburah and Hod)

- Path 11 Teth, Lust and Strength, Leo (connects Geburah and Chesed),
  Durga, Archangel Ariel, Thor
- Path 10 Kaph, Wheel of Fortune (connects Netzach and Chesed),
  Claire of Assisi
- Path 9 Yod, the Hermit, Virgo (connects Tiphareth and Chesed),
  Eir
- Path 8 Lamed, Adjustment and Justice, Libra (connects Tiphareth and Geburah),
  Deborah, Forseti
- Path 7 Cheth, the Chariot, Cancer (connects Geburah and Binah),
  Bernadette of Lourdes, Enoch
- Path 6 Zain, the Lovers, Gemini (connects Tiphareth and Binah),
  Oengus mac Og
- Path 5 Vav, the Hierophant, Taurus (connects Chesed and Chokma)
- Path 4 Tzaddi, the Emperor, Aries (connects Tiphareth and Chokma),
  Charlemagne, Arjuna
- Path 3 Da'leth, the Empress (connects Binah and Chokma),
  Angel Hasdiel, Rebecca, Hera, Parvati, Guinevere, Frigg
- Path 2 Gimel, the Priestess (connects Tiphareth and Kether),
  Gefjun, Ariadne, Miriam, Lady of the Lake, Miriam
- Path 1 Beth, the Magician (connects Binah and Kether),
  Hermes-Thoth
- Path 0 Aleph, the Fool, Hebrew mother letter, root of air (connects Binah and Kether)
- Hidden path of the pink ray, no tarot correspondence (connects Geburah and Kether),
  Angel Chamuel
- Hidden path of the blue ray, no tarot correspondence (connects Kether and Chesed), Saint Mary, mother of Jesus/Yeshua, Gullveig/Heid

- First Hidden path of the white ray, no tarot correspondence (connects Kether and Yesod), White Tara
- Second Hidden path of the white ray, no tarot correspondence (connects Yesod and Chesed) Buddha Locana

---

Masters for Your Current Tarot Growth-Year Path (from Birthday to Birthday)

Also in the system of tarot, each birthday begins a specific yearly focus of development that is an overlay on your lifetime path(s). It begins on one birthday and ends on the following birthday, when you move into the next year of evolutionary growth. You can chart these cycles of development over your whole lifetime. The masters who correspond to your current tarot growth year may be helpful during that time. Even if you are not drawn to work with them for some reason, they can be a model for the energy that is present.

To calculate your current tarot growth year, you use almost the same approach used to find your tarot lifetime symbols, adding the day and month of your birth, but instead of your birth year, use the current year when your most recent birthday occurred.

For example, an individual born on January 6 who has a birthday in 2020 is beginning a Lust and Strength year:

> **Month 1**
> **Day + 6**
> **= 7**
> **+ 2020**
> **= 2027**
> **2 + 0 + 2 + 7 = 11**

The number 11 corresponds to Teth, a Lust and Strength growth year, connecting the spheres of Geburah and Chesed. Masters for either sphere and/or a master for Teth (Archangel Ariel or Durga) might be helpful.

Discovering Potentially Helpful Masters through Your Western Astrology Birth Chart

---

While working from astrology to identify potential masters involves more factors, in my experience, it brings masters to your attention who are not highlighted by tarot. I spent more than twenty years doing astrological consultation, but you don't have to be an expert in astrology to use it to identify potentially helpful masters and angels.

By working with the rising sign, north node, and a few planets that are in close conjunction (located within a few degrees of each other in the 360-degree circle of my birth chart), I came to understand why certain masters are on my personal team of guides. My tarot lifetime symbols do not reveal this group, and they are immensely helpful.

If you are not familiar with astrology, a professional astrologer can provide you with information about which planets are naturally strong in your natal chart and those that might require personal effort to express their energies in a harmonious way, so you can look up potentially helpful beings to work with.

Alternatively, you can use a computerized chart summary that includes an assessment of planetary strength. Then consult the chart below to find masters who support your strengths. It may be even more helpful to identify those who can support you to develop greater strength where it is needed.

Astrological Planets and Qabalah Correspondence

Masters can support your natural strengths or can support you to develop greater strength. As discussed in the last chapter, the levels of mastery differ among the beings listed below, so pay attention to which level of support is most helpful for you at this time.

Earth: Malkuth, the tenth (bottom) sphere, grounding, and personal integration (Masters and angels can appear but are not at home in earth's dense vibration.)

Moon: Yesod, the ninth sphere (also paths of Qoph, Cheth, and Gimel and First and Second Hidden Paths of the White Ray), emotions, female fertility cycle, intuition, mediumship, and manifestation

- Rhiannon, Huldah, Leah, Themistoclea, Arianrhod, Aine, Archangel Haniel, Artemis,
- Path of Cheth: Enoch, Bernadette of Lourdes
- Path of Gimel: Ariadne, Gefjun, Miriam, Lady of the Lake
- First Hidden Path of the White Ray: White Tara
- Second Hidden Path of the White Ray: Buddha Locana

Mercury: Hod, the eighth sphere (also paths of Zain and Beth), inspiration, intellect, study, learning, creative expression

- Archangel Uriel, Sarasvati, Archangel Jeremiel, Niguma, Mira Bai, Orpheus, King Solomon
- Path of Beth: Hermes-Thoth
- Path of Zain – Oengus mac Og

Venus: Netzach, the seventh sphere (also path of Da'leth), love, beauty, abundance, healing, desire nature

- Green Tara, Archangel Raphael, Amoghasiddi Buddha, Lakshmi, Aphrodite, Freya, Asclepius, Brigit, Radha
- Path of Da'leth: Angel Hasdiel, Guinevere, Parvati, Hera, Rebecca, Frigg

Sun: Tiphareth, the sixth sphere (also paths of Resh and Teth), leadership, confidence, logic, will, intellectual brilliance, and (at mental and spiritual levels) higher self

- Archangel Gabriel, Mamaki Buddha, Paramahansa Yogananda, Vishnu, Siddhartha Gautama (the Buddha), Hildegard of Bingen, Teresa of Avila, Apollo, Athena, Lugh, Belenus, Fionn mac Cumhail
- Path of Teth: Durga, Archangel Ariel, Thor

Mars: Geburah, the fifth sphere (also paths of Peh and Tzaddi), assertive action, the warrior, overcoming fear, setting firm boundaries, healthy sexual relationships

- Penthesilia, Kali, Archangel Camael, Archangel Raguel, Pandara Buddha, Ares, Tyre
- Path of Tzaddi: Charlemagne, Arjuna

Jupiter: Chesed, the fourth sphere (also paths of Samech Kaph, and Hidden Path of the Blue Ray, and Second Hidden Path of the White Ray), politics and rulership, spiritual wisdom, study and teaching, sacred masculine, high ethical and moral principles, connecting heaven and earth

- Archangel Michael, Angel Nuriel, John the Baptist, Francis of Assisi, King David of Jerusalem, Plato, King Arthur, Francis of Assisi, Moses, Avalokitshvara, Krishna, Rama, Ganesha, Baldur the Beautiful
- Path of Kaph: Clare of Assisi
- Hidden Path of the Blue Ray: Mother Mary, Gullveig/Heid
- Second Hidden Path of the White Ray: Buddha Locana

Saturn: Binah, the third sphere (also path of Tau and path of Da'leth), direct experience of spiritual reality, skills that develop best in later life, bringing light to the personal shadow, spiritual context for physical death, overcoming grief, Divine Mother

- Danu, Mary Magdalene, Saint Germain, Archangel Azrael, Jesus/Yeshua, Ezekiel, Isaac, Sarah, Machig Labdron, Yeshe Tsogyal
- Path of Da'leth: Frigg, Angel Hasdiel, Guinevere, Hera, Parvati, Rebecca

Uranus/realm of fixed stars: Chokma, the second sphere (also Path of Tzaddi and Path of Vav) transcendent wisdom, male potency and power, experiencing the nature of reality before and after an embodied lifetime

- Odin, Ailill mac Mata, Abraham, Manjushri, Vairocana Buddha, Shiva, the Dagda, King Nuada, Njord, Archangel Raziel
- Path of Tzaddi: Charlemagne, Arjuna

Neptune: Kether, the first sphere, gateway to Creator Source, extending to uplift humankind (also Paths of Gimel, Hidden Blue, White and Pink Ray)

- Archangel Metatron
- Path of Gimel: Ariadne, Gefjun, Lady of the Lake, Miriam
- Hidden Path of the Blue Ray: Saint Mary, Gullveig/Heid
- Hidden Path of the White Ray: White Tara
- Hidden Path of the Pink Ray: Angel Chamuel

Masters to Support You During Outer-Planet Astrological Transits

---

In Western astrology, the term *transit* refers to a period when the current position of a planet in the sky (viewed from Earth's perspective) arrives at one of many possible angular relationships with the locations of planets in your birth chart. The transiting planets are astrological indicators to note the timing in your continuing development, during which you transform the way you express a specific energy to a higher level.

Outer planet transits (involving Pluto, Neptune, Uranus, Saturn, and the asteroid Chiron) mark noticeable periods of evolution that are in effect for one to two years. During such times, you might find that masters and angels corresponding to the planet *receiving the transit* (the energy being transformed) can be quite helpful.

Important to Remember: How Can the Qabalah Be Used?

To notice spiritual progress and to mark and remember your meditation experiences

To identify which angels or masters might be most helpful or comforting

To understand more about the energy you are learning to express in your life

To gain deeper insight into current life choices or help with challenging situations

---

CHAPTER 10

A METHOD TO INVITE SPECIFIC ASCENDED MASTERS AND ANGELS CLOSER IN MEDITATION

Methods to Contact Angels and Masters

Different approaches are offered in all the spiritual and esoteric literature that addresses working with angels or masters. All of them include some form of meditation practice or method to enter trance and become aware of the higher dimensions. Some approaches suggest symbols, some use specific types of incense or essential oils, and some use gemstones or mantras. Many of these practices can work, and they are not all the same. A mix-and-match approach taken from multiple traditions may not be especially effective.

Another classic approach that may be used by some readers is known as pathworking. I want to say a bit about pathworking before I introduce the system offered in this book.

Pathworking

Pathworking is a form of aural induction to what is usually a group trance experience. Experienced practitioners create pathworking scripts to be read aloud to a focused group who intend to experience a specific path. Some pathworking scripts are published, and some are reserved for use in a specific tradition or mystery school. They provide a form of guided meditation in which the words become a launching pad for consciousness so that at least some in the group can reach the same dimensions of consciousness as the practitioner who wrote them. Within the working group, it is likely that individual experiences vary, according to each person's level of spiritual experience. A pathworking script can also be recorded and played when one is working alone.

The beginning and ending of each pathworking includes certain words that invite consciousness to move beyond normal awareness and return to normal awareness at the end, passing by the same series of markers. (Some of the Monroe Institute guided meditations offer similar markers, combined with the type of binaural sound technology that facilitates out-of-body experience.)

When a group is pathworking together, the guided meditation script utilizes words that describe colors, patterns, or symbols that may be encountered during the inner journey on a specific path. A group event can sometimes enhance individual learning when individual experiences are shared. Pathworkings sometimes mention beings who may be encountered, but those I am familiar with are not designed to reach specific masters or angels.

It is possible one could modify a pathworking technique to reach a specific master on that path if one is working alone. However, a whole group working together may or may not want to reach out to the same being. Instead, group members may wish to contact the one they are most closely attracted to who expresses energy on that path.

Pathworking, as the name implies, arose from initiatory traditions that focus attention on attuning consciousness to each of the paths as a method to develop higher consciousness. This is a valid approach. However, it is not the only approach. It is also possible to align consciousness to experience the pure energy of each sphere and the many masters and angels who extend each of those energies toward humankind.

My Method to Focus on an Individual Angel or Master

The system my guides brought me to share is to visualize a specific symbol within a field of color that corresponds to the Qabalah dimension where a master or angel can be met in consciousness. Both the color and symbol to visualize are included at the end of each angel's and master's profile in part 2. These two factors constitute what I call their *higher-dimensional address*. It can be used by an individual working alone or as part of a focused group approach. Before I describe how to use it, I want to provide an overview of why symbols are helpful.

How and Why Symbols Work

Symbols can open a psychic door with us to access higher dimensions of consciousness. When we quiet the mind's inner dialogue, we can move through that door to intuitively access, receive, and extend communication.

Many symbols are illustrated by artists, found in popular decks or wall art. I enjoy many of these forms. When a symbol is described only in words and we are then invited to visualize it, what appears in our mind's eye arises from forms that already exist within us. Symbols bypass the thinking mind, or intellect; we can feel them diving deep into the potent waters of inner consciousness. They have effects.

According to transpersonal psychologist Frances Vaughn (see page 164 in her book *Shadows of the Sacred*), psychologist Carl Jung observed that the incidence of meaningful synchronicities increased as his patients became aware of the symbolic dimension.

There are many types of symbols. Hebrew letters, astrological glyphs, geometric forms, and common everyday objects are just a few of the many forms. Any symbol can be a psychic doorway.

Symbols That Are a Mnemonic

A mnemonic (pronounced with the first *m* silent: nem-onic) is a memory device that features a pattern of letters, ideas, or associations that can help increase our ability to recall and retain information. This learning style dates to ancient Greek times.

> Mnemonic techniques act as memory aids to help us translate pieces of information from short-term memory into long-term memory.

Mnemonic devices can be created through a process known as chunking. Chunking is a form of organization mnemonics wherein you learn pieces of information and then put them together into a symbol that represents the whole.

For example, in this book, one can read about the details of masters' physical lives, their accomplishments and challenges, where they lived, their family relationships, their Qabalah correspondences, and the colors present in their energy fields. This is an application of the chunking technique, and then the symbol and colored field put all this information together in simple psychic shorthand. Using the symbol and color to reach out to them in meditation (along with your intention and inner preparation) sends a clear and focused invitation for them to draw closer.

As you reach the stage of contacting a master directly, your consciousness will record the way their energy feels to you or a message they may bring to you. Each experience you have with them is automatically added to your inner storehouse of memory, organized around their symbol. Later, when you want to return to them in meditation, you can focus on their symbol and color, and you're in contact with them more quickly. Learning the symbol and color provides a simple process that can be applied instantly, wherever you are, to invite them closer. A technique that includes chunking mnemonics is useful for surpassing the average short-term memory limit of seven pieces of information that can be used together.

The Intuitive Mind Works Best with Simplicity

I love visionary art and have always filled my home with it. Symbols appear in visionary art, but visionary art usually includes a whole collection of symbols, backgrounds, and effects shown together. Visionary art decks (whether tarot or angels and ascended masters) often present us with images that are inspiring. It can be helpful to draw one of those beautiful cards and intuitively recognize it as a sign of energies that are present in our lives right now. Doing that can validate our intuitive knowing.

Meditation in front of a complex mandala or deity image is another practice present in different spiritual traditions. However, to remember and use a symbol to extend an invitation to a specific master or angel, it is better to use something simpler. The symbols I received from each master and angel are simple. I like to think of them as higher-dimensional clip art.

It is well known that human consciousness can access a vast storehouse of archetypal symbols. Until we try, we may not recognize what can occur when given a few simple words as a guide. The symbols I was given are presented in words only, so your own consciousness will come up with the configuration—the specific form—that works best for you. The symbols that your mind presents to you are potent. When used with intention, they can open psychic doorways to communicate with ascended-realm beings. The master will recognize that you are attempting to reach him or her through the form that your own mind selects.

Methods to Discover Your Most Effective Image to Visualize

To find the symbols offered at the end of each angel's and master's profile, I worked with each being individually to ask what he or she would prefer to use for this system. Some symbols will be familiar to you and are mentioned in other sources, while other symbols are not currently found in any other resource or book, to my knowledge.

When masters bring me the symbols to use for them, sometimes I see the symbols with inner vision. After the experience, I do a quick sketch and label each symbol so I can remember it later. Other times, their symbols are communicated as concepts, or they tell me specific objects to use for them. I may be unfamiliar with them. This was especially true when a type of ritual object used in the spiritual tradition a master founded or followed was unknown to me because I hadn't practiced the tradition in which it is commonly known.

161

When I was unfamiliar with the symbol a master wanted, I used the internet to locate images of that type of object. Other times, I searched for a clip art image that reminded me of what the master showed me in spiritual vision. You can do the same thing if one of the symbols I suggest is unfamiliar to you. If you can call an image forward from the words given, there is no need to look further. It will work—for you.

If you do need to do an image search, you might find many versions. Yet there will be one that immediately resonates more effectively for you than others. You will recognize yours because it impacts you in some way. You can feel it. Print that one out if you are guided, to remind yourself.

Create an Index Card or Object with the Master's or Angel's Symbol and Color

I have discovered that I can recall information to visualize most effectively by creating an object that expresses whatever I want to remember. It isn't art; it's a process of programming my inner levels. Doing this deepens my ability to remember all the information that the chunking mnemonic provides. It's fun, and I also do the process with intention. Making a card that represents our own visualization symbol is a more powerful process than using anyone else's version.

If I am using an image from the internet, I add the correct Qabalah color of the being's field with a bit of paint or colored marker around the symbol. Then I tape it onto an index card. Once it's complete, I put the card aside and can more easily call it from memory, because I've gone through the process of giving it form. If you enjoy painting or prefer any other medium, you can use that method. Just remember to keep it simple. For this purpose, a collage or vision board is far too complex.

After I finish, I put the card aside until I need reminding. After looking at the card occasionally over a period of days (especially before I reach out to that being in meditation), gradually, I can think of the master's or angel's name and immediately visualize the symbol in my mind's eye. I can use it wherever I happen to be during the day to invite that being close.

Adding the Color of the Qabalah
Dimension to a Master's Symbol

As I've said, many masters and angels are met in a dimension with a color hue. In visualizing a specific color in meditation, we are focusing our intent on a specific Qabalah sphere or path at a specific level. It's like a higher-dimensional address. Each dimension of the Qabalah includes multiple masters and angels. Each level of mastery also has multiple beings. To focus our invitation toward a specific being among all those present there is the function of the symbol. The symbol, plus the color, becomes an invitation extended by your consciousness for that angel or master to come forward from the whole group who extend energy there. The combination of symbol and Qabalah color used together is thus much more specific for an individual master or angel than using the color or symbol alone.

Note that I purposely use the word *invitation*. My approach is not a demonstration of will; it is a request (directed toward your spiritual team, higher self, and Source) aligned with your heart and mind to serve your highest good.

How Do We Visualize the Correct Color?

Everyone describes colors differently, and color names can be imprecise. Some of us are trained to perceive colors, and others haven't needed to develop that ability. To communicate what I mean when I use certain color-descriptive words, I have provided a Pantone color system equivalent designation along with each symbol at the end of the master's or angel's profile. Pantone colors are recognized worldwide, used primarily for printing and color imaging across computer platforms.

If you have internet access, you can quickly look up the Pantone color specified at the end of the master's or angel's profile and glance at it on your computer screen. As graphic artists are aware, colors can appear differently depending upon the way they're produced (e.g., RGB technology on a computer screen versus the CMYK color system for printing). Pantone colors are a bit different again. However, that level of specificity isn't needed for you to reach out to a specific higher being with this approach. The Pantone color, in whatever way your mind recalls it, will get you in the right ballpark.

In some cases, I have given a range of colors that can work, so it isn't absolute. Keep it simple, and remember, the ascended-realm beings will already know you are trying to reach them.

In traditional Qabalah initiations, candidates would need to paint or otherwise identify the specific colors at each of the Qabalah levels as evidence that they were able to experience those dimensions in consciousness. My guides suggested I provide the Pantone colors to make the ascended realm most easily accessible to those of us today who are working with this method. I'm sure some of the ancient practitioners are smiling about this approach!

What to Expect

What we experience through the method using both a symbol and a Qabalah color still depends on our current state of spiritual development, which determines how clear and receptive we are to higher energy. It may take some practice: reaching out this way with sincerity—while you continue your own spiritual development—before you notice some response. As with any other spiritual tool, practice and patience can produce results.

At first, your experience might be subtle, but it can get much more profound. If this process begins to work for you, it is something available instantly to call on a master or angel wherever you happen to be.

Four Steps to Work with the Symbol and Color

1. Before meditation, first intend contact with a specific master, bringing his or her name into mind.
2. Close your eyes and try visualizing his or her symbol first.

3. Behind the symbol, add the colored or white field that is described with the symbol. (If steps two and three combine into one step, that's fine.)
4. After you have sent out that invitation for a minute or two, then let the image go, and turn inward to see what you experience. (If you are in a longer meditation and lose concentration, you can repeat the steps.)

If you receive a different symbol for a master or angel who is part of your higher team, then use that one. Be sure to include the background color I've given (this is the field, which corresponds to the whole dimension of energy where he or she can be met in your inner-world experience).

Recognizing When Symbols Are No Longer Helpful

This book is intended to serve people at various stages of their spiritual journeys. When you have cleared the inner obstacles and developed strong meditative concentration, you may be able to contact a master who works with you simply by sitting down to meditate and reaching out with focused intention toward him or her. Or you may sit down to meditate and find a master or angel reaching for you! It works both ways.

If you are the one reaching out, review in advance the Qabalah dimension in which a master can be found. That can be helpful, as you might see that color in his or her energy field as he or she comes forward in direct contact. If this description reflects your current level of experience, then attempting to use a symbol will simply be distracting to the pure connection you can experience with that being.

Until that state of development is reached, using a specific symbol can enhance your meditative concentration and give your mind a helpful focus. For this reason, visualization practices are part of meditation techniques taught by many different spiritual lineages.

Whether you are currently aware of direct contact with ascended-realm beings or not, the power and focus you extend will call the masters or angels toward you. They may later work with you during nighttime dreams or send you a message in another way they know you will be able to receive.

Twenty-Four Ways to Draw the Ascended Realm Close

The following general ideas cover beginning to more advanced levels of experience. Some of them have been mentioned earlier, but they now appear in the form of potential action steps. Allow your own wisdom to recognize whatever may be helpful to you at this time. This section concludes this book's focus on developing working relationships with your higher spiritual family of ascended masters and angels.

1. **Begin, or deepen, a particular spiritual path.** Work with a teacher, join a group, go on a retreat, and, especially, commit to some form of daily spiritual practice, even if only for a few minutes. There are many different spiritual traditions, so it is essential to find one you love, so you'll want to incorporate it into every day. The beloved mystical poet Rumi suggested that one commit to a daily practice, as knocking on that door repeatedly will produce an answer.

2. **Explore different methods of meditation and trance.** There are many methods to meditate and many methods to enhance trance states, all of which carry one past the Third Dimension and into the higher realms. You can combine meditation with music or use a passage in a spiritual text to focus your meditation. You can try pure contemplation, lifting your thoughts to the divine in inner silence. Sometimes shifting to another type of meditation practice (e.g., sitting up or lying down if you have been doing the opposite) can refresh your practice. Rather than advocating any specific method, I encourage you to discover the forms that work

best for you. Many of us learn best with the physical presence of an embodied teacher of some tradition, but there are online classes, and the company Sounds True offers many downloadable video classes.

3.   **Exercise, eat well, rest, and develop strong grounding skills.** The higher you go in exploring the dimensions beyond physical form, the more necessary this becomes. A stronger physical container can hold higher energies and allow you to work with them. Grounding also includes taking care of all the other responsibilities in your life. Paying bills, having necessary conversations with others to resolve conflicts, resting, and enjoying recreation are all important so you can turn to spiritual practice in the most peaceful inner state.

4.   **Come to meditation or any higher-dimensional experience well rested and avoid foods and beverages that are grounding.** Learning what grounds your energy versus what enhances a higher-dimensional experience is an essential skill. For some, intermittent fasting is helpful, though not for everyone. Proteins, especially animal proteins, are grounding. Practicing meditation first thing in the morning (on an empty stomach) is generally more successful than attempting to meditate after a full meal. Pay attention to your own body and consciousness and discover the approach that works best for you.

5.   **Use the energy of any intense emotions or life events to lean into (deepen) your spiritual practices.** As you read the profiles of the masters ahead in this book, you will find that they all experienced intense life situations. When we learn to use the intensity, it can accelerate our development like nothing else.

6.   **Do a time-management inventory.** Beyond the many responsibilities that fill our days are choices we may not realize we have made. It can be helpful to check in with yourselff periodically

about the overall structure of time in your life. When you do that, it's possible to carve out space for other activities you want to include, such as meditation.

7. **Invite one or more angels and masters to contact you during dreaming and keep a dream journal.** Our consciousness enters the astral realm every night during nighttime dreaming, and ascended masters can contact us there.

8. **Choose a master from your tradition or one you are attracted to and learn more about him or her.** That is part of the purpose for the profiles in this book, but there are always additional resources. If the master left spiritual writings or if other authors wrote about his or her teachings, reading this material will allow the master to work with your consciousness, even if you are not yet aware of his or her presence directly.

9. **After learning something about a master, put your knowledge into some visual form.** This idea allows you to expand into additional forms beyond the master's symbol and color, as suggested above. You might create a collage, a vision board, or some other object. Place it in the room you use for meditation or on your home office desk if you use one, where you'll see it daily. The time spent creating something tangible focuses your thoughts, feelings, and intention toward that master. He or she will feel you reaching out, and you will also remind yourself about whatever attribute or teaching attracts you.

10. **Read more about Qabalah.** There are many books on this subject, and a deeper knowledge can help us to understand the energy extended by a master or angel from a new perspective. If we notice that our current life experiences seem focused in a way represented by a specific sphere or path of the Qabalah, studying the meaning of that energy from various perspectives can help us to gain more insight into life choices that are helpful.

11. **Create sacred space, set up an altar, or create a ritual if that is part of your practice (while appreciating that the masters can also contact you in ordinary daily life).** Many different traditions use altars or power spots in the wilderness as sacred spaces. Within your preferred tradition, by learning from an embodied teacher or reading spiritual books, you can learn how to create your own sacred space. Declaring a sacred intention to contact higher energies in a spot where you won't be disturbed is a worthwhile practice. However, the true sacred space is always within your own consciousness. Learn to value and develop that inner chamber. Your need for specific outer rituals may change over time. Keep your spiritual practice alive and growing. As some form begins to feel complete, let it go. As your ability to contact the ascended realm develops, anytime your mind is quiet, masters may make their presence known.

12. **Use the power of sound to invite the beings of the ascended realm to come forward.** Sacred sound is part of many forms of ritual. You can use a particular invocation, mantra, seed syllable, or chant while focusing your intention on a master. If you don't know with certainty which sacred sounds correspond to which masters, a prayer spoken from the heart in your own words is sufficient. Sometimes people are given some words to use to call their higher teams' presence. Any sound instrument, such as a drum, rattle, bell, chime, Tibetan brass bowl, or crystal singing bowl, can underline your intention for connection. (Ascended beings always respond to your intention, your inner preparation, your availability of attention, and the timing determined by your own higher levels, regardless of the forms you use.)

13. **Learn different techniques to work with breath.** Pranayama (alternate-nostril breathing), which arises from yogic traditions, is one approach. There are different patterns of inhaling through the nose and exhaling through the mouth (using various counts) that work for some people. Inhaling through the crown chakra

and then letting the breath move downward through the front of the body and back up to the crown through the back of the body is another form. Figure-eight breathing can also be used. Try out some different forms to find what works best for you to enter trance.

14. **Play selected meditation music (without lyrics) while you are reaching out to contact masters.** Masters and angels can and do arrive in consciousness anytime our minds are silent. However, for many years, I have created special playlists of music to use during meditation. Selecting music that arises from a certain tradition is part of the invitation I extend, along with intent, to call certain masters forward in consciousness. With the advent of Apple Music and other music apps and websites, it is easier than ever before to preview and select music that is appropriate for specific masters. For Krishna, you would look for bansuri flute music. For ancient Hindu master musician Miyan Tansen, I searched available Hindustani recordings. For members of the angelic kingdom, there are a wide variety of available recordings. There are Celtic themes, Egyptian themes, and Tibetan Buddhist themes, to mention a few. Music can help us to move toward certain vibrations and lineages effectively when it is used with understanding.

15. **Use scents (e.g., incense, essential oils, or flowers) if these are part of your practice—if you know from direct experience that they correspond to the masters you are seeking.** Plant essences have the potential to connect to the higher realms, as do gems and minerals. However, please remember that there are many different systems of correspondence that derive from different traditions.

16. **When spiritual experiences unfold, learn how to work with whatever you experience without calling your mind back to thinking.** As you develop the ability to experience contact with the masters, you will learn how to extend your inner quiet and

concentration to allow them to work with you. It takes practice to discover what allows you to maintain contact versus plunge back into thinking. Some people focus on breath, while others use visualizations to quiet the mind. It is also possible for the mind to become totally silent, an ability that grows with practice. When a master makes contact, one learns to move past the reaction of "Wow" and gently hold and explore what the master wishes to communicate. One can learn to use inner mental prompts, such as "Show me more," or to mentally ask masters for their names without going back into a thinking and evaluating mode. Once you start trying to describe in language what just happened, the experience itself has ended. Through trial and error, you will learn how to stay in the sweet space and make the most of any contact you experience. Come with a willing, gentle, open focus. Don't expect; don't demand.

17. **Be in your experience with all your senses awake.** Notice as many details as you can without trying to describe them. (Describing them will come after the experience.) If you develop the ability to take notes (as a form of automatic writing that bypasses thinking), that can be helpful later. As you observe any phenomenon, mark it in consciousness in some way that will bring it back later. No one can do this automatically and perfectly all the time, as the experience itself takes place in a dimension past language and ordinary consciousness. Afterward, we want to bring back as much detail as we can, so whatever guidance we receive can be applied in our lives.

18. **Thank the angels and masters.** They don't require this; however, gratitude not only is appropriate but also helps us open our hearts, which is always beneficial for us. Many people learn to extend gratitude more widely throughout life, and this is especially true when you experience contact with higher-realm beings. Thank them and the whole spiritual realm for whatever you experience. Remember that each experience is a precious link in the chain of

spiritual certainty you are building. This chain of certainty is not intellectual but experiential. You are discovering all the help that exists beyond physical sight, and the access point is already within you. The ability to learn from the masters, who have already accomplished the whole human journey to spiritual awakening, is a profound blessing.

19. **Record any experiences as soon as possible.** During a profound experience, it seems unforgettable. However, there is a less-than-helpful part of the (ego) mind that conveniently forgets. Referring to what we wrote (or speaking into a recording device) about our spiritual experiences has great value even years later to remind us of what we most want to remember. Writing or journaling will also let the ascended realm know you are paying attention.

20. **Use discernment about sharing spiritual experiences with others.** I have shared many experiences in this book—but not all. I asked for guidance about which ones are appropriate to share. When working within a spiritual group setting where confidentiality is one of the ground rules, sharing a profound spiritual experience can help us to mark and remember it. However, attempting to communicate a deeply sacred experience during an ordinary conversation is usually far from satisfying. That kind of sharing tends to diminish the experience for us. Even when that principle is understood, not all experiences are meant to be shared with others, or at least not at first. Some of what we experience continues to work within us when we simply hold it within our hearts and minds. When in doubt, ask your inner team of guides if something is to be shared, with whom, and in what setting.

21. **Integrate and apply what you learned or were shown in your life.** If a master suggests a particular practice for you or laughs with you (masters never laugh *at* us) about some personal foible, act on the guidance you receive. Higher wisdom is worthless unless we apply it in our lives. Spiritual guidance arrives to show us our

own next steps, but to progress requires our full participation. Trust builds as we notice the results.

22. **Pay attention for subtle signs that your spiritual team is helping in your life.** This can come in the form of quiet thoughts that keep returning to mind (a different tone than the strident voice of personal ego) or new information or a needed resource that arrives serendipitously without effort to make it happen. Notice whatever other personal signs you have come to recognize as your team's presence (e.g., finding a feather, seeing a particular animal that keeps appearing in life, or having certain numbers reoccur repeatedly, such as when you glance at a clock). Write them down in a journal. This is evidence designed for you to recognize that your spiritual team is at work, helping to arrange things that are beneficial and contribute to your life. If you are not experiencing occasional confirmations of spiritual presence in your life, it may be a sign that you need to recognize and release some fear or do some forgiveness to clear your energy.

23. **Release expectations after a profound experience.** After we experience a precious, deeply meaningful spiritual contact, the ego mind can step back in, and it wants more of the same. (Or sometimes it offers a less helpful message, attempting to convince you to doubt or even turn away from what might lead to its undoing.) To remain on an elevating track, we can intend progress while surrendering expectations about the form and timing. Releasing expectations is the best way to progress on to higher states of consciousness.

24. **Extend trust. Trust your higher spiritual team and your higher self.** Trust is closely allied with the presence of love. When we are close to love's presence, trust is a natural state. We can extend trust as an active way to choose again for love if fear is attempting to gain a foothold.

ANGEL AND ASCENDED
MASTER PROFILES

Abraham: Judaic Founding Patriarch
Chokma, Mental Level

Abraham first came into my consciousness to correct my misunderstanding of the potential placement I had given him in the Qabalah. I was not even working with the Judaic lineage at the time; in fact, I was working with some of the Christian and Greek masters when Abraham made contact. I had previously associated Abraham only with strict monotheism and carried some judgments about how those traditions were applied. While associating him with monotheism wasn't wrong, it wasn't the whole story either. The ideas that any of us have inherited from religions can be limiting to a deeper understanding of their masters.

Abraham's entire family lived in Ur of the Chaldees (situated about 140 miles, or 225 kilometers, southeast of the site of Babylon, in modern-day Iraq). In his youth, he worked in his family's idol shop. His eventual spiritual calling, as founder of an entirely new spiritual tradition, thus was a radical change from the beliefs of his ancestors. He was a reformer! This gave me a different basis to understand him. The power to enact radical change takes a certain kind of leader who can follow his or her own independent path, tearing down old institutions and replacing them with new forms. These leaders march to their own drummer (inner Source) and are impervious to outer-world obstacles and the opinions of others. Abraham was this sort of spiritual pioneer. Abraham is honored today in Judaic, Christian, and Islamic traditions—the three so-called Abrahamic religions, which follow a monotheistic belief system.

Abraham married Sarah, who remained childless for many years. According to the story told in the biblical book of Genesis, Abraham was called by God to leave the house of his father and settle in the land originally given to Canaan. He and Sarah made this move when Abraham was already seventy-five years old! There was a famine in Canaan, so they went to Egypt, where Pharaoh was tempted by Sarah's beauty and offered Abraham rich gifts to obtain her. Abraham at first said she was his sister (true but not the whole truth), but when Pharaoh found out she was also his wife, they were permitted to leave. Abraham went south to Hebron and settled in the plain of Mamre.

According to the traditional biblical tale, after many adventures, once again, Abraham received a vision that repeated the promise of the land and the birth of descendants "as numerous as the stars." At the ages of one hundred and ninety, respectively, Abraham and Sarah, we are told, had their first child, as prophesied by three mysterious visitors who were passing through the land. Such a miraculous conception is difficult for modern minds to understand literally.

Abraham is frequently remembered for the spiritual test he was presented regarding offering up his son Isaac as a human sacrifice. The traditional story begins with him traveling with Isaac for three days, until he came to the mount that God had directed him to visit for this purpose. He then commanded the servants to remain behind while he and Isaac proceeded alone up the mountain. Isaac carried the wood upon which he would be sacrificed. The story tells that Isaac was already bound, and just as Abraham was about to sacrifice his son, his hand was stayed by an angel sent to intervene.

I will admit I found this story troubling at face value and didn't understand how a father could do this. When Abraham made contact in meditation, he communicated that it was his final spiritual initiation to surrender his attachment to his beloved son in this fashion and that it wasn't easy for him to do!

Attachments are aptly named. They hold us like glue to a third-dimensional perspective, and they include many different patterns tightly woven into an individual personality. We mostly don't see them, until we do. As we see them, it's possible to choose again. As Buddhist wisdom also recognizes, attachments are one of the roots of suffering in the human realm, where change is the sole constant.

Advanced spiritual practitioners are presented with insight into their remaining attachments to move past those attachments and claim their senior spiritual identity. Abraham demonstrated his own moment of truth when he was asked to choose between a treasured earthly identity and trust in the Absolute. Finding the spiritual discipline to pass such a test is a big evolutionary step. Abraham provides an example of achieving it.

Keywords: Abraham supports the development of powerful male spiritual leadership that can usher in profound change. He supports those who are asked to be spiritual fathers to their people and supports all who are developing the habit of seeking and following only guidance, so higher wisdom can take the lead in our lives. The symbol Abraham brought me (below) refers to the releasing of attachments, rather than the sacrifice of a son. The symbol of an altar with flames is also found in other traditions, including tarot.

Suggested Meditation Symbol: Sacrificial altar with plumes of smoke rising against a radiant white field

Ailill mac Mata: Celtic Lineage
Chokma, Emotional Level Two

Ailill mac Mata is introduced in the famous Irish saga *Táin bó Cuailnge*, which translates as *The Cattle Raid of Cooley*. He became king of Connaught by marrying the lusty Queen Maeve. He is said to have been her fourth husband. While he claimed the right to rule Connaught through his mother's lineage and his father had been king of another tribe, in some versions of his tale, he was initially Maeve's bodyguard. He challenged her then husband in single combat, killed him, and then married her. We learn little about his personality from the tale, other than that he was "without jealousy," which was a practical necessity because of Maeve's many lovers. Together they had seven sons and at least one daughter, ruling from Cruachan (now Rathcroghan, County Roscommon).

The Táin is believed to have originated in the first century, a heroic age in Ireland. It is the longest tale that is considered part of the Ulster cycle of Irish myth, which focuses on the exploits of heroes. It deals with the conflict between Ulster and Connaught over possession of the Brown Bull of Cooley. Composed in prose with verse passages during the seventh and eighth centuries, it is partially preserved in *The Book of the Dun Cow* (circa 1100) and is also found in *The Book of Leinster* (circa 1160) and *The Yellow Book of Lecan* (late fourteenth century).

The conflict came about because of a conversation between Ailill and Maeve about their respective wealth. In that period, wealth was measured by the number of cattle one possessed. Maeve's prize stud bull Finnbhennach did not want to be owned by a woman and departed her herd for Ailill's. She was determined to be equal to Ailill in power, and the only bull of potency equal to Finnbhennach's belonged to the Ulaid. Typical of the warrior ethos of that period, she determined to steal him. When the Ulaid heard her plan, war ensued.

The Ulaid were under a temporary curse that rendered all their warriors powerless. As a result, the youthful warrior Cuchulainn had to fight the mighty warriors of Connaught by himself. He did this by requesting the right of single combat and defeated a series of warriors in this way, until the Ulaid warriors could overcome the curse and join the effort. Despite their valiant efforts, the Connaught warriors were able to carry off the Brown Bull of Cooley.

As their tale ends, we learn that Maeve had the great Ulaid warrior Conall Cernach kill Ailill for his extramarital affair, while retaining her right to choose successive partners. Conall was then killed to avenge Ailill's death.

When I sought Ailill in the ascended realm, he came forward to identify himself and told me the Cattle Raid of Cooley was an actual event recorded by bards. While this cannot be proven by known evidence, it certainly fits what is known about bards who were present to witness ancient battles and afterward create tales that memorialized the greatest warriors.

Keywords: Ailill supports men to develop their warrior leadership, combining fighting ability and strategy to create effective rulership of one's domain. As with many masters at Chokma, his male potency is a strong creational force. He also works with women who are developing their own inner masculine leadership capacity.

Suggested Meditation Symbol: Powerful white bull (like Finnbhennach) against a radiant white field

Aine: Celtic Lineage
Yesod, Mental Level

Aine, whose name may mean "Brightness" or "Splendor," is one of the most famous fairy queens of Ireland. Her pagan traditions persisted well into the twentieth century, and she was never Christianized. Some trace her to the province of Munster in southwest Ireland, but her popularity spread throughout Ireland and to Scotland.

Aine has been celebrated since ancient times. Under the full moon's light on Midsummer Eve, farmers waved lit torches over their fields in a celebration to guard against sickness and ensure fertility. She is also associated with the sacred hill Cnoc Aine in Knockainey, County Limerick, which is described as having three ring barrows upon its summit. At Samhain, Aine is believed to emerge from the sidhe of Aine, a cairn located to the east of the barrows. Bonfires were lit in her honor on all the surrounding hills at that time.

An enchanted lake known as Lough Gur is a site where people who were ill once gathered at the full moon in the hope of receiving a cure as they were exposed to the moon's reflection off the water. At that location, Aine was believed to assume a mermaid form, and there are reports from those who saw her come out of the water and sit on a rock to comb her long hair, which became woven into local folklore.

As with many beings mentioned in myth, there are conflicting stories of her origin. She was said to be sometimes a human woman taken by the fairies and other times a member of the Tuatha Dé

Danann. She was sometimes known as ruler of the faeries, while other stories told of her turning herself into a fairy and mating with mortal men while holding them under enchantment, thus getting them to do whatever she commanded. (This is a rather misogynistic perspective, though her energy is indeed enchanting.) One ancient story relates that she was raped by a Munster king named Ailill Aulom and got payback for the misadventure by biting off his ear.

However we understand her, Aine is generally acknowledged as a female master of human love and fertility and as a protector of women. She had a long list of lovers, some mortal and some gods. In some tales, the sea god Mannan mac Lir exchanged his wife for her charms. Although portrayed as lustful, she was a woman expressing independent choice about sexual partners. She was continually conspiring with mortals in passionate affairs but also had a maternal side. Her birth chair (a natural rock formation) can be seen on the hill of Knockadoon.

In my first direct experience with Aine, she came close in a field of brilliant, sparkling white light, whose texture was lush, "velvety" and feminine. While the vision was abstract, the feeling was utterly exquisite, and it was wonderful to be bathed in her field of energy. I wanted to remain there indefinitely. It is no wonder that she has been so powerfully attractive to others!

Part of Aine's special mastery is enhanced intuitive receptivity. On later occasions she was helping when I was contacting other mental level female masters on some of the Qabalah paths at the top of the Tree (and one spiritual level male master), supporting me to receive their communications and record them through automatic writing.

Keywords: Aine is an ally of women, supporting beauty, fertility, dreaming skills and psychic-intuitive abilities. She can also be called upon to support mental level healing for issues involving sexual abuse. She works through the capacity to direct kundalini energy upward from the bases of the spine, lifting consciousness to the pineal gland **in the** sixth chakra (third eye).

Suggested Meditation Symbol: Rustic birthing chair (used for millennia by birthing women to maintain an upright position and allow gravity to aid in delivery of the child) against a radiant white field.

Amoghasiddi Buddha: Buddhist Lineage
Netzach, Emotional Level Two

Amoghasiddi is one of the Buddhas in the Dhyani Buddhist tradition. He extends the green ray of Netzach in the Qabalah. Within Vajrayana tradition, he is the male Buddha of the karma family and represents the ability to transform the poison of envy and jealousy into the wisdom to produce material success. His name means "He Whose Accomplishment Is Not in Vain," or sometimes it is given as "Infallible Success."

As one of the masters at Netzach, Amoghasiddi helps us to purify emotions associated with what we desire. In Buddhist principles, desire can be associated with craving, preference and aversion, and unhelpful comparisons with the resources of others. These emotions can block success, so when they are cleared, the natural flow of abundance is restored. Lessening material attachments can also help one progress toward spiritual realization.

In direct experience, Amoghasiddi arrived in an abstract rich green light form. My primary impression was of his connection to the earth—he was amazingly grounded for a higher-dimensional master. He extends a pure invitation to all humankind to enjoy abundance, based upon learning to make lifestyle choices and using material resources that consider the needs of all.

He urges us to recognize that earthly resources have finite limits. Rather than focusing on an endless pattern of fulfilling personal desires (excess, or more, more, more), we could focus on sharing resources with others. This would transform the way humankind presently operates—in scarcity consciousness and lack—to an enlightened approach that achieves abundance for all.

In iconography, Amoghasiddi may be seated, with an upraised right

181

palm facing forward in the mudra of fearlessness, symbolizing his and his devotees' fearlessness toward what are called poisons or delusions. He may be radiating a green light, symbolic of nature, a color that, when one meditates on it, calms fear and anxiety so that the wisdom of accomplishment can be revealed.

Keywords: Working to uplift the human desire nature, Amoghasiddi urges us to overcome any tendency to compare our resources with those of others, thus eliminating envy, and to release our attachment to strictly material values. When those inclinations are eliminated, then he supports us to achieve success through wise application of personal effort. He also urges us to progress in spiritual development, so we are better able to use the earth's resources wisely, achieving lasting abundance for all humankind.

Suggested Meditation Symbol: The double vajra, composed of two golden vajras that form an equilateral cross shape, against a medium forest-green field (Pantone 371 or 378)

Angel Chamuel: Angelic Kingdom
Hidden Path of the Pink Ray (not shown on Qabalah diagrams), Emotional Level Two

Angel Chamuel works beside male and female ascended masters, extending the pink ray of unconditional love, which links spiritual Source with all humankind. Working with him helps us bring peace to the tensions that can be experienced in human life.

His energy extends in a fiery burst that conveys the simple yet profound message "God is." This is a reminder that beyond every scene in human perception, love is. This truth is like a melodious tone that resounds through all dimensions. When we attune to that vibration, all sense of worry and care dissolves like morning mist.

Chamuel supports us to leave the past behind—especially any experience that made us doubt the reality that we are loved and lovable—now and evermore. Love is our own truest essence, despite whatever illusions our personality might temporarily entertain. We were created by love, and so we remain, despite all the changing perceptions that appear to human sight. He supports us to extend self-compassion and appreciate ourselves for undertaking the sometimes-demanding journey of human life.

Chamuel is always near when we are willing to turn away from fear and join in the vast wave of love that extends through all creation. As we extend that wave, so too we remain aware of that harmonious flow coming to and through us.

Keywords: Chamuel supports all humankind to choose to align with the truth of love through the feeling nature. He is a special guide to those whose spiritual practice includes any divine love tradition (using poetry, song, mantras, or meditation).

Suggested Meditation Symbol: Pink sacred heart symbol (a heart with golden flames from the top) against a slightly violet-pink field (Pantone 2365)

Angel Hasdiel: Angelic Kingdom
Path of Da'leth (Tarot – Empress), Emotional Level Two

Although angels never took on a human gender, they can be experienced through human senses as strongly yin or yang. Hasdiel's yin energy is a delight to experience. She extends qualities of grace, beauty, and harmony. She supports women to claim their own style of feminine beauty (without using it to control others or becoming identified with it). She supports those who cultivate benevolence, generosity, and kindness and extend those qualities to a human partner. In one experience with her, my consciousness merged into a vast, sparkling, feminine emerald-green stream of divine love and beauty.

My first awareness of contact with Hasdiel came when I began to have a sense that my current relationship partner was going to transition.

Not surprisingly, she was the one who responded to my inner call for guidance on how to cope with this. She reminded me that the only true solace would be to direct my attention to the flow of divine love. In doing so, I would experience that love can never be lost, because we all remain eternally connected through a wholly loving Creator Source.

As an agent of divine love, she reminds us that there are many romantic relationship patterns still present in collective humankind that don't produce harmonious relationships. To create new models, she encourages us to stop searching for love and fulfillment outside ourselves and instead turn within to discover love's true divine Source.

No human partner can carry our romantic projections perfectly or all the time, and when those projections slip (which they inevitably do, even with the most committed love partner), it can be a painful experience. When we relieve our earthly beloved from the role that no human being can possibly fulfill, we remain eternally filled by the Source of love itself and can share that love with our earthly partner.

Keywords: Hasdiel extends pure female life force, supporting renewal and regeneration, beauty, grace, and harmony. She is an agent to help us understand and open to the divine Source of love, which can be shared with an earthly partner.

Suggested Meditation Symbol: Flowing cosmic stream composed of millions of tiny, sparkling emerald-green hearts (Pantone green 363)

Angel Nuriel: Angelic Kingdom
Chesed, Emotional Level Two

Like many of the male masters at Chesed, Nuriel extends a noble, sacred energy that carries a strong yang polarity. I refer to this elsewhere as *sacred masculine*. Such beings may develop warrior capabilities, which are used to uphold the possibility of peace.

When seen in spiritual vision, Nuriel appeared in a dark blue field, with an impression of warrior attire (a chain-mail helmet draped around his head and chest), emitting a strong silvery-white light into the surrounding darkness. His energy felt strong, immensely protective, and spiritually uplifting. He helps us to walk through all the appearances of human life while remembering the higher realms.

Nuriel's name translates as "Fire of the Lord." We can call for his support if we find ourselves in a dramatic scene we don't know how to solve. He reminds us that by lifting our perceived problems up to divine Source, we can move into a state of trust that matters are being worked out. We can execute this handoff to Spirit by adopting the attitude of spiritual surrender.

Surrender does not imply that we are caving in to forces seemingly outside our control. As I use the word *surrender*, this doesn't imply being passive or a victim but, rather, refers to a powerful spiritual practice of releasing our perception of what needs to happen and waiting to be guided about any actions. Doing this bypasses the personality's wiring, which tries to control outcomes, and provides an opening that can allow miraculous solutions. The ability to surrender comes from a practical acknowledgment that from the (limited) view of human perception, we cannot know which outcome is best for us or anyone else.

Willingness to surrender our view opens a door to solutions that serve the highest good of all concerned. Becoming able to do this when it's most needed requires that we learn and practice some spiritual tools. Nuriel supports us to be disciplined in making time for spiritual practice, since this is how we learn what takes care of us in all situations.

Prayer is an effective form that can be used when we need to surrender our pictures or expectations about what a solution should look like. We can supercharge our prayers when we learn to channel the energy of a demanding situation toward the spiritual realm. Praying with words or in the silence of our hearts, we can recognize we have done our part in turning the situation over when a welcome state of inner peace arrives.

As you were invited to explore through one of the writing exercises in chapter 6, in looking back over the dramatic turns of our lives, we can observe evidence that some other force was at work besides our personality, because we got through tight spots without knowing in advance how it could be done. Unexpected doors sometimes opened. That kind of observation builds trust that there is a divine Source that knows the highest good for all—when we step out of the way and allow it to happen.

Each time we choose to ask for higher help and trust instead of trying to figure it all out, we make space for divine energy to move in our lives. We will be given lots of opportunities to grow in our capacity to trust divine Source by experiencing situations in which we recognize our human mind doesn't know the best solution.

Keywords: When we ask, Nuriel can be close as we build a foundation of spiritual trust that can be applied to every apparently challenging life event. He extends powerful support to help us be dedicated to learning and applying spiritual principles that help us in all areas of life.

Suggested Meditation Symbol: Dark blue warrior angel with huge, fully opened wings, dressed in chain-mail armor, emitting silvery-white light into surrounding darkness (brighter to darker blues, Pantone 281–295)

Aphrodite: Greek Lineage
Netzach, Spiritual Level

Aphrodite, who comes to us in myth as part of the Olympian pantheon, is a major figure known throughout Western culture. She extends the qualities of love, beauty, pleasure, and procreation, which are also associated with the planet Venus. She was often depicted in iconography with the sea, dolphins, doves, swans, pomegranates, scepters, apples, myrtle, rose trees, lime trees, clams, scallop shells, and pearls, many of which were considered sacred to her.

There are at least two different creation stories about her. In Hesiod's *Theogony*, Aphrodite was said to be created from sea foam when Cronus severed Uranus's genitals, which dropped into the sea. In Homer's *Iliad*, however, she is the daughter of Zeus and Dione.

Wherever she was known, Aphrodite was the patroness of the

hetaera and courtesan. She is consistently portrayed in art as a nubile, infinitely desirable, youthful adult female and often is depicted nude. At the temple of Aphrodite on the summit above Corinth (before the Roman destruction of the city in 146 BCE), sexual intercourse with one of her priestesses was considered a method of worshipping her. Ritual prostitution is also attested in association with Aphrodite on the islands of Cyprus, Cythera, and Sicily but not in Athens. (Modern writers have used the term *sacred prostitutes* to recognize these ancient temple priestesses.)

In many of the later Greek myths, she is portrayed as vain, ill-tempered, and easily offended. However, masters at the spiritual level display no human ego quirks. Turning to what was known of the planet Venus, we have a different model to understand Aphrodite's two different mythological moods. Venus was understood by many cultures to have two opposite natures, depending upon whether it was currently appearing in the sky as a morning star or as an evening star. Venus as morning star was more warlike.

In Aphrodite's myths, we read about concerns among the other gods, who feared her beauty might lead to conflict and war through rivalry for her favors. As a result, it was said that Zeus married her off to Hephaestus. (This was typical of the period of myth, when even female divinities were portrayed as losing power and independence.) Despite this, Aphrodite followed her own inclinations and had many lovers—both those identified as gods, such as Ares, and men, such as Anchises. Aphrodite also played a role in the Eros and Psyche legend and was both lover and surrogate mother of Adonis.

In my experiences with her, Aphrodite helped me appreciate that, as Ralph Waldo Emerson said, "beauty is its own excuse for being." She helped me understand her connection to some male artists who became famous throughout the Western world for masterpiece paintings using dark tones and light (the chiaroscuro technique). Artists such as Leonardo da Vinci, Caravaggio, Rembrandt, Vermeer, and Goya often had a female muse in earthly form. Sometimes it was the artist's model (who often became his lover), yet behind the scenes, it was Aphrodite herself, who was connecting with the artist's consciousness.

Keywords: Aphrodite supports us to examine our values, which shape our desires, assembling astral images that manifest in form on the physical plane. She helps us open ourselves to love, lovers, and abundance; and helps us express beauty in some physical appearance.

Suggested Meditation Symbol: White lion's paw scallop (largest scallop variety, which can measure eight inches in diameter) against a radiant white field

Apollo: Greek Lineage
Tiphareth, Spiritual Level

Apollo is one of the most familiar names in the Olympian pantheon that comes to us through Greek myth. Credited with the seemingly diverse roles of healer, musician, and oracle, Apollo, along with Athena, was claimed as patron god by more of the Greek city-states than Zeus.

As confirmed by Greek myths and countless iconic representations, Apollo was depicted as a beautiful male, beardless, athletic, and eternally young, with blue eyes and golden hair. Not only gods but also humans, both women and men, fell in love with him.

In one of Apollo's myths, Daphne, a daughter of the river god Peneus, rejected his advances and ran away from him. When he chased her, she changed herself (or the mother goddess, Gaia, changed her) into a laurel tree. From then on, Apollo admired laurel leaves, which became a sacred symbol of success, triumph, and victory; laurel wreaths were also given to the winners of contests.

Author and university professor Fritz Graf's book *Apollo* helps us trace Apollo's association with healing from inscriptions in Mycenaean Linear B script that refer to a still earlier Bronze Age god. Whatever Apollo's origins, his cult spread widely, including to Black Sea colonies and Southern Italy and likely to the Etruscans.

In the Roman period, a statue of Apollo in a doctors' club showed him with his lyre.

Music was considered healing for psychic troubles. It was customary for some Romans to worship the triad that included his mother, Leto, and his sister Artemis. Romans regarded him as a bringer of health and a provider of medicine, and the Roman vestal virgins said a daily prayer to Apollo. Beginning in the fifth century BCE, the rise of Apollo's son Asclepius came to fulfill humankind's need for healing more than Apollo himself did.

As the genius who spoke through the priestesses at the Delphic oracle, Apollo was an authority relied upon for more than a thousand years throughout the Greek world. Consulted by the rich and powerful, including Alexander the Great, the oracle was in continuous (but not daily) use from the eighth century BCE until Emperor Theodosius shut down all pagan sites in 381 CE.

In Western thought, Apollo has come to symbolize the intellectual, logical, and orderly side of humankind, diametrically opposite to the ecstatic (Dionysian) polarity. His forename, Phoebus, means "Bright" or "Pure," and the view became current that he was associated with the sun. (At the spiritual level of Tiphareth, he extends energy from what is known metaphysically as the Great Central Sun, far beyond the sun in our solar system.)

In direct experience, Apollo has come into spiritual vision on a few occasions as an abstract, visual, huge male form, lithe and attractive, with golden skin. I found that nothing I had studied in researching him adequately prepared me for contact with his powerfully enlivening energy. Far more inclusive than the meaning of *intellectual*, his energy provides a powerful lift to merge with higher-self consciousness. As with many ascended masters, myth and archaeology leave many gaps in our understanding, which can best be answered in a spiritual practitioner's direct experience.

Keywords: Apollo inspires prophetic knowledge (strengthening the third chakra increases psychic sensitivity) and is a vitalizing influence that promotes health, intellectual achievement, and all forms of cultural expression, including music and poetry. He remains committed to the awakening and integration of the higher self and human personality to assist the evolution of humankind.

Suggested Meditation Symbol: Golden laurel wreath against a radiant white field

Archangel Ariel: Angelic Kingdom
Path of Teth (Tarot: Lust and Strength), Spiritual Level

Ariel is an archangel whose name is found primarily in Jewish and Christian mysticism and the Apocrypha. The name Ariel is translated as "Lion of God." Ariel's energy is a powerful, fiery extension of white light on the spiritual level of Teth, close to divine Source. While angels did not incarnate in human earthly form and, thus, do not correspond to a single gender (male or female), Ariel's energy is strongly yin, and her images are often female.

The path of Teth includes strength and power that mediate between the pure, divine warrior force of Geburah and the noble, sacred king energy of Chesed. She is sometimes portrayed either beside a lion or with a lion's head. Those who are spiritual practitioners gradually awaken awareness that all of life is one. She is a dedicated protector of that oneness, whether its individual sparks exist in human, animal, or plant form. She is a special ally who supports the natural world, wilderness, and the earth herself.

In iconography, Ariel may appear with a globe representing Earth or with elements of nature (such as water, fire, or rocks) to symbolize her role in caring for God's creation on Earth. Her most common symbol is the lion.

Teth, at the spiritual level, utilizes the power of awakened kundalini. It has a lusty, sexual component that fills the entire energy field, yet in all cases, the individual who can transmit power at this level has already dedicated its use to assignments received from spiritual guidance. These assignments may take the form of a powerful leadership role or an agent of divinely inspired creativity. Ariel supports those who are ready to dedicate their gifts to be used at this level.

Ariel has been a companion who has gotten my attention for some years. At first, I could only catch her name coming into my awareness, sometimes during daily life. In recent years, I have been able to experience her more directly as her protective presence surrounds me with a huge, impenetrable white shield and points me toward spiritual experiences in the higher realms of consciousness.

Keywords: Ariel provides a protective shield from influences that would interfere with your optimal spiritual development. She helps you become a more conscious custodian of the environment, wild animals, and all life. She can also help you assume a powerful leadership role or perfect a form of creative expression that serves the spiritual world in some way.

Suggested Meditation Symbol: Lion with white angel wings against a radiant white field

Archangel Azrael: Angelic Kingdom
Binah, Mental Level

Azrael is an archangel whose Hebrew name translates as "Whom God Helps." He extends the vibration of Binah through the violet ray on the mental plane. Binah is the first gateway (moving up the Qabalah tree) between our personal earthly identity and the transpersonal, formless realms that hold our eternal identity.

Azrael is sometimes called the Angel of Death, but it might be more accurate to think of him as one who helps us to remember eternal life. He supports us to learn and practice methods to develop spiritual awareness, guides our consciousness in meditation, and is beside us (or a loved one) when we complete physical life and awaken to our already-existing higher levels. This beloved angel also supports caregivers (professionals or loved ones) who are assisting someone's death transition.

His symbol of the purple scythe reminds us that to make the

smoothest transition to eternity, we must surrender any remaining attachments to physical life and release beliefs that conflict with awakening into the eternal self. Ideally, the process of awakening to our true, eternal spiritual identity begins during our physical lifetimes by our adopting some form of spiritual practice we enjoy.

When I experience Azrael's energy, it is immense, exploding in purple-white bursts of light, lifting from the crown chakra like a fountain. He helps to lift human consciousness toward the divine. His energy is an invitation to step into the immense blessings of eternity, where divine comfort is found. Part of his function is to help us master the mental discipline to hold only thoughts consistent with our highest spiritual essence, rather than those of limitation that arise from the human ego, so we enter the higher dimensions with ease and grace.

He supports us to deepen in spiritual wisdom through study, meditation, and regular daily practice, rather than allowing worldly diversions to capture all our attention. As we do our part, we are more able to receive the divine help he and all the angels and masters extend.

Keywords: Azrael supports those gaining spiritual knowledge and practicing meditation. He is a guide to those making their death transitions and those who support others in that process to be able to let go of physical life at the appointed time and reunite full awareness with the already existing eternal self.

Suggested Meditation Symbol: Scythe with purple angel wings against a purple field (Pantone 265–266)

Archangel Camael: Angelic Kingdom
Green Geburah, Mental Level

Archangel Camael extends the green ray of Geburah at the mental level. (Geburah includes both red and green ray masters and angels who work at the root chakra and the heart chakra in the human energy system.) Camael supports men and women who take on heroic assignments. He is protective of the world's natural environment. This includes forested wilderness all over the earth (the Amazon rain forest as well as other forested lands). He supports us to discover how to live on this planet with growing ecological awareness and become wise stewards of natural resources.

Working on the mental level, he is a warrior who helps us to correct our perception. He helps us to free the mind of judgment (deciding that something shouldn't be happening when it is happening) and cut through our own illusions (seeing what we want to be true but isn't true) to develop clear discernment. He supports us to accept matters just as they are, so we are best able to receive guidance about how to proceed.

Heroic actions are not always visible to the outside world. We are heroic in our own lives when we confront a seemingly daunting task and find a courageous and self-empowering way to approach it. The truth is, we never do anything alone! There is always higher help coming through, especially when we remember to ask. If we are asked to take on a project, we will be given the resources and ability to accomplish it. By holding this truth firmly in mind and keeping an open heart, we will be able to receive guidance that will help us move through the assignment in the best way.

When I experience Camael, I sometimes glimpse an abstract warrior-clad angel in a deep forest-green energy field. He demonstrates how to be courageous in every life scene by consistently remembering the spiritual truth that fear is only a thought in our own mind when we momentarily forget our eternal nature. He is a constant support to maintain Earth's resources.

Keywords: Camael brings the warrior's skilled protection and fearless courage to act on the assignments we are given while being mindful of the power of our thoughts. He reminds us that we will experience situations as we believe them to be, so our part is to choose thoughts that are empowering.

Suggested Meditation Symbol: Deep green warrior's shield with white angel wings against a glowing green field (Pantone green 350)

Archangel Gabriel: Angelic Kingdom
Tiphareth, Spiritual Level

Archangel Gabriel, whose name translates as "God Is My Strength," is one of the most well-known angels. In the Bible, he was the divine messenger who delivered the news to Mary about the coming birth of her son, Jesus (who is also known to some as Yeshua). Gabriel holds the spiritual level of Tiphareth, a portal of beauty and light to what is metaphysically called the Great Central Sun.

Ascended masters and angels who extend energy at the emotional levels of Tiphareth are linked to the electromagnetic energy of our sun, which connects in the human energy anatomy to the solar plexus chakra. This center corresponds with our sense of an individual self who was born on a certain month, day, and year and has certain personality characteristics. While one's personality self may shine with high ability in human life, there is a level of self (sometimes called higher self) that can be discovered through spiritual practice. This level of advanced development connects the solar plexus to chakras over the physical head. This is the process Gabriel helps to oversee.

Those who commit to an ongoing spiritual path are gradually led toward awareness of their senior identity. As those levels come into play, the fixed ideas and seeming limitations of the personality become more and more transparent, allowing the light and consciousness of the higher self to shine through the individual, finding expression in some unique way.

Gabriel holds the knowledge about our life mission—the one we chose to manifest during our lifetime. In polishing our natural gifts and talents and building a strong solar plexus chakra, we develop readiness to recognize it when it arrives. When we release the blocks of unworthiness or pride and move past personal ambition into willingness to place our abilities in service to a greater good, the path toward fulfilling our life mission will arrive.

When we have sudden insights or profound dreams or receive valuable guidance about our future, it may be Gabriel sending us a message. To amplify our ability to receive Gabriel's messages, spiritual practices, such as meditation, are invaluable. It may also be helpful to try journaling and automatic writing to guide you to the next step in achieving your life mission.

Gabriel can arrive in consciousness like a voice speaking. When he reminds us about what we came into life to accomplish, there is no more confusion or doubt that we can fulfill it perfectly. Whatever it may be, we feel joyful and grateful to have the assignment. As a patron of inspired communications, Gabriel can assist writers, teachers, journalists, and others to receive and convey their messages, find motivation and confidence, and market their skills. He also assists in overcoming issues of fear and procrastination in communication.

Gabriel is often artistically portrayed (and may be seen in spiritual vision) as golden, surrounded by brilliant white light. In imagery, he often carries a copper trumpet, which is symbolic of a sound that can gather collective attention before an important announcement.

My experiences of Gabriel, along with those of other angels and masters, has continued to deepen through the years. My first awareness of him was as a tiny ball of golden-white light, with his trumpet, in dimensions that seemed far overhead. Gradually, he appeared more often and in more powerful ways, sometimes along with archangel Metatron. I sensed them extending downloads of energy I couldn't fully comprehend at the time, which would come to consciousness when the time was right.

Keywords: Gabriel is a messenger from Source who delivers important communications from the higher realms. His energy powerfully links our higher levels and our navel chakra to help us appreciate the unique brilliance of the spark of divine light that only we can express. It matters—to us and to all creation—that we express our gifts! This is the purpose for which we came into physical form. In claiming the part we came to play, we tap a massive current that fills us from Source and extends an arc of light toward whatever we can contribute that serves the greater good.

Suggested Meditation Symbol: Golden orb with white wings, with Gabriel's horn floating above, in a radiant white field

Archangel Haniel: Angelic Kingdom
Yesod, Mental Level

Haniel, sometimes spelled Anael, extends the energy of Yesod on the mental level. Her name translates as "God's Pleasure or Joy" or as "Grace of God." While angels are essentially androgynous, if clairsentient senses are strong, we experience their energy as yin or yang, which the human mind interprets as female or male. With Haniel, I felt blessed to experience her powerful, lofty yin energy.

At the mental level of this sphere, the emotional body has been purified, and inner calm is the established state. The third-eye chakra has become active, and awareness of our connection to the spiritual dimension is established. Haniel supports all who are seeking the higher realms, ushering our consciousness toward eternity. She is helpful for anyone practicing meditation and for receiving intuitive information through the subtle senses. She supports women with strong intuitive abilities to develop them fully and then direct them into channels that can assist others.

On one occasion, I was working with a crystal for Haniel and one for Metatron simultaneously. She came through, announcing her name. The divine energy was exquisite, radiant, and iridescent. Together they were holding the current that can carry consciousness all the way home to Creator. On another occasion, while working with her, I was able to see the weaving of divine light currents known as the Merkabah over the crown of my head, which connect us directly with Source consciousness.

Keywords: Haniel supports those who enter higher states of awareness in meditation; assists those who develop intuition as a faculty to assist others, working with men and women who have this potential; and supports consciousness during the transition at the end of physical life.

Suggested Meditation Symbol: Winged Merkabah outline (two interpenetrating three-dimensional pyramids, one pointing upward and the other downward) glowing in iridescent white against a field of radiant white light

Archangel Jeremiel: Angelic Kingdom
Hod, Mental Level

Jeremiel helps us to refine the flame of passion within to claim our ability to enjoy healthy and pleasurable sexual experiences, experience joy and playfulness in life, and express inspired creativity. To do this, he helps us to clear any thoughts or beliefs that hinder the fullest connection between the human sacral (second) chakra and transpersonal chakras over the head.

The second chakra is associated with the lower abdomen. Observed from the back, relative to the spine, this area is the sacrum, thus the name *sacral chakra*. Notice that the word *sacral* and the word *sacred* share a common vibration. Awakening the full potential of this energy begins with the observation that it is indeed sacred.

The second chakra initially develops during childhood to adolescence, between the ages of seven and fourteen, culminating in human reproductive capability. For a long time, spiritual awareness about how to awaken this energy has been absent from our remaining coming-of-age traditions. Collective advertising, social media, and entertainment trends focus on the sexual component of this energy only, and women especially are encouraged to sexualize their appearance from an early age. Prevailing modes of authority, whether church or family, have also attempted to impose control of this awakening energy, creating repression. With dominant models that range from erotic to repressive, it is little wonder that few individuals have come to adulthood without incurring experiences that produce sexual wounds and creative blocks. For most human beings, some healing in this area is an essential process.

Both genders experience difficulties; however, I can only speak to the female experience. Wherever we begin on the spectrum of expression, returning awareness to the fact that this energy is sacred is a key context for the healing process. Healing does not imply that we adopt anyone else's standards without questioning their relevance for us. Developing higher consciousness begins with self-awareness. How have we expressed this energy to date, and which experiences are authentic for us now? Jeremiel's name is sometimes translated to mean "God Shall Have Mercy." It is essential that we are merciful with ourselves as we do this healing.

When an energy flame is generated in our sexual parts, we are not required to express it there. There are times when we might choose to contain the spark of passion and direct it upward along the inner channels that facilitate higher consciousness. As one clears the shadows of the past (through forgiveness) and continues spiritual development, the individual becomes a channel to receive inspiration. Creative ideas arrive in a sudden, illuminating flash.

Jeremiel can be an ally to complete the mental level of this process. He can help us to clear any remaining thoughts or beliefs that identify us with shame and guilt or keep us identified with forms of sexual expression that no longer serve us. One method to work with him is through a journaling process. Through questions that allow us to review our previous experiences, anything still present in our energy field that is an inner obstacle can come to light. This helps us to identify where to apply forgiveness.

Creative activities themselves can also be part of a successful transformation process. Many authors have found the act of writing their stories or poetry to be healing. What are the creative activities that light up your inspiration? What makes you feel joyful and playful and brings a juiciness to life? Is it time to explore a new creative passion you have never tried?

Coloring books for adults, learning to draw with the nondominant hand, writing or poetry workshops, creating in clay, dance classes, drum workshops, and a host of other activities are available to explore. I highly recommend the classic book *The Artist's Way* by Julia Cameron. I gave this book as a gift to several women friends before I finally did the whole set of exercises she outlines. It was transformative and revealing!

During the period when I was writing this book, Jeremiel appeared in spiritual vision in an abstract, muscular male form. The flames of creative passion were intense, and I was aware of their rhythmic nature—a bit like wings fluttering. There was a sense of soaring into fiery, visionary, creative realms that were colored orange and white. I could only be profoundly grateful.

Keywords: Jeremiel helps us to claim our fullest capacity for sexual passion and divine inspiration and consciously direct them toward forms of self-expression that contribute to all.

Suggested Meditation Symbol: Upward-pointing pure-orange triangle emitting fiery golden-white flames against an orange field (Pantone 165–167 or 170)

Archangel Metatron: Angelic Kingdom
Kether (Always Spiritual Level)

Archangel Metatron corresponds to the sphere of Kether, the white sphere at the top of the Qabalah diagram. Kether symbolizes the point from which divine energy streams toward manifested form, gradually differentiating into the colored spheres and paths of the whole tree of life. Metatron is strongly associated with the sacred geometric diagram called Metatron's cube, which contains within it the flower-of-life pattern, the five Platonic solids, and many other shapes that are the building blocks of all physical matter. Sometimes known as the chief of the archangels, he has been given many high descriptive names appropriate to recognize his significance.

There is a great deal of speculation about the origin of archangel Metatron, including various theories that he was once embodied in a human form. Some sources connect him to the biblical patriarch Enoch.

The story of Enoch reports that he was taken by God without going through death.

Since I have contacted both Enoch and Metatron on several occasions, using different minerals, my experience is that they are not one and the same. Their energies feel distinct. Both extend energy at the spiritual level, and the path of Cheth (Enoch) is a high-vibration path, though it's not the same energy as Kether (Metatron).

Whatever you may believe about his origins is fine. Contact with archangel Metatron is an exceptional experience, among many exceptional members of the angelic kingdom. I experience him as a massive, abstract pillar of white light that rises to great heights above my point of view. I have sometimes glimpsed what appears like a golden sash through his radiant white light field.

While he represents a vast spiritual consciousness, I am deeply grateful that he is accessible and always involved with humankind in practical and helpful ways. He is engaged in helping us to awaken to our highest spiritual essence while we are still in physical form. On a personal level, he works with me in daily meditation and enhances contact with many of the masters when I work with them.

Keywords: Sometimes known as the chief of the archangels, Metatron extends vast energy from Source through the domain of Kether to support the highest potential outcomes for those committed to spiritual evolution.

Suggested Meditation Symbol: The sacred geometric diagram known as Metatron's cube, outlined in gold against a radiant white field

Archangel Michael: Angelic Kingdom
Chesed, Mental Level

Michael, one of the most beloved and familiar of all the archangels, extends the blue ray on the mental level of Chesed. He is one of a few angels envisioned and portrayed with a sword, which is wielded to dispel ignorance and negativity. His purpose with humankind is to help us awaken the energy of Creator consciousness, which is contained within each spark of human-divine incarnate. He is a sacred warrior who upholds faith, spiritual truth, mercy, and beneficence. He helps us to be vigilant to allow only the highest spiritual thoughts to fill our minds, so we can experience the peace and power that are present when we remember the spiritual levels of existence.

Remembering we are eternal spirit temporarily animating a physical bodies so we can play the role we chose to play in the earthly realm, we remain aware that we exist before, during, and after physical life, at a metalevel of reality. Our eternal essence can never be harmed or changed in any way, no matter what seems to occur at the level of the body. Holding our senior spiritual identity firmly in mind means the end of fear in any form. Although we are eternally safe, it is up to us, moment by moment, to choose between spiritual truth and acceptance of fearful appearances as our reality.

I have been aware of Michael's presence over many years. He has been wise, merciful, and patient with me as I learned to hold spiritual truth more consistently. At times, he appears in spiritual vision as a rapidly moving energy against a field of sapphire blue, holding a flashing sword. In addition to helping me to be vigilant with my own thoughts, I've called upon him for psychic protection and the setting of strong psychic boundaries when they were needed. Nothing negative can penetrate his shield when we ask that it surround us. Michael can also be invoked to ensure that only the highest energies can enter a ceremonial space. This is essential when seeking contact with ascended masters or undertaking any sort of astral travel.

Michael understands that the world perceived by the human senses is not ultimate reality. His energy reminds us to awaken—now! While we develop awareness of our eternal safety, he works in practical ways to guard our homes, possessions, and loved ones. He is aware that practical needs must be met before humans can focus on spiritual matters. He is accessible and available to everyone as soon as we ask and serves all humankind.

On one occasion, Michael communicated about the purpose of sacred-masculine energy as it relates to women. It can be used to create a protective field around a woman (when she asks for this). Male energy used against a woman's will—as an attempt to control her—is a misapplication of its purpose.

At the level of higher self, gender is no longer perceived. As we evolve toward those levels, finding ways to interact with those of the opposite gender, with mutual respect, is important. In every age, there have always been men who extend the highest respect and complete safety to women. As women heal any experiences that have been less than this, we attract more highly evolved men into our lives. I have been blessed to know more than a few dear spiritual brothers who have polished those levels through diligent effort.

Michael can also teach us about the death-transition mysteries. He showed me a tunnel of light near a dear one who was about to complete his physical life. If one is present at a loved one's transition, by remembering that death is only how the process appears from the limited perspective of human sight, it is possible to hold awareness on the individual's eternal reality, creating a sacred space for his or her grace-filled awakening.

Keywords: Michael offers his sword of truth to help us choose the reality of love over the illusion of fear, protects us from negativity in any form, and supports the full manifestation of spiritual awakening, which brings our higher self into awareness during life.

Suggested Meditation Symbol: Upright sword of blue flame with white angel wings (Pantone 281–295, brighter to darker blues)

Archangel Raguel: Angelic Kingdom
Red Geburah, Mental Level

Raguel extends a pure, sacred warrior energy on the red ray that corresponds to the sphere of Geburah. Some beings at Geburah work through the heart and the green ray to manifest courage, while others extend the red ray through mastery of physical energy, strength, and endurance. At the mental level, Raguel's highly refined warrior energy is also linked to higher chakras and used only according to guidance received. He can protect and serve by dispelling negative influences.

Archangel Raguel is a powerful, practical, and realistic agent for change, helping call a firm halt to situations that are unjust (at home, at work, or in the outer world). He can help us channel anger (rather than trying to suppress it) into clearing obstacles and revealing constructive solutions.

Raguel's name translates as "Friend of God." He supports us to live, work, and interact with others in a context of mutual respect and integrity. If you ever are involved in a situation where you feel mistreated or unheard or encounter dishonesty or gossip, he can help steer you down a path to rectify the situation. You can recognize Raguel's guidance in thoughts, visions, or signs that lead you to action to create a more balanced power dynamic in your relationship with a boss, coworker, friend, or relationship partner. He is stalwart in helping you to set boundaries that are appropriate and defend them if they are violated. Working with his guidance, from the midst of conflict, you can emerge empowered.

My first experience of Raguel occurred along with some ascended masters who share his Qabalah placement. He finally came into full solo contact with an abstract sense of flashing armor moving within a field of red. He demonstrates the power available when there is a union of mind (powerful, spiritually guided thoughts and beliefs) and a physically strong body (energy, endurance, and finely honed skill) entirely focused on serving spiritual intent. Those in female bodies can also cultivate both endurance and skill that allow this energy to be transmitted effectively.

Keywords: Call upon archangel Raguel when you need help in changing the dynamics with a boss or friend or in your relationship. He can help you channel anger into a mighty force for change and empowered actions and carry out any assignments you may be given to serve and protect with integrity.

Suggested Meditation Symbol: Red angel wings on either side of an upraised sword, against a pure red field (Pantone 711 or 703–704)

Archangel Raphael: Angelic Kingdom
Netzach, Mental Level

Raphael is one of the most well-known archangels. His name translates as "God Healed." He helps us to recognize the origin of optimal health and wholeness, which results from awareness of our eternal connection to a divinely loving Source.

Within the human experience, when we lose sight of our connection to Source, guilt can arise in the mind for things done and undone over the course of human life. Unaddressed, guilt interferes with our natural ability to maintain optimum health. To restore balance, Raphael helps us to clear the mind of any residue of guilt, which is toxic to the human spirit, energetically regenerating and restoring our energy. Completing a deep-healing assignment can result in higher levels of functioning than ever before.

It is often helpful to approach healing from many levels while searching for the root cause of disharmony. Working at the physical level with a traditional Western medicine or integrative medical approach may be an essential part of any healing process. Alternative or energy healers and professionals who work with human emotions may also be an essential part of one's healing. Those who pursue the deeper causes of physical discomfort from a spiritual-healing perspective may find the help of archangel Raphael highly beneficial.

Raphael is an agent for the art of forgiveness. He supports us as we learn to forgive others involved in our life dramas. Extending forgiveness to others is how we ultimately learn that we are forgiven—for anything and everything that has appeared to occur from the perspective of life in a body.

As we become willing for forgiveness to occur, we release the charges that those events produced, which we may still be carrying in our energy fields. To help us with this, Raphael is one of the beings who ushers in a massive current of divine, unconditional love. Any direct experience of being loved by Creator is healing because it undoes the illusion that humankind is separate from our Source. When divine love flows in to massively surround us, despite our past story of what we did or others did, we begin to realize that all that appears in human life is not as final as we once thought. Healing arrives, along with great relief that we cannot lose the love of our Source, regardless of what seems to have happened in physical life. From such experiences we arise fully regenerated.

Raphael has been a powerful ally during my life for all types of healing and forgiveness work. For the most part, I experience him as a massive emerald-green torch burning away what no longer serves. On occasion when he comes close I see his multiple sets of wings (six wings). I deeply appreciate the powerful currents of regeneration he elicits and the profound renewal they bring forth.

Keywords: Raphael supports those who seek personal healing and supports healing professionals who transmit the healing energies of God's love to facilitate healing for others.

Suggested Meditation Symbol: Gold caduceus symbol against a large emerald-green heart (Pantone 354–355)

Archangel Raziel: Angelic Kingdom
Chokma, Mental Level

Archangel Raziel comes to our attention among the angels known in Judaic tradition. I am deeply grateful to those in that tradition who transmitted the names of many angels we might not have otherwise known.

Judaic scholar Rachael Elior's *The Three Temples* provides a well-researched framework to understand three different Judaic temple periods, during which the wave of Judaism evolved as it did. (She serves as a professor of Jewish philosophy and Jewish mystical thought at the Hebrew University of Jerusalem.)

She describes a concept that arises from the first temple period (that of King Solomon), which is evidenced in a series of mystical and poetic writings known as the Heikhalot literature. It is dated variously by scholars to the first through third centuries CE or the fifth and sixth centuries CE. I was intrigued by her descriptions of the Heikhalot temples as a connected series of higher-dimensional energies, with each level presided over by specific angels. This is consistent with ideas embedded in the Qabalah. I had no idea I would experience the Heikhalot temples directly but was deeply moved when my consciousness landed there.

Raziel holds a special place of leadership among the Judaic angels, which I came to appreciate directly. His name translates as "God Is My Mystery," and I have indeed experienced him as a keeper of the (Judaic) mysteries. In my strongest connection with him, he showed me the legendary object known as the breastplate of the high priest (worn by Aaron, the brother of Moses, and likely others who served that function). It is mentioned in the biblical book of Exodus. The description of it as square, made of gold, and set with twelve equal-sized gemstones was exactly what he showed me. I was aware of it from my research but had been unable to discern its meaning or use. Scholars have debated the specific types of gems it contained and the meaning of this sacred object for years, providing different interpretations.

Raziel allowed me to experience its use during this profound encounter, but he does not want me to share the details in this book. If you connect with him in a powerful way, if it serves your spiritual development or life purpose, at the perfect time, he will communicate it directly to you. This is the nature of mystery teachings, many of which exist whole and complete in the higher realms and can be discovered when one raises consciousness to connect at their level.

Working with Raziel is an experience of connecting with pure power. This is characteristic of all beings at the mental level of Chokma, who receive and extend energy of Source toward manifested form. Power is sometimes misdirected and misunderstood in the human world. In its purest form, power is simply awareness of connection to Source energy.

In later experiences, Raziel arrived in my consciousness with clear, succinct, and highly elevated guidance. One communication was "Nothing is more powerful than a being who is awake!" He has become a trusted and highly valued member of my spiritual family. After connecting with him, I connected more easily with additional angels known from Judaic traditions. I experienced him as a leader in this group, analogous to how Metatron is a leader amoung angels better known in other traditions.

Raziel is also an archangel of spiritual initiation. As we grow spiritually, we may reach points where the old structures of our lives no longer serve us. When this occurs, those forms come to some ending. With Raziel, life change can occur suddenly, when power works like a surgeon's knife, eliminating all that has outlived its usefulness, so something new can come into form. You may be expecting this change; however, it may arrive in a way you don't expect.

The human mind is subject to attachment to how things appear in physical form. For that reason, the apparent endings that register in human perception can trigger strong emotions. However, human perception is not the final arbiter of reality. When one's consciousness is attuned to the realm where Raziel is met, one is in touch with the unchanging reality of eternal existence, where all of us remain connected to one another and to spiritual Source. If major life changes present themselves, the key is not to resist but, rather, to surrender, trust, and embrace them!

As we become more able to accept changes in worldly form with grace, remembering that in the highest spiritual reality, nothing changes or can be lost, we are released from human suffering. Our attachment to worldly sights as reality is the only sacrifice we are asked to make to achieve the state of peace that is senior to anything that appears to human perception.

You can call upon Raziel to help you hold this higher truth, especially during times of profound life transition. His energy is massive and powerful. He is like a protective and wise spiritual grandfather whose commitment to serve spiritual Source is total. His razor-sharp discernment can penetrate any subterfuge and make you aware of anything you might otherwise have missed, so your transition unfolds smoothly along its intended course.

Keywords: Raziel oversees the mental-level initiation at Chokma, where transcendent vision (clairvoyance) can sometimes overlay the limited band of human perception in moments outside time. He oversees direct flashes of intuitive knowing (revelation) and supports all humankind to move through life (and the death transition) with consciousness about the eternal nature of ultimate reality.

Suggested Meditation Symbol: Breastplate of the high priest (twelve squarish colored stones set in a large gold breastplate) against a radiant white field

Archangel Uriel: Angelic Kingdom
Hod, Spiritual Level

One translation of Uriel's name is "God Is My Light." Light and understanding are one in the sphere of Hod. Hod is the realm that denotes the human mind, which, at the highest levels, can operate in a perfect interface with divine mind. Uriel's name also translates as "Fire of God," which refers to his special ability to help us receive divine guidance and directly connect with our spiritual team and the ascended masters.

To access those levels, we learn to enter states of inner quiet, moving past all our personality's thinking—beliefs and preconceived ideas about ourselves, everyone else, and judgments about what should or shouldn't happen.

As we do this, we begin to access our own higher levels and our spiritual team of angels and ascended masters who can guide us toward inspired thoughts and ideas we might never have otherwise considered. By following the inner guidance we receive, we discover, through experience, a far better way to proceed in life than relying entirely on our minds' thinking, which is largely conditioned according to patterns that have developed in the past. Learning to ask, receive an answer, and move forward deepens our trust in the divine help that always surrounds us.

Doing this requires a lot of trust in the spiritual realm, which builds slowly over time until it becomes an ongoing state. By following a spiritual path, we are given many opportunities to practice, and we experience that asking for guidance produces a better outcome than we would otherwise have achieved. Learning to surrender our ego's best ideas about what needs to happen in a specific situation, we arrive at the spiritual state known as of being in the world but not of it.

I was reaching out for archangel Uriel for a long time before I was able to connect with him directly. Finally on one occasion, I was able to focus on him alone: a magnificently large, abstract presence scintillating in brilliant, fiery hues against a radiant white light. Since that experience I have been more aware of the many times he helps me to receive messages and visions from other masters.

During another direct contact I asked him to clarify how we can recognize the best direction to follow in life. I was shown a glowing, abstract purplish energy line gently unfolding ahead. His message was that when one is sincerely asking for guidance, the personality is simultaneously releasing its agenda. As that occurs, following the energy that wants to unfold is the right move since everything that occurs is orchestrated by our higher Self.

Keywords: Uriel helps us remember to cultivate inner stillness, release our egos' agendas, and ask to receive divine guidance about all the matters in our lives. He helps to awaken our higher mind so that our spiritual team can communicate with our consciousness, translating messages and direct knowing into information we can understand and follow.

Suggested Meditation Symbol: Radiant sphere of iridescent rainbow-colored sparkles in a field of pure-white light

Ares: Greek Lineage
Geburah, Emotional Level Two

In Greek mythology, Ares is introduced as the god of war, one of the twelve Olympians, and the son of Zeus and Hera. He represents an active, assertive, and primal constellation of warrior energy who mastered his red ray at the final emotional level.

To develop warrior skills, one develops the fullest potential of the root chakra, a foundational energy important for anyone, male or female. This chakra governs physical strength and endurance, our ability to be resilient in the face of challenges, our capacity to set and hold firm boundaries (a firm no from which one doesn't back down), and our capacity to choose healthy and fulfilling sexual relationships.

Some who carry this energy as a major life ray may develop skills with weapons when their life assignments include military service or apply their strength and endurance in athletic accomplishments.

Warriors hone power to provide for their basic needs. They fight only when better options do not exist and never from anger. They are not impetuous, brash, or arrogant but can move with alacrity when the time is right. They can work with others but function well independently, demonstrating self-reliance. They maintain a state of readiness and recognize optimal timing. Once they embark on a mission, there is no hesitation, and they persevere through obstacles that would dismay others.

Those who master the emotional level of Geburah may also have life learning assignments that require them to develop greater discipline in the expression of sexual energy or clear old patterns that have interfered with its full development. They may be required to learn to transmute anger or develop the means to channel it toward a cause they are guided to serve.

Martial arts are an expression of Geburah's energy, and some of them arose around a leader whom the warrior pledges to serve. Others discover they can develop the capacity to receive guidance to inform the optimal timing and direction for their actions. When these qualities all come together, successful expression will occur.

As Ares succeeded with this path, we can learn from some of the challenges he faced. In Greek tales, he was not always appreciated for his efforts. Although he embodied the physical valor necessary to achieve victory, he was considered a dangerous force. An association with him endowed places and objects with a savage, dangerous, or militarized quality. His value as a war god was placed in doubt during the Trojan War, when he supported the losing side, while Athena, often depicted in Greek art as holding Nike (Victory) in her hand, favored the triumphant Greeks.

Ares is also represented in a less-than-flattering way in literary narratives, through his numerous love affairs and abundant offspring. When he does appear in myths, he typically faces humiliation. He is familiar in some tales as the lover of Aphrodite, the goddess of love, who was married to Hephaestus, the god of craftsmanship. The most famous story related to Ares and Aphrodite shows them exposed to ridicule through the wronged husband.

As is the case with female masters portrayed in Greek myth, when one encounters Ares in the ascended realm, he doesn't reflect any remaining emotional challenges like those his myths describe. My experiences with him have revealed a warrior par excellence, who mastered all the emotional dynamics associated with his energy.

It took me some time to confirm his correspondence in the Qabalah and to discover the correct mineral. To do this, I had to peel back the layers of Greek myth to his earliest role on the stage of human life. While he fought capably with the Olympians during the battle known as the Titanomachy, he showed me an earlier scene in which he served as the head of a school that trained young men of the right temperament and natural ability in the art of war. He was matter-of-fact about the ease of using the energy he extends to make things happen in the world—when one is guided to do so.

He was also clear about his willingness to support women with the important task of honing their own inner warrior capabilities. He offered that if a woman has experienced the shadow side of male force, she will need to forgive (not condone) the outer-world events and people involved to fully claim and empower her own inner sacred warrior.

Keywords: Call upon Ares to guide you (whether you are male or female) to develop your warrior capabilities. Learn to set boundaries with your time, energy, and resources that meet your needs first. From there, you can assist others. Act when and where needed to achieve your goals. Learn skills to defuse anger or channel it into worthwhile actions when appropriate. Purify your emotional levels so that the ability to fight is governed by an inner moral code and spiritual guidance. Clear any blocks at the first chakra to contribute to optimal sexual experience while also developing the discipline to express that energy in ways that are healthy and consistent with your personal code. For those with clairsentient abilities, bringing the first chakra into optimal functioning opens new levels of clarity with the intuitive information one receives.

Suggested Meditation Symbol: Round shield with a metallic gold border design surrounding a pair of crossed swords (with the points upward) against a red field (Pantone 214–215)

Ariadne: Greek Lineage
Path of Gimel (Tarot: High Priestess), Spiritual Level

Those who are familiar with Ariadne recognize the story which includes Theseus and the monster known as the Minotaur, as told in Homeric myth. The ancient Greek authors Homer and Hesiod made invaluable contributions that provided the basis for learning about beings honored in the Greek pantheon of gods, and both of them ascended at the mental level of Hod for their contributions. However, I was able to confirm Ariadne's existence in the ascended realm, and thus following the footsteps of another ancient Greek, Euhemus of Messene, came to understand her as a being who lived a lifetime in an earthly form. We can appreciate that the Greek myths may have been written long after some of these figures lived, told from whatever details remained in collective memory during a later age. Yet when one contacts the consciousness of a master directly, a different story might emerge.

I began my attempts to contact her from Homer's traditional

tale. There she is introduced as the daughter of King Minos of Crete. According to an Athenian version of the legend, Minos attacked Athens after his son was killed there. The Athenians asked for terms, and to grant them peace, Minos required that every seven or nine years, they send seven young men and seven maidens to his kingdom, to be sacrificed to a fearsome bull known as the Minotaur. Ariadne was said to preside over the labyrinth where the sacrifices were made.

This tale continues with what happened when those to be sacrificed arrived. The sacrificial party who arrived in Minos's kingdom included Theseus, the son of King Aegeus, who had volunteered to come kill the Minotaur. According to the story, Ariadne fell in love with this hero and helped him by giving him a sword and a ball of thread (Ariadne's thread), but he ultimately rejected her. Many women who are called to discover Ariadne are familiar with some version of this tale and find it wanting. I was determined to connect with Ariadne if I could and discover my own truth. Fortunately, she assisted me and made different levels of contact as I persisted with the desire to understand more about her.

I began with some research on Knossos and found Rodney Castleden's book *The Knossos Labyrinth: A New View of the "Palace of Minos" at Knossos* most interesting. He provides evidence to support that it was a temple, rather than a palace. Some sources also refer to the labyrinth as a sacred dancing ground for ritual use. No one knows when the first labyrinth was created, but by 1200 BCE, the familiar pattern had already appeared on coins of Crete. After examining surviving myths, customs, and ancient accounts, scholars have concluded that labyrinths were used to celebrate resurrection, perform fertility dances, and mark the annual cycle of the sun's and moon's passage through the sky. Some women today experience that walking or dancing through a labyrinth can help them to enter an altered state of consciousness and receive guidance

Perhaps, as I have, you will tap into your own higher-dimensional confirmation about the role of priestesses at Knossos. Before reading Castleden's book, during one experience, I connected deeply to Ariadne, traveling in consciousness to Minoan Crete. I felt the lovely, temperate climate and visually toured the Knossos temple, whose design allowed light and currents of air to circulate through the structure. Spiritual vision reviewed the beautiful frescoes painted on all the interior walls—of vines, flowers, and leaping dolphins. Everything showed the extraordinary quality of civilized development that flourished there, which would not be equaled for long eons to follow. I experienced that in accessing the higher dimensions, the priestesses remembered Ariadne as a highly evolved female who had transmitted still earlier female spiritual initiation practices to their culture.

Over succeeding weeks I was drawn to penetrate more deeply and eventually experienced that Ariadne did not originate in Crete but was part of a still earlier strata of masters who transmitted spiritual knowledge, some of which was brought to that area of the ancient world.

Many female masters who possess high spiritual knowledge correspond with the energy of the path of Gimel in the Qabalah (High Priestess in tarot). They occur at different levels, with Ariadne and others in this book extending energy at the spiritual level. This correspondence represents the most evolved state of spiritual development possible in a female body, wherein a woman opens the channel to spiritual reality with every cell of her being.

My ultimate connection with the being we know today as Ariadne located her presiding in a temple environment. As I said earlier in this book, not all sacred experiences are meant to be shared. I will say only that during my deepest contact with her consciousness, amid exquisite feelings of joy and bliss, she gave me the symbol below to use in meditation. Using it on subsequent occasions has lifted my consciousness to meet her again, and I hope it is useful for those of you reading these words.

Keywords: Ariadne is an advanced inner-world guide for female spiritual initiation. Her mind knows the way, and she can help us to claim our own female spiritual power and use it to serve the spiritual realm and the course of human evolution.

Suggested Meditation Symbol: A crown comprised of a simple polished silver metal headband containing three upright, huge, marquise-shaped gems (pale blue) emitting brilliant light against a radiant white field

Arianrhod: Celtic Lineage
Yesod, Spiritual Level

The name Arianrhod comes from the Welsh *arian*, meaning "silver," and *rhod*, meaning "wheel." Arianrhod comes to modern awareness in myth in the fourth branch of the (Welsh) Mabinogi. It was written at a time when the Christian church had already established a strong foothold, including the tendency to try to control the "evil" of women's sexuality.

The tales say she had a brother named Gwydion, who was a magician and placed her in a shameful, unfortunate situation. Her uncle Math fab Mathonwy was under a spell that would cause him to die if he did not keep his feet in the lap of a virgin when he was not at war. His original virgin was desired by a man named Goewin and raped. Gwydion proposed Arianrhod as a replacement. (This part of the story is questionable, as a female who ascended at the spiritual level of Yesod would make up her own mind about any such liaison, rather than be forced into one by her brother.)

Math decided to test Arianrhod's virginity by asking her to "step over his magician's rod." As she did so, she was surprised to give birth to two boys (one became Llew Law Gyffes). Some interpretations suggest that this child was forcibly and incestuously conceived with her brother, Gwydion. Supporting this interpretation, Gwydion hid the boy in a chest and raised him in secret. In the myth, Arianrhod was angry about her humiliation and placed several *geis*, or taboos, on the boy, denying him three aspects of masculinity: a name, the ability to bear arms, and a wife. However, she was outwitted by Gwydion's trickery on each count. Her behavior toward her son seems less than that of an ideal mother, but it is impossible to know from the myth itself where the truth lies.

While this tale is likely altered by time and later beliefs, we can

215

observe that some women who heal patterns of incest develop complete mastery of kundalini energy, which is a powerful psychic-spiritual force. In the traditions of Indian and Buddhist tantra, kundalini is called the serpent energy, coiled at the base of the spine.

As Arianrhod's myth offers, many women today are called to heal sexual trauma. including incest. Sometimes this trauma runs through one's whole ancestral female lineage, until finally, one woman completes the healing for herself and thus breaks the pattern for her whole family line. If the necessity for that type of healing comes forward, Arianrhod can be a beacon of light to be called upon if one is such a pattern breaker.

Kundalini energy is present in everyone but usually lies dormant until awakened by spiritual practice or during the final stages of healing sexual trauma. As kundalini awakens, consciousness can be carried far beyond any experiences of victimhood and into union with our higher self. From that elevated perspective, consciousness is aware we remain exactly as we were created. Nothing that appears to occur in human life can change that divine radiance in any way.

As this state of awakening is reached, kundalini energy is then available as an ongoing resource that can be directed toward healing, accessing higher states of consciousness, and manifesting forms in the physical plane. Female masters at this level of Yesod claim their fullest intuitive and prophetic abilities and are virgin in the original meaning of the term—they may choose sexual relationships when they wish but are not defined by a relationship to any partner in form or the lack thereof.

My first experience of working with Arianrhod occurred during a time when I was trying to manifest something important in my life. Manifestation is one of the attributes of Yesod, which shapes forms from astral mater. Outdoors, the full moon shone in glory, filtering through the window amid moving shadows of wind in the trees. I could feel Arianrhod and sent out my prayers, and the desired life path manifested a few months later.

Some years later, I had a glimpse of Arianrhod with spiritual vision: a huge, abstract energy presence in an iridescent white field, also with moving shadows. More recently, she appeared, still abstract, extending silvery energy in outward-flowing circles, which became a transdimensional portal that my consciousness could enter. I am deeply grateful to experience her powerful presence and beneficial influence, as she supports many of my explorations in higher dimensions.

Keywords: Arianrhod supports women who attain the spiritual level of development at Yesod, helping them to use the power of awakened kundalini to lift consciousness toward the divine realms; claim female power; access direct intuitive knowing; become skillful in manifesting; and make free, independent sexual choices when they wish that.

Suggested Meditation Symbol: An abstract silver wheel in circular motion, opening a transdimensional portal containing a gleaming full moon surrounded by stars against the cosmic void

Arjuna: Hindu Lineage
Path of Tzaddi (Tarot: Emperor), Mental Level

Arjuna, who features prominently in the classic Hindu spiritual text Bhagavad Gita, was an ancient warrior leader of great renown. Arjuna's dialogues with Krishna comprise an important part of the teachings of the Bhagavad Gita, a key part of the Mahabharata, which is considered a holy scripture of Hinduism.

By all accounts, Arjuna's skill with weaponry was legendary. He was the son of Pandu and Kunti of the Kuru Kingdom and the spiritual son of Indra. (Indra is not included in this book, but I have experienced his incredibly powerful presence at the sphere of Chokma.)

Arjuna was the favorite disciple of his guru, Drona, who taught weaponry. He was ambidextrous and perhaps the greatest of all archers (archery was the foremost of all fighting disciplines in that time and culture). He was also a supreme chariot warrior (war chariots were the mobile battle stations used in ancient warfare.) He obtained near-perfect mastery over almost all divine, celestial, and esoteric weapons, along with the secrets of invoking and recalling them. There are accounts that interpret this to include nuclear weapons, and indeed, some unexplained ancient sites in India that show evidence of nuclear warfare.

Arjuna was also known for his great devotion to Krishna. (All masters at the mental level of any sphere or path have awakened their relationship with spiritual forces.) The friendship bond of Krishna and Arj una is the most celebrated in Hindu mythology (followed closely by the bond between Rama and Hanuman). Krishna, being a friend of the Pandava clan, helped them in various ways during the time of their ordeals. When the great war for succession was going to begin, both Arjuna (on behalf of the Pandavas) and his cousin Duryodhan (on behalf of the rival Kaurava clan) went to Krishna to seek his help.

They told him of the coming war and said they had come to him seeking military help. To this Krishna replied that he had seen Arjuna first, so he would give him first choice between two options. He could choose either Krishna's entire fit and healthy army or Krishna's company alone as driver of his war chariot. Arjuna immediately opted for Krishna himself, and Duryodhan was given Krishna's large army.

Arjuna's dilemma about the coming war was about following dharma. He was of the Kshatriya (warrior) caste, so in that culture, it was considered his duty to fight, which was also his greatest skill. Yet he was distraught at the thought of having to fight with his friends and family, which included his dear teacher, Drona, and grandsire Bhishma. Fighting against one's only family put him in conflict with a different set of teachings, so he faced a moral dilemma. Neither choice, to fight or not fight, was entirely correct. Seeking the advice of Krishna on this matter produced dialogue between them that is considered of great importance in Hindu thought.

Aside from how this text may be interpreted within traditional Hindu religion, we can consider this tale as an illustration of the Qabalah structure. Both beings correspond to the mental level of development. We can observe that by offering to drive Arjuna's war chariot, Krishna was symbolically offering him access to direct spiritual guidance. Arjuna was truly devoted and open to receiving what was being extended.

Warriors at the mental level of Tzaddi long ago mastered requisite skills with weapons, physical strength, courage, and endurance. At the mental level, success is gained by holding only the thoughts that are consistent with victory. Any doubts about engaging in the battle had to be settled before one began to fight, or they would be one's undoing. The direct spiritual guidance Krishna offered ultimately opened the path to victory. Success could be won not by the leader who directed a larger army but by one who had access to greater spiritual insight.

As I experienced more and more masters at Tzaddi—including Charlemagne, who is profiled ahead—I came to appreciate that mastery here is attained when a warrior leaders' singular devotion to spiritual reality set them apart from others. As a result, some of the Tzaddi masters played key roles throughout human history, winning important battles that shaped the future for humankind.

Meeting Arjuna in consciousness was an experience of the penultimate spiritual warrior leader. His state of absolute fearlessness is an energy different from that of one who is still learning to overcome fear. Yes, he entered battle with great skill, years of experience, and Krishna's guidance. But his complete freedom from fear arises from the certainty that he is one with what is sometimes called the Limitless Light.

Soon in this meditation, Arjuna was asking for Krishna to come forward. As I held minerals that correspond to both these masters, together they opened a channel all the way to the white light, extending the purest qualities of the sacred warrior and the sacred masculine.

Keywords: Arjuna supports the mental development of fearless male warrior skills that are paired with spiritual guidance to serve a high holy purpose.

Suggested Meditation Symbol: Arjuna's huge golden bow named Gandiva against a red field (Pantone 711 or 703–704)

Artemis: Greek Lineage
Yesod, Spiritual Level

Artemis is one of the most well-known and widely venerated beings known in the Greek pantheon. Greek myth introduces her as a second-generation Olympian, the daughter of Zeus and Leto and the twin sister of Apollo. Her image appeared on the coinage of fifty cities throughout the Greek world, and her veneration is attested in ninety-two surviving texts and inscriptions.

Artemis Orthia (worshipped at a small sanctuary at Messene) was associated with wilderness and the hunting of wild beasts. The earliest offerings at her shrine go back to the protogeometric period in the ninth century BCE.

Athenian festivals in honor of Artemis included the Elaphebolia, Mounikhia, Kharisteria, and Brauronia. Prepubescent and adolescent Athenian girls were sent to the sanctuary of Artemis at Brauron to serve the goddess for one year. During this time, the girls were known as little she-bears.

Arcadian Artemis (Arcadia was part of the Peloponnese region of the Greek mainland) was celebrated in the forest and portrayed as riding in a chariot drawn by four stags with golden antlers or as a beautiful, tall woman with a hunting dog by her side. She was the Hellenic goddess of the hunt, wild animals, and wilderness, often depicted as a huntress carrying a bow and arrows. She was also associated with virginity and was a protector of young girls. The deer and the cypress were sacred to her. Her best-known cult centers were on the island of Delos and at Ephesus (modern-day Turkey), both of which claimed to be her birthplace.

Author Guy Maclean Rogers, in his book *The Mysteries of Artemis of Ephesus*, describes how the mysteries of Artemis were celebrated for nearly seven hundred years at the gigantic Temple of Artemis (mid-fourth century BCE to 262 CE). Ephesus was a prosperous trading port that connected to the well-traveled Silk Road. While other Greek deities also had cults at Ephesus, Artemis was considered the tutelary, divine, protective goddess of the city. The Ephesian temple was both a Vatican and a Fort Knox of beautiful objects and wealth. Married women were banned in the sanctuary (emphasizing female independence). Artemis's mystery tradition finally ended after a plague, a famine, and, finally, a major earthquake felt throughout the whole Aegean destroyed the magnificent temple.

Those who are familiar with Artemis today honor her as a protector of maidens and associate her with the new moon phase of the moon's cycle. Those who study goddess spirituality are accustomed to triple moon goddesses, and the maiden phase, or new moon phase, often has to do with female coming-of-age ceremonies and customs. Those who have written on feminine spiritual themes in the past two decades remind us of the original meaning of *virgin*: a woman who is self-renewing. Such a woman chooses her own sexual partners and may have many lovers, yet she does not define herself by relationship to any male. Far from man-hating or simply a moon goddess, Artemis represents the ultimate powerful, completely self-sufficient, and self-defined woman.

I was strongly attracted to Artemis at the beginning of my spiritual path. Through her, I found the connection to wild nature that I had not yet claimed in life. It took many years of spiritual development, however, before the most direct experiences of her came about. On one occasion, she appeared in a visual abstract form that was unmistakably her. I could see her connection with wild nature and the moonlit wilderness settings in which she can be sought. She reminded me of a vision quest I did twenty-five years ago with a group of women, which was a powerful experience.

In recent years, she came through again, bringing the words "Artemis, mistress of wild things" clearly into my consciousness. Later, I returned to work with her, and she responded again, taking form as an abstract Greek sculpture, tall and graceful. She was a virgin queen who mated with whomever she wanted whenever she wanted, not the property of any man. She extends a field of energy that has amazing strength and white-light protection.

Keywords: Artemis supports women to claim their independence and to be self-renewing virgins who choose lovers when they do—or remain intentionally celibate—without being defined by any partner relationship or lack thereof. She supports women who are equally at home in wilderness settings and with their own wild (independent) nature and is protective of young women and women's rites of passage.

Suggested Meditation Symbol: Silver-tipped arrow crossing a radiant white crescent moon (forming a bow-and-arrow effect)

Asclepius: Greek Lineage
Netzach, Emotional Level Two

In Greek myth, Asclepius is the god who represents the healing aspect of the medical arts. His daughters are Hygeia (Hygiene, the goddess and personification of health, cleanliness, and sanitation); Iaso (the goddess of recuperation from illness); Aceso (the goddess of the healing process); Aglæa (the goddess of the glow of good health); and Panacea (the goddess of universal remedy).

Asclepius was one of Apollo's sons, sharing with Apollo the epithet Paean, or the Healer. The rod of Asclepius, a snake-entwined staff, remains a symbol of medicine today. According to myth, Apollo carried his baby son Asclepius to the centaur Chiron, who raised him and instructed him in the art of medicine. It is said that in return for some kindness rendered by Asclepius, a snake licked Asclepius's ears clean and taught him secret knowledge (to the ancient Greeks, snakes were sacred beings of wisdom, healing, and resurrection). Asclepius became so proficient as a healer that he surpassed both Chiron and his father, Apollo. Asclepius was therefore able to evade death and to bring others back to life from the brink of death and beyond.

The healing temples where people sought the healing intervention of Asclepius were known as Asclepieia, which were located throughout Greece and in the wider Hellenistic and Roman world. Archaeological evidence has revealed more than three hundred different Asclepieia.

These temples were often located in secluded locations, surrounded by spas or mountain sanatoriums. The most famous temple of Asclepius was at Epidaurus in northeastern Peloponnese, dated to the fourth century BCE. Another famous Asclepieion was built approximately a century later on the island of Kos, where Hippocrates, the legendary so-called father of medicine, may have begun his career. Other Asclepieia were situated in Trikala, Gortys in Crete, and Pergamum in Asia.

From the fifth century BC onward, the cult of Asclepius grew popular, and pilgrims flocked to his healing temples to be cured of their ills. Ritual purification would be followed by offerings or sacrifices to the god (according to one's means), and the supplicant would then spend the night in the holiest part of the sanctuary: the abaton (or adyton). Any dreams or visions would be reported to a priest, who would prescribe the appropriate therapy by a process of interpretation. Some healing temples also used sacred dogs to lick the wounds of sick petitioners. In honor of Asclepius, a particular type of nonvenomous snake was often used in healing rituals, and these snakes—the Aesculapian snakes—slithered around freely on the floor in dormitories where the sick and injured slept. These snakes were introduced at the founding of each new temple of Asclepius throughout the classical world.

In iconography, Asclepius is pictured holding a staff wreathed with a snake, which has associations with healing in many different traditions. When I experienced his powerful energy directly (using a crystal), I could feel emotional debris from a demanding life situation I'd recently experienced fly off my energy field. I joined my intention to release whatever was there to release, and the powerful result was regenerating. He has been helpful to me several times in a similar manner. His energy is as strengthening as it is transformational.

Keywords: Call upon Asclepius to support you as you train or work in some healing modality that includes emotional healing or during any life stage in which clearing emotional charges from your energy field is needed.

Suggested Meditation Symbol: Strong wooden rod or staff wrapped with a single entwined green serpent, against a forest-green field (Pantone 371 or 378)

Athena: Greek Lineage
Tiphareth, Spiritual Level

Athena, like Apollo, is one of the most well-known figures in Greek mythology, and she is the tutelary deity of the important city of Athens. Myths relate that Athena and Poseidon competed for patronage of the city of Athens by each giving the people one gift. Poseidon struck the ground with his trident so that a spring of water sprang up, but Athena gave them the olive tree, which was considered even more valuable, and thus won the competition.

The earliest known evidence for Athena is found in inscriptions in Mycenaean Linear B, which date from the late Bronze Age (circa 1450 BCE), before the introduction of Greek letters. Greek myth places her in a warrior role, and we understand that she was likely part of the force we know as the Olympians, who were called to fight the earlier group we know as the Greek Titans.

In iconography, Athena is portrayed as a tall and lovely woman holding a spear and sometimes a shield, dressed in full battle armor. She is sometimes accompanied by a small, winged Nike (symbol of victory), an owl (symbol of wisdom), a serpent (symbol of female power), or an olive branch (her gift to the Athenians). Traditionally, she is associated with wisdom; crafts, such as weaving; and the strategic ability to successfully wage war.

Another tale reports that Hephaestus wanted to marry Athena, for she was beautiful as well as intellectually gifted, but she was one of the virgin goddesses and refused him. Another part of her myth tells of a weaving contest between Athena and the mortal woman Arachne, who had boasted that her talent was equal to Athena's. When the mortal woman lost their contest, Athena turned her into a spider. This part of the tale reveals Athena's skill with crafts.

Athena's birth story introduces her as a child of Zeus but via a different mother, named Metis. In some versions of her tale, Athena was not born in the usual way. Before her birth, Zeus was told that any child born to Metis would be more powerful than his or her father. He was worried by this prophecy and decided to swallow Metis before she could give birth to their child. He did this, but sometime later, he began to have terrible headaches. The pain grew so unbearable that Zeus asked Hephaestus to cut his head open to see what was wrong. When Hephaestus opened Zeus's skull, Athena emerged, fully grown, and dressed for battle. This tale about her birth is symbolic, reflecting that she was a unique individual, with mental qualities that Homer could only describe as arising directly from the mind of a male progenitor!

We can appreciate that many myths, even those that attempt to tell of beings who once walked on earth, have incorporated elements to entertain. Any author might be at a loss to explain the lives of those who lived in another period. Whatever the case, I have found that the mythological birth stories and family relationships introduced in Greek tales do not always hold up in direct contact with their masters. That was my experience with Athena.

In sometimes pointing out gender perceptions woven into myths, I don't imply that females have always been denigrated, and it will be clear in my experiences with male masters that I value their contributions greatly. I am simply pointing out that behind the myths, when one contacts the masters directly, new insights may be gained.

As I worked with certain masters, I was guided to keep seeking their earliest contributions to humankind. As I pursued deeper contact with Athena, she showed me another layer, during which she presided over what I could only call a college of knowledge. Spiritual vision revealed a vast complex containing ancient scrolls and texts, with domed rooftops of gleaming golden color. The powerful energy radiating from this dimension is still potent and is the origin of Athena's association with wisdom.

Keywords: Athena is a powerful leader who champions women's right to gain higher knowledge and express their unique brilliance. She supports women who are developing strong leadership and discernment to contribute to the world in different ways that advance humankind. Every woman has access to her support.

Suggested Meditation Symbol: Oval, highly domed, gleaming golden helmet against a field of radiant white

Avalokitesvara: Buddhist Lineage
Chesed, Spiritual Level

Avalokitesvara is among the most popular of all Buddhist deities throughout the world today. His name means "Lord Who Looks Down with Compassion." Western scholars have not reached a consensus on the origin of the reverence for Avalokitesvara, though this being has been recognized since the rise of the Mahayana doctrines, early in the Common Era (nearly two thousand years). It is easy to understand his widespread appeal, as in every era and culture, the quality of compassion is greatly needed and highly valued.

In Mahayana Buddhism, Avalokitesvara is recognized as a bodhisattva. The concept of a bodhisattva describes a being who is dedicated to collective human awakening, expressing profound qualities of mercy and compassion. Bodhisattvas are often understood within Buddhist traditions to have postponed their own Buddhahood (fully realized enlightenment) until they have helped every sentient being on earth to achieve liberation.

Like some other masters, Avalokitesvara is known by different names in different cultures. Lokanatha, whose name means "Lord of the Universe," was well known at fourth-century-CE Nalanda (a Buddhist university) as he who protects the world. Chenrezig, known in Tibet, is also identified with Avalokitesvara in many interpretations. His meditation, with 108 prayer beads, is practiced in all the great lineages of Tibetan Buddhism.

Avalokitesvara is also sometimes identified with Quan Yin. As the worship of Guanyin (or Quan Yin) evolved during the first millennium in China, this bodhisattva began to exhibit traditional female traits, such as kindness and thoughtfulness. In my direct experience with both Quan Yin and Avalokitesvara, she has an entirely different Qabalah correspondence (at the spiritual level of the path of Gimel, the High Priestess in tarot), while Avalokitesvara is met at the spiritual level of the sphere of Chesed. I have contacted both, using different crystals that correspond to those distinct parts of the Qabalah. Please follow whatever tradition you wish, but I suggest you simply orient your meditation to the name Avalokitesvara when you wish to contact the master described here.

As Mahayana texts, such as *The Lotus Sutra* and *The Flower Garland Sutra*, were arriving via the Silk Road, Chinese artists shaped Avalokitesvara in culturally specific forms: sometimes male or female but mostly genderless. Sometimes portrayed in an androgynous form dressed in flowing robes, adorned with a bodhisattva's intricate pendant headdress and necklace, he appears to meditate with great grace and gentleness, with downcast eyes softly saddened by human distress.

This androgynous portrayal is apt, as in my experience, the closer masters are to the spiritual level at any part of the Qabalah, the less they display gender differences—because they are so closely connected to Source energy, which moves beyond gender entirely.

One prominent Buddhist story tells of Avalokitesvara vowing never to rest until he had freed all sentient beings from samsara (cyclic rebirth into the physical world). Despite strenuous effort, he realized that many unhappy beings were yet to be saved. After hes struggled to comprehend the needs of so many, his head split into eleven pieces.

Also part of the Mahayana tradition, Buddha Amitabha, seeing his plight, gave him eleven heads with which to hear the cries of the suffering. Upon hearing the cries and comprehending them, Avalokitesvara tried to reach out to all those who needed aid but found that his two arms shattered into pieces. Once more, Amitabha came to his aid and invested him with a thousand arms with which to aid the suffering multitudes.

This story of multiple heads and thousands of arms also reminds me of a higher spiritual truth that is difficult for the human mind to grasp: the ascended masters, as well as angels, especially those at the highest levels, can work with large groups of people simultaneously, yet our experience of them may be individual. Human language, which is based in time and duality, fails to convey this truth easily, but from nondual awareness (oneness with Source and all creation), it makes perfect sense that any part of divine Source is continuously in touch with every other part.

I've had several experiences with Avalokitesvara. Each time he comes into mind, he simply introduces himself as "the white Buddha." His energy is as pure and pristine as a Himalayan mountaintop. In my most recent experience, he appeared as a gold figure with a thousand arms, like some of his statues.

As I've experienced with some other spiritual-level masters who correspond to different parts of the Qabalah, he brought a few words to help me remain awake to the spiritual levels, no matter what scenes present themselves in human perception. It was a simple, personal teaching that my mind could understand and remember, which is consistent with how any master works with our consciousness.

Aligning with the energy of any of the masters at spiritual level, one can experience a mind that is one with Source. Such experiences are always powerful, because we realize we couldn't register that unless our consciousness is also part of the One, in the dimensions beyond time and space. When it happens once, it's amazing and illuminating. As this experience recurs during repeated experiences, we grow in the certainty that being an extension of that Oneness is our truest essence.

Keywords: Avalokitesvara shows us how to model new ways to express ultimate compassion for oneself and for all humankind while we awaken from the perception that we are separate from our divine Source.

Suggested Meditation Symbol: A 108-bead mala prayer necklace of colorless quartz beads, with a red silk tassel against a radiant white field

Baldur (the Beautiful): Norse Lineage
Chesed, Mental Level

Norse myth introduces Baldur as a member of the Aesir group of beings, the second son of Odin and Frigg (after Thor), and the husband of Nanna. Forseti was said to be his son. According to the Icelandic tales (Snorri Sturluson in *The Prose Edda*), Baldur was an entirely beneficent being. All praised him; he was so fair of face and bright that he seemed to shine; and he was wise and eloquent as well as merciful and so did not judge others harshly. The story of his death and the attempt to retrieve him from the underworld is one of the most important tales in Norse mythology.

As Snorri's version goes, Baldur was having disturbing dreams of a nature that perhaps foretold his death. His mother, Frigg, acted on this foreknowledge by obtaining oaths from all things in creation that they would not harm him. After she did this, the Aesir beings made a sport of attempting to kill Baldur, watching with enjoyment as he remained unhurt!

Loki (not an ascended master in that lifetime) was displeased by this and discovered that the mistletoe plant was the one thing Frigg considered so harmless that she did not make it participate in the oath. (We should keep in mind that mistletoe was sacred to the druids, and this death story may refer to a shamanic initiation into the higher realms.)

Loki fashioned a spear from the mistletoe and gave it to Hod, Baldur's blind half brother, inciting him to throw it at Baldur. It pierced him, and he fell dead—a great misfortune done.

Distraught, Frigg called for a volunteer to travel to the underworld to plead with Hel, Loki's daughter, who reigned there, to try to persuade her to return Baldur to the Aesir. Hermdor was the valiant warrior who volunteered for this assignment, borrowing Odin's eight-legged magical horse named Sleipnir for the journey.

Hel agreed to release Baldur, providing that all things, living and dead, wept for him. Hermdor returned with this news, and emissaries were sent out with the request. One old lady (perhaps Loki in disguise) refused to weep, so Baldur remained in the underworld. As in many Viking tales, vengeance was taken on Loki, and he was chained up, with a venomous serpent dripping poison onto his head, which brought him great pain. Loki's loyal wife held a bowl over his head that captured most of the venom before it touched him, but when she had to empty her bowl, his pain was intense.

While Hermdor was on his mission, Baldur's funeral took place, and it was a magnificent one, including a Viking funeral pyre lit on Baldur's ship. Baldur's wife, Nanna, died of grief and went up in flames beside her beloved. Consistent with other ascended-master beings at Chesed, one of the qualities that Baldur models for us is spiritual devotion. He is aligned with the higher realms, rather than human motivations of greed, revenge, and personal gain. Like other sons of divine parents (within the mythic structure), he plays the role of sacrificial son.

John Lindow, in *Norse Mythology*, mentions that the description of Baldur given by Danish historian Saxo Grammaticus was significantly different from Snorri's Icelandic tale. According to the Danish version, Hod and Baldur vied for the hand of Nanna (who first became Hod's wife and then, after another battle, became Baldur's wife); Hod was not blind; and there was no mistletoe. No attempt was made to regain Baldur from the underworld, and the story of his funeral is far less dramatic. The stories overlap in some areas, including the detail that Odin sired a son by Rind, overcoming her through magical means, which was essentially a rape that would avenge Baldur. Both accounts present Baldur's death as a disaster that led to Ragnarok. As with many myths that survive in different accounts, there is no way to determine the most accurate version.

In direct experience, Baldur came into consciousness with a (now familiar from other masters at this level) feeling of sacred-masculine beneficence. His presence was an abstract deep blue field with many tiny, sparkling golden dots. It was easy to understand that such beings are called radiant from the spiritual light they extend.

Keywords: Baldur reminds us of the value of the spiritual qualities of purity, mercy, compassion, and holiness, which uplift us whenever we extend them to others. Call on him to help you rise above petty human considerations, release judgment held against others, and embody a truly uplifting high vibration that extends universally to everyone.

Suggested Meditation Symbol: Sprig of mistletoe (green leaves and creamy white berries) against a sapphire-blue field (brighter to darker blues, Pantone 281–295)

Belenus: Celtic Lineage
Tiphareth, Mental Level

Belenus, sometimes given as Bel or Belenos, means "the Bright One" or "the Shining God." The annual festival of Beltane, celebrated on May 1, which marks the return of the full light of the sun at the beginning of summer, was named for him. This important day in the Wheel of the Year celebrates the returning season of fertility for the land. In this context, we can appreciate how later generations could memorialize Belenus as a symbol of fire, light, and the promise of abundant new life.

Existing evidence shows that Belenus was worshipped by the Celts across Italy, Austria, Gaul, Britain, and Ireland. There are fifty-one known inscriptions dedicated to him, mainly concentrated in Gaul but also some extending far beyond into Celtic Britain and Iberia. The known archaeological finds relating to him are more numerous than for any other Celtic being, demonstrating his popularity in pre-Christian times. Besides inscriptions, artifacts include a coin bearing his image and a carved article of jewelry. He is associated with a horse (found among clay votive offerings in Burgundy) and a wheel.

Belenus is often described as a sun god and was often equated with Apollo by the Romans. (I found that Apollo corresponds to the spiritual level at Tiphareth, and Belenus corresponds to the mental level.) Ancient authors Tertullian and Herodotus and the Roman poet Ausonius also mentioned Belenus. Certain early races were understood in terms of radiant physical strength and dominance, which often produced success.

When I first contacted Belenus, my initial impression was of bright light. I understood why others had called him the Bright One, and his light and warmth seemed to be growing in power. He appeared in an abstract form, dressed in a peculiar style of ancient armor I had never seen. His upper torso armor seemed to be made from bronze-colored metal strips that had a wide scrolling design which partially covered his upper body but left gaps showing his skin. Some of the designs in the metal were circular, a bit like a bull's-eye pattern. I felt a strong and familiar connection with him and was energized and uplifted by the experience.

Many types of Beltane celebrations have existed; most use fire. It remains one of the most important days in the Wheel of the Year, celebrated by people within various spiritual traditions.

Keywords: Belenus is available to support those who develop powerful warrior leadership to follow a destiny path that serves humankind and the higher planes. He works at the mental level, bringing higher-dimensional inspiration through the individual, helping people to fulfill their unique life missions.

Suggested Meditation Symbol: An ancient war-chariot wheel with golden overlay, against a radiant white field

Bernadette of Lourdes, Saint: Christian Lineage
Path of Cheth (Tarot: Chariot), Mental Level

Bernadette Soubirous (1844–1879 CE) was the firstborn daughter of a miller from Lourdes. She was a sickly child who suffered from both cholera and asthma and was too ill to practice the austerity of nuns but lived a quiet life of service, making altar cloths. She became a beloved patron of healing, and her name was given to the spiritual healing center in Lourdes, France. She is also venerated as a saint in the Catholic church.

Bernadette is best known to history for her clairvoyant visions of a young lady (later identified as Mother Mary), who asked for a chapel to be built at the nearby garbage dump of the cave grotto at Massabielle. Her spiritual visions of Mary are said to have occurred between February 11 and July 16, 1858. Bernadette received recognition when the lady who appeared to her identified herself as the Immaculate Conception. Despite initial skepticism from the Catholic church, her claims were eventually declared worthy of belief after a canonical investigation, and the Marian apparition is now known as Our Lady of Lourdes.

So many mystical adepts and healers have experienced severe health crises that the interpretation has sometimes been made that this level of sacrifice is required for spiritual progress—which is not the case. It is true that some form of life challenge is often the impetus to develop spiritually. Those challenges sometimes take the form of personal healing crises, which help us disengage from worldly concerns to discover the spiritual realm.

The Marian shrine in Lourdes, Midi-Pyrénées, France, went on to become a major pilgrimage site, attracting more than five million pilgrims of all denominations each year. Remaining focused on the divine for healing help can often be facilitated by physically traveling to a healing center, where one is free of worldly distractions, but it is not the only option.

Bernadette came into consciousness one day during my walk to ask me to say that it is not necessary to go to her healing sanctuary to work with her. She will work with anyone who lifts his or her mind and heart to the divine in sincere prayer, wherever he or she may be. My deepest experience with Bernadette also included the presence of Mary, the mother of Jesus. The feelings of love and rapport that flowed between them were precious to experience.

Keywords: Bernadette supports women's psychic-intuitive development and the emergence of abilities that can benefit others. One can call upon her compassionate support in all matters of healing and to learn the habit of turning to the divine presence of love through prayer and contemplation.

Suggested Meditation Symbol: Marian altar cloth symbol: blue scrolling letter *M* with a golden crown above, against a field of radiant white

Brigit: Celtic Lineage and Christian Saint
Netzach, Mental Level

The name Brigit means "Exalted One." She is called Bride in Scotland and is also known under the spellings Brigid, Brid, Bridget, and others. She was originally known as a member of the Tuatha Dé Danann (a daughter of the Dagda) and married the tyrannical half-Fomorian Bres, but she evolved over time from a pagan goddess into a revered Catholic saint. (She didn't change, but beliefs about her changed, allowing for more universal acceptance.)

Brigit was the territorial deity of Leinster, but unlike most Celtic beings, who were bound to a single place, Brigit was venerated at many sites all over Ireland. She was venerated for an especially wide variety of matters, which I believe reflects her long evolution in human understanding from Tuatha member to Catholic saint. Some experience her support in matters of healing. Also, like other beautiful women, Brigit, as a muse, can inspire the creative flow of male artists and poets. As one example, a man I have known for years who is both a gifted healer (in alternative approaches) and a published poet and who has strong connections to Ireland and a strong inner relationship with Brigit.

Brigit is linked to perpetual sacred flames, such as one maintained at her sanctuary in Kildare, Ireland. Evidence suggests there was a pagan shrine at Kildare before Catholic times. Some plains in the area were left untilled, meaning they belonged to the goddess. It is likely that a group of priestesses lived in or near Kildare and performed rites associated with Brigit.

Her imagery includes the sun, the moon, cows, sheep, vultures, baths, sacred fires, and serpents (healing and sexual energy). Her festival is at Imbolc, celebrated on February 1 each year. To fully grasp the significance of Imbolc, it is necessary to understand the life-and-death struggle represented by winter in any northern agrarian society, such as Ireland. In a world lit only by fire, the snow, cold, and ice literally hold you in their grip, only relaxing with the arrival of spring. Imbolc divides winter in half; the Crone months of winter are departing, and the promise of the Spring Maiden—and renewed abundance—is around the corner. Imbolc is the beginning of lambing season and spring sowing, which will lead to renewed abundance.

On recent occasions, my consciousness made a deeper connection to Brigit. The result of contact was healing on the mental level, more deeply than I realized was needed. We are all entirely beloved in the higher dimensions, though our human personality finds many ways to block that love from our experience. To experience the love of Creator Source is the ultimate form of healing. She extends that blessing through a warm and loving feminine presence, like a perpetual flame dedicated to the divine.

Keywords: Brigit helps us to tend the perpetual sacred flame within our thoughts to personally experience how much we are loved by our Source. She supports health, enhances our ability to manifest abundance, and can also serve as a poetic muse. Like all ascended masters, she is equally available to guide those who participate in pagan traditions, celebrate her as a Catholic saint, or follow another path altogether.

Suggested Meditation Symbol: Brigit's perpetual flame brightly glowing in a field of emerald-green (Pantone 354–355)

Buddha (Siddhartha Gautama): Buddhist Lineage
Tiphareth, Spiritual Level

Siddhartha Gautama is the name of the being who came into an earthly lifetime to achieve full enlightenment and become the Buddha (fully enlightened one). According to traditional information, Siddhartha was born in the sixth century BCE in the area that is now modern-day Nepal. His earthly father was the king who ruled the local tribe, who were economically poor and lived in conditions of hardship in that geographically remote area. His mother, Queen Maya, died just seven days after giving birth to him, but a holy man prophesied great things for the young Siddhartha: he would be either a great king and military leader or a great spiritual leader.

Siddhartha's father raised him in a palace built just for the boy and sheltered him from knowledge of religion and human hardship. According to custom, he married at the age of sixteen, but his life of total seclusion continued for another thirteen years.

One day he began to secretly venture out, and he encountered an old man, a diseased man, a decaying corpse, and an ascetic. His charioteer explained that the ascetic had renounced the world to seek release from the human fear of death and suffering. Siddhartha was overcome by these sights, and the next day, at age twenty-nine, he left his kingdom, wife, and son to lead an ascetic life, determined to find a way to relieve the universal suffering that he now understood to be one of the defining traits of humanity.

For the next six years, Siddhartha studied and meditated, using the words of various religious teachers as his guide. When answers to his questions did not appear, he redoubled his efforts, enduring pain, fasting nearly to starvation, and refusing water. Whatever he tried, Siddhartha could not reach the level of satisfaction he sought, until one day a young girl offered him a bowl of rice. As he accepted it, he suddenly realized that corporeal austerity was not the means to achieve inner liberation and that living under harsh physical constraints was not helping him to achieve spiritual release. So he had his rice, drank water, and bathed in the river.

From that time on, Siddhartha encouraged people to follow a path of balance instead of one characterized by extremism. He called this path the Middle Way. Siddhartha sat under the Bodhi tree, vowing not to get up until the truths he sought came to him. He meditated, seeing his entire life and previous lives and overcoming internal demons in his mind. He finally saw the answer to the questions of suffering that he had been seeking for so many years. In that moment of pure enlightenment, Siddhartha Gautama became the Buddha ("the who is awake"). Armed with his new knowledge, he preached his first sermon (henceforth known as "Setting in Motion the Wheel of the Dharma"), in which he explained the Four Noble Truths and the Eightfold Path, which became the pillars of Buddhism.

In my first direct experience with this master, I came to a deep meditation, seeking healing for unhappy experiences in a transpersonal lifetime as female Buddhist nun. While many people do not experience transpersonal lives, some of us do. I have found it important to clear these as they arise in consciousness.

Working with a crystal that corresponds to the Buddha, I lifted the issue up in meditation. I certainly did not expect it, but Buddha responded, coming fully into consciousness. He appeared as a massive, illuminated, abstract white presence, and I was showered with pure, unconditional love. Within this blessed experience, the lifetime of hardship melted away, and the nun's devotion to him as a great spiritual master was validated. After this experience, I experienced a stronger connection to him as well as many masters who are known from Buddhist teachings.

I have connected with Buddha on several other occasions, consciousness entering a massive, sparkling field of white light. Sometimes the words *Buddha mind* form in my consciousness during the experience. I am deeply grateful to experience his presence, especially when he comes into my meditation spontaneously, without me reaching out for him. Like all masters, he is available to support people who follow many traditions, when they can meet him without judgment.

Keywords: Siddhartha Gautama came into a physical form with the life mission to achieve full enlightenment and initiate a new spiritual lineage for humankind. Call upon the Buddha as you develop your own capacity to receive and extend unconditional love, develop advanced understanding of Buddhist practices, and cultivate inner peace through nonattachment.

Suggested Meditation Symbol: Golden eight-spoked Buddhist dharma wheel against a radiant white field

Cerridwen: Celtic Lineage
Path of Ayin (Tarot: Devil), Emotional Level Two

Cerridwen, who comes to us from Welsh tales, is associated with shape-shifting, life transformation, wisdom, prophecy, inspiration, and poetry. Her name translates as "Cauldron," one of the central Celtic symbols associated with female witches, in which they brew up a mixture that will bring inspiration and knowledge.

Cerridwen is frequently linked to the moon cycle (the dark moon phase), which is a familiar symbol for endings in the cycle of transformation. She represents the crone, the elder woman possessing power and knowledge, who channels sexual energy toward spiritual enlightenment.

An important facet of Celtic wisdom is the cyclical nature of human life experience. When one door closes, another will open. When this truth is absent from human consciousness, endings are feared, which is simply an error in perception. Endings come about in human experience (though not in ultimate reality, which is eternally changeless) so that a new cycle of life can begin. Cerridwen walks with us through some of those endings so that something new can begin.

Cerridwen's myth tells how she was brewing up a magical remedy intended for her son, Afagddu, to make him into a wise seer to compensate for his ugly physical appearance. The cauldron needed to be tended for a full year, so she gave this task to her servant boy, Gwion Bach. By accident, three drops of the liquid splashed onto his fingers, and as he licked his fingers, he instantly attained all knowledge. Frightened of Cerridwen's reaction, he turned himself into a rabbit.

Cerridwen shape-shifted and gave chase in the form of a greyhound. Gwion then became a fish and jumped into a river, and she became an otter, continuing to pursue him. He turned into a bird, and she followed as a hawk. Eventually, Gwion transformed himself into a grain of corn, and she ate him, as she had by then become a hen. The grain took seed in her womb, and nine moons later, she gave birth to the bard known as Taliesin. She was unable to kill the child; instead, she wrapped him

238

up in a leather bag and set him out to sea. He survived and became the famous Welsh poet bard.

This tale symbolically evokes many themes that were important to Celtic peoples. First, Cerridwen's awesome power is demonstrated by multiple acts of shape-shifting. Like other masters at her level, she works directly with astral fluid to create changing forms and appearances.

Others have observed that within Celtic spiritual traditions, there are common roots shared with other indigenous shamanic practices. Both male and female shamans (as well as male or female druids) possessed the spiritual power to move between the worlds, sometimes in various power animal forms, which were allies during astral travel. Through shape-shifting, Cerridwen settled a matter that was of significance to her. The most skilled enchantresses always inspired both awe and a bit of fear, for to trifle with them always had consequences!

Cerridwen came into my inner-world consciousness to offer wisdom about the most effective way to move through a major life transition that was ahead. She took me to a point of observation where I could see the fabric of my current life being ripped open. All sorts of roles and activities that had been part of my life up to that time were beside me on one side of the tear. To move ahead meant stepping into the dark void—by actively surrendering (offering up) all I had been before.

Having gone through deep times of transformation previously, within the vision, I stepped into the void without hesitation. I saw some of the different roles I would no longer enact flying off. I understood that by my willingly surrendering to the process, the astral matter that gave those precious things form in the physical world was being returned to the cauldron of all-possibility. Actively letting go with joy, love, and trust that a beautiful new cycle of experience will arrive is the attitude that best serves the journey ahead.

For every human being, this approach to endings is a learned skill. It becomes easier as we develop trust in the spiritual world to guide us. The human tendency of clinging to the familiar (which is essentially a patterned, fear-based reaction) doesn't help us when transitions arrive. Actively cooperating with the process of letting go helps our spiritual team to create the next stage of our journey quickly and helps us arrive there with minimum angst. All forms in life are created on the astral level, and Cerridwen teaches us how to become skilled shape-shifters.

Keywords: With Cerridwen's help, we can navigate endings with power and grace, shape-shifting into a positive new cycle of life. She can also be an ally to assist with various issues related to motherhood.

Suggested Meditation Symbol: Cosmic wormhole tunnel opening into the nighttime starry void, scattered with multiple pinpoints of starlight

Charlemagne: Christian Lineage
Path of Tzaddi (Tarot: Emperor), Spiritual Level

In the eighth century CE, Charlemagne was the powerful and skilled military strategist who united parts of modern-day France, Belgium, Luxembourg, the Netherlands, and Western Germany into what became the Holy Roman Empire. It was a Christian-centered earthly kingdom.

To conquer people and territory always involves bloodshed. There is a vast difference between a powerful human ego ambitiously seeking more power and glory and one who fulfills a destiny that serves a higher spiritual purpose. We can assume that those who reach ascension on this path made many choices along the way between brutality and more humane treatment of those they conquered. Few human beings are asked to carry out life missions that literally change the course of history, and few can do it while maintaining an inner moral code. Apparently, Charlemagne was one of those few. His efforts ushered in a period of accelerated artistic and literary output that advanced human civilization in a significant way.

Like some other great historical leaders, Charlemagne had a physical stature and bearing that were described as impressive. He was broad, strong, and exceptionally tall. He had many wives and mistresses and fathered some eighteen children. He enjoyed robust good health until the final four years of his life, when he suffered from fevers and a limp. He was independent until the end, refusing his doctor's orders to give up roasted meat, which he enjoyed.

He gave money and land to the Christian church and protected the popes. In return, the papacy crowned him emperor of the Romans on December 25 in the year 800 and canonized him—for political reasons—after his death. Today the church doesn't recognize his sainthood. As I have noted elsewhere, the religious designation of sainthood is not at all significant to ascended masters, who keep extending their gifts to humankind with or without such designations.

What sort of inner compass guided Charlemagne's life? According to an article called "The Talisman of Charlemagne" (see the spring 2019 issue of the journal *Gems and Gemology*, published by the Gemological Institute of America), Charlemagne wore a specific talisman. It was a reliquary pendant set with two massive cabochon sapphires. Pressed between them was a wooden sliver, purportedly from the true cross of Jesus. He rode into each battle while wearing this object, indicating that it was of great spiritual significance to him.

I knew of Charlemagne but was surprised when he contacted my consciousness. Spiritual vision revealed a somewhat abstract, physically large, and powerful male master, all gold-and-white energy, senior in apparent age, with a regal bearing. He brought his name clearly into my mind. It is difficult to describe in words the high holy dimension he inhabits. He communicated that yes, he was a sacred warrior leader, but his mission was to create a space for spiritual light during a period that was otherwise somewhat dark. I returned to experience him again later in the evening and was shown glimpses of my personal life ahead during a period of major life transition.

Keywords: Charlemagne supports the development of exceptional male leaders who are to carry out significant worldly assignments that serve a higher spiritual purpose. When one can align with his high-vibrational energy, he can also appear in consciousness (whether one is male or female) as a guide, especially when a major life transition is about to unfold.

Suggested Meditation Symbol: The jeweled crown of Charlemagne (Holy Roman Empire) against a radiant white field

Clare of Assisi: Christian Lineage
Path of Kaph (Tarot: Wheel of Fortune), Emotional Level Two

Clare of Assisi (1194–1253 CE) became the founder of a female spiritual order of nuns called the Order of Saint Clare, commonly referred to today as the Poor Clares. She wrote their Rule of Life, the first set of monastic guidelines known to have been written by a woman. She was inspired by, and a close associate of, Francis of Assisi. These like minds focused on a spiritual path of material simplicity, removing material distractions so that one could more easily focus on God. (Some beings who ascended from lifetimes in Buddhist, Hindu, and other traditions followed ascetic traditions for similar reasons.)

Traditional accounts say that Clare's father was a wealthy Roman aristocrat, and her mother was a devout noblewoman who had undertaken pilgrimages. As a child, Clare was devoted to prayer. It is assumed she was to be married, according to family tradition. However, at the age of eighteen, she heard Francis preach during a Lenten service in the Church of San Giorgio at Assisi and asked him to help her to live after the manner of the gospel.

On the evening of Palm Sunday, March 20, 1212, she left her father's house and proceeded to the chapel of the Porziuncola to meet Francis. Her hair was cut, and she exchanged her rich gown for a plain robe and veil. Francis then placed Clare in the convent of the Benedictine nuns of San Paulo, near Bastia. Her father attempted to force her to return home, but she resisted, professing that she would have no other husband but Jesus Christ.

To provide the greater solitude Clare desired, a few days later, Francis sent her to the monastery of Sant'Angelo in Panzo, where she was soon joined by her sister. They remained with the Benedictines until a small dwelling was built for them next to the church of San Damiano. Other women joined them, and they were known as the Poor Ladies of San

Damiano. They lived in enclosure, devoting themselves to a simple life of prayer and manual labor. They went barefoot, slept on the ground, ate no meat, and observed almost complete silence. While this austerity doesn't sound appealing to most of us today, we must realize that for one with mystical inclinations, it fostered the states of mystical spiritual ecstasy that women such as Clare experienced.

For a short period, the female order was directed by Francis himself. Then, in 1216, Clare accepted the role of abbess of San Damiano. As abbess, Clare had more authority to lead the order than she'd had as the prioress. Clare sought to imitate Francis's virtues and way of life. She also played a significant role in encouraging and aiding Francis and took care of him during his final illness. After Francis's death, Clare continued to promote the growth of her order.

Clare was made famous for courageously resisting the army of Frederick II when they threatened to plunder Assisi in 1224. Clare went out to meet the armed force, carrying a religious-worship object called a monstrance, or a pyx. She warded away the soldiers at the gates of her convent by displaying the Blessed Sacrament and kneeling in prayer. This act of faith brought a mysterious terror to the enemies, who fled without harming anybody in the city.

I have connected with Clare on a few occasions, usually along with Francis, experiencing the joy and deep rapport these two lights still share. Contact with them helped me understand that divine simplicity is an easy condition in which to awaken a deep personal connection with spiritual Source.

Keywords: Clare supports women who commit to spiritual devotion (within an order or not) by adopting simple lives and undertaking disciplined practices that can open spiritual vision and clairvoyance, mystical experience, ecstasy, joy, and spiritual rapture. She supports those who undertake spiritual leadership with groups of women and can protect retreat centers or other sacred meeting places.

Suggested Meditation Symbol: Golden monstrance (sacred spiritual object) radiating light against a radiant white field

Dagda (Tuatha Dé Danann): Celtic Ireland
Chokma, Mental Level

The Dagda (a title meaning "the good god") is the familiar all-father leader of the Tuatha Dé Danann. He ruled the Tuatha after King Nuada and after Lugh (see both below). According to myth, he was also the father of Brigit and Oengus (perhaps by different mothers).

The Dagda is associated with immense power; fertility; agriculture (seasons, weather, and crops); manliness; strength; magic; druidry; and great wisdom. All of these qualities are associated with other masters at Chokma.

He was believed to reside in the hill of Uisneach, in the barony of Rathconrath in County Westmeath. Today this ancient ceremonial site is a protected national monument consisting of numerous prehistoric and medieval earthworks: a probable megalithic tomb, burial mounds, enclosures, standing stones, holy wells, and a medieval road. Uisneach is near the geographic center of Ireland, and in Irish mythology, it is deemed to be the symbolic and sacred center of the island. It was said to be the burial place of mythical figures and a place of assembly associated with the druids and the festival of Beltane.

The Dagda is typically portrayed as a large man who was known for a tendency to overeat. He enthusiastically expressed his virility by mating with various goddesses. One of his liaisons was with Boann, which produced their son, Oengus mac Og (see below). Another was with the Morrigan, after which she helped the Tuatha to gain victory in battle. When the Tuatha were defeated by the Milesians, the Dagda led the Tuatha underground to the fairy mounds (symbolizing leading them into a higher dimension).

He is often pictured wearing a hooded cloak and holding his club. His club is also a powerful symbol; one end killed the living, and the other revived the dead. A common characteristic of otherworld beings at Chokma is that they help the spirit of one who has left incarnation to awaken to his or her eternal reality. Spiritual awakening can also occur for those still in human incarnation when some initiation carries awareness into the higher planes of formless reality.

The Dagda was associated with several magical objects: an immense cauldron called the Cauldron of Abundance, the Stone of Destiny, and the Sword of Nuada. The fourth object he retrieved from the otherworld was a magic harp that could change men's emotions.

I experienced Dagda as a large, abstract white energy field who radiated powerful and beneficent energy. I understand why he was called an all-father to the Celtic people, from the absolute goodness he extends. Contact with his energy is a strong push upward for consciousness, toward the higher transpersonal realms where one can experience the eternal nature of spiritual reality that exists before and after human life.

Keywords: The Dagda supports those who seek the wisdom of the realms beyond physical form to inspire their leadership and extend material abundance to a wider spectrum of humanity. He is a guide to the mysteries of the Tuatha Dé Danann and a welcoming presence for those awakening after physical life (or during a deep meditation or spiritual initiation) into their own eternal essence.

Suggested Meditation Symbol: Wooden Celtic harp carved with Celtic motifs, on a radiant white field

Danu: Celtic Lineage
Binah, Mental Level

As I became ready to attempt direct contact the masters among the Tuatha Dé Danann, I felt it was appropriate to begin with their leader, the female master named Danu. Some sources translate the name Tuatha Dé Danann as "People of Danu." After several unsuccessful attempts, I made a connection with her, experiencing an enormously strong female presence accustomed to holding considerable power and knowledge. She seemed to understand my purpose in reaching out to her and was willing to be known.

After I connected with her consciousness, some of the powerful males who are part of that lineage then came forward. The respect and unquestioned authority they still extend to their female leader is clear. I have encountered other female leaders (Russian empress Catherine the Great, Chinese empress Dowager Xi-Chi, Egyptian queen Hatshepsut, and others) who brought their powerful female leadership forward to govern earthly nations. It is one of the possible expressions of the energy of Binah. Many other female masters express female leadership in this sphere by founding new spiritual traditions.

There are various theories about Danu's origin. Various myths present her among one of the waves of conquest that came into Ireland from elsewhere. In whatever way she arrived, she became a spiritual mother and ancestral progenitor of her race, beginning a whole new chapter in a new land. This is essentially an act of mothering, albeit at the scale of a whole race.

Danu is associated with the ancient site called Newgrange, a Neolithic monument in the Boyne Valley, located in County Meath, Ireland. Conventional archaeologists date it circa 3200 BCE (which may or may not be accurate) and classify it as a passage tomb, which doesn't accurately describe its importance as a site of astrological, spiritual, and ceremonial significance.

The physical site of Newgrange today consists of a large, kidney-shaped mound covering an area of more than one acre, retained at the base by ninety-seven stones, some of which are richly decorated with megalithic art. The inner passage, nineteen meters in length, leads to a cruciform inner chamber with a corbeled roof. At dawn, from December 19 to 23, a narrow beam of light penetrates the roof box and reaches the floor of the chamber, gradually extending to the rear of the chamber. As the sun rises higher, the beam widens within the chamber so that the whole room becomes dramatically illuminated. This event (in the physical dimension) lasts for seventeen minutes, beginning around nine o'clock in the morning. The astronomical accuracy of Newgrange is remarkable, pointing to ancient builders in possession of advanced knowledge. Its full spiritual significance remains for seekers to discover with the help of Danu.

I experienced an interdimensional visit to Newgrange during one of my most profound experiences with Danu. It began as the well-known triple spiral carved into the entrance stone came into full inner vision. Her energy was present in an abstract way, with radiant colors streaming from that triple-spiral carving. My field of view then shifted to observe the inside of the tunnel—from within the innermost chamber—just as the solstice ray of light entered the tunnel opening. I had known this phenomenon existed but never had imagined witnessing it in this way.

Keywords: Danu supports women to develop and claim advanced spiritual knowledge, leadership, and power. She is a guide to the mysteries of the Tuatha Dé Danann and supports women who initiate a new chapter of life in a new land.

Suggested Meditation Symbol: The Newgrange triple spiral in deep purple (Pantone 265–266), against a deep blue cosmos (Pantone 282) with sparkling white stars

Deborah: Judaic Lineage
Path of Lamed (Tarot: Adjustment and Balance), Emotional Level Two

According to biblical accounts in Judges 4 and 5, in the twelfth century BCE, a female leader named Deborah became the fourth judge (a charismatic leader) of premonarchic Israel. She is the only female mentioned in the Bible who served in that capacity. The name Deborah means "Bee" or "Honeybee." She was stated to be the wife of Lapidoth and was described as a prophet, judge, military leader, songwriter, and minstrel. Deborah is introduced, as are the other eleven male judges, in the biblical book of Judges—without fanfare. However, in a text remarkably poor in roles for female leaders, she is therefore remarkable, and the Bible records no dissent or rebellion against her leadership.

The Bible reports that the Israelites recognized her abilities and prospered under her tenure. She led Israel for sixty years. Her oversight covered approximately twenty years of national hardship before the Canaanite war and then a peaceful aftermath of forty years. She is portrayed as a decisive figure in the defeat of the Canaanites, a victory told in two accounts: a prose narrative in Judges 4 and an ancient song known as "The Song of Deborah," a victory hymn probably composed not long after the original events, possibly by Deborah herself (which is preserved in Judges 5). The song describes the chaotic conditions that existed until "you arose, Deborah, arose as a mother in Israel."

Deborah judged while under a palm tree—a setting, as rabbinic tradition maintains, that validated her fairness, openness, and refusal to show partiality. Her arbitration powers as judge were parental, even maternal. The text in Judges that describes her is of great importance for providing a contemporary glimpse of Israelite civilization in the twelfth century BCE. According to rabbinic tradition, she was also a keeper of tabernacle lamps.

Like each of the masters I've encountered, Deborah has a distinctive energy when met in consciousness. As I felt into her energy, my hand did automatic writing. Later, I found that I had written, "What a pistol she is." Others might have used words like "A strong, sharp mind who wasn't fazed by anything and held to her opinions with gusto!" I could also feel that she had great compassion, expressed through the decisions she made. She gave people a second chance when that was possible, especially first offenders who broke the law or those whose circumstances mitigated what they had done. Her personal qualities made her outstanding in a time when few such opportunities were available for women, but those qualities would serve any judge equally well today.

Keywords: Deborah supports women who claim their connection to inner wisdom, justice, and fairness and serve in a public capacity as outspoken, charismatic leaders to guide their people (politically) toward peace and a more abundant life.

Suggested Meditation Symbol: Palm tree against a radiant white field

Demeter: Greek Lineage
Binah, Emotional Level Two

Greek myth includes Demeter among the original twelve Olympians. She was celebrated annually in the ancient Greek mystery tradition known as the Eleusinian Mysteries for nearly a thousand years. Her cultural importance was summarized by the ancient Athenian rhetorician Isocrates, who concluded that Demeter's greatest gifts to humankind were the mysteries, which give the spiritual initiate higher hopes in this life and the afterlife, and agriculture, particularly cereal grains, which nurture humanity during their physical lifetime.

Major cults to Demeter are known in a great many Greek locations. Her cult titles include Sito, meaning "She of the Grain," and Thesmophoros, which translates as "Divine Order, Unwritten Law."

According to Joan Breton Connelly in *Portrait of a Priestess*, Demeter's priestesses were among the most highly respected in Greece, surpassed only by the Athenian priestesses of Athena Polis. They held the dual title priestess of Demeter and Kore. (Greek Kore is better known to us today under her Roman name, Persephone.) As one indication of the importance of Demeter, the personal names of the women who presided over Demeter's sanctuaries were used to date important Greek events that took place during their tenancy.

Some scholars believe that the name we understand today as Demeter appears in Linear A (a writing system used by the ancient Minoans of Crete from about 1800 to 1450 BCE). Linear A has still not been satisfactorily translated, so this remains a theory. Demeter is also attested in the Linear B Mycenean Greek tablets dated circa 1400–1200 BCE that were found at Pylos. Clearly, she dates from an ancient period.

Demeter's Thesmophoria festival (October 11–13) was for women only, while her Eleusinian Mysteries were open to initiates of any gender or social class. At the heart of both festivals were myths concerning Demeter as mother and Kore (Persephone) as her daughter.

The Eleusinian Mysteries took place in September of each year. Her priestess would set out from Eleusis, accompanied by other priestesses and many others assisting, carrying holy objects in a long eighteen-mile procession to their sanctuary in the center of Athens, at the foot of the Acropolis. They remained there for four days. Anyone could participate in the general ceremony, which began with the washing of piglets that would later be sacrificed. On the fourth day, the new initiates spent the day indoors in seclusion. On the fifth day, they made the long procession back to Eleusis to receive their initiation into the mysteries.

In addition to ripened grain, another of Demeter's symbols is the poppy, a bright red flower that grows among the barley. It is believed that a vision-inducing elixir known as *kykeon* came from ergot that formed on the barley, a substance not unlike LSD. This elixir was served to the most advanced initiates as part of the initiation ceremony. Another of her symbols is the pomegranate (related to Persephone's annual months spent in the underworld). Death and rebirth are also part of the initiate's experience in the mystery cults.

Perhaps from deep transpersonal memories, for many years, I found myself thinking of Demeter each year at the time when the Eleusinian Mysteries had been celebrated. Despite my strong attraction, it took a long time to get her Qabalah and crystal correspondence correct. When I finally did, her incredibly feminine energy gently flowed in to surround and lift my conscious to exquisite realms. I understood why she became a symbol for spiritual as well as seasonal agricultural renewal.

I was also working with Zeus, and after allowing her to come forward alone, he joined in. His energy lit my spiritual vision, and I could see the weblike structure connecting above my crown to the higher realms. As they worked together, the feeling of regeneration to my original template was cellular, strong, and lasting. The result left me no doubt about the nature of their relationship, which was intimate and blessed. I have experienced the combination of more than a few masters who were sexually intimate during life and whose passionate connection can still be experienced in the ascended realm.

Keywords: Call upon Demeter to help you recognize eternal life by opening the crown chakra. She is a guide to the Eleusinian Mystery traditions, supports deep work in mother-daughter relationships, and helps us create life-enhancing abundance during our earthly lives.

Suggested Meditation Symbol: Golden-ripe sheaf of wheat against a rich purple field (Pantone 265–266)

Durga: Hindu Lineage
Path of Teth (Tarot: Lust and Strength), Spiritual Level

Durga is a fierce and beloved Hindu female often portrayed riding on a tiger. She is protective of human life and the spiritual evolution of humankind. She is a central deity in the Shakti tradition and has a significant following all over India and Bangladesh and in Nepal. Archaeological finds in Java have yielded numerous statues of her. She is also known in Cambodia and Vietnam. All known artifacts date from the sixth century CE onward. While she heads some pantheons, in others, she is introduced as one of the wives or consorts of Shiva.

Durga unleashes her destructive side to combat all negative influences to serve the highest expressions of spiritual liberation. At the same time, she is also nurturing and protective. She and other male and female masters at the spiritual level of Teth are all forces to be reckoned with. The word *durga* means "impassable, inaccessible, invincible, unassailable." It is related to the word *durg*, which means "fortress" or "something difficult to access, attain, or pass."

While the word *durga* is found in the Vedas, the descriptions by that name lack the details found about her in later Hindu literature. The Rigveda hymn called "Devi Suktam" may be a description of her. As Devi, she is also linked to the name Durga in the Upanishads.

Durga features prominently in the *Devi Mahatmya*, or *Devi Mahatmyam*, which translates as "Glory of the Goddess." This is a Hindu religious text—part of the Markandeya Purana and estimated to have been composed in Sanskrit between 400 and 600 CE—that describes the goddess as the supreme power and Creator of the universe. The *Devi Mahatmyam* describes a storied battle between good and evil, wherein Devi, manifesting as goddess Durga, led the forces of good against the deceitful buffalo demon Mahishasura. The goddess appeared angry and ruthless, and the forces of good won. By killing him, she saved the world from annihilation and darkness. After this victory, she promised her devotees she would come to their rescue in times of distress and danger, saving them from thieves, assault, fire, lions, tigers, elephants, demons, enemies, imprisonment, execution, shipwreck, and invading armies. No wonder she was so beloved!

I have been attracted to Durga for many years. My first deep experience of her in meditation, occurred when I was working with other female masters from the Hindu lineage. Her energy was as familiar as a dear friend. She simply used the name Devi in my mind, and the experience of being immersed in her powerful and loving energy was sublime.

On a few other occasions, I had a brief vision of her familiar many-armed form, riding a tiger. She communicated that I was to pay attention to the weapons she carried (and reminded me to use them!). All ascended masters invite us to use what they have mastered and, thus, join them in the higher realms.

On another occasion, she communicated that consciousness is the greatest weapon of all that serves spiritual awakening, and she wanted a specific one of the weapons she carries (Shiva's trident) to be part of her meditation symbol in this book. In another experience she communicated that she has many other related forms, which correspond to different parts of the Qabalah. They are known under different names, but just as Buddhist Tara has different forms that emanate from a single higher energy, so does Durga. This made sense to me, as at times, I had sensed some of her other related manifestations.

Durga is celebrated in major annual festivals (lasting four or nine days) in Bengal, Odisha, Assam, Jharkhand, and Bihar. The festivals are scheduled per the Hindu lunisolar calendar in the month of Ashvin and typically fall in September or October. The celebration includes making special colorful images of Durga out of clay, along with recitations of the *Devi Mahatmya* text, prayers, and revelry for nine days, after which the image is taken out in procession with singing and dancing and then immersed in water. The Durga puja is an occasion of major private and public festivity in the eastern and northeastern states of India.

Keywords: Durga offers us tools for self-empowerment so that we can move—fearlessly—through every apparent challenge toward our fullest spiritual potential. While she offers many weapons, each of which represents forces extended by other masters to overcome obstacles to spiritual progress, the most powerful weapon we can use is the ability to direct our own consciousness toward the higher realms.

Suggested Meditation Symbol: The eyes of Durga (dramatic, stylized open female eyes and eyebrows) with a red bindi dot between them and the trident of Shiva on the forehead, against a radiant white field

Eir: Norse Lineage
Path of Yod (Tarot: Hermit), Emotional Level Two

In Norse mythology, Eir (whose name translates from Old Norse as "Protection, Help, Mercy") is a goddess associated with medical skill. Eir is attested in *The Poetic Edda*, which was compiled in the thirteenth century from earlier traditional sources; in *The Prose Edda*, which was written in the thirteenth century by Snorri Sturluson; and in skaldic poetry, including a runic inscription from Bergen, Norway, from around 1300. Her distinction as a servant of both Frigg and Odin and her important function have earned her a place of veneration among those today who honor the Norse pantheon.

Several other Norse deities are sometimes called upon for help with healing. Eir, however, is the preeminent and principal healer in the Northern tradition. The official healer of a warrior people would have had to be skilled in surgery. She was called to the battlefield as the first responder, and her skill could make the difference between life and death. Before the rise of the male-dominated medical institutions of Europe, community healing and medical care in Norse and Germanic countries were largely the sphere of women.

Healing methods included prayers, magic, midwifery practices, surgery, herbalism, home remedies, copper bracelets and detoxes using saunas.

Folk tradition holds that Eir was invoked in healing rituals using a white flower known as an Eir flower. She is also associated with copper, which was used in healing ceremonies. Some of her symbols include mortars and pestles, healing instruments, bandages, saunas, healing herbs, home remedies, folk medicine, copper, and hilltops.

When I contacted Eir in inner-world experience, she was quickly surrounded by wild plants and flowers and communicated that (in addition to all the different healing modalities she supports) she could be called upon by those who use flower essences today to be able to understand the special uses of each one and to make pure remedies.

Keywords: Eir supports women and men who use alternative vibrational remedies, spiritual healing, energy healing, and herbal medicine. For those with a strong lifetime focus on the path of Yod, the need for personal healing may direct them to explore alternative approaches, which, when successful, may then be extended to others.

Suggested Meditation Symbol: A flagon with a stopper, painted with the image of an Eir flower (a small white flower with petals open, in full bloom), against a light pastel-yellow field (Pantone 458 and 459)

Enoch: Judaic Lineage
Path of Cheth (Tarot: Chariot), Spiritual Level

Enoch, son of Jared, is mentioned in the biblical book of Genesis as the seventh of the ten predeluge patriarchs, all of whom are described to have lived lifetimes of phenomenal length that would be considered miraculous by any standards based on human life expectancy. Enoch was said to have lived 365 years, and then he "walked with God: and then he was no more; for God took him." (Genesis 5:21-24)

The Bible is not the only document that mentions Enoch. There are also various Apocryphal books of Enoch (found among the Dead Sea Scrolls), which recount how Enoch was taken up to heaven in a winged chariot; was appointed guardian of all celestial treasures; and returned to share his visions, including the golden four-wheeled Merkabah chariot throne of god. These writings place Enoch as the founder of what came to be known as Merkabah mysticism, or the chariot tradition.

According to the extensive research of Judaic scholar Rachel Elior in *The Three Temples*, Enoch (in a way distinctly different from the accomplishments of Abraham and Moses) carried out a unique role as transmitter of the covenant between the Judaic lineage and the divine realms. Some Jewish groups, while exiled from their native homeland, worked with mystery traditions through Enoch's writings. They studied the writings as preparation for the uplifting of consciousness that occurred during spiritual initiation. In this way, the books of Enoch are evidence for Jewish mystical traditions that didn't emphasize the law of Moses or the sacrificial cult. For that reason, they were later outlawed.

Modern scholars note that fragments of these books, copied by many different hands, have been found, attesting to their widespread popularity from about the third century BCE to the third century of our era (when they were declared heretical). It is believed that Zadokites (the original priesthood established by King Solomon, who were exiled in Egypt), as well as the Essenes, Egyptian Therapeutae, Johannite Christians, and others, were inspired by Enoch's lofty descriptions of the numinous beauty of the divine realms, union with God, meetings with angels, and cosmic flights of conscious.

Enoch's mystical ascent has been interpreted in other ways, including that he experienced a visit with extraterrestrial beings who shared wisdom to assist humanity's evolution. By whatever means his insights arrived, they include topics such as cosmic law; medicine; dreams; astronomy; angelology; and knowledge of sacred numbers, such as seven, twelve, and thirteen. Enoch's number symbolism was part of the revealed basis for the solar calendar used by the Aaronite priesthood (First Temple of King Solomon), which synchronized earthly temple worship with angelic worship in the seven levels of heavenly temples

(Heikhalot). Divine time thus formed a vertical axis that linked heaven and earth based upon the solar calendar.

When I turned toward Enoch in meditation, his energy was huge and powerfully uplifting for consciousness. He communicated that he was a transmitter of the chariot mystical practices and gave me some general impressions of how this prepared the human energy body to be able to transmit higher energies. It is well known in different spiritual traditions that while every member of humanity possesses the ability for ascension in potential, the ability requires spiritual development, which awakens the energy body in specific ways.

Keywords: Enoch assists humankind to develop their advanced subtle energy body capacities (helping to transmit a systems upgrade, so to speak) so that consciousness can lift toward the spiritual realms and be prepared for ascension.

Suggested Meditation Symbol: Gold star of Enoch mystical symbol against a radiant white field

Ezekiel: Judaic Lineage
Binah, Mental Level

Ezekiel was born in the sixth century BCE into a family of priestly lineage. The book of Ezekiel in the Old Testament is named for him. His famous mystical vision of the four-wheeled chariot of God represented his prophetic calling.

Ezekiel is commemorated as a saint or prophet in many religious traditions, including the Eastern Orthodox Church, Eastern Catholic churches that follow the Byzantine Rite, the Calendar of Saints of the Armenian Apostolic Church in the Roman Martyrology, and certain Lutheran churches. He is also among the prophets recognized by Islamic tradition.

According to biblical accounts, Ezekiel demonstrated advanced spiritual power in a scene in which he overcame priests of other religions by causing fire to rain down on an altar and dramatically consume the sacrifice placed there. He could also raise the dead. His miraculous skills ensured an ever-renewing basket of flour and flagon of oil that could care for a widow during times of famine.

Ezekiel's early prophesies (from circa 592 BCE) in Jerusalem were pronouncements of violence and destruction (like those of Jeremiah). In that period, Ezekiel was most likely a functioning priest attached to the Jerusalem Temple.

During the exile period, Ezekiel and his wife lived on the banks of the Chebar River, in what is now Iraq. His later oracles addressed the hopes of the Israelites exiled in Babylon, which resulted in the ultimate establishment of a new covenant between God and the people of Israel. He thus had a profound influence on the postexile reorganization of Judaism. Ezekiel understood that he was going to be taken directly to heaven without dying at the end of his life, so he was guided to seek out Elisha to train as his successor.

According to Judaic scholar Rachel Elior in *The Three Temples*, the biblical book of Ezekiel offers three references in which he specifically affirms Zadokite (rather than later Hasmonaean) priesthood legitimacy: Ezekiel 40:46, 43:10, and 46:15–28. She makes a good argument that the authors of some of the Dead Sea documents, many of which were steeped in Judaic mysticism, were exiled Zadokite priests. Zadok was Aaron's first son, and his hereditary descendants served as priests throughout the whole First Temple period, until they were exiled. Ezekiel came from this mystical background, and in this regard, his compelling vision was no accident.

Another compelling link cited by Elior is that Ezekiel's vision is described to have occurred on Shavuot (which, in Dead Sea Scroll writings, is the important anniversary of the covenant). His vision included a rainbow, which ties it to the rainbow covenant received by Noah, and described the Merkabah chariot throne surrounded by spiritual fire, smoke, and heavenly sounds, not unlike the experience revealed by Enoch (see above). All these examples align Ezekiel with the traditions of the First Temple period.

While some in our time interpret Ezekiel's vision (like Enoch's vision) as a phenomenon of extraterrestrial contact, even if this is true, it doesn't preclude its spiritual significance. The book of Ezekiel also deals with the future temple and Zadokite priests—guardians of the Merkabah tradition. While there were efforts within later Mishnaic tradition to suppress the reading of Ezekiel's vision at Shavuot, it continued to remain important.

In direct experience, Ezekiel appeared as a massive, abstract purple-white presence whose holiness was compellingly attractive. My consciousness simply wanted to remain united with his energy forever. While we cannot maintain such states during daily life, when the opportunity presents itself, the experience of such contact calls forth the same vibration from within us. (We all contain these energies, which can emerge into full manifestation as we evolve spiritually.) Practicing holding and extending—only this—is how we develop certainty about the divine energy that connects each of us to our Source exactly as we are.

Keywords: Within a life as a priest and prophet, Ezekiel experienced initiation into the higher realms beyond human experience. As a result, he became a key to the restoration and revision of faith, a beacon to guide humanity toward our divine essence. Now, from the nonphysical realms, he supports all humanity to lift their thoughts toward the divine.

Suggested Meditation Symbol: Fiery chariot wheels with eyes, against a purple field (Pantone 265–266)

Fionn mac Cumhail: Celtic Lineage
Tiphareth, Mental Level

Fionn, whose name is often anglicized as Finn McCool or Finn MacCool, was arguably the greatest hunter-warrior leader in Irish mythology. He also appears in stories from Scotland and the Isle of Man. He grew up to lead the fierce band of Iron Age warriors known as the Fianna. For most of the year, these small bands of young men lived in the wild, hunting, raiding other communities and lands, training, and fighting as mercenaries. Some scholars believe the *fian* was a rite of passage into manhood. The stories about Fionn form the Fenian Cycle, much of it narrated in the voice of Fionn's son, the poet Oisín.

According to myth, Fionn was born under trying circumstances. His father, who had also been a leader of the Fianna, asked for the hand in marriage of Muirne, Fionn's mother, from her father, who was a powerful druid in Kildaire. Muirne's father refused him, but she was already pregnant with their child. As a result, Fionn's father was hunted and killed. Muirne was forced to flee, leaving her son in the care of his druidess aunt, a warrior woman called Liath Luachra. The two women raised Fionn in secret in a forest, teaching him how to hunt and fight from an early age. When he was old enough, they sent him to serve the local king, without revealing his identity. Fionn charmed everyone he met, but when they discovered his parentage, he was sent away.

While wandering the lands of various kings, he came across a druid called Finnegas by the River Boyne. Finnegas had spent several years searching for a certain salmon that, while passing through the Well of Wisdom, had eaten nine hazelnuts that had fallen into the well and, in doing so, had gained all the wisdom of the world.

Finnegas became Fionn's teacher in the druidic arts while he cast his line into the River Boyne every day in the hope of hooking the fish. Suddenly, one day, it happened: he hooked a giant salmon. He was overjoyed! Exhausted by his great deed, he took to his bed and left Fionn to cook it.

Somewhat like the tale of Cerridwen and her assistant Gwion Bach, the tale of Fionn claims that some fat from the fish splashed onto Fionn's thumb, burning him. Fionn then stuck his thumb into his mouth, as one does with such a burn; licked his finger; and received the great wisdom.

Armed with natural fighting and hunting ability and now with all knowledge at his disposal, Fionn was poised to be a remarkable leader. He lacked, however, the trust of those who blamed him for his father's death. During one Samhain feast when Fionn was a young adult, he gained the admiration of all by defeating a fire-breathing fairy called Aillen, who had been tormenting Tara (seat of the high kings of Ireland) for the previous twenty-three years. His prowess was celebrated, his heritage finally was recognized, and he was given command of the fierce band of warriors known as the Fianna.

As leader of the Fianna, he became a larger-than-life presence: a tall, handsome blond leader possessed of athletic prowess and skill in weaponry. He won many battles, cured the sick, hunted abundantly in forests, and gained legendary renown. He was also credited with carving mountain passes, hollowing out caves, and creating various rock formations (including the geologic phenomenon known as the Giant's Causeway) with his superhuman strength.

Fionn is most often associated with the Leinster region, particularly Kildare and the Hill of Allen. Many centuries later, his name (and that of his band) still commands great respect. A variant of his name, Fianna Fail, was adopted in 1926 as the name of the nationalist political party formed during the struggle for independence. It translates as "Warriors of Ireland."

I tried several different warrior correspondences before I was able to contact Fionn.

When I made contact, his energy arrived within a billowing field of white light, in which many minds were present (the Fianna). In automatic writing, "Warriors of the Light" was all I captured, as the energy was so powerful.

Keywords: Fionn supports those (male and female alike) whose spiritual quest for the knowledge of ultimate reality carves out a life of heroic proportions. He can also guide those who learn the ancient druidic arts.

Suggested Meditation Symbol: Many-rayed golden sun against a field of radiant white, with a long metal-tipped spear superimposed horizontally across the sun (similar to the central part of the Fianna Éireann symbol)

Forseti: Norse Lineage
Path of Lamed (Tarot: Adjustment and Justice), Emotional Level Two

The Norse tales introduce Forseti as a member of the Aesir. He was the son of Baldur and Nanna and, thus, the grandson of Odin and Frigg. Typically, in Norse tales, we learn of those who enacted swift vengeance to right a wrong, yet somehow, Forseti approached disputes with fairness, recognizing that there are two sides to any conflict. He was a master of skillful mediation, able to see both sides of an issue and arrive at a just and equitable solution.

Snorri says about him in *The Prose Edda*, "He has that hall in heaven, which is called Glitnir 'shining' [referring to its silver ceiling and golden pillars, which radiated light that could be seen far away], and all who come to him in legal difficulties go away reconciled. That is the best place of judgment of gods and men."

I reached out to Forseti when I was working with other masters in the Norse pantheon. His energy extends from within a field that I could only call "the spirit of fairness." While Norse myth doesn't inform us specifically about matters Forseti helped to resolve, some of the tales mention conflicts that arose among the Aesir. Whenever personalities interact, matters will not always go smoothly. There will be friction, and unexpected complications can arise.

What qualities might have allowed Forseti to be considered a successful mediator among his people? To be fair, one must first grant that everyone has an equal right to be heard and have his or her needs considered, rather than only those who possess much gold or are quick with a sword. Beyond impartiality, he would have needed patience, an ability to ask insightful and penetrating questions, and seasoned wisdom to make whatever adjustments were needed to arrive at practical solutions. He would also have needed the authority to make those decisions binding. A man with such qualities would indeed bring a welcome mastery to any group and thus serve the cause of justice for all.

Keywords: You can call upon Forseti when you are experiencing a conflict with someone that you hope to resolve through mediation or take before an impartial judge in a court of law. He also supports those who train to serve as mediators, attorneys, or judges, helping them to bring common sense as well as skill with legal doctrine forward to help humankind arrive at peaceful solutions to interpersonal conflicts.

Suggested Meditation Symbol: Upright profile of a Norse battle-ax with a wooden handle and a golden blade (symbol of authority to make his decisions binding) against a radiant white field.

Francis of Assisi, Saint: Christian Lineage
Chesed, Mental Level

The man who came to be known as Francis of Assisi (1181/82–1226 CE) is a beloved spiritual figure to many. He embraced a radical lifestyle of material simplicity, attempting to follow in the footsteps of Jesus, which led him to establish the Franciscan order. A true mystic, he experienced spiritual ecstasies, and near the end of his life, he experienced the stigmata (i.e., the physical phenomenon of the wounds of Jesus's crucifixion appearing in his physical body). Following his death, he was quickly canonized (declared a saint) by the Catholic church.

While his holiness appeals to many, some find the notion of sainthood built up around him to be daunting. In *The Saint and the Sultan* by investigative journalist Paul Moses, we move past the religious perspective to discover facts about Francis's personal life that help us relate to him today.

Moses's research paints a startling picture of Francis in his youth. He was a handsome, witty young nobleman from a wealthy family who delighted in fine clothes; was a devotee of troubadours; and wished to become a great knight. In 1202, he had his first opportunity to ride into armed conflict in the battle between Assisi and neighboring Perugia, which was far from glamorous. He was exposed to the horrors of war, which landed him a year in a dark prison cell.

After being released from prison, he made a spiritual pilgrimage to Rome and was inspired by a spiritual vision of Christ to renounce his former worldly life and rebuild churches. With no assets of his own to raise funds, he sold some cloth from his father's store, which drew his father's wrath. He was dragged home, beaten, bound, and locked in a small storeroom. Soon his father brought the case before the city consuls, and Francis renounced his father and his inheritance by way of restitution.

Over the following two years, he embraced the life of a penitent, during which he restored several ruined chapels in the countryside around Assisi with his own hands. Next, he took to nursing lepers. One morning in February 1208, Francis was hearing a mass based on the book of Matthew. The disciples were told to go proclaim that the kingdom of God was at hand, taking no money, second tunic, sandals, or even a walking stick. As he heard those words, he was inspired to devote himself to a life of poverty, bypass the distraction of worldly possessions, and value only the eternal.

Francis discovered gifts as a preacher. Since his inspiration came from within, he was able to address villagers (and later popes and kings) with words that flowed from his heart. The way of life he adopted, following in the footsteps of Jesus, drew others to him, and in 1209, the pope approved the founding of his order.

In 1219, during the Fifth Crusade, Francis traveled to Egypt on a dangerous mission across enemy lines, hoping to convert the sultan to Christianity. While his peace mission did not end the war, it was an example of his radical spiritual philosophy of love—even for one's enemies—that he understood Jesus to advocate. His contact with the sultan also left him with a genuine respect for the religious traditions of others.

Francis returned from his peace mission in Egypt to find that factions within his own order had taken it in directions that were far from his original intent. During the last years of his life, he resigned as its leader. Paul Moses cites ancient sources that show Francis was angry about this, but he forgave all concerned before his death.

I have experienced several contacts with Francis. My heart

immediately responded to his close presence, and my sense was of a spiritual father. Another experience began as a portal opened, and I was flooded with what I could only note as "the light of Assisi." Francis was present within that current, along with other masters from different traditions. On another occasion, he brought one of his practices. It is simply to actively love all of creation as a daily practice—people, the earth, the animal kingdom, the angelic kingdom, and the ascended masters. To stay in this radiant state will eventually open a window in consciousness so that one can experience receiving the divine love that is eternally extended to all by Source.

Keywords: Francis is a guide for those who choose to live simply and focus on spiritual ideals. He supports all who conduct missions of peace and extend unconditional love and compassionate service. He can be an ally to help one overcome conflicts with the values of one's birth family and develop respect for the religious traditions of others.

Suggested Meditation Symbol: Simple wooden crucifix on a sapphire-blue field (blues brighter to darker, Pantone 281–295)

Freya: Norse Lineage
Netzach, Emotional Level Two

Freya (sometimes spelled Freyja) is one of the two most familiar females mentioned in Norse myth (the other being Frigg). She is described as a member of the Vanir tribe, the daughter of Njord (see below), and the sister of Freyr (also an ascended master, though he is not included here). Some sources suggest the names Freya and Frigg refer to the same being; however, I have contacted them in different parts of the Qabalah, through different minerals.

Freya, at the Qabalah sphere of Netzach, offers mastery teachings to help us refine our approach to love, material abundance, and personal values (the nature of things we desire to manifest in life). Norse myths portray her as a beautiful and lusty woman fond of material luxury. She drove a chariot pulled by two cats, was fond of erotic poetry, was known for sexual liaisons with both men and dwarves and was the object of desire for several giants. In some sources, she was said to be married to a man whose name is sometimes translated as Odr. Those working with the Norse pantheon have long been advised to call upon Freya regarding all matters of love.

Both Freya and her brother, Freyr, are understood to be fertility deities—for women and men, respectively. Early Norse culture granted wide acceptance to women surrounding their expression of sexuality. However, even in the more tolerant views of Norse myth, Freya seems to be criticized for being overly lusty.

Myth also describes Freya, like several of the Norse females, as a master of seidr, Norse magic. There are contradictory tales stating that she was the first to bring seidr to the Aesir, although in others, it was already a skill evidenced by Frigg, Gullveig, and the primordial female Gefjun. It is possible Freya's cats, said to pull her chariot through the skies, are symbolic of her magical abilities.

To put Freya's desire for gold into a cultural context, in the raw, challenging Viking culture, material wealth was not a given. Plans for gaining gold were a strategy to help one survive in an otherwise uncertain time. Generosity to guests was also an important cultural value. One of Freya's strategies to gain gold was to make love to each of the four dwarves who crafted a magnificent golden necklace known as Brisingamen. Women throughout the ages have been known to parlay beauty and sexual attractiveness for financial security. Such bargains— even when made by the woman herself—come with a high cost for her in terms of independence, authenticity, and self-worth. Women who have the freedom to make their own choices can learn from Freya's model, rather than playing this principle out in their own lives.

All Freya's best (and worst) qualities come together in the part of *The Poetic Edda* wherein the king of the Jotun (giants) steals Thor's hammer, Mjolnir. Freya lends Loki her falcon cloak (a magical object) to search for it, but upon returning, Loki tells Freya the king has hidden the hammer and demanded to marry her in return for it. Freya is so angry that all the Aesir's halls beneath her are shaken, and the necklace Brisingamen breaks off from her neck. The storyline of being married off against her will evokes the issue (still present in many cultures today) of women being denied the ability to decide their own marriage partners.

My own experience with Freya was like bathing in green currents of divine feminine energy. She helps women to appreciate their beauty and the gift of being in a female body (on a female planet), enjoy healthy sexual pleasure, and maintain a quality of eternal youth despite chronological age. She teaches us that we can tap into the pure essence and female life force as we give up self-limiting ideas about aging. As with all ascended masters, there was no experience of any personality flaws like those described in some of her myths. Her energy was pure and regenerative to experience.

Keywords: Call upon Freya to create material abundance without excess, maintain your own ageless physical beauty (without being identified with it), and grow discernment that channels your desire toward sexual partners and possessions that serve your highest good.

Suggested Meditation Symbol: Freya's chariot pulled by two cats against an emerald-green field (Pantone 347)

Frigg: Norse Lineage
Path of Da'leth (Tarot: Empress), Mental Level

Frigg appears in Norse myth as the wise queen of Asgard (wife of Odin and mother of Baldur), one of the two most well-known females in Norse myth, with the other being Freya. They are described in myth with some overlapping attributes, though each of them corresponds to a different part of the Qabalah.

Frigg can be met on the path of Da'leth. Understanding her mastery begins with reviewing all the activities of a highly esteemed queen who is married to a powerful male partner. Such women develop a nurturing sphere of influence all their own and maintain power and autonomy within that arena. The path of a partner relationship can produce powerful evolution, which may include life lessons about fidelity and developing the wisdom to run a kingdom.

Such queens also may give birth to significant heirs (Frigg birthed the prince named Baldur, described above). Frigg unsuccessfully attempted to protect her son by making everything in creation take a sacred oath not to harm him. In the Icelandic accounts, she forgot the mistletoe, and Loki used the plant to do away with him. Though she sent Hermod to attempt to retrieve Baldur from the underworld, she had to ultimately accept her son's death (which also makes her a compassionate ally for women facing a similar grief process).

As a wise queen, Frigg established her own sphere of influence by engaging in battles of wit with Odin. Sometimes this resulted in her ideas being carried out. She held authority over management of the palace resources and demonstrated her ability to provide earthly abundance through her association with weaving. (Weaving was Iceland's primary export and source of economic stability from medieval times until at least 1600 CE.) She developed a retinue of trusted helpers (many females are listed as handmaidens of Frigg), whom she sent out on various special errands. She also had the gift of prophecy but did not reveal all she knew.

However, Frigg is much more than an earthly queen. In iconography, she is often depicted with a distaff (used for spinning and weaving). The distaff also has another meaning. It is also a symbol for time, beginnings and endings, birth and death, and the light of heaven. All this is appropriate for the lofty sphere of Da'leth at the mental level, where the higher realms become firmly anchored in consciousness.

In my first experience with Frigg, she came forward in my consciousness along with Odin. Their energies were joined in a seamless partnership, yet I could distinguish each of them individually. She matched him in power, and the result was an ecstatic soaring in the higher dimensions. My deepest personal experience with her came months later. She let me know she preferred one of the other translations of her name: Frija, from High German, which translates as "Beloved." The sound of the name Frigg did feel a bit harsh for the regal, feminine presence that is her energy. I extended a lot of love and gratitude as

267

I merged with her consciousness, and at some point, she turned all that energy around and flooded me with love. Then she proceeded to bring me a personal practice to move through scenes that appear challenging to human perception. Even after many different experiences with masters, this level of contact is more precious than can be conveyed in words.

Keywords: Call upon Frigg to assist you in developing wit and wisdom to manifest a balanced and successful relationship with a powerful male partner. She can support you to run your kingdom wisely, create abundance, and fulfill the role of motherhood to your children. She is also a guide between the worlds of life and the heavenly realm, whose love and guidance help to remind consciousness of the eternal view as human life concludes.

Suggested Meditation Symbol: Distaff weaving white clouds, against a radiant white field

Ganesha: Hindu Lineage
Chesed, Mental Level

Ganesha is an immensely popular being in the Hindu pantheon and beyond, known as a lord of good fortune and the remover of obstacles, both material and spiritual. Within Hindu teachings, he is known as the son of Shiva and Parvati. Several Hindu texts relate anecdotes that purport to explain his distinct iconographic form: an elephant head with a broken tusk.

In one story, Parvati, wishing to bathe, created a boy and assigned him the task of guarding the entrance to her bathroom. When her husband, Shiva, returned home, he was denied access and killed the boy, striking his head off with a sword. Parvati was understandably upset, so Shiva sent out his warriors to obtain the head of the first dead creature they could find. They happened to find an elephant. The head was attached to the body of the boy, and he was brought back to life.

Two different stories about Ganesha relate how his tusk came to be broken. In one, he broke it off himself to write down the Hindu epic tale Mahabharata, as was being relayed to him by higher spiritual forces. In a different tale, Ganesha's father, Shiva, decided to take a nap and asked his son to guard him. Sleeping Shiva was attacked by a Brahman warrior, but Ganesha stopped the attack with his tusk, which broke as the intruder's ax hit it. This incident was interpreted as a demonstration of Ganesha's loyalty and devotion. For this reason, Ganesha statues are typically placed facing doorways, as protective symbols.

The energy-medicine symbolized by elephants has always included the qualities of loyalty, wisdom, and longevity. Set against the ancient landscape of India, elephants were a symbol of material abundance and power, as only the wealthiest ruling class had them.

Good fortune, luck, and abundance can result from being devoted to spiritual pursuits, overcoming obstacles, and receiving spiritual grace. Universal attraction to these benefits explains why Ganesha is so popular.

Every human being, confronting various life experiences, develops some blocks, specific to certain chakras. They are part of our personal evolutionary work to clear. We can cooperate in this inner work, helped by the ascended masters. Ganesha supports mental-body energy purification at the fifth and sixth chakras.

As we clear the fifth and sixth chakras—our access to spiritual vision—our ability to study, teach, or write about spiritual practices; manifest greater devotion to the spiritual realms; and experience spiritual grace and know peace and abundance in earthly life increases. Ganesha is a divine-masculine master who provides a lot of strength to help clear any mental patterns that are not aligned with the purest expression of this energy.

In direct experience, Ganesha came into consciousness during a quiet moment just after I was writing about him. I have experienced this phenomenon with several different masters, which illustrates that when we focus on reading, writing, or studying about them, we call them near. Another time, I was aware of an abstract glimpse of an elephant-headed male figure. Another time, he was in an abstract human male form, without the elephant head. His energy was fiery, purifying, strong, and a blessing to experience. He supports needed refinements in the human male journey but also works with a woman's inner masculine nature.

Keywords: Ganesha supports inner mental purification so that we can refine and perfect our experience of the (inner or outer) masculine, facilitating spiritual wisdom; the ability to share spiritual principles with others through teaching, speaking, or writing; and the development of loyalty and devotion to the divine so that spiritual grace and abundance may increase.

Suggested Meditation Symbol: Broken elephant's tusk against a sapphire-blue background (brighter to darker blues, Pantone 281–295)

Gefjun: Norse Lineage
Path of Gimel (Tarot: High Priestess), Spiritual Level

Gefjun is introduced in myth as a member of the Aesir tribe and frequently associated with plowing, foreknowledge, and virginity. She is described in many ancient sources, including *The Poetic Edda, The Prose Edda*, and *Beowulf.*

Her association with plowing was brought forth in *The Prose Edda* account "Gylfaginning." It states that King Gylfi was once the ruler of "what is now called Sweden" and that he was said to have given "a certain vagrant woman, as reward for his entertainment, as much land as she could plough up in a day and a night." In various mythologies, there is often a being associated with bringing agricultural cultivation to humankind in some early period. Clearly, that is one understanding of Gefjun's contributions. However, her path is not that of other agricultural goddesses, as the land she plowed (by transforming four of her giant sons into oxen) was an enormous tract. She opened the way for agriculture, but her means of doing so was clearly a magical act—or a higher cosmological truth.

Symbolism of course played a part in creating mythic structure, conveying ancient knowledge in the form of stories that could be told to all. In the book *Hamlet's Mill* by Giorgio de Santillana, ancient knowledge of stars and constellations flowed in to color the world of myth. The Plough—the constellation Ursa Major, commonly called the Big Dipper—was one of the most important to the ancient world. Are we to understand that the true origin of the being who brought agriculture to the Norse was in the starry Plough?

In addition to the emphasis on her magical power, Gefjun's attributes of foreknowledge and virginity are two other key parts of the path of the priestess. Foreknowledge meant the ability to prophesy, to know the direction that would unfold in advance of actual events happening. Many of the Norse female beings were experts in seidr, the Norse magic, and knowing in advance what things were going to happen was part of seidr.

On behalf of all the female masters, it's important to clarify that virginity does not necessarily mean one is sexually uninitiated or require sexual abstinence. Instead, it describes a woman who makes her own choices irrespective of the dictates of society or any male partner. Priestesses lived outside the social expectations of marriage and motherhood. They sought times of solitude, which is required to open the highest portals within consciousness and draw upon the spiritual world. Such women become literal conduits, facilitating a descent of power that comes through them. Far from being virgin according to modern understanding, some types of priestesses engaged in periodic ritual sex, serving the higher mysteries of their goddess.

During one deep meditation on the Norse pantheon, I was contacted by Gefjun and Frigg together. The experience of Gefjun left no doubt about her presence at the spiritual level of Gimel (the High Priestess). Her energy field was a high-vibration, feminine field of white light, and she was happy to work with Frigg. On another occasion, Gefjun came forward alone, communicating that she was one of the most ancient ancestresses of humankind. I understood that she was a star being who came to Earth in an ancient period to clear the far northern land, preparing it for human habitation and agriculture.

She carried me into divine light and returned later to demonstrate a unique form of interdimensional travel. Spiritual vision revealed a tubelike wormhole in front of my field of view, which had a few smaller tubes inside that were swirling and rotating inward and forward. She led my consciousness to enter that field of motion. It was easy to do once I began. After I entered the portal, any ability to describe the dimension was eclipsed by white light.

Keywords: Call on Gefjun to develop the highest possible spiritual abilities and leadership in a female lifetime (the priestess within), perfect abilities to receive foreknowledge of events, and make prophecies when called to do so. Gefjun possesses ritual knowledge of ancient Norse traditions and can be an ally for those who are learning different forms of interdimensional travel.

Suggested Meditation Symbol: Ancient wooden plow pulled by oxen on a radiant white field

Guinevere: Celtic (Arthurian) Lineage
Path of Da'leth (Tarot: Empress), Mental Level

Guinevere is the beautiful queen of King Arthur, familiar to many from Arthurian myth. Some authors have recognized her as a sovereignty goddess. Such women had a relationship with the land itself, and alliances between them and earthly kings were necessary during certain periods to provide the kings with a genuine right to rule.

Guinevere, like the being known as King Arthur, who is described below, may have lived during the fourth to fifth centuries of our era. Along with Arthur and Sir Lancelot, she is part of one of the most famous love triangles in Western culture. While love triangles often have difficult consequences and produce human sadness, they have been a favorite subject in literature, art, movies, and television for many centuries. They also may provide strong energy for individual evolution.

The tales of Arthur and Guinevere emerged into modern awareness through the writings of Chretien de Troyes in the tenth century

CE. He was a writer associated with Marie de Troyes, countess of Champagne, a key figure in the courtly love tradition. One cannot appreciate Guinevere without understanding that love within this genre was defined by unrequited longing and inevitable challenges. It rarely had a happy ending for those involved. Medieval marriages were made for dynastic and political reasons, rather than for love as we conceive of it in Western culture today.

Outside of marriage, courtly love gave its blessing to other types of male-female relationships. Knights who served the king chose women to admire, flirt with, and champion, wearing the women's colors into battle or tournaments. Such knights placed their beloveds on a pedestal. For the possibility of the women's affections, they fought bravely on the battlefield as well as under the flowing banners of court tournaments. There was an edge of danger that made such alliances titillating; the potential for conquest vied with the more likely outcome of rejection by the object of one's desire.

The game was played out with social rules of conduct that fueled underground currents of gossip and provided entertainment for the whole court. These ideas of love inspired the songs of troubadours and have filtered down to influence relationship dynamics (mostly unconsciously) even in our present time—for better or worse. They are embedded in the collective male-female psyche—until we choose to follow a different model.

Guinevere's life was not as glamorous as we might imagine. In direct contact with her, I could look through her eyes at a scene of Arthur and his best knights dressed in armor and going off to battle. I could feel how difficult it was for her and all the women to send their beloveds to war, never knowing if they would return alive or injured beyond repair. It took a lot of courage on the women's part, as their fate often depended upon what happened to their champions.

Keywords: Guinevere supports women to embrace and express their own feminine qualities of beauty, grace, fertility, and abundance while recognizing and refusing the model of courtly love and to manifest a timeless, sacred human love relationship.

Suggested Meditation Symbol: Golden circlet tiara with green forehead jewel, on a radiant white field

Gullveig/Heid): Norse Lineage
Hidden Path of the Blue Ray, Mental Level

Gullvieg (at the mental level), along with the being known as Mother Mary, or Saint Mary (at the spiritual level), share one of the hidden paths that are not illustrated in the conventional Qabalah diagram. This hidden path directly connects the uppermost sphere of Kether with the sphere of Chesed. Chesed is an all-male sphere of masters, but this unique hidden path allows some high-dimensional yin energy to connect to the spiritual wisdom path of Chesed, through a female master.

In Gullveigs myth, we are told only that she possessed powerful ritual knowledge was conversant with words of power and From her myth, I anticipated that she would be met at Gimel, on the path of the Priestess, but she didn't respond there. She immediately came forward (before I was even actively seeking her) when I used a mineral whose correspondence relates to the hidden path of the blue ray.

Gullveig's myth comes from "Voluspa" in *The Poetic Edda*. Her experiences are the root of the Aesir-Vanir War. The name Gullveig is variously interpreted as meaning "Strength," "Intoxication," "Power," or "Gold Branch." In the Northern tradition of paganism, Gullveig might be called a volva or seeress, (although practitioners today have various definitions of *volva*).

Gullveig carried a unique body of knowledge, was a wise woman of great power yet did not use her power to harm. She was a bridge between the unseen and the physical world who was skilled at entering trance. Since the myths that brought her name forward originated in a late mythological period, they were likely influenced by Christianity (which tended to label all such abilities in a negative way).

According to her myth, Gullveig was said to be of the Vanir tribe. For some reason she was traveling among the Aesir. Many ancient volvas were traveling seers who visited different homes. We don't know exactly where she came from or what she did to provoke them (the tale about her talking repeatedly about her love for gold as a reason for attacking her seems an unlikely overlay.) Whatever happened, the Aesir riddled her with spears and then burned her three times but couldn't kill her. Three times she was burned, and three times she stepped from the flames unscathed—reborn. Clearly this was a miraculous feat that is being reported. Upon her third rebirth, Gullveig became known as Heid, or Heidr. Taking a new name after a profound spiritual initiation was, and still is, practiced in many cultures.

While the mythological descriptions of the attempts to kill her are not pleasant, we know from research that women and men accused of practicing magic were treated wretchedly by different times and cultures. (The Inquisition was, of course, a prime example of this.) Moving past those unfortunate human actions, we can interpret her tale symbolically to glimpse a higher spiritual truth. Though a human body may be put to death, there is an eternal spirit that survives.

Most spiritual traditions point to an eternal spirit—perhaps we can simply call it *consciousness*—that exists before birth and after death. Given the period in which Norse myth was written down we can appreciate that Gullveig was awake to the higher levels of spiritual truth. Though killed repeatedly, she doesn't die.

When the Vanir tribe learned about how the Aesir had treated Gullveig, they became incensed with anger. They swore vengeance and began to prepare for war. The Aesir heard about this and moved against the Vanir tribe. This was the first war in the world. (An interesting part of the myth, suggesting a primordial period.)

For a long time, the battle raged back and forth, with neither side gaining much ground. Eventually, the gods became weary of war and began to talk of peace. Hostages were exchanged from one tribe to the other to ensure that both sides would honor their oath to live side by side in peace.

In direct experience, Gullveig was the first of the Norse pantheon to come forward in my consciousness. I had not yet researched Norse myth and was not aware of her before she made contact. She announced her name in my mind as I felt a huge and powerful presence. entirely in service to the light. Since that time she has returned on other occasions.

Keywords: Women who have been committed to developing their ability to enter trance and deliver inspired communications from the spiritual realm for some time, can call upon Gullveig when they are polishing mental level development. She supports those who do individual consulting work or speak to groups, especially on topics of women's spirituality.

Suggested Meditation Symbol: Radiant outpouring of white light, descending through an aqua-colored field (Pantone 550)

Hera: Greek Lineage
Path of Da'leth (Tarot: Empress), Emotional Level Two

Greek myth (which reflects the mindset of the 8th C BCE when Homer lived) introduces Hera as the sister and wife of Zeus, who, because of Zeus's repeated betrayals with other women, became jealous and vengeful. However, considerable scholarship over the past two hundred years has refuted this interpretation by uncovering how Hera was originally honored.

In iconography, Hera is portrayed as majestic, often enthroned, and wearing a crown, sometimes with sacred animals that included the cow, lion, or peacock. One of her epithets was Queen of Heaven. While we cannot know exactly how early she was venerated, traces of her worship in the form of cult bowls in late Mycenaean style that date to the second millennium BCE were found on the Greek island of Samos. Much later remnants of the enclosed, roofed temple sanctuary called the Heraion, dating to 800 BCE (Homer's era), still stand on the same site. The earliest sanctuaries to her (and to other female ascended masters) were under the open sky.

Johann Jakob Bachofen, a Swiss anthropologist of the mid-nineteenth century of our era, believed Hera was a goddess of a matriarchal people who inhabited Greece before the Hellenes. Samos excavations have revealed votive offerings dating from late eighth to early seventh centuries BCE, which demonstrate that Hera was more than a local Greek goddess of the Aegean. These votive offerings come from Armenia, Babylon, Iran, Assyria, and Egypt, showing that she had a wide following.

Hera was also worshipped in the earliest temple at Olympia and two of the great fifth- and sixth-century temples of Paestum. According to scholar Joan Breton Connelly in *Portrait of a Priestess*, priestesses of Hera enjoyed great prestige at Argos, with their tenure serving as historical date markers for other events.

The most enlightening evidence about Hera comes from Ken Dowden in his small book entitled *Zeus*. He cites the ancient Greek historian Pausanias, reporting that Zeus and Hera were honored in a *hieros gamos* tradition (sacred marriage) that was ritually enacted at many locations throughout Greece. Evidence from ancient Boeotia shows that this ritual took place every fifty-nine years over a long period of time. It was a festival of renewal, in which society made a new start, and the world was seen to begin again. The ritual took place on Mount Cithaeron, on the border with Attica. Many Greek marriages took place at this significant time of year (which would not have been the case if Hera's energy had been somehow tainted).

So where did the idea of Hera as a jealous wife come from? During the ancient festival, Zeus had to win Hera's favors again. To do this, he pretended to be about to wed another woman, to gain Hera's attention and attract her to his side once again. A wooden statue was dressed as his intended bride and carried to the mountaintop in a great procession. As the portrayal unfolded, Hera arrived in a fit of jealousy but discovered his joke. She then reconciled with him, and the hieros gamos took place. Over the course of the ensuing fifty-eight years, she had to become distanced from him once more for the ritual cycle to repeat. Homer's telling of her myth (during a period when powerful females were poorly represented) stressed her negative emotional reactions without giving their ritual context.

In direct experience, my first contact with Hera confirmed the reason she was so honored. I experienced a regal, lofty presence who was fully a master of great feminine wisdom, with no shred of arrogance or negative emotions—truly a queen of heaven. I felt blessed. On a later occasion, I was able to contact Hera and Zeus together. The result was an instantaneous uniting of their energies in total splendor, offering spiritual regeneration to humankind and blessings to those who follow the demanding path of a sacred partnership relationship. Although on another occasion I experienced Zeus's relationship with Demeter, there was no element of jealousy present in Hera's energy.

Keywords: Hera supports women to develop deep feminine love-wisdom to support the path of sacred relationship with a powerful male partner with whom an equal and respectful balance can flourish. She supports women valuing their own worth without losing their own identities.

Suggested Meditation Symbol: Golden crown set with five white stars on peaks across the front, against a green field (Pantone 364)

Hermes (also known as Thoth or Hermes-Thoth): Greek Lineage
Path of Beth (Tarot: Magician), Mental Level

Hermes, also known as Hermes Trismegistus or Hermes the Thrice Great to the Greeks, was the transmitter of divine wisdom sent to assist humankind. A Mycenaean Greek reference to a deity or semideity as "thrice or triple hero" found on Linear B clay tablets at Pylos, Knossos, and Thebes is sometimes interpreted as referring to him, although the full name Hermes Trismegistus appeared with more certainty in later Hellenistic Alexandria.

The hermetic wisdom stream, part of the perennial philosophy, is named for him. This wisdom passed through a series of adepts native to many lands and cultures so that humankind would have tools for spiritual evolution in our present day.

Greek myth portrays Hermes, like many Greek gods, as a humanlike personality subject to moods, whims, and mischief. He was thought of as having a diverse bag of attributes and could be invoked as a god of trade, wealth, luck, fertility, animal husbandry, sleep, language, thieves, and travel. He was the patron of shepherds; invented the lyre; and was, above all, the herald and messenger of Mount Olympus. He came to symbolize the crossing of boundaries in his role as a guide between the two realms of gods and humanity.

In Qabalah correspondence, Hermes extends energy at the mental level on the path of Beth (the Magician in tarot). He is a conduit for knowledge about how the forces of divine creation take form in the human world. Information about the cosmic laws of creation is embedded in the Qabalah; sacred sounds (music, chanting, letters, and language); sacred numbers (geometric shapes and relationships); and colors. Each of these vibrational forms is part of a single universal matrix of knowledge.

Understanding how to recognize the cosmic principles inherent in each type and their interrelationships (correspondence with one another) allows us to use these subtle vibrational energies for spiritual evolution. Western astrology, tarot, alchemy, and many other wisdom systems that are part of the Western esoteric tradition descend from the hermetic root.

Hermes has many attributes and symbols. One is the herma, an archaic form that consisted of a pile of rocks or, if more elaborate, a statue form with a head and perhaps a torso above a plain, usually squared lower section, perhaps with a penis, which was placed at borders or crossings. Quadrilinear in overall shape, the herma form associated him with number four, as in presiding over the four directions.

He has also been associated with the rooster (fertility), the tortoise (wisdom and creation), the satchel or pouch (messages from the gods), and winged sandals and a winged helmet (speed in traveling through the higher realms of consciousness as a divine emissary). Among his many symbols, his main one is the caduceus, a winged staff intertwined with two snakes (symbolic of both Qabalah and the human subtle energy system).

I was drawn to study the hermetic wisdom stream for twenty-plus years before beginning work on this book. Hermes was working with me long before I was aware of him directly. My first awareness of his presence was during a private wilderness retreat in the high desert of Nevada years ago. I had not intended any contact, but he appeared spontaneously on that occasion in the thrice-great form in which he is pictured in Greek iconography. This included a conical sort of hat and flowing robes. I felt blessed!

Years later, during an extended visit to a healing center in Brazil, he appeared in his earlier Egyptian form (Thoth) in the dark of early morning beside my bed, holding the tall caduceus-shaped staff. During that period, I was learning specifics of gem and mineral correspondence according to hermetic principles.

In the period when I was working on this book, he appeared again, showing me a still earlier form, when he first brought this knowledge to humankind.

Keywords: Hermes is the bringer of knowledge of the cosmic forces of creation to humankind.

Suggested Meditation Symbol: Egyptian ibis bird in a side-view profile, against a light lemon-yellow field (Pantone 1225)

Hildegard von Bingen, Saint: Christian Lineage
Tiphareth, Mental Level

Hildegard of Bingen (1098–1179 CE), also known as the Sibyl of the Rhine, was a German Benedictine abbess, writer, composer, philosopher, Christian mystic, visionary, and polymath. Hildegard founded several monasteries, including Rupertsberg and Eibingen, and traveled widely, corresponding with popes; statesmen; German emperors, such as Frederick I Barbarossa; and other notable figures, such as Saint Bernard of Clairvaux.

Her written works include three great volumes of visionary theology, and she is also known for a variety of musical compositions and contributions to healing arts and natural sciences. Her tremendous range of expertise spanned a breadth of categories yet had the single aim of expressing the divine. She has been recognized as a saint by branches of the Roman Catholic Church for centuries.

Hildegard's parents were a family of the free lower nobility in the service of Count Meginhard of Sponheim. Sickly from birth, Hildegard experienced spiritual visions from a young age. She was placed in a Benedictine monastery at the age of fourteen, along with an older woman, Jutta, the daughter of Count Stephan II of Sponheim.

Upon Jutta's death in 1136, Hildegard was unanimously elected as *magistra* of the community by her fellow nuns. Abbot Kuno of Disibodenberg asked Hildegard to be prioress, which would have put her under his authority. Hildegard, however, was a woman with remarkably strong convictions who followed only her inner guidance. She asked Abbot Kuno to allow them to move to Rupertsberg, which would allow them more independence. The abbot initially declined Hildegard's proposition yet eventually relented when she was stricken by an illness that kept her paralyzed and unable to move from her bed, an event she attributed to God's unhappiness at her not following his order to move her nuns to Rupertsberg.

Hildegard's remarkable intellectual brilliance and unique abilities allowed her to become an accepted female teacher, theological writer, and preacher during a time when women were not permitted these forms of spiritual expression. She conducted four preaching tours throughout Germany, speaking to both clergy and laity in chapter houses and in public, mainly denouncing clerical corruption and calling for reform.

When I sought contact with her while using a corresponding crystal in meditation, she responded right away. It was amazing to be in contact with her mind; I felt both its range and its mental mastery, along with the single-pointed focus on expressing God's will. Her unique gifts and spiritual dedication are more than enough to inspire both women and men.

There was no grandness or sense of her authority in our interaction; she was warm and willing to be known. While this egolessness is characteristic of all in the ascended realm, it is no doubt the sort of selfless model that inspired others. She was beloved among the women to whom she was dedicated and received the respect of male spiritual colleagues and world leaders—both in her lifetime and after.

Keywords: Hildegard von Bingen supports women to develop both their minds and their spiritual sensibilities and then offer their abilities in service to the higher realms. Her mental mastery and intellectual works; visionary gifts; and strong, independent leadership are still extended to assist human spiritual development.

Suggested Meditation Symbol: Crosier staff (with a curving golden top), which is the symbol of the spiritual authority of a bishop or abbot, against a white field with golden highlights

Huldah: Judaic Lineage
Yesod, Spiritual Level

Huldah, who lived during the reign of King Josiah (641/640 to 610/609 BCE), was an example of a woman who had profound abilities as a psychic medium. She was called a prophet for her ability to receive clear information, and her pronouncements were acknowledged by the highest authorities, including both king and high priest.

The Bible relates that Huldah was the wife of Shallum, son of Takhath; they lived in the second quarter of Jerusalem; and she was a keeper of the wardrobe. After a discovery of a book of the law (Deuteronomy) was found during a renovation at the Temple of Solomon, the king sent Hilkiah the priest and other high officials to consult her as to its authenticity. She authenticated it and prophesied a future of destruction for all who failed to follow it. (Deborah was the first female author of scripture, but Huldah was the first to declare that a certain writing was scripture.) This was no small thing, and her word (the message that came through her from a higher source) was considered final and universally accepted. At the same time, she also prophesied the fate of King Josiah himself, saying that "due to his piety, he would be gathered into his grave in peace."

When we consider how few women are mentioned in the Hebrew Bible and the fact that Huldah is mentioned in only a few verses (2 Kings 22:13–20 and 2 Chronicles 34:22–28), the fact that she had the authority to speak the Word of God directly to the high priest and royal officials about what was to be considered scripture and could foretell the fate of a king is remarkable. It is hard to fully appreciate her position of authority, other than noting that other (male) prophets, such as Jeremiah, who was also preaching during the time she lived, are mentioned even more briefly in the Bible than she is. (Jeremiah is mentioned in 2 Chronicles 35:25.)

As she was an outstanding biblical holy woman, the location of the tomb of Huldah is of interest to some today. One view holds that she was buried between the walls in Jerusalem, while another locates her tomb in a rock cave beneath a mosque on the Mount of Olives, a site that is sacred to Jews, Muslims, and Christians alike. The Huldah Gates, one of the sets of gates that led into the Jerusalem temple compound in the Old City of Jerusalem in the Hasmonean period, were named for her.

My experience with Huldah began by my being immersed in high female energy. I saw her in spiritual vision as a small, olive-skinned, and dark-haired woman in a peasant-style, rough tan cloth skirt with a heavy veil wrapped around her head. Yes, she had the power to tap in (the highest intuitive mediumship) and get answers from the place of all knowledge. She was powerful and strong, and she visited me twice more.

Keywords: Huldah supports those with psychic-spiritual potential to develop their gifts to their fullest and use them as an instrument to serve the spiritual realm and humankind.

Suggested Meditation Symbol: Ancient biblical scroll against a radiant white field

Isaac: Judaic Lineage
Binah, Emotional Level Two

Isaac, who may have lived circa the thirteenth century BCE, is known as the son of Abraham and Sarah; thus, he was the second generation of the men known today as the Jewish patriarchs. Isaac was the focus of his father's great test of faith: he was going to be sacrificed, until an angel intervened at the last moment to prevent it. It was said to be a test of his faith also, as he understood what was being asked and didn't attempt to resist.

According to the biblical sources, Isaac's parents were both past the age of childbearing when he was born on Shavuot, one year after his birth was prophesied by divine messengers. According to Jewish tradition, he was born in Canaan. Canaan was situated in the territory of the southern Levant, which today encompasses Israel, the West Bank and Gaza, Jordan, and the southern portions of Syria and Lebanon.

Isaac married Rebecca, who gave birth to Jacob. Isaac was the only patriarch who stayed in Canaan during his whole life, and though once he tried to leave, it was said that God told him not to do so. He was the oldest of the biblical patriarchs at the time of his death (said to be 160 years old) and the only patriarch whose name was not changed. He is considered a saint by both the Eastern Orthodox Church and the Roman Catholic Church and is also a prophet of Islam, mentioned fifteen times in the Koran, along with his father, Abraham, and his son Jacob. Despite the number of lineages who recognize Isaac, some modern scholars question his historical existence at all, while one speculates that he lived in a much earlier period.

Isaac was the first of the masters known in Judaism to come into direct contact with me during meditation. I wasn't seeking him, but I experienced a high holy presence who gave me the name Isaac and communicated that he was one of the Jewish patriarchs.

On another occasion, I connected with Isaac and Abraham together. I was aware of the importance of their spiritual agreement, which manifested itself through the roles of father and son but was a spiritual partnership forged on the higher levels. Isaac brought a profound holiness and spiritual strength that sent the wave they were bringing in forward in time. I was shown their temple, which appears different in the astral than King Solomon's temple. Both temples are present in high holy dimensions that can be visited by consciousness.

According to some sources (historical information is scarce), Isaac may have helped to create the institution of Jewish synagogues to serve as alternative houses of worship when temples were not available. This became of practical value during the period of exile known as the Babylonian Captivity.

Keywords: A spiritual prophet and forefather of the Judaic religion, Isaac supports all humankind to complete their emotional purification to move into direct experience of the divine realms. He is there as a shoulder to lean on as we polish our connection to divinity.

Suggested Meditation Symbol: Ner Tamid (eternal light) lamp that hangs in each Jewish synagogue, seen against a purple field (Pantone 265–266)

Jesus (also known as Yeshua or Jeshua): Christian Lineage
Binah, Spiritual Level

The master whom history commonly knows by the name Jesus, or Jesus ben Joseph (Jesus, son of Joseph), who came into a physical form some two thousand years ago, was—and is—both a beloved and a controversial figure. Learning to recognize masters independent of the religious teachings that grew up after their lives is how some of us best connect with them. This is especially applicable to Jesus, as some find a gap between the application of his teachings within religion and the message of love he advocated.

When I first began spiritual practice, I discovered a need to heal my own less-than-ideal experiences with Christianity to create a clear space to discover Yeshua. Like all the masters, he was patient with me as I did that inner work. Gradually, moments of undeniable contact with his mind began to arrive, especially when I needed them most. I find it helpful to call him Yeshua (also spelled Jeshua), but you can call him by whatever name you are most comfortable with—and he will understand you!

Even when we consider only traditional biblical accounts, we discover that Yeshua was a controversial figure in his own day. He was a reformer who, even as a young man, debated spiritual matters with those much older (and supposedly wiser) than he. He was passionate about his beliefs and didn't live up to the expectation of some of his contemporaries (to become a literal king of the Jewish people). When he took up his life mission, he was accessible, in ways that defied the cultural traditions of his day, to people of other races, women, and little children. He told inspired stories (parables) that taught new principles of human brotherhood and spoke of the divine as a Source of unconditional love, rather than a God to be feared. He performed miracles of healing and raising the dead and turned a few loaves and fishes into food to feed the masses. He was not the only biblical figure (or ascended master) who demonstrated spiritual power, but his level of accomplishment was profound.

When learning from ascended masters, we want to know what they accomplished and be shown how they achieved it. During one moment of contact, when I wanted to know more about him, he gently urged me to read about the miracles he performed. Healing, raising the dead, and miraculous transformations of physical substance are described in many biblical passages.

Today we can observe that among the gifts he brought to humankind was a new universal access to Christ consciousness. Yeshua came into the experience of human life, overcame the perception of separation from Source, became fully identified with Creator consciousness, and solidified that awareness as an ongoing state within his being. From that state of enlightenment, he offered teachings and demonstrations—which, as happened with masters of other ancient traditions, were sometimes misunderstood and sometimes transmitted less than accurately or completely by those who later wrote about him.

Some understand his ascension as proof of our own spiritual reality—which is eternal—existing far beyond the physical body. These gifts are not just for a select few disciples or spiritual initiates but available to all races and all classes and irrespective of gender identification.

My earliest direct contact with the mind of Yeshua was early one Easter morning while walking alone in a wilderness area. Other treasured moments of contact (with him and the Magdalene) gradually followed. Over many years, I was given various insights about some of the circumstances of their lives that are not mentioned in traditional texts. I asked for Yeshua's presence beside me as I faced some deep personal healing. I have received clairaudient messages from him, and appreciate the healing balm of his love and presence. As I continued to evolve, my experiences with him deepened.

As I discovered repeatedly, Yeshua does not require our exclusive attention on him for us to experience his presence. I have experienced him working alongside ascended masters from all traditions. I am deeply grateful to receive from him, thoughts and practices that help me to prepare consciousness to awaken in the realms of limitless light.

In whatever ways we understand him, his help didn't end when he was no longer in physical form. His mind is still available to those who seek him and prepare for that connection. He welcomes all humankind to invite his close presence, regardless of the spiritual path you follow.

Keywords: At any time, you can call upon Yeshua to help you shift perception to higher reality when things in the human sphere appear challenging. He is a master teacher of divine love who can provide healing, spiritual wisdom, and a supportive presence to remind and help us claim our own higher essence.

Suggested Meditation Symbol: Radiant white Christmas star above a wooden shepherds staff, surrounded by radiant white light

John the Baptist, Saint: Christian Lineage
Chesed, Spiritual Level

John the Baptist was a traveling Jewish preacher and prophet who lived in the late first century BCE. He followed a simple life devoted to spiritual pursuits, and his message was for people to set their lives straight to prepare for the coming of one who would be much greater than he. The Bible says he performed a river baptism for his younger cousin Jesus, during which the Holy Spirit descended in the form of a dove. This scene became the origin of the sacrament of baptism, which was incorporated into later Christian traditions. John is venerated today by Christians, Mandean sects, mystical Judaic sects, and other groups, for various reasons.

The Bible introduces John as the son of a priest named Zacharias and his wife, Elizabeth. His birth was prophesied to his father by an angel when the formerly childless couple were both elderly. According to the Edgar Cayce readings, John's parents both died when he was young, and he was adopted by the mystic community of Essenes and lived among them for many years near the Jordan River. His spiritual training in that desert community prepared him well to deliver a message about the need to reform.

Like the messages of other spiritual teachers who advocated uplifting moral changes in human behavior, the messages John delivered were not universally welcomed. He rebuked King Herod Antipas for living a sinful life—Herod had "put away" his wife and married his brother Phillip's wife. This message made Herod angry, and he had John put in prison. Herod would have put him to death, but he was afraid of the reaction of others who considered John a prophet.

Then Herod gave a birthday party during which the daughter of his new wife, Herodias, danced before him and so pleased him that he promised her anything she might ask. Herodias, also angry with John the Baptist for condemning her and Herod, told her daughter to ask for the head of John the Baptist on a platter. Herod complied with her request, and John was beheaded.

To open the direct channel to John, I had to first forgive the scene in which he met his death, wherein his decapitated head was placed on a platter. This came into visual form, but he was beside me, reminding me that from human perception, we can never judge what appears in human life as "wrong," because we have no idea of the higher purpose that even challenging appearances may represent. He wasn't at all disturbed about it!

Before connecting with him, I had been wondering what sort of initiation John's rite of baptism really was for those in his time. We have all experienced the normal human condition in which we know we haven't always done the right thing in life. Or we have participated in another normal human habit of blaming others for our problems. Both patterns result in guilt we carry, although we try to keep it well out of mind (mostly unconscious).

John then showed me how powerful the rite of river baptism had been in his time. Most people were in a rough state in that period and not very conscious. To be bathed in waters of purification and told to "arise, go forth, and sin no more" was a powerful practice to release the past. John thus delivered an important practice to prepare people for Jesus's mission.

Keywords: John provides powerful support for spiritually cleansing and uplifting one's energy field as preparation for further spiritual development. He supports those who have spiritual messages to deliver, and he can help to identify practices to develop spiritual consciousness and inspired words to communicate what one has experienced.

Suggested Meditation Symbol: White dove flying above the blue Jordan River

Kali: Hindu Lineage
Geburah, Spiritual Level

The master known as Kali is a powerful expression of shakti, the feminine principle, who is recognized throughout India and worldwide. She is considered a dark mother, meaning a destroyer of evil forces, and she is often portrayed with a fierce appearance (in the same way some of the Buddhist karmapalas at Geburah have fierce appearances).

Kali has been worshipped in various roles by devotional movements and tantric sects; she is one of the ten Mahavidyas—great wisdom goddesses of the Shakti (goddess) tradition. Despite her sometimes fearsome depictions and raw transformational power, she is a great blessing to experience when we need assistance to release attachments to things that hold us back.

Kālī shares the meaning of "time" or "the fullness of time" with the masculine noun *kāla*. She is one who carries out the changing aspect of nature that brings things to life or death. In iconography, she is portrayed mostly in one of two forms: the popular four-armed form and the ten-armed Mahakali form. In both of her forms, she is described as black in color, but she is most often depicted as blue in popular Indian art. Her eyes are described as red with intoxication, her hair is shown disheveled, small fangs sometimes protrude out of her mouth, and her tongue is lolling. She is often shown naked or wearing a skirt made of human arms and a garland of human heads.

Kali is often shown standing or dancing on her consort, Shiva, who lies calm and prostrate beneath her. (He is not dead!) Her right foot is on Shiva's chest. This represents an episode in which Kali was so out of control on the battlefield that she was about to destroy the entire universe. Shiva pacified her by lying down under her foot, both to receive her blessing and to pacify and calm her. Shiva is sometimes shown with a blissful smile on his face.

Delivering energy that helps us to overcome what no longer serves us (attachments, destructive habits, negative thought patterns, and material forms), she is a being associated with the death of old forms.

She is thus a true, powerful, and loving protector of the divine nature hidden within each human personality—the one who bestows moksha, or liberation.

Like many, I have experienced the power of Kali at different times in my life, since long before I was able to contact her consciousness directly. Each time, beyond the human personality's resistance to change, I experienced a welcome transformation. When old forms are cleared, something better for who we truly are can manifest.

I experienced the most powerful contacts with Kali during the later stages of writing this book. While abstract, she did appear blackish, while the active part of her energy was like a white laser. Her powerful divine-feminine aspect is unmistakable. Vision carried me to ancient tantric enclaves in which she was worshipped at night with red-hued statues and pigments.

On two occasions, she helped me to clear an attachment to something I had not consciously recognized was present in my consciousness. To do this, she first brought the matter up from my unconscious levels into clear focus. When I could see what was there, I was willing to let it go, recognizing that it was holding me back.

In one case, I was shown unconscious beliefs about the order in which anticipated life changes needed to occur. Those beliefs were making it more difficult for my spiritual team to arrange events in the optimal manner. As I became willing to surrender my ideas about the optimal order of events, then Kali's powerful, laser-like white light cut those beliefs from my energy field. I could both see the process and feel its benefit energetically. There was no doubt the work was accomplished, and I held a state of trust without knowing what would manifest ahead in my life. In the weeks following, outer-world changes occurred that were entirely beneficial. I was and am deeply grateful!

Keywords: Kali extends the power to destroy our attachment to what no longer serves us, helping us to recognize what is interfering with our continuing evolution. Despite some of her portrayals, she is only fierce with negativity and helps us to end only what has outlived its usefulness, so a higher-level experience can unfold.

Suggested Meditation Symbol: Hindu sacrificial sword (see images online of the unique shape of the blade) against a radiant white field

King Arthur: Celtic (Arthurian) Lineage
Chesed, Emotional Level Two

King Arthur is the semilegendary figure who appears in Arthurian myth. There have been many theories put forward to identify the historical Arthur, one of which identifies him with a fifth-century-CE high king of the Britons known as Riothamus. Another school of thought, stemming from the writing of Gildas, identifies him as the warrior leader Ambrosius Aurelianus. These figures were part of the historical landscape during the period of the fifth century CE. This was a key period that marked the end of four hundred years of Roman rule in Britain. As the Romans withdrew to deal with unrest in other parts of the Roman Empire, a vacuum of leadership was created, during which various British tribes allied for protection.

It is not the purpose of this book to try to prove any specific theory but, rather, to direct you toward direct contact with the ascended masters themselves to experience your own truth. For those who resonate with the Arthurian masters, cultivating contact with Arthur and Guinevere will be meaningful, and they have a lot to teach us now.

Whatever his historical name, Arthur is one model of the beneficial warrior king committed to uplifting those under his care. He extended qualities that are sometimes called the *sacred masculine* today, inspiring and personifying the chivalric ethos, wherein a knight's military prowess, leadership, courage, truthfulness, moral character, honor, and faith in God were presented in a unique assemblage.

Arthur was granted kingship via his union with Guinevere and through the auspices of (and sword provided by) the Lady of the Lake or Merlin, depending on which tale you follow. The greatest ancient kings received their right to rule via the sacred feminine. When true sacred kingship manifested through an outstanding leader, other outstanding individuals were attracted to the light; this was the essence of Camelot.

Such an epoch marked a peak in human civilization, wherein some reflection of the divine was anchored (temporarily) on earth, and miraculous levels of culture, peace, and prosperity could flourish.

Despite the unhappy love-triangle drama that Arthur, Guinevere, and Lancelot embodied (a dynamic common to courtly love traditions), those who experience these masters in the higher dimensions can discover that the great love between Arthur and Guinevere is radiantly intact. (Love does not end when physical bodies are laid down.) That the love shared between sacred partners remains in the higher dimensions when one or both partners leave physical form behind is a far more worthwhile truth than courtly love traditions could possibly express.

In Arthurian tales, when Arthur died, in the manner of other sacrificial kings, his body was said to have been carried to Avalon. It was believed that Arthur would return to support future generations when he was needed. Even though Avalon disappeared from the physical plane into the mists, it can be experienced in higher dimensions. All the minds of the Arthurian masters still exist on the higher planes, available for those who resonate with their frequency to call upon.

I had many experiences of contact with Arthur, Guinevere, Lancelot, the Lady of the Lake, and some of Arthur's knights during an early period when working on this book. In direct experience, Arthur's beneficent, sacred-masculine energy is profound. Part of the sacred masculine includes a commitment to honor the feminine, including giving her full choice about whether and when to consummate an intimate relationship. This provides the woman a sense of safety that is palpable and inviolate. To answer an ancient rhetorical question, this is one thing women want, today more than ever.

Keywords: Arthur extends qualities of the sacred masculine: spiritual devotion; courage; skill; successful war leadership; and wise, benevolent rulership to produce peace and abundance and inspire the development of culture. He can be a guide for men who develop these admirable qualities and he can also contribute to a woman's inner masculine. Arthur also supports those today who are evolving male-female love relationship dynamics past conflict toward a mutually respectful, holy partnership.

Suggested Meditation Symbol: Medieval king's crown against a sapphire-blue field (brighter to darker blues, Pantone 281–295)

King David of Jerusalem: Judaic Lineage
Chesed, Emotional Level Two

According to biblical narrative, David (circa the eleventh to tenth century BCE) was originally a shepherd who faced and killed a Philistine giant named Goliath in single combat. He was a powerful warrior who became the second king of a united Jerusalem (following Saul), founding a theocracy whose model connected earthly rulership to divine principles and inspiring others to follow his leadership.

The ideal of sacred kingship was based upon a leader with high moral principles who valued peace as the condition in which humankind could flourish (but who could skillfully conduct war to obtain it). David possessed wisdom, and as evidence for his spiritual commitment, we find him acknowledged as the author of at least seventy of the 150 psalms in the Old Testament book of Psalms. The psalms were sacred poems conveying meaning to influence human behavior for the better, intended to be sung as part of worship. Many masters at Chesed authored some form of sacred text within their traditions.

Some believe David was inspired and strengthened by his custody of the mysterious object known as the Ark of the Covenant. He is richly represented in postbiblical Jewish written and oral tradition, is discussed in the Koran, and figures in Islamic oral and written tradition as well. He and his second wife, Bathsheba, were the parents of King Solomon.

Until recently, there was no evidence outside the Bible for the existence of King David. In 1993, a team of archaeologists led by Professor Avraham Biran, excavating the site known as Tel Dan in northern Galilee, found a triangular piece of basalt rock measuring twenty-three by thirty-six centimeters and inscribed in Aramaic.

This ninth-century-BCE artifact, known as the Tel Dan Stele, has an inscription containing the words *Beit David* ("House [or Dynasty] of David"). This is the first near-contemporaneous reference to David ever discovered. While not conclusive, it does strongly indicate that a king called David established a dynasty in Israel during the relevant period.

Another piece of significant evidence comes from Dr. Avi Ofer's archaeological survey conducted in the hills of Judea during the last decade. It determined that in the eleventh and tenth centuries BCE (David's supposed period), the population of Judah almost doubled compared to the preceding period. It was most likely centered in Jerusalem, a previously settled site important enough to be mentioned in Egyptian documents. There is plenty of evidence of the antiquity of the city of Jerusalem. Excavations in the City of David, especially the village of Silwan, show that the site has been continuously occupied for some five thousand years.

Like the tales we received about masters known in other spiritual traditions, the Bible leaves many of our questions about David unanswered. It says he observed Bathsheba bathing and had her husband, Uriah, killed so he could possess her. In some accounts, we are told he realized this was an error and later believed that the death of his first child he conceived with her was justified punishment for his actions. While it would reflect a belief in guilt, we cannot know what actually occurred.

The traditional story also tells us that King David was known for enormous compassion, expressed even toward those who opposed him. He knew how to forgive and to love his enemies. Many who learn the art of true forgiveness find that they develop extraordinary compassion for all who share the human journey. These are among the gifts of the sphere of Chesed, shared by many masters.

In direct experience, David came through during one meditation. I didn't intend to contact him, but he arrived anyway. I was moved by the combination of warrior strength, wisdom, and compassion he extends.

Keywords: David supports the development of skill and wisdom in male leaders who seek to bring spiritual values and high moral standards into earthly governing institutions. He supports all humankind (male and female) to practice universal compassion and can assist those who compose spiritual texts.

Suggested Meditation Symbol: Gold Jerusalem cross against a sapphire-blue field (brighter to darker blues, Pantone 281–295)

King Solomon: Judaic Lineage
Hod, Mental Level

Solomon, who lived in the tenth century BCE, was the son of King David and Bathsheba and became the third and final priest-king of the united monarchy of Israel. He oversaw the building of the magnificent Temple of Solomon and is remembered for both esoteric wisdom and rulership acumen. After his death, the kingdom broke apart into the northern Kingdom of Israel and the southern Kingdom of Judah.

Some believe Solomon studied spiritual wisdom extensively in Tibet, India, and Persia for many years as preparation to assume rulership. Wherever his knowledge came from, he understood how to use gems and minerals for their spiritual energetic qualities and had healing abilities. One of his most well-known esoteric symbols is the seal of Solomon, showing the solar influence of Tiphareth in the center of a six-pointed star that radiates to and through the surrounding six planetary spheres. The meaning of this symbol is reflected in the Qabalah.

Solomon began his reign with an extensive purge of the ruling administrators and then consolidated his position by appointing friends throughout his administration, including in religious positions as well as in civic and military posts. He greatly expanded his kingdom's military strength, especially the cavalry and chariot arms. He founded numerous colonies, some of which doubled as trading posts and military outposts, and developed successful trade relationships. He continued his father's profitable relationship with the Phoenician king Hiram I of Tyre (a Phoenician port city), trading in luxury products such as gold, silver, sandalwood, pearls, ivory, apes, and peacocks. This allowed him to build a strong business empire that provided abundantly for his kingdom.

During his life, Solomon was known to have many wives, plus a harem of concubines numbering three hundred more women. This practice was not unusual among the most powerful male rulers during certain periods and cultures. However, among these many women, Solomon formed an important love relationship with one powerful woman known only to history as the queen of Sheba. (She isn't listed separately in this book but is an ascended master.) Some who study the esoteric traditions of Judaism suggest that Solomon may have been part of a tradition that still practiced hieros gamos (sacred marriage) with a female priestess and that the sensuous language of the Song of Songs (sometimes attributed to him) relates to that type of initiation.

Solomon has come into my consciousness on several occasions over the past twenty years, sometimes alone, sometimes with Sheba, and once with his mother, Bathsheba. The love shared with Sheba can still be experienced on the inner planes. When they come forward together, the kinesthetic and visual experience leaves no doubt they share a cosmic and still passionate love. I have also experienced his healing support on several occasions.

The energy set in motion by the building of Solomon's temple still attracts our attention some three thousand years since it existed in physical form. It was built according to sacred geometric principles, which made it a place of high initiation for the Judaic mysteries, perhaps supported energetically by the presence of the Ark of the Covenant. The temple's buried secrets were a focus for certain Templar Knights, who regained control of Jerusalem during the First Crusade in the eleventh century CE. The temple is still part of various mystery school teachings. I have visited this temple in consciousness on two occasions to date. Like some other legendary spiritual places, it is a temple of initiation, where one can wake up to the higher dimensions and one's own spiritual reality.

Keywords: Solomon is an initiate and guide to esoteric knowledge. He can support the development of business acumen and practical decision-making to build wealth. He can inspire a deeply sacred, intimate partner relationship and help one to express inspiring messages through lyrical means.

Suggested Meditation Symbol: Gold seal of Solomon against an orange field (Pantone 165–167 or 170)

Krishna: Hindu Lineage
Chesed, Mental Level

Krishna is familiar to people worldwide as well as within the Vaishnavite Hindu traditions. Vaishnavites worship him along with Radha in two forms: sometimes she is his love consort or wife, and elsewhere she is the feminine component of a single Radha-Krishna soul.

According to devotees, Krishna lived about five thousand years ago and was a fully enlightened being. He was a spiritual teacher, savior figure, skilled warrior who could overcome any adversary, and adviser to kings. Some consider him an avatar of Vishnu. A comprehensive yet easy-to-read collection of the life stories of Krishna can be found in the book *The Complete Life of Krishna* by female devotee and author Mataji Devi Vanamali. *The Illustrated Mahabharata* also offers a delightful collection of tales about Krishna.

In iconography, Krishna is depicted in blue or black form, often playing the bansuri flute, and accompanied by a peacock feather. He grew up in the country with a foster mother and was a playful, mischievous youth who was fond of butter and could already work miracles. As a young man, he became a shepherd, and he went into the forest by day, playing the bansuri (Indian flute) and sometimes dancing with the *gopis* (milkmaids), especially Radha.

According to tradition, Krishna's virgin birth was foretold by prophecy: his purpose was to bring a message to humanity about the infinite sweetness of divine love (the bhakti tradition) and its role in the attainment of spiritual consciousness. He represents spiritual success (moksha, or deliverance from the cycle of rebirth), which can be achieved through a combination of praying, being devoted, trusting in the divine, and receiving and following inner guidance.

Krishna's universal appeal has always included the simplicity of his message, which can be understood by anyone. Women engaged in the daily tasks of child raising and household chores can picture him as the engaging child who answered every need placed before him. Female devotees, such as sixteenth-century mystical poet Mira Bai (see below), turned to Krishna in their quests for the infinite. Despite Mira Bai's example of renouncing worldly expectations, such as marriage, children, and even clothing, contact with Krishna does not require renunciation or an ascetic lifestyle.

Krishna is associated with the Vrindavan forest in Uttar Pradesh in northern India, a city known today for its multitudinous temples. He is also believed to have founded the ancient island city of Dwarka, off the northwest coast of India (Gujarat). He prophesied that Dwarka would be reclaimed by the sea after his death. Modern archaeological discoveries of an ancient, submerged site off the coast of the present-day city are cited as evidence for Krishna's authenticity. This area remains one of the most important pilgrimage sites for him today.

In the Bhagavad Gita, Krishna becomes the charioteer of the Pandava prince Arjuna. He helps Arjuna to resolve moral questions about whether he should participate in the war (his dharma as a member of the warrior caste, even though doing so would mean he would face his own family members in battle).

In many tales, Krishna comes to the aid of women. He helped Draupadi the disgraced wife when she became a bounty won in a game of dice, and he aided the mother of future King Parikshit, reviving her stillborn child and thus ensuring the continuation of the Kuru clan. In various tales, Krishna is portrayed as marrying eight primary wives who desired him as husband and then sixteen thousand more women who desired him when he released them from a demon. Some interpret these marriages as a demonstration that no one who approaches Krishna is denied the relationship he or she desires.

When I began working on this book, Krishna came into consciousness many times, simply extending love. Later, I glimpsed him in a visionary form as a yogi prince: a tender, sacred-masculine presence who joined heart and mind to soar toward the white light of Source. In one deep experience, I touched the heart of what I could only call Krishna-consciousness, which was pure bliss. He works beside many other masters to increase awareness of joy and spiritual ecstasy and radiates goodness and spiritual grace.

Keywords: Krishna supports one to develop the highest spiritual consciousness, make prayer and meditation a daily practice, develop trust, and follow inner guidance. He can provide a sacred-masculine model that is healing for women and can inspire men to extend the qualities he embodies.

Suggested Meditation Symbol: Bansuri (flute) against a sapphire blue-field (Pantone 280, 281, 287, or 288)

Lakshmi: Hindu (and Buddhist) Lineage
Netzach, Spiritual Level

Lakshmi, sometimes known simply as Shri, is known for holiness, authority, auspiciousness, beauty, grace, fertility, luxury, abundance, and long life. She was incorporated into the Hindu Tridevi (along with Sarasvati and Parvati), where she is considered the consort or partner of Vishnu (who is part of the Trimurti of male deities, along with Shiva and Brahma). One of her earliest hymns is recorded in the Rig Veda. She also appeared in some of the earliest Buddhist stupa carvings in India and continued with Buddhist sects in Tibet and Nepal and throughout southeast Asia.

Archaeological discoveries and coins attest to her presence from the first millennium BCE. She was part of the Pancharatra tantra, which originated in the late first millennium BCE around the ideas of Narayana, with the various avatars of Vishnu as their central deities. The movement later merged with the ancient Bhagavata tradition and contributed to the development of Vaishnavism.

Images of Lakshmi started appearing around the third century BCE in sculptures found in Kosambi, an ancient city in northern India, and on coins issued during the reign of the Gupta dynasty around the fourth century CE. She became a favorite of kings as more and more people believed she was the bestower of power, wealth, and sovereignty.

Lakshmi's attributes are developed further in the Atharva Veda (1000–900 BCE), in which she is a beautiful, resplendent woman trembling with immense energy and power. She is portrayed similarly in the Mahabharata, is mentioned in the Ramayana, and features prominently in the Puranas.

The mythology of Lakshmi acquired full form in the Puranas, chronicles of gods, kings, and sages that were compiled between 500 and 1500 CE. Separate shrines to Lakshmi within the precincts of Vishnu temples may have been built as early as the seventh century; such shrines were certainly in existence by the tenth century CE.

The practice of personifying the beauty and bounty of earth as a goddess was prevalent in all ancient cultures. In iconography, Lakshmi is often depicted as a four-armed woman elegantly dressed in a red sari embroidered with golden threads (sometimes accompanied by an owl), sitting or standing on a lotus pedestal and holding a lotus in her hand. She is one of many deities associated with the lotus, which is a symbol for self-knowledge and spiritual liberation.

Lakshmi first arrived in consciousness during a meditation devoted to many of the Hindu masters. She announced herself by name, extending a strong, loving presence that was familiar. On another occasion, she appeared in spiritual vision in a female form, holding a lotus blossom. The words she communicated in my mind were "Source of all life." She holds the ultimate potential for abundance (which, historically, arises from abundance produced by the plant kingdom). This is the fountain for the life-giving energy that extends to all humankind. She showed me a way to honor her on an altar through multicolored lotus candleholders, showed me an array of precious jewels and crystals, and provided an image of a mala that would be appropriate to make for her.

Keywords: Lakshmi can be understood as a powerful female transmitter of spiritual and material abundance to humankind, a fountain of life force that can produce an auspicious and long life so that we awaken into the highest spiritual levels.

Suggested Meditation Symbol: Pink lotus blossom in full bloom against a radiant white field

Leah: Judaic Matriarch, Wife of Jacob/Israel
Yesod, Emotional Level Two

The biblical figure of Leah, introduced in Genesis, presents us with a story of a love triangle involving Jewish patriarch Jacob (later known as Israel); his first wife, Leah; and her more beautiful sister, Rachel. According to the traditional tale, Jacob initially was attracted to Rachel and asked her father, Laban, for her hand in marriage, agreeing to work for Laban for seven years in lieu of a bride price. Rachel's father agreed, Laban fulfilled their bargain, and the promised marriage day finally arrived.

Somehow, at the last minute, Laban substituted the older sister for the younger. (We might assume this was to rid himself of the financial obligation of continuing to provide for a less marriageable daughter.) Jacob consummated the marriage with Leah yet did not discover her identity until the morning. He thus became husband in a consummated marriage with a wife not of his choosing! When Jacob learned of this deception, he still wanted Rachel, and Laban agreed to let him marry her too, for the price of seven more years of work.

We cannot know from the story how willing a participant Leah was in her father's deceptive scheme. Leah lived in a time and culture in which multiple wives were commonplace. We can understand that unfortunately, in some families, one child may be considered more beautiful than another. As a result, Leah's self-esteem likely suffered. Perhaps she hoped Jacob would learn to love her (we can all be blind in

302

the face of strong attractions), but we are told this never occurred. Yet he lay with her often enough for six sons and one daughter to be born.

Leah thus became an important foremother whose DNA still echoes throughout a whole cultural group today. Her sons became the progenitors of six of the twelve tribes of Israel. Her third son, Levi, an ascended master who is not listed here, was the grandfather of Moses, Aaron, and Miriam (each of whom ascended at their life's end). Aaron became the head of the Levitical priesthood, whose descendants were given charge of watching over the tabernacle. Leah's daughter Dinah, known from biblical tales for being raped, also ascended at the end of her lifetime (though she is not listed in this book).

When I contacted Leah in the ascended realm, my first impression was of the roburst and strong physical form she had inhabited in life. She possessed an ideal constitution to give birth to six sons and one daughter. Then I was given a spiritual view of motherhood. I saw the mother's part, contributing her DNA to form the child's body. (Some genetic schools of thought maintain that our physical form is most strongly influenced by maternal DNA.) Leah's DNA appeared in a beautiful form, like etheric white lace. In the journey of a spark of divine light into physical incarnation, giving birth is a sacred act. The mother's physical body is the conduit between worlds—a feat truly worthy of respect.

Leah shows us that coming to accept the roads *not* walked in life can be an important spiritual accomplishment. Setting aside religious interpretations, we can understand her role as one of arriving at acceptance of the spiritual assignment she was given. We can find joy and peace when we can accept what is, rather than suffering over the personality's unfulfilled expectations.

Keywords: Leah supports women who recognize the sacred dimensions of birth and motherhood and whose biological children may have a significant spiritual destiny. She helps anyone learning to accept and find joy in his or her life assignments, rather than suffering over his or her personality's unfulfilled expectations.

Suggested Meditation Symbol: Lacy white DNA strand in a field of radiant white light

Locana Buddha: Buddhist Lineage
Hidden Path White Ray (Two)
Yesod to Chesed, Mental Level

Locana, is one of the five female Dhyani Buddhas and, in that system, the partner of Buddha Akshobya. Her name is translated as "Clear Seeing" and sometimes given as "White-Robed One." She is met on one of the Hidden paths of the Qabala, this one connecting the sphere of Yesod (intuition at the mental level) with the sphere of Chesed (spiritual wisdom), where Buddha Akshobya can be met.

In iconography, Locana holds her hands together at her breast in the anjali mudra (prayer-hands mudra) and clasps the stems of two lotuses. Upon the lotus at her left shoulder rests a vajra bell, and on the lotus at her right shoulder rests a vase of immortality.

One of the visualization practices that can be used to work with Locana involves picturing a water mandala: a circle of clear, pure, still water that forms a mirrorlike reflecting surface. Water is often a symbol of emotions. We cannot see clearly when our emotions are turbulent. Locana's mirrorlike wisdom teaches us that by calming emotions, we can access deeper levels of wisdom. Working with her visualization practice gives us a steady point of focus that helps to develop calm concentration.

Close your eyes and visualize a large body of water, at night, with a full moon above. Watch for the surface of the water to become perfectly still, while being aware of the gentle rhythm of inhalation and exhalation of your breath. As this occurs, you can direct attention to observe the mirrorlike surface of the water with your inner vision. Symbols may appear on the waters surface, or other information may arrive, depending upon your strongest skills and level of experience.

To hold spiritual vision at this level requires that you come with the willingness to simply observe things as they are with objectivity

304

and equanimity, overcoming the obstacles of attraction and aversion to various events. Locana's mirrorlike wisdom allows us to see all things with detachment, remaining unaffected by what we see. This allows human consciousness to step back behind the personality's emotional reactivity to the neutral Observer, a state that is a great blessing to attain.

Objective witnessing is not denial, nor is it lacking in compassion. We are not asked to deny what our eyes report. Stepping back gives us a bit of distance and a wider perspective. It recognizes that there is always a higher purpose at work beyond all appearances and that human sight does not reveal those levels. Spiritual experience in the higher dimensions provides this sort of vantage point to glimpse levels of reality beyond what the body's eyes perceive.

In personal experience, Locana arrived in consciousness during one experience as a feminine stream of white light, connecting to Source. A later experience took me to a vast expanse of water, which was a bit below my point of observation. I was looking down at it, and the surface was dark, as if at nighttime. I could see that the surface of the water had some ripples—reactions in the emotional body to some perception. She then demonstrated how to pull my awareness back (behind my previous point of vision) and simply observe the scene from there. The ability to make the shift is based on calming the emotional body by remembering higher reality (i.e., shifting from the emotional body to access the mental body). The ripples in my vision smoothed out and became glassy. I maintained mental stillness, waiting for a symbol to appear on the water's surface, aware that by my accessing those (intuitive) depths from stillness, helpful guidance could emerge.

Keywords: Locana extends an outpouring of divine feminine energy to help us calm emotions and step back to access mirrorlike wisdom.

Suggested Meditation Symbol: Body of perfectly still water reflecting a full moon above as clearly as a mirror

Lugh/Llew/Lugus: Celtic Lineage
Tiphareth, Spiritual Level

In Celtic myth, Lugh is the great warrior leader, possessed of magical objects and the power to use them, who led the Tuatha Dé Danann in the Second Battle of Mag Tuireadh to victory over the Fomorians. He ruled the Tuatha after King Nuada was killed and before the Dagda. Known as Lugh of the Long Arm, he is celebrated at the harvest festival of Lughnasa, one of the most important seasonal celebrations in the Wheel of the Year throughout Ireland, Scotland, and the Isle of Man. In Wales, Lugh was worshipped as Lleu law Gyffes, while in the regions of Gaul, he was known as Lugus.

Lugh was generally described as bright and is often pictured through solar imagery: a tall, young, handsome, and vital man with wavy flaxen hair, sometimes riding a yellow horse. He is attested in many forms throughout the Celtic world, and his influence can be recognized in the names of many historic cities and sites throughout the European continent.

Lugh's mythological biography identifies him as a mixture of two races, and his father gave him to Tailtiu, queen of the Fir Bolg, to foster and raise. (It was common in ancient Celtic societies to have one's children raised by another.)

As a young man, Lugh traveled to Tara, the ancient seat of the high kings of Ireland, to join the court of King Nuada of the Tuatha Dé Danann. Only those who were masters of some recognized skill were admitted to their company.

At first, the Tuatha didn't want to accept him. As he mentioned each of his skills in turn, the gatekeeper replied that they already had a master of that skill. Then Lugh ingeniously asked if they had any single person who'd mastered all those skills together. There were none who had them all, so he was accepted.

Lugh was said to be in possession of various magical objects gathered from various sources. They included the spear of Assal, one of the four jewels of the Tuatha Dé Danann; his slingshot, wielded in battle against Balor of the Evil Eye; Fragarach, or the Answerer, the sword of Manannan mac Lir, which forced those it was pointed at to answer questions truthfully; Sguaba Tuinne, the Wind Sweeper, a boat of considerable speed; several horses, including Manannán's horse, Énbarr of the Flowing Mane, who could travel land and sea; and Failinis, a greyhound of great renown. Through magic and inspiring leadership, Lugh's forces overcame the Fomorians, though King Nuada was killed during the battle by Balor. Lugh then killed Balor, which fulfilled a prophecy. After that, Lugh ruled the Tuatha for a period. He finally retired from public life, along with his wives, making way for the Dagda to assume kingship of the Tuatha.

In my first experience with Lugh, he appeared in an abstract male form with reddish-flaxen hair, attired in gleaming battle armor. I kept receiving the words "Lugh of the bright countenance" and the idea that simply being around his fiery energy was revitalizing for anyone. After a bit, he was joined by a strong female presence whose name comes down to us as Buach—said to be one of his wives. The love-relationship energy between them was powerful to feel.

My strongest connection to Lugh took me behind the Celtic tradition entirely. His earliest appearance on earth was one in which he was a master of solar forces, using more advanced technology than is known today. The technology was designed to maintain a higher-dimensional energy field on a portion of the earth's surface. While some misused that power, causing a great cataclysm, Lugh never misused it. He continues to support the beneficial expression of higher dimensional light and yang power in the world today, which can be called upon by women as well as men.

Keywords: Lugh extends the power of the Great Central Sun to support advanced leadership, helping females and males to express the power of higher self in an entirely beneficial, balanced way. He is also a guide to ancient knowledge (Atlantean and Tuatha traditions).

Suggested Meditation Symbol: Round shield with a central Atlantean golden sun symbol, against a red field encircled by a golden pattern

Machig Labdron: Buddhist Lineage
Mental Level

Machig Labdron, known by the epithet Singular Mother Torch (1055–1149 CE), was a renowned eleventh-century Tibetan tantric Buddhist practitioner, teacher, and yogini who originated several Tibetan lineages of the Vajrayana practice of chod.

Hers were the first Buddhist teachings that originated in Tibet (brought forth by a male or a female). This identifies her as a significant spiritual foremother. She gave birth to a new and disciplined form of spiritual practice so that practitioners could experience the divine realms directly. It is easy to imagine that her independence, strength, and commitment to spiritual practice were (and are) profound to experience.

Some sources suggest she may have come from a family that practiced Bon spiritual traditions. She may have developed chod by combining native shamanism with the Dzogchen teachings. She went through many struggles to avoid traditional marriage and eventually left home to practice Buddhism as her life's calling. She was in a monastic order in Yuchong but eventually left and married Indian pandita Topa Draya, who was also a Buddhist practitioner. She and her husband practiced tantric union and raised a family.

During the period when she lived, it was believed that all authentic Buddhist teachings came from India, so her teachings were controversial. A delegation of Brahmans came from India to assess her qualifications as a teacher. Her students gathered with her at her home, where she successfully debated with the pandits. Thereafter, her practice spread even to India.

In iconography, Machig is often depicted like a dakini, holding a drum in her right hand and a bell in her left, with her right leg lifted. She is portrayed as white in color and wears the six bone ornaments of the charnel grounds, which is traditional for a practicing yogini. Her practice remains popular up to the present day in Tibet, Mongolia, and the Indian Himalayas.

In direct experience, she came rushing into consciousness while announcing her name in my mind. Her independence, strength, and commitment to spiritual practice were profound to experience. Another time, connecting with her mind, I noted an Asian energy that had a powerful edge. She is not one to be taken lightly. In another visit some weeks later, she arrived in consciousness conveying the qualities of a spiritual foremother, one who is profoundly focused on supporting spiritual awakening in a disciplined way.

Keywords: Machig Labdron supports those who practice chod (or shamanic) traditions and can be an ally to support those who teach women's spiritual practices.

Suggested Meditation Symbol: Chod drum against a rich purple field (Pantone 265–266)

Mamaki Buddha: Buddhist Lineage
Tiphareth, Mental Level

Mamaki is the golden-yellow female Buddha of the ratna, or jewel, family. In the Dhyani Buddha tradition, she is paired with male Buddha Ratnasambhava. Her name means "She Who Makes Everything Her Own," because she knows the true spiritual unity (the higher self) that unites all humankind.

Every life begins by developing the capacities of the individual self. In the beginning there are distortions in self perception. One extreme produces excessive pride; the other extreme is characterized by lack of self-worth and confidence. The process of developing one's unique qualities and achieving personal power is concluded at the second emotional level.

As one continues spiritual practice, although the ego may offer temporary resistance to giving up it's individual perspective, persistence will eventually move one toward experiences of the higher self. Mystics through the ages have sometimes used the word *annihilation* to describe a temporary ego death which might be experienced along the way. Annihilation describes an experience in which the customary locus of individual self dissolves (through the agency of spiritual grace) into timeless no-self.

Working on the mental level, Mamaki supports us as we transition from wielding personal power to being a point of expression for transcendent power, *through* our gifts. To make the shift, one lays down personal ambition, pride in one's unique achievements, and the need to receive acknowledgment from others. Adopting attitudes that grant equal worth (through different forms and at different levels of expression) to everyone, along with continuing spiritual practice, assists the process. As the higher self descends into full physical manifestation, it becomes possible to momentarily experience the spiritual state known as oneness.

In iconography, Mamaki may be depicted in two-, six-, eight-, or twelve-armed forms. In two-armed form, she may be shown holding a jewel. In certain Buddhist meditation practices, she is visualized as emerging on a square earth mandala made of yellow jewels, emerging from a blue sky, or emerging on a golden throne supported by four camels, which symbolizes the riches of her mind being extended toward physical manifestation.

In direct experience with Mamaki on several occasions, my consciousness was showered with her white-golden light. Once, she arrived by announcing her name within my mind. Contact is powerfully energizing, restoring the spiritual perspective by which one can look upon all the dramas of the physical world and remain in a centered, clear state.

This is the dimension where the individual mind is already attuned with divine mind, From that radiant meeting point, equanimity shines its benevolent light toward everything we encounter ahead as we become ready to serve as an outlet for a unique life mission.

Keywords: Mamaki works on the mental level to help us clear any remaining thoughts and beliefs (the personality's perceived limitations) and appreciate our natural gifts without feeding specialness, arrogance, or excessive pride. She helps prepare us to be a conduit for some higher spiritual purpose

Suggested Meditation Symbol: A central circle of clear golden light surrounded by a vast expanse of abstract, radiant white light extending everywhere, (Pantone 1225 or 1235)

Manjushri: Buddhist Lineage
Chokma, Spiritual Level

Manjushri is one of the most familiar and significant masters acknowledged in several branches of Buddhism. He was said to bestow spectacular visionary experience to those meditating on select mountain peaks and caves therein. He is the earliest known and most important bodhisattva (of wisdom) in Mahayana Buddhism. Within Vajrayana Buddhism, he is a meditational deity, considered a fully enlightened Buddha. In Chinese Buddhism, he is one of the four great bodhisattvas, associated with the sacred mountain called Mount Wutai.

In Tibetan Buddhism, Manjushri is sometimes depicted in a trinity with Avalokitesvara (at the Chesed spiritual level) and Vajrapani (an ascended master not included in this book). An example of Manjushri's wisdom teachings includes how to enter samadhi naturally through transcendent wisdom. Arriving at transcendent wisdom is the special gift of all Chokma masters. Sometimes called omniscience, this wisdom includes the means (spiritual techniques) for moving past the personality level and awakening to prelife and postlife awareness.

One of Manuhiri's practices is to contemplate the five skandhas (form, sensation and feeling, perception, mental activity, and consciousness) as originally empty and quiescent, nonarising, by day or night. It is said this practice—if engaged over time—leads toward the inconceivable state (inconceivable because it is beyond thinking and language) without any obstruction or form. This is called the samadhi of one act.

When consciousness momentarily arrives at this inconceivable state, it recognizes that there are metalevels of existence beyond the individual personality self. When one realizes that the personality self is merely a temporary grouping of the aggregates, each of which is negated by the mental choice "Not I," then human suffering is extinguished. (In this view, suffering comes from clinging to the aggregates to define both self and reality.) The emptiness approach is unique to Buddhism.

In iconography, Manjushri is depicted as a male bodhisattva wielding a flaming sword in his right hand, representing the realization of transcendent wisdom, which cuts through ignorance and duality. The scripture supported by the padma (lotus) held in his left hand is a *Prajnaparamita* sutra, representing his attainment of ultimate realization from the blossoming of wisdom.

My first contact with Manjushri in consciousness occurred in a field of total darkness, while his mind was alive with flashing mirrors of radiant white light. During my strongest contact with him, I entered a field where my consciousness was like a ball whose entire surface was an organ of vision. In every direction—all 360 degrees—full vision was possible simultaneously. Nothing in any universe was hidden, yet there was also no personal aspect of mind active or asking any question.

Keywords: Manjushri is a pure extension of the wisdom and power to claim ultimate reality. Compassion is an essential spiritual quality but not enough by itself. Manjushri's fiery sword provides spiritual power that clears the way for practitioners of all paths to access the highest states of consciousness. He can also provide specific wisdom about Buddhist teachings for those who study Mahayana traditions.

Suggested Meditation Symbol: Raised Buddhist flaming sword against a radiant white field

Mary, the Mother of Jesus, Saint Mary: Christian Lineage
Hidden Blue Ray (No Tarot Equivalent), Spiritual Level

During the past two thousand years, Mary has been consistently venerated as the blessed mother of Jesus/Yeshua. Whether one believes in the concept of virgin birth or not, she was clearly the mother of his childhood and witnessed his crucifixion. She is honored within all major Christian traditions and is granted a revered position in Islam, in which one of the longest chapters of the Koran is devoted to her.

Mary has miraculously appeared to certain people at different times over the centuries since her physical lifetime. She can appear in a regal form or in a simple form to those who perceive her with visionary senses.

As is the case with many of the ascended masters who were incorporated into various religious traditions, there are conflicting beliefs about her life. According to the apocryphal Gospel of James, Mary was the daughter of Joachim and Anne, whose name is sometimes written as Anna. According to this source, before Mary's conception, Anna was barren and was far advanced in years. Without attempting to resolve our questions about this, we can simply note that as a young child, Mary was taken to live at the temple in Jerusalem to serve as a consecrated virgin.

Perhaps this parting from her parents at such a tender age is partly what made her such a compassionate ally for life challenges and traumas faced by children. She was also a key figure in the intense drama of the crucifixion. We can hardly imagine what it was like for her to witness Jesus's crucifixion. We can appreciate that however she did it brought forth mastery that makes her an ally when parents face times of challenge with their children.

Mary has provided comfort and support throughout much of my life. She first came to me in childhood, although it wasn't until the second half of my life that I became aware of her again directly. As my spiritual senses developed, I was more able to receive communications about other times when she had been near.

During the time when I was preparing this book, she communicated that she came into the human experience as part of a first wave to rebalance the feminine energy on earth. As a spiritual mother, she could gently open hearts so that a rebalancing of polarities could begin to occur. Currently, it is her mission to hold all of humankind collectively while we are shedding old hurts and waking up to our eternal reality, where no hurts exist. In this way, she is a divine mother whose gifts wrap around the entire world with infinite and tender care.

Though I first experienced Mary many years before I began to write this book, it was important that I was able to confirm her classification and level through a mineral. However, I made errors for a long time. She made occasional contact without any mineral, which all masters can do.

At first, I thought she might correspond to the one hidden path I already knew at the time, which was the hidden path of the pink ray. Later, when she made contact I could see in spiritual vision that her energy field carried pale blue as well as white light. This color combination is found with some female masters on the path of Gimel at the mental level (tarot High Priestess), and I next thought those females included her. But she did not respond through the minerals that work for that group.

I had recently discovered another of the hidden paths, connecting the sphere of Binah and Chesed, through a rare blue mineral with unusual chemical composition and fluorescence that connected me with two masters there. This opened my awareness to the possibility of additional hidden paths. Indeed there are more, not all of them are included in this book.

At that point, Mary herself helped me to realize that one of my so-far-unexplored colorless quartz specimens corresponded to her (and told me the specific trace-element chemistry within colorless quartz that linked the spheres of Kether and Chesed). When I went into meditation with that crystal she appeared immediately, with a clarity of contact beyond anything I'd yet experienced.

She has sometimes been called the Queen of Heaven, and indeed she is, extending a spiritual level colorless ray directly from the uppermost sphere of Kether, to the sphere of Chesed, where spiritual teachings uplift humankind.

Keywords: Mary is available to comfort anyone on any spiritual path who is facing challenges and asks for her support. She can be an ally in all matters that pertain to children. Her gift of divine (unconditional) love and compassion can be the panacea that breaks generational patterns of hurt that are passed through ancestral family lines.

Suggested Meditation Symbol: Faint white-light outline of the vesica piscis symbol against the starry void. It is oriented with the points of central almond shape where the circles intersect pointing up and down. The central shape is a portal of radiant pure-white light, which becomes light blue as it meets the surrounding cosmic space. This symbol typically represents the intersection of the spiritual and physical worlds, and the cosmic womb of creation— appropriate for one who expresses an aspect of the Divine Mother.

Mary Magdalene: Christian Lineage
Binah, Mental Level

Despite the efforts to suppress accurate information about her for some two thousand years, as Mary Magdalene has reemerged into collective awareness in the past few decades, she has become an iconic divine-feminine figure precious to many. Among several key biblical Marys, she is sometimes identified as Mary of Bethany, sister of Lazarus.

Magdalene provides a uniquely significant model for women that combines spiritual wisdom, female leadership, and (as some believe) an intimate and energetically powerful sexual relationship with Jesus, also known as Yeshua, as her beloved partner.

Her reinterpretation has come about as formerly unknown ancient texts mentioning her have emerged. One of these, called the Gospel of Mary, was discovered in 1896 in a fifth-century papyrus codex written in Sahidic Coptic. This Berlin Codex was purchased in Cairo by German diplomat Carl Reinhardt. The translation of this work portrays Magdalene as a female spiritual leader ("the woman who knew the All") and suggests she received teachings directly from Jesus/Yeshua that were not shared with others. She is also mentioned in a tantalizing passage in the Gospel of Philip (another of the ancient documents retrieved in the Nag Hammadi find), described as "the one who called [Jesus] companion" and claimed he "used to kiss her on her [mouth]."

After those discoveries, Magdalene's importance could no longer be denied. Many other books have been written since then, such as the 1982 book *Holy Blood, Holy Grail* by authors Michael Baigent, Richard Leigh, and Henry Lincoln. The more recent, widely read Dan Brown novel *The Da Vinci Code* and the movie of the same name proposed that her lineage (and the child conceived with Yeshua) was protected throughout certain periods by the Templar Knights. She is also linked to the Sinclair (or Saint Clair) family in Scotland, who built Rosslyn Chapel. According to these theories, the holy bloodline (her child conceived with Yeshua) was the secret preserved by the mysterious order known as the Priory of Sion.

As with many masters, the most compelling evidence for who she was and what she achieved comes about when we become able to contact her in the ascended realm. Like many women, I wanted to discover as much as I could about her soon after beginning my spiritual path. Reading what I could find and continuing my spiritual work, after some years, I felt divinely blessed to experience a brief touch of her energy. It was many years before there was more.

Magdalene is listed in the Gospel of Matthew as being present at Jesus's crucifixion (Matthew 27:56). In the Gospel of John, she is recorded as the first witness of Jesus's resurrection (John 20:14–16; Mark 16:9 in later manuscripts). What sort of spiritual training allowed her to witness the crucifixion, be greeted by Yeshua when she visited his tomb the next day (as reported in the Bible), and then be able to move thousands of miles away from her homeland soon after? Evidence suggests she may have traveled by boat, along with Joseph of Arimathea and a few others, initially arriving in Southern France near Marseilles and then continuing to the British Isles, to begin a new chapter of life. Clearly, she mastered the art of graceful life transitions, something all of us must learn.

In *The Cult of the Black Virgin* by Ean Begg (2006), she is linked to the mysterious Black Madonna icons, which originally numbered about four hundred and a few of which remain in ancient cathedrals scattered in Southern France. These icons are linked to Magdalene, the Merovingian Dynasty, and the Knights Templar. Authors who had unique access to research the ancestral genealogies of the European aristocracy, such as Laurence Gardner, author of *Bloodline of the Holy*

Grail and other books, also contributed to these theories about Yeshua, Magdalene, and their purported descendants.

Our hearts' deepest questions about Magdalene will not likely be answered by research. Through multiple experiences over many years, I received my own answers regarding the nature of the intimate relationship she shared with Yeshua in life, which still exists energetically on the higher planes. She has been a teacher of high sexual-energetic practices and a model for a truly holy relationship. She also taught me how to hold a priestess role when ushering a beloved partner through the transition at the end of life. Holding awareness in the spiritual realm while supporting the physical process invites a state of grace, rather than grief, to be present. Magdalene's spiritual support is unfailingly valuable in my life.

Keywords: Custodian of high spiritual knowledge, Magdalene supports women to awaken their spiritual potential and power and manifest the full range of expression possible within a female body, including a sacred sexual relationship. She can support us to assist a loved one with the death transition and support those who teach about the divine feminine.

Suggested Meditation Symbol: Deep purple Holy Grail (chalice) flooded with white light coming down from above, against a violet field (Pantone 265–266)

Mira Bai: Hindu Lineage
Hod, Mental Level

Mira Bai, also known as Meera, is a historically known sixteenth-century Hindu mystic poet and devotee of Krishna. In the absence of other sources, scholars have attempted to establish Meera's biography from secondary literature that mentions her. She is mentioned in "Bhaktamal," a fifteenth-century poem by Nabha Dass that gives short biographies of more than two hundred bhaktas, confirming she was widely known and a cherished figure in the bhakti movement.

Bhakti refers to a passionate love-devotion to a deity. It was expressed in personal terms, constituted an individual path to enlightenment, and was mystically inspired, grounded in individual experience. The bhakti movement emerged in the eighth century in Tamil Nadu and Kerala (South India) and spread northward, reaching a peak between the fifteenth and seventeenth centuries in the North Indian Hindu tradition. It produced a surge in Hindu literature written in regional languages, particularly in the form of devotional poems and music. Mira Bai's poetry is one of the most enduring and popular examples that came forth during this potent time.

Some accounts say she was born into a Rajput royal family in the Kudki district of Pali, Rajasthan, India. Most legends about Meera mention her fearless disregard for social and family conventions; her passionate commitment to Krishna, whom she treated as her husband; and her persecution by her in-laws for her religious devotion. While historical evidence is slim, she is believed to have gone on many pilgrimages in later life and may have lived either in Dwarka (sacred to Krishna) or in Vindrevan.

The spiritual voice of her poetry marks Mira Bai as a vessel through which divine inspiration flowed into words. Thousands of devotional poems in praise of Lord Krishna are attributed to her, but scholars believe just a few hundred are authentic. Many poems attributed to Meera were likely composed later by others who admired her. These poems are commonly known as *bhajans* and are popular across India.

Mira Bai was one of the first of the Hindu masters to connect with my consciousness in meditation, long before I understood her Qabalah correspondence. While I was working on this book, I eventually heard her name in my mind and felt a loving presence come forward. Several years later, I was working with her in meditation, and her devotion to Krishna came through in a strong wave of feeling. As I aligned with her feeling for him, I began to see abstract images of her, naked in the forest in a moonlit setting, expressing her (now fulfilled) desire for her spiritual beloved in poetic words, within my mind.

Meera's poetry often referred to her spiritual longing for Krishna in erotic terms, like that of a lover and beloved, and she often referred to herself in the third person. Her continued influence in our time underscores her message of freedom, her dedication to Krishna, and her commitment to express her spiritual beliefs despite persecution. She lived and wrote about what she felt, doing so with a vivid language of love that illustrates the full range of human emotions between human and the divine.

During one other experience, she brought me poetic lines before I sat down to meditate. Connecting with her more deeply, my mind went soaring up to a high mental-plane dimension. I was told I was visiting the Well of Words, the dimension where all the words used in one's language reside, accessible for those who write. I could see the tremendous (and practical) value for a spiritual author to connect with her.

Keywords: Call upon Mira Bai to open your mind to divine inspiration; support your own emerging spiritual-creative voice (poetry, music, creativity); and hold fast to your right to choose the spiritual path most meaningful for you to experience the divine realms.

Suggested Meditation Symbol: Ektara (long-handled Indian string instrument with rounded base used to accompany verse) against a slightly pinkish-orange field (Pantone 170)

Miriam: Judaic Lineage
Purple Path of Gimel (Tarot: High Priestess), Emotional Level Two

Miriam comes to our attention in several biblical passages as the sister of Moses (mystical law giver associated with the Ten Commandments) and Aaron (high priest). Her first well-known exploit is told in Exodus 2:1–10, wherein an unnamed sister of Moses helps to deliver him to the Nile River. We can use two genealogies listing Moses, Aaron, and Miriam as the sole children of Amram (Numbers 26:59; 1 Chronicles 6:3) to identify this sister as Miriam.

Miriam first appears by name, however, in the crossing of the Red Sea (Exodus 15:20–21), wherein she is called "the prophet Miriam, Aaron's sister." She led the Hebrew women in singing, dancing, and playing drums. This passage identifies her as the biblical equivalent of the high priestess, who often leads other women in spiritual practices such as those described.

To fulfill a priestess role requires that a woman have her own direct relationship with spiritual forces. She becomes a living link that can access higher reality through the subtle energy channels in the human body. Biblical sources do not tell us how she developed this ability, but both her brothers manifested their own mystical abilities. Such gifts often run in families even in the present day.

Priestesses also are women with truly independent spirits. They don't easily accept being told what to do and are able to speak truth to power, to borrow an expression that is understood today. However, the period in which Miriam lived did not easily accept such a woman. She is described as outspoken, and she was the first biblical woman to be given the epithet *prophet*.

Huldah (in chapter 10, the sphere of Yesod) and Hannah (also an ascended master but not listed in this book) were also known as prophets. We might guess that Miriam was a gifted intuitive who shared the information she received from the higher realms—although when it challenged cultural or religious boundaries it was not universally welcomed!

Biblical narrative (Numbers 12:2) tells us that Miriam (along with Aaron) challenged the sole prophetic authority of Moses. She asked a telling question: "Has the Lord spoken only through Moses? Has he not spoken through us also?" She understood spiritual leadership to embrace diverse voices, female, and male. But the price of speaking out at that time was severe, and she was punished for her audacity, while Aaron was not.

While the Bible says she was punished by God, all who experience the divine as an entirely loving Creator will question the meaning of this assertion. Punishment from an earthly "authority" of spiritual law was more likely. Whatever happened, Miriam's voice was effectively silenced, and she was disgraced. We are told she never spoke again, nor was she spoken to—she thus became a warning to control future generations of women.

When I connected with her in the ascended realm, she was a tower of purple-white light. My consciousness simply wanted to join in that holy extension—forever. My point is not to critique the customs or beliefs around her story. Those of us living today who express spiritual energy in any priestess role can thank her for her accomplishments in a time when expressing her gifts was far from easy.

Keywords: Miriam supports women to polish their abilities to become living links to higher spiritual forces and to share those methods with other women when that is appropriate. She reminds us that the access point to Spirit is within our own consciousness. We can access the divine directly as we release limiting cultural beliefs and maintain disciplined practices.

Suggested Meditation Symbol: Early hand drum against a violet field (Pantone 270 or 265–266)

Moses: Judaic Lineage
Chesed, Mental Level

As described in the Bible, Moses was of the tribe of Levi. Levi was the third son of patriarch Jacob and his first wife, Leah. Moses; his brother, the high priest Aaron; and their sister, Miriam, were descendants of biblical patriarch Jacob (Israel). Moses's mother was named Jochebed (she is an ascended master at Yesod but is not listed individually in this book).

The Talmud holds that the Torah (the first books of the Old Testament of the Bible) were written by Moses, with the exception of the last eight verses of Deuteronomy, which describe his death and burial and were written by Joshua. While I understood that the Ten Commandments formed the basis for upholding Judaic tradition (and were also incorporated into Christianity), I must admit I held some negative judgments about how they had been used during centuries of repressive Christian teachings. Some unexpected experiences with Moses during meditation led me to step behind those judgments and see him from a different perspective.

Since Moses was born in Egypt during the period when all male Hebrew children were ordered put to death, the Bible tells that as an infant, Moses was placed in a reed basket by his mother and sent downstream to preserve his life. The basket was found by Pharaoh's daughter, who then raised him. According to some accounts, it was Moses's older sister, Miriam, who led Pharaoh's daughter to find the basket.

As an adult, Moses possessed genuine spiritual power and could demonstrate that fact. Moses was a prophet whose word was believed, and others followed him. He was the prophesied liberator who led his people (as the energy of Chesed always does) toward a better and more abundant life, based on spiritual principles. In a dramatic scene, Moses famously threw down his staff, which became a serpent, and parted the Red Sea, allowing his people to make their exodus. As they passed through the parted sea, the Israelites were physically separated from their troubled past as exiles in Egypt.

I wasn't intending contact with Moses the first time he came forward in consciousness. I hadn't yet shaken my judgments about how the Ten Commandments had been used. Our contact was brief, and I was focused on contacting other masters at the same level.

During his second more extended visit, he showed me a flash of his mystical experience on the mountain. Masters understand us very well and communicate in a way most likely to capture our attention. Now he had my full attention. Whatever its source, I was shown that visionary information came to him, imprinting his consciousness in a way that was like engraving it in stone. (I have no idea about actual stone tablets, but he showed me the symbolic import of what he experienced.)

It was a significant part of his life mission to share something from that profound mystical experience, which is always difficult to do. In that period, there were few individuals who experienced higher consciousness directly. His energy field was strongly oriented to teach higher knowledge in terms of spiritual laws.

The purpose of Moses's laws was to show humankind how to draw the spiritual world closer. Doing the things prohibited by the Ten Commandments produces guilt for most human beings. Guilt is one of the biggest obstacles that humans must clear so their consciousness can experience the higher realms. Thus, it is logical that *not doing* the things the commandments prohibit eliminates potential guilt, thus outlining a path of human choices that could lead one back to direct awareness of the divine.

Contact with his mind gave me reason to release my former negative judgments. As we liberate Moses (and other masters) from how their teachings have been used, we can better appreciate the possibility of developing our own mystical relationship with the divine. We may not go into the wilderness or receive revelations from within a burning bush, but the spiritual realms are waiting for us to pay attention in whatever way we can. Moses also reminds us that the kingdom is within us and that we each contain the means to recognize this, even though we must polish away any blocks to claim it.

Keywords: Moses supports all who choose to uplift and purify their habits and conduct to become available to receive divine guidance. He supports those who have an assignment to bring forth prophecies, written principles, or teachings that help humankind experience greater spiritual love and light, develop human relationships based in brotherhood and sisterhood, and respect all creation.

Suggested Meditation Symbol: Engraved stone tablets against a sapphire-blue field (brighter to darker blues, Pantone 281–295)

Niguma: Buddhist Lineage
Hod, Mental Level

Niguma, a woman who lived in the tenth to eleventh centuries CE, is acknowledged as one of two female founders of the Shangpa Kagyu school of Vajrayana Buddhism. She became an accomplished spiritual mystic-adept who left behind a legacy of teachings (taken down by others) that made her one of the most important and influential yoginis and Vajrayana teachers of the period.

Biographical information about Niguma is scarce (see *Niguma Lady of Illusion*, translated by Sarah Harding). Her birth name may have been Shrijnana or Palgyi Yeshe, and she may have been born into a rich Brahman-caste family in the town of Pema in Kashmir. This area was a hub of Buddhist activity, particularly of the tantric type, and probably in close quarters with the Shaivite tradition and other forms of esoteric Hinduism. Some reports are that she was the consort of Naropa.

The tantric path is one that offers the possibility of enlightenment in a single lifetime (as opposed to other Buddhist traditions that suggest the attainment of Buddhahood is accomplished over many lifetimes). Masters of the tantric path display certain signs that allow their spiritual advancement to be recognized. Niguma manifested the signs of progress in the secret mantra Vajrayana and attained the rainbow-like body of union. She had the ability to directly receive teachings from the great male Buddhist deity known as Vajradhara.

Niguma had many students, some of whom left accounts of meetings with her. Marpa Lotsawa, the master translator of Buddhist scripture, received teachings from her. To preserve the teachings in purest form, she allowed only a single individual to serve as lineage holder for seven consecutive generations. Vajradhara initiated the lineage, Niguma was the second, and five male adepts continued after her. Together these masters are known as the Seven Jewels. It was noteworthy to me when I was able to discover that all five in the lineage after her also ascended at the end of their lifetimes. The Shangpa Kagyu tradition continues to this day, more than one thousand years after her lifetime, known as one of the eight great practice lineages of Tibet.

She is known by the epithet Lady of Illusion since she advises practitioners to meet every observed manifestation as both deity and Illusion. Perceiving the outer world visible to human eyes as an illusion (the Hindu term is *maya*) is a teaching found in many Buddhist and Hindu traditions. Her approach actively uses the illusion, rather than attempting to escape from it, to awaken illumination.

Her own meditative practices were clearly advanced, as her teachings refer to advanced practices using breath and cultivating inner heat, energetically stimulating the three channels within human subtle energy anatomy to achieve the final stages of enlightenment. The translations are obscure (likely intentionally) to those who have not received an empowerment (i.e., been initiated by a teacher of that tradition).

Niguma is considered a dakini—a fierce female sky dancer—alluding to her ability to travel in higher astral realms and ferociously cut away spiritual ignorance and human ego. Pictured in iconography, dakinis typically brandish a flaying knife in one hand and a skullcap in the other.

Niguma was one of the last among the masters I experienced while writing this book. She had been on my spreadsheet for a long time, but I was unsure of her correspondence. She came into consciousness during a long walk to encourage me to discover her. When I finally understood her correspondence correctly, she arrived in a powerful way. The words I jotted down during the experience (using automatic writing) included *tremendous spiritual knowledge, voluptuous,* and *powerful.*

Cemeteries were a location favored by dakinis for spiritual practice. Vajrayana practice is known for breaking custom and engaging practices that are conventionally taboo. Niguma communicated that there was also a practical reason why those who were serious about achieving enlightenment in a single lifetime would seek such an intense practice environment: the ability to hold one's practices and spiritual light in such a setting developed great spiritual strength and ability.

Keywords: Call upon Niguma to provide inspiration into tantric practice and to inspire you in your own spiritual studies or in teaching others if that is your assignment.

Suggested Meditation Symbol: Shangpa Kagyu symbol in gold (like Shiva's three-pronged trisula) against a slightly pinkish-orange field (Pantone 170)

Njord: Norse Lineage
Chokma, Mental Level

Njord is introduced in Norse myth as a member of the Vanir race, who came to live among the Aesir because of the truce that ended the Aesir-Vanir War (both he and Hoenir were part of the Vanir's side of an exchange of hostages that ensured hostilities would end).

Njord is also known as the father of Freya and Freyr and was chosen as a husband by Skadi, who was from the Jotun race of giants, to compensate her for the Aesir's killing of her father. The tales report that their marriage was not a good match for either of them, as Skadi preferred to live in the far mountains, and Njord preferred to live by the sea. These scant bits of information seem to place him in a secondary position, even to his children, who are popular figures to those who follow Norse tradition. When I contacted him, I completely revised my understanding of his significance.

Njord is further described in *The Poetic Edda* as a future survivor of Ragnarok, which implies great courage and skill as a warrior. The poem "Grímnismál" describes him in a complimentary way as a "prince of men ... lacking in malice" and adds that he "rules over the high-timbered temple." *The Prose Edda* introduces Njord in chapter 23 of the book *Gylfaginning*. In this chapter, Njord is described as living in the heavens, ruling over the winds, and having the ability to calm both sea and air. These qualities begin to reveal a master of genuine importance.

An additional fact to note is that Njord's reputation as a beneficent force was remembered in Norwegian folk practice as recently as the eighteenth and nineteenth centuries. His name is also linked to an Icelandic ring oath and to many place names throughout Scandinavia, indicating that he was more important than we can understand simply from his scant mention in *The Prose Edda* and *The Poetic Edda*.

Ring oaths were pledges of loyalty made by warriors who followed a powerful war leader. The leader sometimes wore a neck or arm ring made of metal shaped to snugly fit his bicep. The ring was a symbol of the leader's authority, and those he commanded swore an oath, using the ring.

When I first attempted to contact Njord, I hadn't put these clues together, and I tried several other Qabalah placements that include warriors before seeking him at Chokma. Once again, I would not have discovered his high level without using crystals I had previously classified. When I finally tried one at the mental level, he came through with incredible power and strength—pure male potency in a massive, ongoing current. He invited me to notice that part of the abundance he extends to all humankind includes his son, Freyr, and daughter, Freya, who help humankind to manifest abundance at levels further down the Qabalah tree (at Netzach). I am glad I persisted and was able to confirm he is indeed far more important than myth indicates.

Keywords: Njord supports the development of male leaders who use power in beneficial ways, inspire loyalty, and build strong teams to provide abundance and improve the quality of life for their time.

Suggested Meditation Symbol: Silver metal arm band on a strong male bicep, against a field of radiant white light

Nuada: Celtic Lineage
Chokma, Mental Level

Nuada is known in myth as the first king of the Tuatha Dé Danann, who led his people to Ireland. We have no archaeological evidence from the (early) period in which he lived. He appears in tales that have been grouped into what is known as the Mythological Cycle within Irish mythology. This grouping includes works such as *The Book of Invasions*, *The Battle of Moytura*, *The Children of Lir*, and *The Wooing of Etain*. All these stories tell of the Tuatha Dé Danann and other mythical races, such as the Fomorians and Fir Bolg.

Nuada was described as large-breasted and flaxen-maned. (Many ancient warrior leaders were of physically imposing stature.) When Nuada and the Tuatha arrived in Ireland, the island's earlier inhabitants, known as the Fir Bolg, refused his request to be given half the territory. As a result, the two groups went to war.

Nuada possessed a magical sword from which none could escape (one of the four treasures of the Tuatha), which was later passed on to Lugh. Nuada lost a hand during the battle, in combat with the Fir Bolg champion Sreng. The Tuatha's primary healer, Dian Cecht, made Nuada a silver hand to replace the one he'd lost; however, he had to give up kingship since to fill the kingly role required complete physical perfection that he no longer possessed. Kingship passed to Bres, a half Fomorian, who ruled for a time, though he was not respected, because he levied heavy burdens of tribute (taxes) on the Tuatha.

Ultimately, Dian Cecht's son Miach, who was even more skilled than his father, made Nuada a hand of flesh and blood, with which he was able to regain kingship. Bres set off events that led to a second battle. In the second battle, Nuada and his wife, Macha, were slain by Balor, or the Evil Eye. Lugh then roused the Tuatha to seek revenge, killed Balor in the ensuing melee, and became king of the Tuatha for a time. Ultimately, he retired and turned rulership over to the Dagda.

In every cultural mythology, we meet tales of heroic and skilled leaders who orchestrated great battles. Some of those leaders ascended at the end of their lifetimes. It is well known that many leaders were killed or lost limbs in carrying out their life assignments. More than a few of the masters who express the energy of Chokma (including Osiris, though the Egyptian lineage is not included in this book) are presented in tales in which they are killed yet live on, ruling the otherworld that exists beyond form. These tales in which slain leaders reule in the afterlife remind us that the physical body is not our senior reality. Our ultimate spiritual essence cannot be changed or harmed in any way, no matter what happens in human life.

My experience with Nuada came near the end of this book's preparation. I had previously sought him in other parts of the Qabalah unsuccessfully. When I approached him again, using the right crystal and working with a symbol I intuitively felt would be appropriate, a sword of light, the experience was spectacular. He instantly communicated that each of us possesses a sword of light, referring to the energy channels that can be awakened that lie parallel to the human spine. He was with me as those channels lit within, sending my consciousness soaring. He reminds us that each of us has this access within, which can carry consciousness to a vastly different perspective on All That Is than human eyesight.

Keywords: Nuada is a skilled guide when consciousness is prepared to experience the omniscient wisdom of ultimate reality. He supports the evolution of courageous and skilled leadership (which manifests in women as well as men). He can provide insight into the mysteries of the Tuatha Dé Danann and supports those who lose a limb during earthly warfare (a limb may be replaced with a prosthetic, an artificial body part). He invites all of us to cultivate the mental attitudes that allow us to remember our eternal wholeness in the dimensions outside time.

Suggested Meditation Symbol: Nuada's sword of white light glowing against a radiant white field

Odin: Norse Lineage
Chokma, Mental Level

In Norse myth, Odin (also known by the name Woden or Woten in Germanic tales) is the all-father of the gods and the ruler of the Aesir. He is a shape-shifter who speaks in verse and is skilled in magic. He led his people in the Aesir-Vanir War and established the great hall known as Valhalla, to which the souls of valiant warriors slain in battle are taken by Valkyrie shield maidens, where they enjoy an honorable and happy afterlife.

From Odin's high seat (Chokma is the realm of transcendent wisdom in the Qabalah), he can survey all the nine dimensions and knows what is going on in all of them. He makes many journeys into the world, into the land of men, and is shrewd and calculating as well as helpful, often described as both a trickster and a protector. He is frequently shown wielding a spear named Gungnir and wearing a cloak and a broad hat. He rides the flying eight-legged steed Sleipnir across the sky and into the underworld and has two raven companions named Huginn and Muninn, whose names represent thought and memory.

As author John Lindow points out in *Norse Mythology*, many of the characteristics accorded to Odin describe a shaman. Lindow cites a twelfth-century work called *Historia Norvegiae*, which offers descriptions of shamans among the Sami, an indigenous people inhabiting northern Sweden; Denmark; Norway; and Murmansk Oblast, Russia, and the Kola Peninsula. Some practitioners of Norse traditions today object to comparing the higher abilities of Norse masters to shamanism. Whatever terms you prefer, we can note that both the Norse masters and shamans learned to travel through the astral dimensions.

As is typical of myths, Odin is introduced in a family structure, as the son of Bestla and the husband of Frigg (see both above). Together he and Frigg appear as father and mother of Baldur (see above). Thor (see below) is said to be Odin's son with Jord.

The myths relate that Odin gained his great wisdom by venturing to the mystical well at the base of the world tree. Mimir (also an ascended master) was the guardian of the well and had become all-wise by drinking the magical waters. Odin asked for a drink of the water, and Mimir replied that Odin must sacrifice an eye. Odin gouged out his own eye, dropped it into the well, and was allowed to drink from the waters of cosmic knowledge. One-eyed Odin is thus a symbol of our need to temporarily sacrifice human perception to gain metalevel wisdom. Like Osiris, Odin presides over the afterline dimensions and welcomes those whose consciousness is prepared to join him for experiences of the higher realms while they still live.

I've experienced Odin in spiritual vision as a hooded figure circling high on his familiar horse, Sleipnir. My deepest contact with him began by seeing a single cosmic eye descending toward my point of observation. As the eye came closer, I was aware of pure sentient consciousness. It became a portal; entire stars, planets, and universes were within it, and it could see into all dimensions. As I entered this realm, I experienced exquisite journeys and understandings that took place beyond any ability to describe them in words.

I was also aware of Odin's mind in union with divine Source and shown how dedicated he is to serve the divine plan. Nothing I had read, especially about his supposed trickster side, prepared me for the sacredness I felt. I was aware of the nearness of divine Source and my own higher essence. From this metalevel perspective, all the scenes unfolding in human incarnation appear strung together like individual frames in a movie film unfurling against infinity. All of one's life events have a higher purpose, and by choosing to see them that way (rather than as something wrong) one can extend into whatever life presents—with power and presence. In my experience, the master we know as Odin takes an extraordinary interest in assisting the evolutionary development of humankind.

Keywords: Odin is a custodian who holds a gateway to the dimension of all-knowledge, where reality before and after physical life can be seen and where insight into the spiritual purpose of one's present life journey can be gained.

Suggested Meditation Symbol: Odin's eye (cosmic nebula), whose inner portal is a radiant white field

Oengus mac Og: Celtic Lineage
Path of Zain, Emotional Level Two

Oengus (also spelled Angus or Aonghus) is known in Celtic myth as the handsome and witty harpist member of Tuatha Dé Danann who is a patron of poets, musicians, and especially lovers. He is featured in five tales, either helping lovers or as a lover himself. These events produced a deep understanding of the challenges presented by love, which allows him to assist human lovers when they face adversity.

In myth, Oengus was born of an illicit union between the Dagda and Boann, a female master associated with the Boyne River. She was married at the time to Nechtan. The Dagda concealed the pregnancy by causing the sun to stand still for nine months, so the child was conceived as well as born on the same day. Oengus was then given to Midir to raise (fostering children out to be raised by someone other than their birth parents was a common practice in Celtic tradition). A different version of his parentage states that his mother was Boann, and his foster father was Elcmar. In both versions of his story, Oengus grew up to be a skilled magician.

Typical of the bard (harpist, poet, magician, shape-shifter, and creative thinker), Oengus is wildly clever and somewhat of a trickster. When he discovered his true father was the Dagda, his cleverness won him the finest of his father's halls.

Oengus arranged this scheme by asking the Dagda to give him the hall for a day and a night. In one version, possibly *The Wooing of Etain*, we learn that the next day, when the Dagda came to take the hall back, Oengus replied that "all time consisted of a day and a night following each other forever"—so he kept the fine hall as his permanent abode.

Celtic myth presents Oengus in three different love stories. He helped to woo Etain on Midir's behalf; intervened to help Grainne and Diarmuid against Finn, who desired Grainne for himself; and spirited her away to safety on two occasions when her discovery was threatened by Finn.

Oengus fell in love himself (in the eighth-century-CE *Dream of Oengus*), dreaming of a beautiful young woman he didn't recognize. He awakened and, not knowing how to find her, began to waste away in yearning. A search was made to locate her. Her name was Caer Ibormeith; she was a fairy maiden and shape-changer who transformed from human female form to that of a swan every other year or, in some versions, for one day a year. The tale concludes with Oengus seeking her out and wooing her, recognizing her among many other swan companions; becoming a swan himself; and flying off with her. In my deepest contact with Oengus, I was also working with a mineral for Caer Ibormeith, who corresponds to the priestess path of Gimel.

Male and female masters who, like Oengus, correspond to the second emotional level on the path of Zain possess an airy, intellectual, inspired mental potential that includes originality, brilliance, and insight. They are so clever that this ability needs a worthwhile focus. There is a lusty, passionate side to their energy, which is instinctual and primal in the body. Their mental agility, imagination, and capacity to connect with divine inspiration produces flashes of fire in the head that empower inner vision and can directly tap spiritual knowledge.

During the contact with Oengus and Caer Ibormeith, Oengus demonstrated how fanning the flames of passion can light the lower chakras, allowing energy to rise upward along the spine and extend through the crown chakra. My consciousness joined his, and the word *illumination* exploded in consciousness as an area above my field of view that had previously been dark was now fully visible.

When illumination comes, we awaken spiritual sight and become directly cognizant of the higher dimensions that cannot be perceived with physical eyes. Seeing the true nature of higher reality, we can then relax and release the grip of the ego mind, which believes matters are up to us to figure out. Seeing that we are eternally safe and loved by our Source, we awaken the seer within and, like Oengus, can receive ingenious solutions from a higher plane.

Keywords: Oengus is a poet-seer who can support you to direct the flame of love-passion to experience moments of spiritual illumination and receive inspiration that can flow into all forms of communication that reflect the beauty and truth of spiritual reality. He is also a guide to Celtic esoteric knowledge and supports those whose experience with the challenges of love relationships helps them be of assistance to others.

Suggested Meditation Symbol: Awen symbol (a circle containing three straight lines and three dots, used by Celtic bards) whose interior is an orange field (Pantone 165–167)

Orpheus: Greek Lineage
Hod, Mental Level

Orpheus is a well-known figure in Greek mythology and Western culture. His historical reality was acknowledged by many ancient authors (though not by Aristotle), although it has been questioned by some scholars today. I was aware of what are known as the Orphic mysteries from research into ancient forms of spiritual initiation, but I had no idea whether or not Orpheus was an ascended master, until he made contact.

Orpheus is most famous in myth for a heroic but ultimately unsuccessful journey to the underworld to try to regain his wife, Eurydice, after she perished. As the story goes, as the time for his marriage to Eurydice was approaching, she happened to be out walking and attracted the unwelcome attention of a satyr, a lustful male nature spirit who had ears and a tail resembling those of a horse and possessed a permanent, exaggerated erection. Running through the tall grass to escape him, she fell into a nest of vipers and suffered a fatal bite on her heel. Her body was discovered by Orpheus.

Orpheus had received a golden lyre from Apollo, who had taught him how to play it. It was said that his melodies were so divine they charmed even wild animals. After Eurydice's death, he was so overcome with grief and played such sad and mournful songs that the nymphs and gods wept. On their advice, he traveled to the underworld in a quest to bring Eurydice back. His music softened the hearts of Hades and Persephone, who agreed to allow Eurydice to return with him to earth on one condition: he was to walk in front of her and not look back until they both had reached the upper world.

Orpheus set off toward the upper world with Eurydice following, but in his haste to be reunited with her, as soon as he regained the upper world, he turned to look for her. Following behind him, she had not yet emerged from the underworld, and with the conditions for her return not met, she vanished for a second time, this time for good.

Although Orpheus ultimately failed in bringing his beloved

Eurydice back from the underworld, his heroic journey into those realms was transformative. Many ancient forms of spiritual initiation involve some level of ordeal that the initiate passes through to gain high consciousness.

The eighty-seven *Orphic Hymns* describe extraordinary mystical phenomena and rituals that perfectly symbolize the journey of individual spiritual initiation. They include a death and rebirth experience, followed by returning to the world with a more divinified awareness. Initiates in the Orphic mysteries used these texts to raise consciousness toward higher spiritual realities. They are believed to have been composed in either the late Hellenistic period (circa the third or second century BCE) or the early Roman period (circa the first to second century CE).

Orpheus concretized for the fifth century BCE some of the rites and rituals for propitiating Demeter (in her grief over the loss of Persephone) and similar Great Mother figures. Important pan-Greek rituals, such as the famous Eleusinian Mysteries, incorporated Orphic poems.

It is also believed that Orpheus may have created mystery initiations that celebrated Dionysus or similar Bacchic figures. As described in various myths, Dionysus was dismembered by the Titans while still an infant and then saved by Zeus, who had his limbs gathered up by Apollo for burial. This gathering up of pieces may symbolize the ending of the experience of separation from spiritual Source as an initiate is able to experience the higher realms of consciousness. (The tale of Dionysus is somewhat like the mysteries of Isis/Osiris, except the restored Dionysus went on to establish his power as a god in the lands of the living, rather than remaining in the underworld.)

My most powerful experience with Orpheus came unexpectedly. In deep meditation, working with a new mineral, my consciousness entered a column of white light with orange glints. Orpheus was present, and I received the information that I was in the vortex of the Orphic mysteries. As if I were viewing a movie film, I was shown that in one ritual, an initiate had to travel alone underground through tunnels in total darkness. Making this journey certainly required the ability to conquer fear! As initiates continued through the darkness, they eventually found their way upward to a trapdoor. It opened upward through the floor of a cave's inner chamber. Emerging from the gloom, they were suddenly thrust into a brightly illuminated space lit by fires built around the circumference. All those who had previously received initiation (males and females both) were gathered to welcome the new initiate into the light of higher self (in contrast to the darkness of ignorance they had just passed through). While this sounds like a typical mystery school initiation, the detailed vision I experienced was completely unexpected. Orpheus wanted me to be able to share that this path of spiritual initiation still exists in the higher planes.

The symbol described below, known as the Orphic egg, relates to their creation myth. It represents the cosmic egg from which hatched the primordial hermaphroditic deity Phanes, who, in Orphic belief, created the other gods.

Keywords: Orpheus supports those who write about mystical experiences (often in poetic forms) to point others toward the higher realms. He can be a guide to the Orphic mystery tradition to discover the nature of transcendent reality and one's own eternal existence.

Suggested Meditation Symbol: White Orphic egg wrapped with a coiled serpent, against an orange field (Pantone 159–160, 165–167, or 170)

Pandara: Buddhist Lineage
Red Geburah, Emotional Level Two

Pandara, one of the five female Dhyani Buddhas, is the tantric consort of Amitabha Buddha. The group of five male Dhyani Buddhas and their female counterparts are said to represent a group of celestial Buddhas who have always existed from the beginning of time. In this system, they correspond to the four directions, plus center, and have a specific color and element correspondence.

In this system, Pandara is red in color, the embodiment of the element of fire; belongs to the lotus (padma) family; and supports us to transform unhealthy attachments in intimate relationships. In the Qabalah, she extends through the red ray at the second emotional level of Geburah.

Every human being needs closeness and warmth. When early life circumstances interfere with the establishment of healthy boundaries or produce fears of abandonment, these needs can become distorted into forms that interfere with happiness. Feelings of depression or loneliness can fuel needy or seductive behaviors to magnetize someone to fill the inner void. There can be lots of passion to attract a romance, without the discernment that helps us recognize what type of relationship is healthy and nurturing. This can interfere with long-term satisfaction and lead to negative self-judgments about choices that were made.

As these patterns are recognized and cleared, compassion—for self and others—grows. Healthy boundaries are developed, and one is more able to organize practical matters to build a strong life foundation. The individual learns to choose intimate partners with greater discernment and build long-term happiness with a committed partner. One also learns to recognize subtle nuances with great precision and create aesthetically pleasing environments. The ability to express warmth and friendliness without the need to be loved back in a specific way by a special person removes striving and produces freedom.

In iconography, Pandara is often portrayed in the form of a dakini, naked, wearing a garland of skulls. In my most powerful contact with her to date, I brought the symbol I'd been given to mind, and she responded immediately. She was red fire, extending an intense sexual current that flooded through me yet was under perfect control. She is a reminder of the power of sexual energy and how important it is for a woman to both awaken and direct it with consciousness to serve her highest good.

Keywords: Pandara supports those who heal any emotional wounds that affect their ability to form healthy relationships and express female sexuality. She helps one open to the wisdom of discernment, choose a healthy sexual relationship, and become able to love another without neediness or attachment. When this healing is done, one result is a boost in clairsentient abilities.

Suggested Meditation Symbol: Red lotus flower (stylized flower profile opened in full bloom) against a slightly pinkish-red field (Pantone 191)

Parvati: Hindu Lineage
Path of Da'leth (Tarot: Empress), Spiritual Level

Da'leth is the path that connects the spheres of Binah and Chokma, which, in the Qabalah diagram, are uppermost on the outer columns. It is a path where one's attraction to cultivate balance and harmony with a love-relationship partner becomes a spiritual evolutionary journey.

Parvati is one of the highest emanations of the divine feminine principle among the masters who came to us from Hindu traditions in India. She extends beauty, bliss, abundance, strength, and power and is sometimes called the "mother of the world." Her sacred sexual pairing with Shiva is symbolized by the sacred lingam and yoni. She is typically understood as the gentle and nurturing aspect of the Hindu goddess and is one of the central deities of the goddess-oriented Shakta sect. Along with Lakshmi (spiritual level at Netzach) and Sarasvati (spiritual level at Hod), Parvati is part of the trinity of Hindu goddesses known as the Tridevi.

Extending the spiritual level of the path of Da'leth, Parvati holds the ultimate awareness of divine, unconditional love that can be developed through intimate partner relationship. As the spiritual level of Da'leth is attained, awareness graduates upward beyond a partner in physical form to experience union with the divine Source of love itself. As she developed this ability, some of the Hindu texts say, Shiva required her to pass strict ascetic tests to become his partner. Sacred sexual partners in various traditions recognize that love is a divine emanation that can be shared with a partner, while its Source is Creator.

Developing one's energy to this level with a sacred partner in form allows the energy of love to be shared without creating dependency.

338

When one or the other completes physical life or if the earthly relationship ends for another reason, the connection to the divine Source of love remains. This is the ultimate evolutionary potential within all partnership relationships.

Sati-Parvati appears in the epic period (400 BC–400 CE), present in both the Ramayana and the Mahabharata as Shiva's wife. However, it is not until the plays of Kalidasa (fifth and sixth centuries) and the Puranas (fourth through the thirteenth centuries) that the stories of Sati-Parvati and Shiva acquire more comprehensive details.

In those scriptures, Parvati is the wife of the Hindu god Shiva and the mother of Hindu deities Ganesha and Kartikeya (both are ascended masters, though only Ganesha is included in this book). Each of Parvati's aspects is expressed with a different name, giving her more than one hundred different names in regional Hindu stories of India. In Hindu temples dedicated to her and Shiva, she symbolizes the yoni—the female polarity in creation.

In iconography, Parvati is usually represented as fair, beautiful, and benevolent. She typically wears a red dress (often a sari) and may have a headband. When depicted alongside Shiva, she generally appears with two arms, but when alone, she may be depicted as having four. These hands may hold a conch; a crown; a mirror; a rosary; a bell; a dish; a farming tool, such as a goad; a sugarcane stalk; or flowers, such as lotuses.

In direct experience, I was first aware of Parvati when I was meditating on the Hindu pantheon. She has also visited on other occasions simply as a loving and familiar presence. Another time, she took form as a white cloud of divine feminine radiance made of sparkling drops—there was a sense of a rare, exquisite fragrance—and then she wanted to work with Shiva. Their energies combined were pure ecstasy and bliss.

Keywords: Women can call upon Parvati to activate the Shakti principle (divine feminine in partnership with male energy). She is a guide to the final level of attainment on the path of partner relationship, where one is drawn to the Source of love itself and may transcend the need for a partner in physical form.

Suggested Meditation Symbol: Downward-pointing triangle with a downward arrow from the top bar (the yoni symbol), outlined in gold, against a radiant white field

Penthesilia: Greek Lineage
Red Geburah, Mental Level

One of the most enjoyable and informative books I read during my research of various masters was *The Amazons* by Adrienne Mayor (2016). She enlightens readers about the long-misunderstood history of this amazing group of female warriors. Her depth of research and academic credibility made it much easier to find many names of these ancient women who met men in battle on their own terms as equals in warfare. As a result, more female masters at Geburah, and on the path of Teth, came into my extended files, and some later came into direct contact.

Mayor makes the case that the Amazons were not man-haters, nor did they cut off one breast. They were Scythian women who grew up within a nomadic culture in which learning to fight from horseback was practiced by woman as well as men.

During the Trojan War, some of the Amazon queens, such as Penthesilia, decided to take part, fighting alongside the Trojans, with whom they felt a certain kinship. The male Greek warriors fighting with Ajax and King Menelaus couldn't understand them, as the only roles available to Greek women were those of wife and mother or temple priestess. Most Greek women remained cloistered behind the walls of their homes. There are many classical Greek painted vases still in existence that show Amazon women fighting against male Greek warriors. In hundreds of examples Mayor surveyed, not one shows any of the women begging for mercy. They were ferocious in battle and tenacious opponents to the end.

The names of some of the Amazon queens have become synonymous with female strength and courage, expressing the first-chakra component of the energy of Geburah. Mayor's research indicates that in the (now lost) five-book epic *Aethiopis*, which was part of the Epic Cycle (or Cycle of Troy) on the Trojan War, Penthesilia's coming to Troy was described in detail. She was also mentioned in the works of several other respected ancient authors. According to several of these sources, her death arrived during personal combat with Achilles.

I did not expect to contact Penthesilia directly, but she came forward when I was reaching out for Palden Lhamo, since they share the same energy and level in the Qabalah and the same type of mineral correspondence. She was an immensely potent and powerful presence who resolutely communicated the message "The warrior always fights— for peace!" This offers a uniquely female perspective on the purpose of war, from one of the most accomplished female warrior masters.

Keywords: Penthesilia supports women to achieve ultimate physical strength and endurance and can help one to develop skill with weapons or advanced athletic abilities. She supports mental attitudes that allow one to access energy at heightened levels and, if called to do so, to fight fearlessly and resolutely to uphold the possibility of peace.

Suggested Meditation Symbol: Profile of an ancient Greek–helmeted Amazon warrior against a medium-dark slightly purplish-red field (Pantone 1935 and 1945)

Persephone: Greek Lineage
Path of Nun (Tarot: Death and Rebirth), Emotional Level Two

The myth of Demeter and Persephone was annually reenacted for nearly a thousand years in the ancient Greek Eleusinian Mysteries. The earliest recorded version of their myth comes from the Homeric "Hymn to Demeter," dated from the seventh century BCE. The name Persephone is how she was known later, duringin Roman times, while the ancient Greeks knew her as Kore.

In their myth, Persephone/Kore is introduced as a beautiful young woman who was the daughter of Demeter. One day she was innocently picking white narcissus flowers, which Hades had planted to lure her, when he abducted her, carrying her off into the underworld. Hades was the brother of Zeus and was Persephone's uncle. Myth relates that Zeus had agreed to allow Hades to claim her in this way as his underworld queen. This myth was traditionally called the Rape of Persephone, and she is usually portrayed in iconography in the process of being carried off. As with many myths, we are left to wonder if all the details are accurate.

Persephone's mother, Demeter, was heartbroken at her daughter's disappearance and searched for the girl everywhere in the upper world, depriving the earth of her attention—and its agricultural bounty—in her grief. This produced a dire situation for humankind, who now lacked food. Myth tells us that Zeus stepped in, sending Hermes to the underworld to negotiate with Hades for Persephone's release.

However, Hades had tricked Persephone into eating a few pomegranate seeds while she was in the underworld, and she was fated to return there each year for a period equal in months to the number of seeds she had consumed. According to this compromise, she was queen beside Hades for one-third of the year and could return to the upper world for two-thirds of each year. With this agreement, Persephone then returned and was reunited with her mother near Eleusis.

The Eleusinian rite portrayed Persephone as a robed mystical divinity carrying a scepter and small box. Portions of the rite were open to the public, both male and female. On the mass level, it was a celebration that reenacted the seasonal death and rebirth of the agricultural cycle. People came to understand that after a cold, dark winter, crops would once again begin to sprout in spring. There were mystery traditions for men (the rites of Attis and Adonis) that portrayed a similar principle.

Those who pursued the secret, esoteric initiations offered at Eleusis were guided through a process that temporarily extinguished identification with their normal personality and consciousness. They drank an elixir called kykeon, which was made from grain. Many researchers over the last few decades suggest that the liquid contained ergot. Ergot is a fungus possessing certain alkaloids that can produce an LSD-type experience. In undergoing this initiation process, one could review and release unconscious psychic blocks, awakening to his or her higher spiritual levels.

Psychology recognizes the deep journey into the personal shadow to reclaim buried psychic energy by the term *descent process*. Persephone has come to symbolize this journey for women today—a deep dive into the unconscious to work with life trauma that could not be processed and released when it originally occurred. When traumatic events happen during childhood, a natural protective response is repression, especially when adult resources are not made available to help the child. It is always possible to clear this unconscious material later in life, which brings great renewal. Like many women, I experienced some of my own deep journeys to uncover parts of my shadow. By the time I did so, I was blessed to have a spiritual context that recognized the evolutionary potential the process offered.

As I was writing this book, Persephone appeared in consciousness to demonstrate the process in a different way. I had been working with Demeter and Zeus and felt they could help bring her forward in my consciousness, and they did. Persephone appeared in a brilliant white field of energy. As I focused on her, I became aware of a massive, dark, chthonic male energy reaching up toward her from the depths. I could feel its pull, and gradually, it had the effect of pulling her slowly downward into increasing darkness. While dense, the energy surrounding this scene was transparent. The pure whiteness of her energy glowed through the gloom. She finally disappeared from my field of view into the darkness.

My consciousness was still present with Demeter and Zeus. They made no attempt to intervene; they simply kept extending the truth of love's presence. At some point, Persephone emerged from the depths and rejoined them. The three of them lit up in a glorious display of divine energy. It was classic, although I never had expected to witness that whole process in spiritual vision.

Demeter and Zeus demonstrated the valuable role of the witness. When loved ones are carried into their unconscious depths, simply standing by as witness, anchored in love and light *but not interfering*, will best support them. Their return will occur in their own perfect time, with purified psychic energy available to function at unprecedented levels.

Keywords: Persephone supports women to develop their psychic-intuitive gifts by making the inner journey to address repressed trauma and reclaim the energy that facilitates heighted states of consciousness. As this occurs, we reemerge with certainty that our spiritual essence remains unchanged, no matter what seems to occur in human life.

Suggested Meditation Symbol: Black-and-white outline of pomegranate sliced open, revealing seeds, against a radiant white field

Plato: Greek Lineage
Chesed, Emotional Level Two

Plato, who lived circa 428–348 BCE, is widely known as a pivotal figure in the development of Western philosophy and the Western esoteric tradition. He was the student of Socrates, a teacher of Aristotle, and the founder of the Academy in Athens, the first institution of higher learning in the Western world. Unlike nearly all his contemporaries' work, his entire work is believed to have survived intact for more than 2,400 years, serving as a foundation of Western philosophy and science.

Plato was born into an aristocratic and wealthy family. Although Socrates influenced him directly, as he related in the dialogues, the influence of Pythagoras upon Plato also appears to have been significant. Plato's Academy operated until it was destroyed by Lucius Cornelius Sulla in 84 BCE. Neo-Platonists revived the Academy in the early fifth century, and it operated until 529 CE, when it was closed by Justinian I of Byzantium, who saw it as a threat to the propagation of Christianity.

Many ancient Greek intellectuals were schooled in Plato's Academy, with the most prominent one being Aristotle. Plato's work, through the teachings offered by the Academy, provided just as much an initiation into the higher mysteries of metaphysical reality (the spiritual laws that underlie all existence) as many spiritual priests and initiators accomplished through other means.

Plato urges us to remember that there is a metareality that lies beyond what physical senses perceive. In advocating this principle, he joins spiritual luminaries from Buddhist, Hindu, and many other mystical lineages who have experienced the higher spiritual dimensions.

One of Plato's most well-known symbols is a collection of five geometric forms known as the platonic solids, which symbolize the classical elements: fire, air, water, earth, and ether. In one experience, Plato came forward as a helping-father presence. He took me through the doorway that he holds into the dark void, where I glimpsed the dimly glowing outlines of the platonic solids against the surrounding blackness, and then awareness merged with this exquisite pattern. He communicated that "mathematics is a form and symbol system that describes how energy moves. Geometry illustrates how it moves through regular polygons."

Plato's famous Allegory of the Cave is still a helpful concept that illustrates the difference between ultimate reality and human perception. The allegory asks us to imagine some prisoners chained together in a cave. Behind the prisoners is a fire, and between the fire and the prisoners are people carrying puppets or other objects, which cast moving shadows on the other side of the wall. The prisoners watch the shadows, believing them to be real. Plato then posits that one prisoner could become free. The prisoner finally sees the fire and realizes the shadows are fake. This prisoner could escape from the cave and discover there is a whole new world outside that they were previously unaware of. To illustrate this, Plato escorted my consciousness into the cave. I was aware of a huge outpouring of light behind me (pouring through to cast shadows on the cave wall). This underscored the difference between human perception (the moving shadows defined as life viewed by the personality in a body) and our true spiritual reality.

Keywords: Plato is a wise helping father who supports the collective awakening of humankind. He is a guide who helps us understand our own eternal nature. He offers understanding about the principles of sacred geometry and assists those who study or write about the great spiritual truths that underlie all existence.

Suggested Meditation Symbol: The five platonic solids against a sapphire-blue field (Pantone 281–282, 286–287, or 294–295)

Radha: Hindu Lineage
Netzach, Mental Level

Radha is a well-known female master who comes to us through Hindu traditions who has also been embraced as a model for women outside of Hinduism. She corresponds to the mental level where ones thoughts about female beauty, grace, and ones loveability, are polished to support an elevated life experience.

In Vaishnavite worship (representing some six hundred million Hindus today), she is venerated alongside Krishna in the cojoined form Radha-Krishna. She appears in many of the ancient texts known as the Puranas, including the Padma Purana, the Devi-Bhagavata Purana, the Brahma Vaivarta Purana, the Matsya Purana, the Linga Purana, the Varaha Purana, the Narada Purana, the Skanda Purana, and the Shiva Purana—all generally dated to the third to tenth centuries CE.

Radha is also part of the Hindu Shakti, or goddess-centered, traditions. In some of these texts, she is Krishna's greatest devotee and consort, and in others, she's an individual deity with power superior to his. Some believe she is an avatar of Lakshmi (who can be met at the spiritual level of the same sphere, Netzach).

One popular tale relates that Radha was born inside a golden lotus floating on the Yamuna River and opened her eyes for the first time as Krishna came near. Other information tells that she was born in Raval, a small town near Gokul in Uttar Pradesh, and her father was a distinguished Yadava chieftain. The Yadava clan, one of ancient India's illustrious lineages, were known for their worship of Krishna.

Radha is a central character in the stories of Krishna's childhood, during the time when he was raised by a surrogate mother in the countryside near the Vrindavan forest. Radha is portrayed as one of the gopis who tended the cattle, the epitome of feminine beauty manifest in form, possessed of every quality considered desirable in a woman. It can be useful for women to consider her model as a next-level stage development, from of Norse Freya, who mastered the second emotional level of Netzach.

In his tales, Krishna's divine nature is expressed through flute playing, a handsome appearance, a mischievous sense of humor during childhood, and immense power and wisdom when grown. These qualities, along with his respectful treatment of women, made him universally attractive to all the gopis.

Despite the fact that every woman desires Krishna, Radha has no jealousy of the other milkmaids; she is filled with the knowledge of her own lovability, which arises from knowing she is beloved at divine levels. Thus, she is beyond all thought of using any of her charms to try to control Krishna. These distinctions—being past all tendencies to be jealous of others, being fully self-loving, and not using beauty to attempt to control a partner—are evidence of an evolved feminine nature.

In direct experience, Radha has connected with my mind on several occasions, both with and without Krishna. Their energies are well honed to operate together—in a fusion of fiery blue and green light. In this current, he leads, moving upward toward Source, while she provides constant support beneath him.

Keywords: Radha is an ally as we develop certainty about our divine lovability, which is an unchangeable part of our eternal essence. Everyone is fully loveable, irrespective of our actions in physical form or the actions of any relationship partner in physical form. As one becomes certain of this inner state, jealousy is impossible. One cultivates beauty as an elevating force without misusing it to obtain power or control another. When thoughts are elevated to this level, stability in love, beauty and abundance can surround and uplift one's life experience.

Suggested Meditation Symbol: Gleaming golden lotus flower in stylized profile against an emerald-green (Pantone 354-355)

Rama: Hindu Lineage
Chesed, Spiritual Level

Rama, also known as Ramachandra, is considered the first avatar of Vishnu the Protector (who corresponds to Tiphareth at the spiritual level). Within Indian culture, Rama is the most popular symbol of chivalry and virtue; an embodiment of truth and morality; the ideal son; and, above all, the ideal king. He and his wife, Sita, are popular symbols of purity and marital devotion.

Rama is widely believed to have been a historical figure—a tribal hero of ancient India who lived during the Treta Yuga, the second of the four great epochs of humankind. Despite the belief about Rama's ancient presence on earth, it is thought that special worship of him did not begin until the eleventh century, and it was not until the fourteenth and fifteenth centuries that distinct sects venerating him as the supreme god appeared.

The adventures of Rama, notably the slaying of the demon king Ravena, are recounted in the Vana Parva of the Mahabharata and in the Ramayana, which was written sometime in the fifth century BCE (dating varies among scholars) but with some later additions. However, it is believed Rama was on the earth at the end of the Treta Yuga, which, according to Mahabharata, came to an end in 867100 BCE.

The duration of the Treta Yuga is variously interpreted as 1,728,000 or 1,080,000 years, based on Hindu astronomical calculations. Rama was said to have ruled the country for eleven thousand years. This is one example of the vastly lengthier time periods accorded to earth's history found in Hindu traditions.

The adventures of Rama illustrate above all the importance and rewards of fulfilling one's pious duty, or dharma. His first adventure began when the sage Vishvamitra asked for help in fighting a demon, or rakshasa. Rama succeeded in killing it and was given divine weapons. He met and won the hand of a king's beautiful daughter, Sita, by not only bending but also breaking in two the huge bow of Shiva with his divine strength.

Although he was a prince, circumstances within his family did not allow Rama to assume rulership. He was exiled for fourteen years to the forest, accompanied by Sita and other companions. During that time, he visited many sages. (A commitment to gathering spiritual wisdom from teachers is one of the characteristics common to masters at Chesed.)

At one point, Sita was abducted by a demon. A series of titanic battles between Rama's forces and the demons followed, weaving a powerful tale that reveals elements of his mastery. Eventually, Rama was reunited with his wife. However, he was not entirely convinced she had remained loyal to him during her abduction, so she was determined to prove her honor in a trial by fire. Though she emerged from the flames unscathed, Rama still exiled her, and during that time, she gave birth to his twin sons. When Rama saw them grown and noted their physical resemblance to him, he realized his mistake and reconciled with Sita.

In yet another dramatic scene, Sita swore her virtue on the earth itself, which then promptly swallowed her by opening beneath her feet. Rama, now even more distraught, vowed to follow his wife to heaven, but Time appeared to him in the guise of an ascetic and called for him to remain and fulfill his duty on earth. Nevertheless, Rama waded into the river and, from there, was welcomed into heaven by Brahma. From a modern Western worldview (and to some feminists in modern India), some of Rama's conduct with Sita, and hers with him, seems far from ideal. When we release judgment and can meet him in direct experience, the experience of his energy eclipses any such questions.

When I was working with the Hindu pantheon, a chant spontaneously came through my consciousness, based on the name of Rama. As I gave it voice, a portal opened, and I joined the dimension where his consciousness is ablaze in white light. It was a visionary dimension of knowledge and power above and outside all forms, extending a fountain of the sacred masculine toward all humankind.

In another precious experience, Rama communicated that "the true purpose of the sacred-masculine energy is to protect women, not control them." This was similar to a message I received from Archangel Michael. Many men today follow, and many throughout time have followed, that guideline, though it is not universally understood or honored. As a woman heals any difficult experiences with men, she is more able to attract a male partner who can express sacred-masculine qualities.

Keywords: Rama supports men to develop sacred-masculine qualities: upholding truth, virtue, and morality; cultivating divinely guided leadership and warrior skills; and protecting, not controlling, women.

Suggested Meditation Symbol: Golden paduka sandals (a unique style associated with India's gurus) against radiant white

Rebecca: Judaic Matriarch
Path of Da'leth (Tarot: Empress), Emotional Level Two

After what is known as the Binding of Isaac (his near sacrifice), his mother, Sarah, died. After taking care of her burial, Abraham went about finding a wife for his son Isaac, who was thirty-seven years old. To accomplish this, he sent one of his servants back to the area where he had been born, Ur of the Chaldees, to look for a bride there instead of among the Canaanites.

He gave the servant many rich gifts, including jewelry, clothing, and other fine things, to present to the prospective bride and her family. The servant traveled with ten laden camels to the central well of the city, having been inspired to conduct a certain test to find a woman of suitable character. He was looking for a young woman who offered, without being asked, to water all the camels.

Amazingly, a young woman did come forward as he prayed and graciously fulfilled these conditions. After this kindness, the servant immediately gave her a golden nose ring and two golden bracelets, which Rebecca hurried to show her mother. Seeing the jewelry, Rebecca's brother Laban went out to greet the guest and bring him inside. By the next day, according to Rebecca's own decision, she accompanied the servant back to Abraham. As they were approaching, she saw a man praying from a distance, and when told it was her future husband, she was pleased. They were soon married, but it was twenty years before any children were born.

What must it have been like for Rebecca to marry a man who lived in a culture different from hers? Some interpretations see her as a dynamic, proactive woman, which was somewhat unique for that time and culture. Even though her parents had reservations about her going off with Abraham's servant, she immediately chose to go. It is believed she and Isaac shared a loving relationship. Yet her life was not without challenge. Like Sarah, she experienced many years of infertility, when bearing children was considered a measure of worth for every wife in that time and culture.

When the long-hoped-for pregnancy finally arrived, just as some women today experience, Rebecca was uncomfortable. Eventually, she gave birth to twin boys: Esau came out first, followed by Jacob. The boys were different in nature. When they were a bit older, Isaac was on the verge of giving Esau, the elder, his birthright, but Rebecca intervened because she had learned from an oracle before their birth that the older son was meant to serve the younger. Consequently, Rebecca arranged a deception so that Isaac, who now had poor eyesight, believed he was passing on his blessing to Esau, though she substituted Jacob at the crucial moment.

We cannot know from biblical sources exactly how to understand this, but succession in families in many ancient cultures often became an issue, and mothers were known to tip the scales toward one son or another for various reasons. Whatever the case, Rebecca acted in a way that arranged an important future for her son Jacob. Jacob's name was changed to Israel, and he eventually fathered the twelve sons who were the progenitors of the twelve tribes of Israel.

Sometimes I find it helpful to work with related masters together to create a deeper level of contact. As I worked with Rebecca and Isaac together, their love for each other was profound and radiant on the higher planes.

Keywords: Rebecca holds a great deal of wisdom about how to create a long-term loving relationship with a powerful mate. She supports women to use the inevitable challenges and transitions that relationships bring (including outliving one's partner, as she experienced) to develop inner strength and spiritual trust. She supports women who give birth to children who have an important destiny to make wise decisions about matters that affect their futures.

Suggested Meditation Symbol: Biblical stone well and a water jar against an emerald- green field (Pantone 355–356)

Rhiannon: Celtic Lineage
Yesod, Emotional Level Two

Rhiannon, a master known in Welsh traditions, is associated with the moon and those who face certain emotionally challenging trials through motherhood. Most of the information we have about her comes from the Mabinogi. The Mabinogi is based upon a fourteenth-century manuscript that contains eleven tales of early Welsh literature.

Rhiannon first appears in these stories as a beautiful and desirable woman dressed in a golden robe who was riding past Pwyll, king of Dyfed, on her horse. Pwyll was immediately infatuated, but no matter how fast he and his men pursued her on their swiftest mounts, they could not overtake her.

Rhiannon's magical abilities (as evidenced by her eluding all forms of pursuit by highly skilled warriors) identify her as an otherworld woman. When Pwyll did get her to stop and converse, she said her errand all along was to meet him; she was choosing him over a man to whom she already was betrothed. Her strategy identifies her as an independent woman in charge of her own lovers and destiny.

After various adventures, Rhiannon married Pwyll, and later, when she arrived at his court, she gave precious gifts to all the nobles. Her image is that of a generous, bountiful queen (symbolizing the full moon, when matters come to fruition).

After three years, she gave birth to a son and heir named Pryderi (his birth is a symbol of her mastery of female fertility). Tragedy struck, however, as the child was stolen from his crib on the third night after his birth. Though she was innocent, the careless nurses felt guilty and implicated her for infanticide. Her punishment was to stand outside the city gates for seven long years, telling her story to each traveler who passed by and offering to carry him or her on her back into the palace like a horse. After many years, her son, Pryderi, was recognized, having been raised elsewhere, and restored to his family, and she was redeemed, to have more adventures.

Rhiannon married a second time after Pwyll's death. Her problems resumed after her second marriage, and the kingdom became a wasteland under the leadership of her son, Pryderi. Finally, they all left that land and moved to a city far away (perhaps London), where they made a living by skilled craftsmanship. Their skill incurred the wrath of the local craftsmen, who drove them away.

They returned to Dyfed, where Rhiannon and Pryderi immediately became enchanted and disappeared. (The family of her first husband had arranged this punishment for her.)

Eventually, her second husband, Manawydan, was able to obtain their release.

Rhiannon is sometimes associated with three magical birds who always fly around her shoulders and sing so sweetly that the dead awaken, and the living fall into a trance. When I contacted Rhiannon, her feminine energy was exquisite to experience.

Keywords: Rhiannon is a guide to magical practices and moon-cycle wisdom and supports women who choose to express female fertility by giving birth. She helps women who must later overcome grief arising from the loss of their children. She also supports emotional mastery as women overcome the challenges of love relationships and claim their full power.

Suggested Meditation Symbol: Mother and child silhouetted against a huge white full moon

Sarah: Judaic Lineage
Binah, Emotional Level Two

Sarah (originally Sarai) was the wife of Abraham. He became the founding patriarch of Judaism, and thus, she is the founding matriarch. While many of the details of her story are given in the biblical description of Abraham above, it is important to emphasize that she was described as a woman of spiritual stature, wisdom, and insight, as well as one possessing physical beauty. The emphasis on wisdom and spiritual leadership is characteristic of female masters who extend the energy of the sphere of Binah in the Qabalah.

Traditional Judaism holds that Sarah was also the biological mother of Isaac—a pregnancy and birth that supposedly happened after she was ninety years old. To modern ears, the idea of Sarah becoming a biological mother and being able to nurse a child herself at the age of ninety requires a leap of faith to consider it literally. However, all debates about this miraculous birth are a distraction from our purpose. As Abrahams wife, and by raising Isaac, she became the spiritual mother of a new religious-cultural identity within human experience.

Sarah was a woman possessed of remarkable inner strength. Along with Abraham, she moved from her homeland to Egypt, only to be subject to the unwelcome and dangerous attention of Pharaoh. Later, she encouraged her handmaiden Hagar to mate with Abraham, which resulted in the son Ishmael, who was born fourteen long years before Isaac's birth. Surely this took great emotional strength. What did it take for her to live through the period when Abraham nearly sacrificed their son? This seems more than any mother could bear, yet she did. We cannot know all the ways in which she supported Abraham to fulfill his destiny in a time and culture in which the role of wife was far from easy.

In direct experience, Sarah came into consciousness conveying great emotional warmth. Feeling her heart extending to me was comforting. She is joyous, happy, uplifting, and solicitous, a Jewish spiritual grandmother with deep wisdom and strength. I find her presence to be both welcoming and stabilizing. On another occasion, I experienced both Sarah and Isaac together, and another time, I experienced Sarah and Abraham together. I could feel the unique mission they were given to bring a new wave of spiritual and cultural identity to humankind. Like each master, Sarah has a completely unique feel to her energy, and I will recognize and welcome her whenever she draws near.

Her symbol is the Hebrew letter tet. Tet's essence is feminine, representing the nine months of pregnancy. It is shaped like a womb, a spiral, a container in which things change and transform. The infinite is contained in tet, and it gives birth to the finite. It includes the kindness and mercy of creation, as well as the principle that everything is eternal, and nothing is ever lost.

Keywords: Sarah is devoted to human spiritual development and helps us to birth our own strength to walk through all emotionally charged life events, uplifted by our connection with and trust in the spiritual realm. She can also be a compassionate ally to women with fertility issues who are having difficulty in becoming mothers. She conveys the loving wisdom of the grandmothers when that is helpful.

Suggested Meditation Symbol: Golden Hebrew letter tet, which has the meaning of a womb and grace, against a purple field (Pantone 265–266)

Sarasvati: Hindu Lineage
Hod, Spiritual Level

Sarasvati is a female master who is revered in multiple spiritual traditions and has remained consistently significant from the Vedic period in India to the present day. She was incorporated into the female highest trinity, the Tridevi, which includes Sarasvati, Lakshmi, and Parvati, wherein she is associated with sacred speech, prayers, mantras, and sacred poetry. Sarasvati has also appeared in Buddhist traditions, with her name unchanged, from the fourth century CE onward. She is also revered by believers of the Jain religion of west and central India and under different names in Burma, China, Japan, and Thailand.

Some trace her origins to the second millennium BCE, where she is linked to the Vedic goddess of creative energy and power, named Vac. (*Vac* is the Sanskrit word for "speech," "voice," "talk," or "language.") Sarasvati was known as the creator of the alphabet and of Sanskrit (the language of the Hindu sacred texts), a first outpouring of sacred sound (chants, music, and language) that extends energy toward the creation of forms. In early Rig Veda, *vac* also refers to the voice of the priest raised in sacrifice. Traditionally, *vac* is present in any sacred words that convey occult power or knowledge, especially mantras. Although prominent in the Rig Veda, the name Vac disappears when she is syncretized with the river goddess Sarasvati.

In Rig Veda hymn 6:61, Sarasvati is called a "canceller of debts" and described as one who digs for lotus stems and "has burst with her strong waves the ridges of the hills" (in my understanding this suggests she has transcended or achieved full enlightenment). She is described further as "marked out by majesty among the mighty Ones." In verse 7:96, she is lauded as "the mightiest, most divine of Streams."

Some Hindus celebrate the festival of Vasant Panchami (the fifth day of spring, also known as Sarasvati Puja) in her honor and mark the day by helping young children learn how to write the letters of the alphabet. People celebrate the day by wearing yellow, eating sweet dishes, and displaying yellow flowers in homes. In Rajasthan, it is customary for people to wear jasmine garlands.

Sarasvati is often pictured in iconography seated and riding on a white swan—a symbol of spiritual transcendence and awakening. Some who build altars for her decorate them with many brightly colored fresh flowers as well as miniature Indian musical instruments, as she is the patron of sacred Indian musicians. She radiates peace and divine blessings to all.

Sarasvati has come near during many meditations, along with other masters from the Hindu lineage (she is often present along with Parvati and Lakshmi). In inner vision, she sometimes descends toward my point of observation, seated upon a regal white swan. It took me a long time to locate a mineral that corresponds to her, but she blessed me with many visits while I continued to look for one. When I did locate the correct specimen, her welcome was a high-energy ecstasy I will not ever forget.

Keywords: Sarasvati holds the ultimate level of female creative power. This includes sacred dance and performance; sacred words (invocations, prayers, chanting, and mantras); and music. Her energy carries a strong component of the divine feminine and is a blessing for any creative person to experience.

Suggested Meditation Symbol: A huge, regal white swan wearing Indian-style gold jewelry, in a radiant white field

Shiva: Hindu Lineage
Chokma, Spiritual Level

Shiva, whose Sanskrit name translates as "Auspicious One," is considered one of the three most exalted male deities of Hinduism. This means he is part of the Trimurti, which also includes Vishnu and Brahma. Shiva is widely revered in India, Nepal, and Sri Lanka and recognized worldwide. Kashmiri Shaivites consider him the supreme god. He is also the male presence (along with Shakti, the female principle) at the top of some tantric pantheons, representing the ultimate union of the energies of the ida and pingala within human subtle anatomy, which launch consciousness beyond duality entirely, into the divine realms.

Perhaps more than any other powerful male master at Chokma, Shiva embodies the polarity of creation and destruction that are experienced in human life. (The eternal realms are formless and eternally unchanging). In his creative form, he can be represented with his consort, Parvati, and sons, Ganesha and Skanda (both ascended masters, though only Ganesha is in this book). In his destructive mode, destroying forms that have outlived their usefulness, Shiva is accompanied by Durga or Kali. In a popular form among the Tamil people, Shiva is portrayed as the cosmic dancer Nataraja, with four arms and a raised left foot, demonstrating five acts or powers of the divine (within Hindu tradition): creation, preservation, dissolution, forgetting, and revelation of spiritual grace.

Shiva is also portrayed as a potent master of male fertility (with consorts or wives or in union with Shakti, the female principle). Alternately, he is a naked ascetic, practicing severe self-denial as a mendicant beggar, a yogi, or Lord of Cattle (in the Pashupata school of Shaivism), who is both the benevolent herdsman and, at times, the merciless slaughterer of the beasts that are the human souls in his care.

Shiva's vehicle in the world, his *vahana*, is the white bull Nandi. Sculptures of Nandi sit opposite the main sanctuaries of many Shiva temples. In temples and in private shrines, Shiva is also worshipped in the form of the lingam, a cylindrical votary stone (representing a penis) that is often embedded in a yoni, which is a spouted dish representing the female principle. One of his most famous pilgrimage sites is the Amarnath cave, located in Jammu and Kashmir, which contains a massive ice lingam, which is the central focus of worship there.

In iconography, Shiva is depicted with three eyes, with the third eye bestowing inward vision but capable of burning destruction when focused outward. He wears a garland of skulls and a serpent around his neck and carries in his two (or sometimes four) hands a deerskin, a trident, a small hand drum, or a club with a skull at the end. Sometimes he is shown with the holy River Ganges flowing from his matted hair. He also carries the trisula (trident). There are different mantras to invoke Shiva's help in various matters.

Women as well as men can experience Shiva when they have prepared consciousness to experience the energy he extends. When I was in the beginning stages of gathering the masters for this book, Shiva unexpectedly came into visionary form, communicating "I'm not on your list" while he paused, waiting for my reaction. Feeling the immense power of his energy, I realized this was a big omission on my part, and I mentally responded that I would correct that oversight immediately. With my response, he exploded into my consciousness with extraordinary power and energy.

Much later in my work, I reached out to him, wanting to confirm what information he wanted me to include in this book. In response, he carried my vision to observe the famous ice lingam in the Amarnath cave. On other occasions, he has appeared in inner vision as a powerful young male yogi with long black hair, once with Nandi, his white bull, beside him. I feel blessed to have such deep contact with him. I find his presence supportive, as my life transitions often involve significant endings in form, followed by new beginnings. Clearing attachment to what was and being able to walk through life transformation with certainty about the nature of higher reality, makes a huge positive difference.

Keywords: Shiva helps us recognize spiritual forces at work when old forms and chapters of life are destroyed, so a new life chapter can begin. His appearance in meditation can indicate that the spiritual forces of destruction and creation are currently unfolding in one's life. Contact with his mind lifts awareness toward ultimate reality, where consciousness merges with bliss in a constant state beyond all apparent change.

Suggested Meditation Symbol: Trisula (three-pronged trident or staff) with an attached drum, shimmering white against a white field

Saint Germain: Christian Lineage
Binah, Emotional Level Two

Saint Germain is a familiar master to many who experience the higher realms of consciousness. He is often envisioned in a violet field, surrounded by alchemical symbols. He is typically called upon when one wishes to transmute lower energies that block spiritual awareness.

Psychologist Carl Jung, who was also a student of the ancient art of alchemy, saw this transformation process as a metaphor for soul work. The symbolic lead, or materia prima, of daily life—depression, disturbances, meaninglessness, emotional struggles—could be actively engaged to develop one's potential for higher consciousness, wholeness and a more satisfying life.

Attempting to learn details about the human life of Saint Germain is difficult. He deliberately spun a confusing web to conceal his actual name and origins, using different pseudonyms in the various places in Europe he visited. Becoming inaccessible isn't unusual behavior for some who choose to focus on spiritual development. Lao Tzu (Laozi) and other masters were similarly inaccessible at certain points in their lives to pursue dedicated practices.

By some accounts, Saint Germain was born circa 1691 or 1712. He grew up to be a European adventurer, with an interest in science, alchemy, and the arts, and achieved prominence in European high society. He was described as a man who dressed in an elegant manner, adorned with a few jewels, and was multilingual, though it was hard to identify his native tongue. He appeared in the French court around 1748. In 1749, he was employed by Louis XV for diplomatic missions. In March 1760, at the height of the Seven Years' War, Saint Germain traveled to The Hague. In Amsterdam, he stayed with the bankers Adrian and Thomas Hope, representing that he was on a mission for Louis XV and using diamonds as collateral to borrow money. There are many associations between Germain and precious jewels.

In 1779, Saint Germain reportedly arrived in Altona in Schleswig, where he made an acquaintance with Prince Charles of Hesse-Kassel, who also had an interest in mysticism and was a member of several secret societies. The count showed the prince several of his gems and convinced him he had invented a method to produce cloth. The prince installed him in an abandoned factory, supplied him with the materials needed to proceed with the project, and later set up a laboratory for alchemical experiments in his nearby summer residence.

Over the past twenty years, my own experiences with Saint Germain have been numerous. I was first aware of him and worked with his violet flame during long meditations at a Brazilian spiritual healing center I visited. On different occasions since, his help as I continue spiritual development has been noticeable. On one occasion, his flame felt like cold fire, and another time, it was like violet bubbles passing through my energy body and scrubbing away debris.

Germain's mastery of the alchemical nature of the gem and mineral kingdom was a good match for my early career training as a gemologist and, later, my passion for using minerals to accelerate spiritual development. He became a primary ally to help me unlock the code to understand the subtle energy of minerals and use them in meditation to enhance connection with the Qabalah and ascended masters.

Keywords: Germain is dedicated to help humankind evolve toward Christ consciousness. He has a profound knowledge of the alchemical nature of gems and minerals and the means to use them to help one progress on his or her spiritual path. Anyone can ask for his help to access the violet flame to purify his or her emotional body to experience the eternal realms directly and assist his or her spiritual growth.

Suggested Meditation Symbol: The violet flame against a darker purple field (Pantone 265–266)

Tara: White (Arya) Tara and Green Tara: Buddhist Lineage

Tara is a beloved spiritual figure known worldwide. Her name is said to mean "Star" or "Planet," and she is recognized as one who has crossed to the other side of the ocean of existence, achieving enlightenment. She is known in multiple forms, two of which are described here.

Tara, White
Hidden Path of the White Ray (Kether to Yesod), Spiritual Level

According to author Miranda Shaw in *Buddhist Goddesses of India*, Tara initially appeared as an attendant of popular bodhisattva Avalokitesvara (and by association was thus assumed to be a bodhisattva).

The bodhisattvas of Mahayana Buddhism are committed to supporting humankind until all beings have been liberated.

In one creation story from this tradition, both White and Green Tara arose as two tears shed by Avalokitesvara, whose compassion overflowed about the suffering of humanity. In this version, the Taras agreed to help him with his mission of liberation. Yet as Shaw points out, by the mid-eighth century CE, Tara had surpassed Avalokitesvara and was known as a Buddha, portrayed in the center of paintings surrounded by her own attendants.

Another of Tara's origin stories comes from the seventeenth-century Buddhist scholar named Taranatha. He describes Tara as a young princess who lived in another star system, under the name of Yeshe Dawa, which means "Moon of Primordial Awareness." For eons, she made offerings to the Buddha of that world and received special instructions from him. After she did so, some monks approached her and suggested that because of her level of attainment, she should pray to be reborn next as a male to progress further. She responded that from the point of view of enlightenment, only the weak-minded saw gender as a barrier to attaining enlightenment.

She also noted that few had wished to work for the welfare of beings in a female form, so she resolved to always be reborn as a female, until samsara (the cycle of birth and death of the human world) was no more. She then stayed in a palace in a state of meditation for some ten million years and released tens of millions of beings from suffering. It is no wonder Tara is a favorite of women among many different spiritual traditions. This story is also consistent with the several types of mineral crystals that can be used for her, which link the hidden path of Kether and Yesod, at the spiritual level.

Tara is also accorded powers of salvation for those who call upon her at their death transitions, and it is believed she will assist with any purification still needed so that individuals embark on their afterlife journeys with ease. As a source of inspired devotion, Tara's mantra is known and practiced throughout the Buddhist world. The white lotus flower, held in her left hand, is one of her most well-known symbols.

In direct experience, Arya Tara is a profound blessing to experience.

It took some years of continuing evolution to open the channel to her. As she connects with my energy field now, there is can be an experience of the thousand-petaled lotus, a giant white lotus blossom, opening at the crown chakra, energy exploding into the highest dimensions over the head. There she is a towering, powerful, abstract form of light with a vague sense of femaleness. She provides great assistance with human ascension. On other occasions, she has burst forth with visions of (and my feeling the full power of) the Himalayas. On another occasion, she worked with Mary, the blessed Mother who corresponds to another hidden path the spiritual level.

While we can be grateful for Tara's great compassion, it is important to clarify that from her state of enlightenment, she has realized (solidified as an ongoing state) the spiritual truth that the turmoil experienced in human life experience isn't final—though most humans believe it is. She understands the mechanism of human perception, but she does not share it. She understands that human suffering arises from an incomplete view (based within the Third Dimension), and she invites us to lift our own awareness to discover the transpersonal levels and, thus, transcend suffering. On one occasion, she invited me to look and see this truth for myself, which my consciousness did, and then bring that memory into any demanding life scene.

Keywords: Tara supports one to complete spiritual enlightenment and, by remembering eternity, liberate oneself from suffering over anything that appears to human sight. She extends great compassion while all humankind is engaged in this process.

Suggested Meditation Symbol: Profile view of a pure-white lotus in full bloom radiating sparkling white light

Tara, Green: Buddhist Lineage
Netzach, Emotional Level Two

Green Tara is one of the most well-known emanations of Tara. In all periods, she has been associated with the natural world, and she extends the gifts of compassion, healing, and enlightenment.

Green Tara appears in Vajrayana Buddhism among the five pairs of Dhyani Buddhas, paired with Buddha Amoghasiddi. Scholars debate Tara's consort status in this tradition since she is acknowledged as a fully enlightened Buddha in others. Perhaps it is best to simply honor that Tara can manifest at many levels, working at different chakras, each of which helps humankind in a specific way.

She is also included as one of the ten Mahavidyas (Great Wisdom Goddesses) of India in the goddess tradition of Shaktism. In each tradition in which she is known, Green Tara is associated with the power of divine love to heal, clearing away what may be blocking us from the fullest experience of an open heart. While there are many different approaches to healing, experiencing the love that is eternally extended by spiritual Source to all beings often restores balance and produces healing results.

Energy-healing practitioners typically transmit energy to those they assist through their hands. The palm chakras are linked through the human body's energy channels to the heart. The heart connects directly to the transpersonal Source of love itself. Such practitioners develop the ability to channel the energy received from Source to temporarily amplify that for others so they can clear their energy field and hold the higher vibration for themselves.

We can reach out to Tara to help us clear whatever is blocking us from our fullest experience of love's presence. In serving this function, Tara came to be identified as a universal mother, always compassionate and always accessible to tend to the wounds of humankind.

Tara's earliest known representation—in the Ellora Caves (dated to the seventh century CE)—took a protective form. Known as Astamahabhaya Tara, she offered protection from the eight mortal perils (lions, elephants, fire, snakes, thieves, drowning, captivity, and evil spirits), as potential calamities were known in the seventh century CE. She was painted in a standing posture, holding a lotus in her left hand and giving the mudra (hand gesture) granting freedom from fear. Scroll paintings show eight different emanations of her, with each depicting resolution of one of the types of fear. Her protective role in overcoming human perils was certainly part of her popularity.

Everyone who embarks on spiritual development learns that fear is a major obstacle that must be resolved for higher awareness to be experienced. Tara can support one through this process.

Traditional in all Buddhist sects is a practice called Praises to the Twenty-One Taras. You can also invite Tara's presence as you walk amid the healing green foliage of nature. As with all ascended masters, reading about her, meditating on her, and, especially, expressing her qualities through your own energy field are some of the ways to draw her close. Connecting with masters in the ascended realm is about attunement; as we learn to hold their vibrations, they are there beside us and extending through us.

In direct experience, I have experienced Tara in a green energy field and also in a human female form that included some softly draping folds of her robe. (This was different from the appearance of Arya Tara above.) She indicated that she simply wants to cover everything with new life—a primordial energy of renewal that is healing and regenerating. On another occasion, Green Tara arrived when I was praying for some spiritual healing energy. Her energy showered me, bringing the mantra in my mind "Peace, love, health, wealth." She extends that same blessing to all humankind.

On one occasion, after working with Green Tara, behind her, I felt the energy of Arya Tara exactly as I had recognized her earlier. She was showing me that both Taras (and all the Taras) are emanations of a single powerful force assisting humankind in many ways. Since that time, I have also experienced Blue Tara, known as Ekadjati, another powerfully protective manifestation.

Keywords: Green Tara promotes emotional mastery of the heart and provides energetic support for regeneration, renewal, and spiritual healing. She transmits the healing power of love, purifying our emotions; opening our hearts; uplifting us past fear; and helping us achieve healing, renewal, and regeneration.

Suggested Meditation Symbol: Single white lotus blossom in full bloom (identical to the one you choose to use for Arya Tara above) against a heart-shaped green field (Pantone 371 or 378)

Teresa of Avila: Christian Lineage
Tiphareth, Mental Level

Teresa of Avila (1515–1582) was born into the life of a Spanish noblewoman but instead chose a monastic life as a Carmelite nun. She is remembered as one of the most prominent medieval mystics, whose exquisite description of the contemplative inner path of prayer and meditation (see *The Interior Castle*, translated by Mirabai Starr) is a spiritual classic that still inspires seekers today.

Teresa's mother died when she was fourteen. At age twenty, she entered a Carmelite convent despite her father's opposition. Within two years, her health collapsed, and she was an invalid for three years, during which time she developed a love for contemplative prayer. After her recovery, however, she stopped praying, until, at age thirty-five, she had a deeper religious awakening.

After this event, in 1558, Teresa began to consider reforming the Carmelite order to return to its original observance of austerity. Her reforms required nuns to commit to lives of utter withdrawal from worldly participation (known as cloistering). In 1562, with Pope Pius IV's authorization, she opened Saint Joseph's, the first convent of the Carmelite reform. Though she faced a lot of backlash, she established an additional sixteen convents over her lifetime.

Teresa ultimately faced controversy even within her own order. In 1579–80 (confirmed by the pope), the Carmelites of the Primitive Rule were given independent jurisdiction. Teresa, broken in health, was then directed to resume her reforms, traveling hundreds of miles between convents. She was canonized (made a saint by the Catholic church) a short forty years after her death and is today recognized as a patron saint of Spain and a doctor of the church.

To appreciate the mastery of Theresa of Avila, we need to first understand that she possessed a strong will. She didn't commit in early life to her spiritual calling, but once she did, the commitment was total. With many masters at Tiphareth, we observe individuals who are essentially extroverts. For example, Hildegard of Bingen (also at the mental level of Tiphareth) became a prioress and, though she lived in medieval times, was known for a remarkable volume of communications with those in authority, from popes to statesmen. She wrote inspired mystical treatises and expressed the multifaced intellectual abilities of a polymath through musical composition, philosophy, and other topics.

In contrast, Teresa focused her will on the mystic's inner introspective journey to unite with spiritual Source. That she succeeded is beyond question. Nuns who lived and worked beside her left amazing accounts of how she wrote the inspired wisdom given her at prodigious speed. During those times, her trance state remained undisturbed, no matter what was occurring around her. Much to the dismay of her spiritual sisters, she had a habit of levitating when in states of spiritual ecstasy!

The same strength of will aided her to continue to travel between the convents she founded, until she finally left her body for the last time while en route. We should realize that as connected as she was on the inner channels, she was likely aware that her physical life would soon end. Yet she was relentless in carrying out to her last breath the spiritual assignment she had undertaken.

In the medieval period in which Teresa (and Hildegard) lived, life choices available to women were limited. Most women could only learn to read and write within the confines of a spiritual order of nuns. Teresa was unique, even among the medieval female mystics. Her spirit was as independent, and her spiritual abilities were as profound, as those of some of the most accomplished priestesses of other spiritual traditions.

For a long while, I misclassified Teresa to the path of Kaph (which is extended by another well-known female mystic, Claire of Assisi). When I returned to consider the accounts that noted her strong will, I was able to make a deep contact with her at Tiphareth. She had clearly mastered the mental level of that sphere, awakening transpersonal levels of light that came forth to guide her.

In one experience, she quickly guided my consciousness to enter the outer chamber of the interior castle described in her book. It was like a tunnel that spiraled inward, and the translucent walls were lit by a radiant white inner glow. I was able to travel partway in while the experience lasted, with growing certainty that the mystics' goal of divine union was possible in the center that lay ahead.

Keywords: Teresa supports all who turn to meditation and contemplation with mystical passion, whether they're part of a religious order or not. She is an inspiring guide who left us written descriptions of the art of contemplation, showing us how to develop the habit of turning inward to divine Source to answer any challenge that human life presents.

Suggested Meditation Symbol: A clockwise spiral of radiant white light leading to an inner chamber of divine fire

Themistoclea: Greek Lineage
Yesod, Mental Level

Themistoclea was a well-known priestess who served the Oracle of Delphi during the sixth century BCE. She is reputed to have been the teacher of Pythagoras. Pythagoras is an ascended master at the mental level of Tiphareth but is not included in this book. He is often called "the father of philosophy" and was also associated with mathematical genius. The Pythagorean triangle was named for him. The name Pythagoras translates as "Spoken by the Pythia," since when his father consulted the oracle, a priestess told him he would have an extraordinary son.

Themistoclea served the Delphic oracle, through which Apollo (a Tiphareth master at the spiritual level) was believed to be the source of prophecy. Delphi was the most famous of the Greek oracle sites in the ancient world, in continuous operation for nearly one thousand years before coming to an end in 391 CE through an edict issued by Emperor Theodosius that banned all oracular shrines.

No parallels that have existed during the last millennium are equivalent to the importance of the Delphic priestesses (known as Pythia). All the ancient writers mentioned the oracle, and they sometimes named one of its priestesses, as they did with Themistoclea.

The first time I recognized Themistoclea in direct experience, she came to consciousness beside Phemonoe, who also served as a pythia at the Delphic oracle center and ascended at the spiritual level of Yesod. On another occasion, Themistoclea came forward alone, bringing me the symbol below to use for her. It is a privilege to connect with her consciousness, which extends to support women today who are developing their higher intuitive gifts.

Keywords: Themistoclea supports women who are developing an advanced capacity to receive psychic-intuitive information offered in service to contribute to the spiritual development and well-being of others.

Suggested Meditation Symbol: A blazing ancient Greek–style torch against a radiant white field

Thor: Norse Lineage
Path of Teth (Tarot: Lust and Strength), Spiritual Level

Thor is one of the most familiar names known today from the Norse pantheon. When I was just beginning my work with Norse masters, I had no idea if he had lived on earth or was simply a character invented to enliven the tales. While the character of Thor was irresistible to the Marvel Comics film franchise, he is indeed a larger-than-life presence who can be met in consciousness among the ascended masters.

To undo our Hollywood projections, we can stop to appreciate that Thor was the single most venerated deity among Viking warriors. Odin was the deity invoked by the elite among the Viking command, but Thor was the ideal model who inspired admiration among the far more numerous crew members. These warriors faced uncertain odds during raids and battles and were fierce in demeanor yet needed a yet-more-forceful resource to inspire them. Thor served that function well.

Thor is introduced in Norse myth as a son of Odin, chief of the gods, birthed through Odin's consort Jord (Earth). Within the Norse pantheon, Thor was known as the mighty champion who wielded thunder. He was regularly dispatched to defend Asgard, realm of the Aesir gods, when evil needed to be brought under control. He accomplished this through an application of enormous force. Male giants in the Norse tales were dispensers of doom and disaster, and it was Thor's chosen duty to rid the world of as many of them as he was able.

To conduct his function, Thor ruled the sky from his great hall, Valhalla, whose name translates as "Power Field" or "Plains of Strength." It was described as a mighty palace of 540 rooms. Such stories also explained natural phenomena, though he is not simply an archetype. The roar of thunder was explained as the rumble of Thor's chariot's wheels across the vault of the heavens. He burst forth in his chariot, drawn by two male goats—Tooth Gnasher and Snarl Tooth—who could be killed and eaten and then brought back to life the next day, as long as their bones remained unbroken. (This is a resurrection symbol.)

Thor was in possession of three magical items. The most well known is his hammer, Mjolnir. He also possessed his belt of strength, Megingjörð, which doubled his strength when he wore it, and the great iron gloves he needed to wield his hammer. Mjolnir always destroyed anything it was sent against and automatically returned to his hand. Miniature talismans of his hammer are known to survive among archaeological finds and are popular symbols worn today by some who follow Norse traditions.

Thor had a quick temper but never acted out of control and was disciplined. Magic could overcome him, but it was an area he never ventured into, because the force he wielded was enormous on its own.

He demonstrated a battle frenzy that rendered him impervious to injury, which made him popular among Viking crew members.

When Thor was not busy dispatching evil, he functioned as the husband of the fertility goddess Sif, with whom he fathered son Modi and daughter Thrud. His other son, Magni, may be the offspring of a union with the giantess Jarnsaxa.

Thor's greatest enemy was the Midgard Serpent, one of the three fearsome children of Loki, which had been cast deep into the sea and had wrapped his tail around the whole world. It was foretold that they would meet at Ragnarok, the ultimate battle that heralded the end of gods and men. Various tales give different accounts of this fatal meeting.

I was working with another master through a crystal, when Thor came into contact, announcing his name. On another occasion, when I reached out to him, his massively large high vibrational energy was magnificent to experience. He communicated that "all in his race look like he does" without explaining where he came from! He is committed to assisting humankind to continue with our spiritual development and is protective to dispel any influences that would hold us back.

Keywords: Call upon Thor as you develop physical strength, endurance, and advanced warrior skills that can be deployed to clear lower energies so your evolution can continue.

Suggested Meditation Symbol: Thor's hammer, Mjolnir, against a radiant white field

Tyr: Norse Lineage
Geburah, Emotional Level Two

If you have read some of the Norse myths, you will likely remember the story of Tyr. He was the courageous warrior who voluntarily gave up his hand to protect the Aesir, so they could bind the terrifying wolf Fenrir.

Fenrir was one of Loki's three children born to the giantess

Angrboda. It had been prophesied that Loki's children might bring harm to the Aesir in the future, so Odin sent Loki's daughter Hel to rule over the underworld and cast the Midgard Serpent into the sea, where it quickly wrapped its tail around the entire world. Despite the prophesy, Fenrir the wolf was kept in Asgard to be raised.

Tyr was the only one brave enough to feed Fenrir. When they all saw how quickly it was growing and how enormous it was becoming, they reconsidered the prophecies and decided they had to chain it before it became impossible to control. They told Fenrir it would be a demonstration of his strength to allow them to chain him and show them how easily he could break the chains. Break them he did as they tried first one and then another heavier chain.

Now really concerned, the Aesir asked the dwarves to fashion a chain that Fenrir could not break. They fashioned one from cat noise, mountain roots, bear sinews, fish breath, and bird spittle. Its slender appearance hid a load of magic.

When it was ready, they invited Fenrir to the game again, but he looked at the chain's narrow gauge, suspicious of a trick. Pride did not allow him to refuse, but this time, he had one condition: he would allow the Aesir to bind him only if one of them put a hand between his jaws as a gesture of good faith.

Tyr knew that chaining the beast was necessary for the safety of the Aesir. With no hesitation, he stepped forward and put a hand between the wolf's mighty jaws. The rest of the Aesir attached the chain, and the more the wolf struggled to break it, the tighter it became. Then all the gods laughed—all but Tyr, who lost his hand. The injury was a serious matter for a man whose specialty was hand-to-hand combat, yet Tyr did not complain and continued to serve the Aesir with dedication and skill.

Warriors are often called upon to rein in something that has become dangerous. When I contacted Tyr, I experienced a warrior who was neither reckless nor arrogant, but he knew his capabilities. He took on assignments that others refused—because someone had to. There was a noble feeling to his energy because his courageous actions were for the benefit of others. Every worthwhile cause depends upon the support of many like him, whose names are not remembered by history.

Whether we agree or not with those who determine going to war, some of the men and women who have lost limbs in military service embody the noble quality of Tyr. While war has no victors and has been used unwisely by those seeking to maintain power, it is always appropriate to respect the valor and courage of those who may experience the loss of a limb, whether in military service or by accidental means.

Keywords: Call upon Tyr for the courage to discern whether a truly noble act is asked of you. This is not the same as willingly accepting sacrifice. Vast amounts of strength and courage are available to women and men (from spiritual Source) when such an assignment is theirs.

Suggested Meditation Symbol: Slender, dwarf-made golden chain against a medium-dark slightly yellowish-green field (Pantone 371 or 378)

Vairocana Buddha: Buddhist Lineage
Chokma, Mental Level

Many spiritual traditions use a metaphysical wisdom concept that refers to ultimate reality as One. One is both omnipresent and omniscient. It exists everywhere yet is not located in space. When consciousness is aligned with this dimension, all knowledge, independent of the mind's thinking function, already exists—now.

Vairocana is a celestial Buddha, at home in this transcendent dimension. He holds the white center of the five Dhyani Buddha families. He is the primordial Buddha in the Chinese schools of Tiantai, Huayan, and Tangmi and appears in later schools, including the Japanese Kegon. His name, translated from Tibetan, means "Maker of Brilliant Light" or "Illuminator."

He is prominent in the Mahayana Buddhist traditions and referred to many times in the Avatamsaka Sutra (Flower Ornament Scripture), translated by Thomas Cleary. Some passages in chapters 3 and 5 relate that Vairocana is always teaching in some of the infinite oceans of worlds, which his vows have purified over eons, so that all minds might know enlightenment. This description is consistent with a master at the mental level of Chokma, who is outside time (beyond the veil of human life and death) but can be experienced by consciousness as it moves beyond body identification toward higher spiritual essence.

Those who master Chokma's sphere of energy can access timeless moments of omniscience, which include wisdom about all the means (we might say the spiritual technology or practices) required to help others arrive at full spiritual enlightenment.

"One who illuminates" is an apt description for a being who guides consciousness to experience transcendent reality. Chokma, in the Qabalah, is the first of the transpesonal spheres through which the light of creation passes, heading toward physical form on the spheres and paths below. Masters there hold direct knowledge of the unmanifest realms one experiences before and after physical incarnation. Direct experience of these realms has always been one of the highest achievements for spiritual adepts of any tradition.

We can see Vairocana's importance within the traditions that honor him, simply by looking at images of the massive size of the Vairocana statues that exist today in various parts of the world. The largest of the famous Buddhas of Bamiyan, estimated by the space for it carved within the rock, was 175 feet (53 meters) tall. The size was a representation conveying the largeness of his teachings. His largest statue existing today is in Ibaraki Prefecture, Japan. Completed in 1993, it measures 393.7 feet (120 meters) in height, including base and lotus. As of 2018, it was ranked as one of the top-five tallest statues in the world.

In direct experience, the mind of Vairocana reached out to connect with me on a few occasions. These experiences were powerful and profound. His mind is a vast, still expanse of pure-white light, wherein consciousness is awake in realms of transcendent wisdom. On some occasions, he announces himself by name before flooding my consciousness with white light.

Keywords: Vairocana, as an emissary of the formless light of divine Source, extends wisdom and power to achieve spiritual illumination at the mental level. He is a unique guide to those studying advanced Buddhist practices but will support all who seek him who have trained their minds to move beyond personal identity into deep states of concentrated meditation.

Suggested Meditation Symbol: The sunyata symbol (an almost-closed circle with emptiness in the center) against a field of radiant white light

Vishnu: Hindu Lineage
Tiphareth, Spiritual Level

Vishnu is the supreme being honored by an estimated six hundred million people today in the Hindu tradition of Vaishnavism. This number represents approximately 60 percent of Hindus, with the next-largest group honoring Shiva. A much smaller sect (still numbering in the millions of people) honors the ten Mahavidya goddesses as supreme.

When we use the Qabalah to move beyond conflicts about which deity is better or more correct, we can observe that both Shiva and Vishnu can be met at the spiritual level: Shiva at the sphere of Chokma and Vishnu at the sphere of Tiphareth. Both of them offer profound experiences of divine light at the spiritual level, though differ a bit in their nature.

Vishnu, among the masters within Hindu tradition represents the development of the energy known as Tiphareth. This energy is first expressed solely at the solar plexus chakra. As an individuals evolution continues to the mental and spiritual levels, the higher self (the transcendent, birthless, deathless self) and chakras over the human head are activated, with lines of light that directly connect to the solar plexus. This allows the higher self to flow into one's vehicle of worldly expression to become the senior guiding identity. Masters, such as Vishnu, can assist with the higher levels of this profound energetic transformation.

Vishnu is part of the Hindu Trimurti, wherein he is known as the Preserver, with Brahma as Creator and Shiva as Destroyer. Vishnu upholds dharma (a word with many meanings, including laws, conduct, virtues, and the right way of living).

As with many masters presumed to have appeared on earth during the most ancient periods, historical evidence for Vishnu is inconsistent and scanty. He is traceable only to the first millennium BCE, where he appears as a Vedic deity. In the Vedic hymns, he is described as residing in the highest home where departed atmans (souls) reside. Vedic hymns invoke Vishnu along with other deities, especially Indra, whom he helped in killing the symbol of evil named Vritra. (I also interpret this tale symbolically as purifying and releasing the less-helpful forces within the personality so that the higher self can be experienced.)

Most of the Gupta kings, beginning with Chandragupta II (third to fourth century CE), were proponents of Vaishnavism. After the Gupta age, Krishnaism, the worship of Krishna as an avatar or emanation of Vishnu, rose to become a major current within Vaishnavism. In the eighth century CE, Vaishnavism encountered the Advaita doctrine of Adi Shankara. During the twentieth century, Vaishnavism spread from India to many places around the globe, including North America, Europe, Africa, Russia, and South America.

In direct experience, Vishnu came into consciousness along with Krishna. My point of observation was in the sphere of Vishnu, and he was demonstrating the avatar relationship he extends through Krishna (who corresponds to the mental level of the sphere of Chesed). I could feel the energy he was sending to Krishna and the link between them. Krishna was an outlet, one of the avatars who brought Vishnu's energy to humankind, through a slightly different channel at Chesed, and with a strong divine love component. Following that experience, I saw Vishnu and Krishna portrayed together in visionary art, also indicating this avatar relationship.

Keywords: Vishnu is one of the masters who assists those who pursue advanced spiritual development, helping to integrate the great light of spiritual self in the physical body. As that birthless, deathless self shines with clarity through an individual, he or she becomes an instrument to deliver a unique gift that contributes to collective humankind.

Suggested Meditation Symbol: Golden portal of divine light high overhead in the cosmos, in a field of radiant white light

Yeshe Tsogyal: Buddhist Lineage
Binah, Mental Level

Yeshe Tsogyal is known by various honorific epithets today, including Mother of Tibetan Buddhism, Queen of Dakinis, Queen of the Ocean of Wisdom, Victorious Ocean of Knowledge, and Queen of Bliss, to name a few.

She was a principle spiritual consort and disciple of Indian Buddhist sage Padmasambhava (also known as Guru Rinpoche), and she transcribed and transmitted his lineage, becoming the first notable Tibetan, man, or woman, to achieve full enlightenment through Buddhist practice. Rinpoche and Tsogyal are known as the father and mother of the Nyingma school (the oldest school of Tibetan Buddhism) and are associated with profound tantric and Dzogchen (Great Perfection) teachings. Within the Nyingma and Karma Kagyu schools of Tibetan Buddhism, Yeshe Tsogyal is recognized as a female Buddha (fully enlightened one).

According to traditional stories, she was born a princess in the region of Karchen, Tibet, in the eighth century CE. There were many auspicious spiritual signs at her birth. Despite her possessing physical beauty and outstanding qualities of temperament, her heart's yearning was to pursue the path of enlightenment rather than follow the cultural expectation of marriage.

However, most sources state that when she came of age, she had to endure a forced marriage to the Tibetan emperor Trisong Detsen. The emperor later invited the Indian sage Padmasambhava (Guru Rinpoche) to come to Tibet, and he gave Tsogyal to the sage. Padmasambhava freed her, after which she became his main disciple and spiritual consort.

The Life and Visions of Yeshe Tsogyal, published in 2017, gives a different account. According to this previously unknown fourteenth-century-CE text, two different princes wanted to marry her. When she refused, her father, the king, had her stripped naked, publicly beaten, and then exiled to live alone in a remote, wild area. One of the suitor princes followed her there and abducted her to become his bride. She prayed for help, and Guru Rinpoche materialized before her. He magically transported her to the Chimpu Caves in Tibet, where he instructed her in the cycle of Great Perfection teachings and left her to meditate alone in the cave for twelve years.

This recently discovered treasure text offers glimpses of stages on her inner path to enlightenment. Even in translation, the language is evocative, describing some of her exquisite spiritual visions. From within her meditation cave, a dakini appeared to guide her to visit the divine dimension known as the Land of Oddiyana. There she confronted her spiritual imperfections and was instructed by higher beings.

Rinpoche returned after twelve years to claim her, assessing her progress as insufficient and instructing her further. She demonstrated the courage to persevere through all inner and outer obstacles. As a final assignment before enlightenment, Tsogyal was asked to rescue the evil minister Shanti from one of the lower astral realms through her meditative skill alone. In fulfilling this task, she proved herself so advanced that she liberated the entire realm!

It is said she took a vow at her death "to respond to all beings, when they ask for protection and blessings while seeking spiritual realization." In my inner-world experience, she came into consciousness as an exotic, powerful spiritual-sexual divine feminine, lifting my consciousness into a field of purple. Like many ascended masters, she had an energy that felt unique. She was demonstrating the type of tantric practice that can lift energy heavenward.

Keywords: Yeshe Tsogyal can provide inspiration to trust one's inherent enlightened nature and worthiness to persist with purification and spiritual practices until the rainbow body is fully manifest. She demonstrates how to use obstacles to further hone devotion, faith, and compassion. She supports those who are refining perception to recognize the illusory nature of all worldly phenomena, and she is a model for women who are developing their capacity for female spiritual leadership.

Suggested Meditation Symbol: A rainbow encircling the silhouette of a woman seated in meditation, against a purple field (Pantone 165–166, 265, and 272)

Yogananda (Paramahansa Yogananda): Hindu Lineage
Tiphareth, Emotional Level Two

Paramahansa Yogananda (1893–1952) was an Indian yogi and guru (spiritual teacher) who spent most of his adult life in America. He introduced millions of Westerners to the teachings of meditation and kriya yoga. His book *Autobiography of a Yogi* is considered one of the spiritual classics and has been read by millions of people. He founded the organization called the Self-Realization Fellowship, which is devoted to human spiritual awakening and is still in existence today.

Yogananda, whose birth name was Mukunda Lal Ghosh, showed an early inclination to spiritual abilities. He found his own guru when he was just seventeen. (His guru lineage connects to Baba Ji and Lahiri Mahasaya via his immediate guru, Swami Sri Yukteswar, all of whom are ascended masters.) One of the characteristics of his lineage points toward focusing on the underlying aspects of unity among world religions, rather than their differences. In Yogananda's center near Santa Barbara, one sees an image of Jesus (Yeshua) on the altar, beside photos of Hindu spiritual luminaries.

It was Paramahansa's life path to move to the United States in 1920 and establish the international center for Self-Realization Fellowship in Los Angeles, California. Male masters at the second emotional level of Tiphareth may be called to found businesses or organizations that have a large impact on the world. Some combination of leadership and charisma attracts attention to individual effforts, timed to meet a collective need and have an impact.

In Paramahans'a case, he served as a spiritual pioneer in a new land.

He was the first Hindu teacher of yoga to spend a major portion of his life in America, living there from 1920 to 1952, interrupted only by an extended visit in 1935–1936 with his guru in India. He taught kriya yoga and meditation practices to help people achieve spiritual understanding, which he called self-realization. Self-realization is the knowing—in body, mind, and soul—that we are one with the omnipresence of God. We do not have to pray that it will come to us, because we are just as much a part of God now as we ever will be. Spiritual realization means to awaken to the experience of our true reality. God's omnipresence is, thus, our omnipresence.

He was only fifty-three years old when, on March 7, 1952, he spoke at a dinner for the visiting Indian ambassador to the United States at the Biltmore Hotel in Los Angeles. His words acknowledged the contributions made by India and America to world peace and human progress and expressed his hope for a united world that would combine the best qualities of "efficient America" and "spiritual India." At the end of that speech, he read one of his poems and then turned his gaze upward toward his third eye while his body slumped to the floor as his consciousness fully rejoined Source.

As has happened with some other spiritual gurus in America, there were controversies regarding his sexual interactions with female devotees that emerged after his death, which were disturbing to his followers. Whatever we understand about those circumstances, he did reach ascension.

In direct experience, Paramahansa first came into consciousness during meditation, amist a glowing golden light. He appeared in a powerful and attractive male form, and I experienced a presence filled with warmth and the highest intentions for humanity. Another time, he shared with me a vision of blue-skinned Krishna dancing among the gopis. During subsequent experiences, he eventually brought others of his guru lineage forward, allowing my consciousness to experience some of them directly. A visionary experience with Lahiri Mahasaya was especially profound.

Keywords: Paramahansa Yogananda supports all of us to open to divine will and put full confidence and power into our life mission. He is an ally to those who are guided to establish a spiritual organization or movement in a highly visible way. He supports spiritual approaches that transcend conflict among those of differing beliefs, thus helping humankind toward the experience of spiritual oneness. He is a skilled guide for certain forms of meditation and yogic practice.

Suggested Meditation Symbol: Golden-yellow yoga practitioner silhouette with light pouring through the chakras, against a bright yellow sun (Pantone 810)

Zeus: Greek Lineage
Chokma Mental Level

Zeus is acknowledged in Homeric myth as the leader of the Greek Olympians, who defeated the earlier race known as the Titans (who had been led by his father, Cronus). Under his leadership the Olympians claimed victory during this war known as the Titomachy. According to Homer, Zeus then assumed authority to oversee heaven and earth from his seat on lofty Mount Olympus. The ancient Greeks regarded him as the supreme god, and he is the most well-known member of the Olympian pantheon today.

Zeus is typically associated with lightning, and one of his symbols is the eagle, which flies the highest of all birds. Many people today understand Zeus (and other masters) as a purely fictional character, rather than a being who was embodied on earth. Among those who do grant him credibility, there are still many prevalent misperceptions.

As I have mentioned in the profiles of other Olympian masters, most of the family relationships presented in Greek myth do not hold up when I experience these masters directly. When I contact other masters—such as Solomon and his mother, Bathsheba, and many others—the type of feeling bonds that I experience, are my indication that they are related.

According to Greek scholar Ken Dowden in his book *Zeus*, our first written evidence for Zeus comes from an inscription in Mycenaean Linear B written circa 1200 BCE. (Although this is the first evidence, I believe the being we know as Zeus was on earth far earlier than this.) As noted earlier, Homer's prodigious later efforts (7th-8th C BCE) to gather information and write about the exploits of the Olympians, took place long after they walked on earth. From experiencng the Greek masters directly, it is my understanding that the members of the Olympian pantheon came together in what is presently known as ancient Greece, from various lands, to share a common purpose; overthrowing the tyranny of the former ruler. If so, theirs would not be the only example where such liaisons occurred.

After the Olympian's victory, Zeus's influence spread beyond present-day Greece as Greek culture extended into new lands under Alexander the Great. This led to many hyphenated names of deities that included Zeus in part. This occurred in Syria and Phoenicia as well as in Egypt. Later, Zeus came to be known as Jupiter by the Romans, a name that shares a linguistic root that translates as "father."

Ken Dowden offers a plausible explanation for how the amorous trickster deity Zeus portrayed by Homer became the lofty power of the universe to whom humankind may pray. This shift may have occurred through the writings of the Roman poet Virgil. Even after Christianity overturned the earlier worship of Greek gods, interest in the classics continued. The widely read compilation prepared by Isidore of Seville, a fifth-century-CE bishop, presented a euhemerist view of Zeus as a man worshipped after his death for exemplary deeds, even though some deeds were far from perfect. Astrology joined the Zeus chorus, relating him to the spiritually uplifting and expansive planet Jupiter. However, Zeus came into repeated contact using a Chokma Mental level crystal and his tale of overthrowing an old order evokes a core theme of Chokma.

During my first direct experience with Zeus, he appeared in an abstract male form—a huge presence amid a temple with columns that were so tall their tops disappeared into the heavenly realms of wisdom above. On two occasions, he came into consciousness, demonstrating the incredibly powerful electrical energy he extends, which some have compared to lightning bolts, which can lift awareness into the heavenly realms.

Keywords: Zeus supports the development of powerful male war leaders who take on an assignment to eliminate an old order, toppling a leader who is brutal and misusing power, replacing it with a different style of governance so that culture and spiritual values can flourish. Zeus can also support men who are overcoming the effects of abusive fathers.

Suggested Meditation Symbol: White eagle soaring in flight, emitting a burst of energy-consciousness, against a radiant white field.